THE
HISTORY
OF
INDIA

UNDERSTANDING INDIA

THE HISTORY OF INDIA

EDITED BY KENNETH PLETCHER, SENIOR EDITOR, GEOGRAPHY AND HISTORY

Educational Publishing

IN ASSOCIATION WITH

EDUCATIONAL SERVICES

Published in 2011 by Britannica Educational Publishing
(a trademark of Encyclopædia Britannica, Inc.)
in association with Rosen Educational Services, LLC
29 East 21st Street, New York, NY 10010.

First Edition

Britannica Educational Publishing
Michael I. Levy: Executive Editor
J.E. Luebering: Senior Manager
Marilyn L. Barton: Senior Coordinator, Production Control
Steven Bosco: Director, Editorial Technologies
Lisa S. Braucher: Senior Producer and Data Editor
Yvette Charboneau: Senior Copy Editor
Kathy Nakamura: Manager, Media Acquisition
Kenneth Pletcher: Senior Editor, Geography and History

Rosen Educational Services
Alexandra Hanson-Harding: Editor
Nelson Sá: Art Director
Cindy Reiman: Photography Manager
Matthew Cauli: Designer, Cover Design
Introduction by Laura LaBella

Library of Congress Cataloging-in-Publication Data

The history of India / edited by Kenneth Pletcher. — 1st ed.
      p. cm. — (Understanding India)
"In association with Britannica Educational Publishing, Rosen Educational Services."
Includes bibliographical references and index.
ISBN 978-1-61530-122-5 (lib. bdg.)
1. India—History. 2. India—Social conditions. I. Pletcher, Kenneth.
DS436.H593 2010
954—dc22

                                                            2009052823

Manufactured in the United States of America

On the cover: *The Taj Mahal is located in the city of Agra, Uttar Pradesh, India.* © www.istockphoto.com

Back cover: *The Temple at Khajuharo, India, is a UNESCO World Heritage Site.*
© www.istockphoto.com/Keith Molloy

Pages: *21, 56, 90, 115, 134, 162, 191, 210, 228, 256, 279, 301, 324, 326, 328, 330 Detail of Akbar tames the Savage Elephant, Hawa'i, outside the Red Fort at Agra, miniature from the 'Akbarnama' of Abul Fazl, c.1590 (gouache on paper)* Victoria & Albert Museum, London, UK/The Bridgeman Art Library/Getty Images

CONTENTS

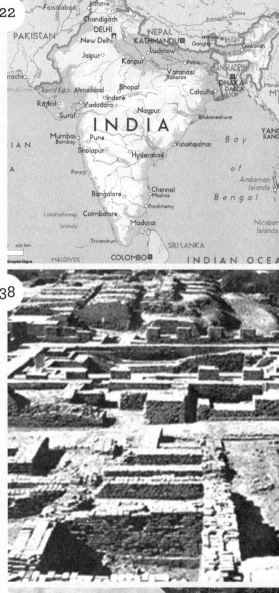

70

71

74

86

88

114

138

145

147

165

169

181

CHAPTER 10: BRITISH INDIA FROM THE MUTINY TO WORLD WAR I 256

CHAPTER 11: BRITISH INDIA FROM WORLD WAR I TO 1947 279

CHAPTER 12: THE REPUBLIC OF INDIA 301

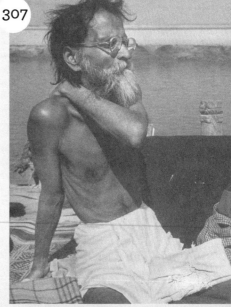

CONCLUSION 324

INTRODUCTION

To outsiders, India is an exotic land, steeped in ancient culture and spirituality. But to focus solely on these often-applied attributes is to ignore the true depth and diversity that make India the rich, vibrant country it is today. India is the second-most populous nation in the world and also the world's largest functioning democracy. It is the birthplace of two major religions—Buddhism and Hinduism—as well as the homeland of Sikhism and Jainism. Over the centuries the subcontinent has endured numerous struggles, not only over religion, but also for self-rule and economic equality. Some of those struggles continue today, but India has nonetheless managed to emerge as a major global force. As readers explore India's long history they will come to understand these struggles.

The writer Mark Twain once said, "India is the cradle of the human race, the birthplace of human speech, the mother of history, the grandmother of legend, and the great grandmother of tradition." Tradition is a key word in this statement. No matter how modern India has become, its traditions have always defined and formed the foundation of this vast nation. Tradition is what has held the country and its people together for thousands of years, despite great differences of religion, language, and socioeconomic status.

Most Indian people practice one of six different religions. They speak hundreds of dialects of 16 officially recognized languages. They are divided into several social castes and thousands of different sects. Yet the traditions that have been passed down for centuries have managed to weave their way through society, politics, and virtually every other aspect of life on the subcontinent.

Hundreds of years of foreign invasion and rule have also left their mark on India and its people. Despite the fact that India is bordered by the massive Himalayas on the north, this barrier was neither high enough nor daunting enough to keep out invaders over the centuries. Those invasions began around 1500 BCE, when the Aryans from Central Asia displaced the Indus valley civilization that had been in existence for a thousand years. Gradually, the Aryans spread their influence throughout the region, creating the Vedas and the first literary records of India's cultures.

In about 325 BCE, Chandragupta Maurya established an empire that spread from Bengal in the east to Afghanistan in the northwest. The Mauryan empire reached its peak around 250 BCE, under the helm of its third emperor, Maurya's

Mohandas K. Gandhi with poet Sarojini Naidu, 1930. Popperfoto/Getty Images

grandson Ashoka. No other group would control so much of the subcontinent for another 2,000 years after the Mauryan empire's demise. And yet other important and formidable empires rose up over time. The Gupta dynasty in the north (320–540 CE) ruled at a time when works of great Hindu literature were written and great advances were made in mathematics and the sciences.

Meanwhile, the Chola civilization united parts of southern India; its kings ruled for more than a millennia, even though by the 3rd century different noble families were battling for ascendancy. Still, there was a flowering of religion, art, architecture, and classical Sanskrit literature. Beautiful temples and institutions of higher education were built.

Islam came to be an important force in India. The first Muslim traders reached Central Asia not long after the Prophet Muhammad's death in 632 CE. Over the next several centuries, waves of Muslim invaders made further inroads southward into the subcontinent, challenging the Hindus for power. The Delhi sultanate controlled much of northern India from the 13th to the 16th centuries. It was succeeded by the great Mughal Empire. In 1525, Bābur, the Muslim ruler of Kabul, crossed the mountains from Afghanistan and attacked the Delhi sultanate. He soon established dominion over all of northern India, laying the foundation of the Mughal Empire (1526–1857). The Mughal rulers were noted for their tolerance of other religions.

However, over time, Mughal power weakened. By the 18th century, dynastic rivalries and incursions from the north were eroding Mughal control. Also a factor in the Mughal's demise was the increasing presence of various European traders who had come and established factories, or trading colonies at Bombay (now Mumbai), Madras (now Chennai), and Calcutta (now Kolkata).

When Europeans first arrived in India, beginning with the Portuguese in the late 15th century, their aim was not empire building but trade, primarily Indian spices but other goods as well. French and English traders followed in the 17th century. But when Mughul power collapsed in the mid-18th century, the English stepped in to fill that vacuum. The East India Company, originally established by Britain to manage its trade with India, came to rule large parts of the subcontinent. However, by the mid-19th century, the company had been abolished and the British government directly controlled virtually all of India.

On the outside, British rule appeared to meet with little resistance. Yet over time, resentment over colonial rule began to bubble up to the surface. Tensions exploded in 1857, when Indian troops in the northern part of the country mutinied and killed their British officers. Indians called it the First Indian War of Independence, while the British referred to it as the Indian Mutiny. Within two years, the British had quashed the rebellion and had enacted a bloody retribution, but the desire of the Indian people for an independent country grew stronger.

The majority of the Indian populace could neither read nor write, but a small group of highly educated people worked their way into the colonial government, and gradually they started a movement toward independence. Over time, the British allowed more participation by Indians.

However, Indian sentiment kept growing for the British to leave India and for Indians to establish self-government. One individual is associated more than any other with India's eventual emancipation from British rule: Mohandas Karamchand Gandhi, known to the world as the Mahatma ("Great Souled"). This slight, unassuming man, with his campaigns of nonviolent civil disobedience, provided a turning point in the nation's final push for independence.

As that goal came closer and closer, tensions increased between Muslims and Hindus. Animosity between these two religious groups in India stretched back centuries, and efforts by one group or the other to rule the subcontinent had long been a source of tension.

In the power struggle between Muslims and Hindus, bloodshed was also nothing new. But the clashes that occurred after the subcontinent finally secured its freedom were among the most violent. By the 1940s, Muslims in India were demanding a separate Muslim state, a campaign that was led by politician Mohammed Ali Jinnah. In 1947, when Britain finally withdrew from the subcontinent, Jinnah's negotiations led to a hastily drawn partition between primarily Hindu India and the Islam-dominated portion that came to be known as Pakistan. This rapid division of borders led to a frantic race to safety, as Hindus and Muslims fled from one land to the other. In the violence that ensued, hundreds of thousands of people were killed.

After having led a campaign of nonviolence, Mahatma Gandhi was dismayed by the bloodshed. Many Hindus held him responsible for the violence because he had failed to prevent the partition. One Hindu extremist took his revenge on January 30, 1948, murdering Gandhi while he was walking to a prayer meeting in Delhi.

As India mourned the death of one leader, they looked hopefully to another. In 1947, Jawaharlal Nehru became independent India's first prime minister. On August 14, when the Indian Constituent Assembly met at Delhi to assume control of their nation's destiny, Nehru made a historic speech, saying, "At the stroke of the midnight hour, when the world sleeps, India will awake to life and freedom. A moment that comes but rarely in history when we step out from the old to the new, when an age ends, and when the soul of a nation long suppressed finds utterance."

Nehru was determined to finally make India self-sufficient. The British had moved the country toward modernization, introducing railroads, modern irrigation methods, and the textile industry. They had helped nurture the first European-style middle class in its cities. And, they had introduced to India a democratic system of government. Yet two centuries of colonial rule had left indelible scars on the subcontinent. Most people still worked as farmers, yet India was unable to feed itself. Much of the population was uneducated. Diseases such as malaria and cholera ran rampant, especially among India's poorest residents.

Nehru's aim was to reshape India's economy. He oversaw the building of dams and factories, referring to them as "the new temples of India." Nehru also attempted to redistribute the land more fairly among the rural population, achieving partial success. Although Nehru prodded Indian industry and created new wealth, it still was not evenly distributed.

Moves toward self-reliance continued under Nehru's daughter, Indira Gandhi, who was elected prime minister in 1966. She pushed for a so-called Green Revolution to ensure that India could support its own food needs. By the 1970s, India had become self-sufficient in grain production and was even exporting some grain by the 1980s. Indian industry also began to expand during this time.

Despite these successes, the public grew increasingly frustrated and disenchanted with Indira Gandhi's administration. Although Gandhi spoke passionately about the continuing problems of disease, poverty, and illiteracy,

she could do little to solve them. A small minority was enjoying the fruits of the nation's labours, while the majority toiled in desperate poverty.

The division of wealth between haves and have-nots is deeply embedded in the caste system, a tightly closed hierarchical social organization that arose out of the Hindu religion. The caste system divides society into four tightly restricted social classes: Brahmins (priests), Kshatriyas (rulers), Vaishyas (merchants and landholders), and Shudras (servants). Another group, traditionally called untouchables (although other names such as Dalit are now used), fall outside the caste system. Under the caste system, the favoured classes enjoy an elite status, while the lowest classes endure a menial existence. Castes are not supposed to intermarry, or even intermingle. Even as modernization was spreading throughout India—and even as the Indian government has made great efforts to outlaw class distinctions—the caste tradition has remained deeply embedded in Indian culture, and it has continued to be difficult for people to escape the lowest rungs of society.

As the country struggled to rise out of poverty and toward self-sufficiency, resurgences of violence between Muslims and Hindus continued to threaten India's security. In 1971, the Bengali population of what was then the eastern portion of Pakistan grew increasingly disaffected and sought independence. The Pakistani army launched a violent campaign, which India eventually countered with a military intervention that put an end to the conflict, and the new country of Bangladesh was created.

Muslim-Hindu tensions have exploded many times since the Bangladesh war, such as in 1992, when a crowd of Hindus in the north Indian city of Ayodha demolished a mosque on land that both religious groups had claimed as their own. That night, a mob rampaged through the city, destroying Muslim-owned shops, homes, and mosques. Two thousand people, most of them Muslims, were killed. In November 2008, 10 Muslim gunmen killed some 174 people and injured more than 300 others in a series of terrorist attacks in Mumbai.

Religion continues to be a contentious element in India, along with income and social stratification. Poverty remains widespread, especially in rural India, where most of the country's population still lives, largely as it has for centuries. Poverty also still exists in the big cities, but life there has changed drastically. Urban India is today a major centre for education, government, modern industry, sophisticated health care, and the technological expertise that has become sought after by nations around the world.

In sheer numbers alone, India has become a major global force—the country being second only to China in population. At the turn of the 20th century it was home to about 238 million inhabitants, but today, India claims more than one billion residents. Though it makes up just over 2 percent of the earth's surface area, more than 16 percent of the world's population—one out of six people on the earth—calls the country home.

In the pages of this book, as readers make their way from the earliest days of the Indus Valley civilization to the modern India that exists today, they will see how the subcontinent has been transformed throughout the years by invaders, by local rulers, and finally, by globalization and the high-tech revolution. They will also discover that, while India embraces modernization, this is a country that still clings tightly to its past. While office buildings and superhighways spring up in India's cities, the ancient monuments and places continue to be preserved. There is no greater testimony to India's past than the one flocks of tourists visit each year. The Taj Mahal, an architectural masterpiece built by the 17th-century Mughal emperor Shah Jahan, is considered one of the greatest wonders of the world. It is evidence that, however much India may change, it will always remain in touch with its past.

CHAPTER 1

THE BEGINNINGS OF INDIA'S HISTORY

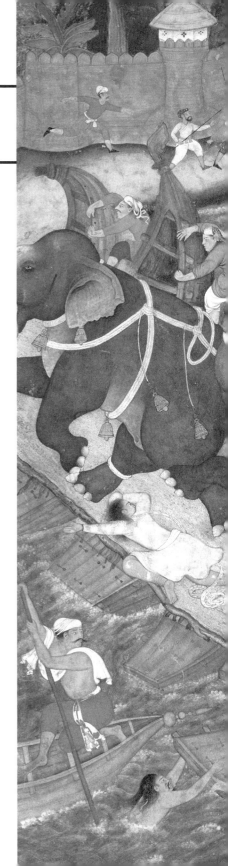

The Indian subcontinent, the great landmass of South Asia, is the home of one of the world's oldest and most influential civilizations. In this book, the subcontinent, which for historical purposes is usually called simply "India," is understood to comprise the areas of not only the present-day Republic of India but also the republics of Pakistan (partitioned from India in 1947) and Bangladesh (which formed the eastern part of Pakistan until its independence in 1971).

Since early times the Indian subcontinent appears to have provided an attractive habitat for human occupation. Toward the south it is effectively sheltered by wide expanses of ocean, which tended to isolate it culturally in ancient times, while to the north it is protected by the massive ranges of the Himalayas, which also sheltered it from the arctic winds and the air currents of Central Asia. Only in the northwest and northeast is there easier access by land, and it was through those two sectors that most of the early contacts with the outside world took place.

Within the framework of hills and mountains represented by the Indo-Iranian borderlands on the west, the Indo-Myanmar borderlands in the east, and the Himalayas to the north, the subcontinent may in broadest terms be divided into two major divisions: in the north, the basins of the Indus and Ganges (Ganga) rivers (the Indo-Gangetic Plain) and, to the south, the block of Archean rocks that forms the Deccan

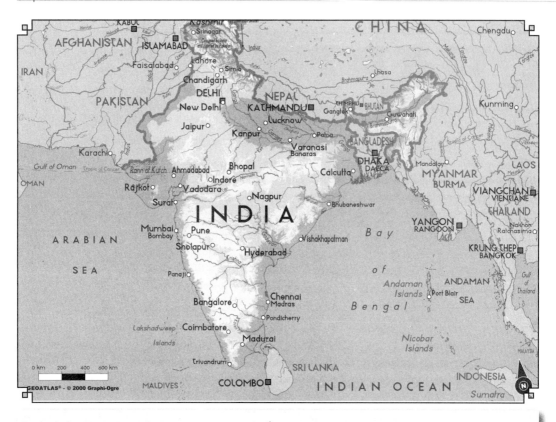

This map of India shows its major geographic features. © GeoAtlas

plateau region. The expansive alluvial plain of the river basins provided the environment and focus for the rise of two great phases of city life: the civilization of the Indus valley, known as the Indus civilization, during the 3rd millennium BCE; and, during the 1st millennium BCE, that of the Ganges. To the south of this zone, and separating it from the peninsula proper, is a belt of hills and forests, running generally from west to east and to this day largely inhabited by tribal people. This belt has played mainly a negative role throughout Indian history in that it remained relatively thinly populated and did not form the focal point of any of the principal regional cultural developments of South Asia. However, it is traversed by various routes linking the more-attractive areas north and south of it. The Narmada (Narbada) River flows through this belt toward the west, mostly along the Vindhya Range, which has long been regarded as the symbolic boundary between northern and southern India. The northern parts of India represent a series of contrasting regions, each with its own distinctive cultural history and its own distinctive population. In the northwest the valleys of the Baluchistan uplands (now largely in Balochistan, Pak.) are a low-rainfall area, producing mainly wheat and barley and having a low density of population. Its residents, mainly tribal people, are in many respects closely akin to their Iranian neighbours. The adjacent Indus plains are also an area of extremely low rainfall, but the annual flooding of the river in ancient times and the exploitation of its waters by canal irrigation in the modern period have enhanced agricultural productivity, and the population is correspondingly denser than that of Baluchistan. The Indus valley may be divided into three parts: in the north are the plains of the five tributary rivers of the Punjab (Persian: Panjab, "Five Waters"); in the centre the consolidated waters of the Indus and its tributaries flow through the alluvial plains of Sind; and in the south the waters pass naturally into the Indus delta. East of the latter is the Great Indian, or Thar, Desert, which is in turn bounded on the east by a hill system known as the Aravali Range, the northernmost extent of the Deccan plateau region. Beyond them is the hilly region of Rajasthan and the Malwa Plateau. To the south is the Kathiawar Peninsula, forming both geographically and culturally an extension of Rajasthan. All of these regions have a relatively denser population than the preceding group, but for topographical reasons they have tended to be somewhat isolated, at least during historical times.

East of the Punjab and Rajasthan, northern India develops into a series of belts running broadly west to east and following the line of the foothills of the Himalayan ranges in the north. The southern belt consists of a hilly, forested area broken by the numerous escarpments in close association with the Vindhya Range, including the Bhander, Rewa, and Kaimur plateaus. Between the hills of central India and the Himalayas lies the Ganges River valley proper, constituting an area of high-density population, moderate rainfall, and high agricultural productivity. Archaeology suggests that, from the beginning of the 1st millennium BCE, rice cultivation has played a large part in supporting this population. The Ganges valley divides into three major parts: to the west is the Ganges-Yamuna Doab (the land area that is formed by the confluence of the two rivers); east of the confluence lies the middle Ganges valley, in which population tends to increase and cultivation of rice predominates; and to the southeast lies the extensive delta of the combined Ganges and Brahmaputra rivers. The Brahmaputra flows from the northeast, rising from the Tibetan Himalayas and emerging from the mountains into the Assam valley, being bounded on the east by the Patkai Bum Range and the Naga Hills and on the south by the Mikir, Khasi, Jaintia, and Garo hills. There is plenty of evidence that influences reached India from the northeast in ancient times, even if they are less prominent than those that arrived from the northwest.

Along the Deccan plateau there is a gradual eastward declivity, which dispenses its major river systems—the Mahanadi, Godavari, Krishna, and Kaveri (Cauvery)—into the Bay of Bengal. Rising some 3,000 feet (1,000 metres) or more along the western edge of the Deccan, the escarpment known as the Western Ghats traps the moisture of winds from the Arabian Sea, most notably during the southwest monsoon, creating a tropical monsoon climate along the narrow western littoral and depriving the Deccan of significant precipitation. The absence of snowpack in the south Indian uplands makes the region dependent entirely on rainfall for its stream flow. The arrival of the southwest monsoon in June is thus a pivotal annual event in peninsular culture.

FROM THE PALEOLITHIC PERIOD TO THE DECLINE OF THE INDUS CIVILIZATION

The earliest periods of Indian history are known only through reconstructions from archaeological evidence. Since the late 20th century, much new data has emerged, allowing a far fuller reconstruction than was formerly possible. This section will discuss five major periods: (1) the early prehistoric period (before the 8th millennium BCE), (2) the period of the prehistoric agriculturalists and pastoralists (approximately the 8th to the mid-4th millennium BCE), (3) the Early Indus, or Early Harappan, Period (so named for the excavated city of Harappa in eastern Pakistan), witnessing

the emergence of the first cities in the IndusRiver system (c. 3500–2600 BCE), (4) the Indus, or Harappan, civilization (c. 2600–2000 BCE, or perhaps ending as late as 1750 BCE), and (5) the Post-Urban Period, which follows the Indus civilization and precedes the rise of cities in northern India during the second quarter of the 1st millennium BCE (c. 1750–750 BCE). The materials available for a reconstruction of the history of India prior to the 3rd century BCE are almost entirely the products of archaeological research. Traditional and textual sources, transmitted orally for many centuries, are available from the closing centuries of the 2nd millennium BCE, but their use depends largely on the extent to which any passage can be dated or associated with archaeological evidence. For the rise of civilization in the Indus valley and for contemporary events in other parts of the subcontinent, the evidence of archaeology is still the principal source of information. Even when it becomes possible to read the short inscriptions of the Harappan seals, it is unlikely that they will provide much information to supplement other sources. In those circumstances it is necessary to approach the early history of India largely through the eyes of the archaeologists, and it will be wise to retain a balance between an objective assessment of archaeological data and its synthetic interpretation.

THE EARLY PREHISTORIC PERIOD

In the mid-19th century, archaeologists in southern India identified hand axes comparable to those of Stone Age Europe. For nearly a century thereafter, evaluation of a burgeoning body of evidence consisted in the attempt to correlate Indian chronologies with the well-documented European and Mediterranean chronologies. As the vast majority of early finds were from surface sites, they long remained without precise dates or cultural contexts. More recently, however, the excavation of numerous cave and dune sites has yielded artifacts in association with organic material that can be dated using the carbon-14 method, and the techniques of thermoluminescent and paleomagnetic analysis now permit dating of pottery fragments and other inorganic materials. Research beginning in the late 20th century has focused on the unique environment of the subcontinent as the context for a cultural evolution analogous to, but not uniform with, that of other regions. Increasing understanding of plate tectonics, to cite one development, has greatly advanced this endeavour.

Most outlines of Indian prehistory have employed nomenclature once thought to reflect a worldwide sequence of human cultural evolution. The European concept of the Old Stone Age, or Paleolithic Period (comprising Lower, Middle, and Upper stages), remains useful with regard to South Asia in identifying levels of technology, apart from any universal time line. Similarly, what has been called the Indian Mesolithic Period (Middle Stone Age) corresponds in general typological terms to that of Europe. For the subsequent periods, the designations Neolithic Period (New Stone Age) and Chalcolithic Age (Copper-Stone Age) also are applied, but increasingly, as archaeology has yielded more-detailed cultural profiles for those periods, scholars have come to emphasize the subsistence bases of early societies—e.g., hunting and gathering, pastoralism, and agriculture. The terms Early Harappan and Harappan (from the site where remains of a major city of the Indus civilization were discovered in 1921) are used primarily in a chronological way but also loosely in a cultural sense, relating respectively to periods or cultures that preceded the appearance of city life in the Indus valley and to the Indus civilization itself.

THE INDIAN PALEOLITHIC

The oldest artifacts yet found on the subcontinent, marking what may be called the beginning of the Indian Lower Paleolithic, come from the western end of the Shiwalik Range, near Rawalpindi in northern Pakistan. These quartzite pebble tools and flakes date to about two million years ago, according to paleomagnetic analysis, and represent a pre-hand-ax industry of a type that appears to have persisted for an extensive period thereafter. The artifacts are associated with extremely rich sedimentary evidence and fossil fauna, but thus far no correlative hominin (i.e., members of the human lineage) remains have been found. In the same region the earliest hand axes (of the type commonly associated with Acheulean industry) have been dated paleomagnetically to about 500,000 years ago.

The Great Indian Desert, straddling what is now the southern half of the India-Pakistan border, supplied significant archaeological materials in the late 20th century. Hand axes found at Didwana, Rajasthan, similar to those from the Shiwalik Range, yield slightly younger dates of about 400,000 years ago. Examination of the desert soil strata and other evidence has revealed a correlation between prevailing climates and the successive levels of technology that constitute the Paleolithic. For example, a prolonged humid phase, as attested by reddish brown soil with a deep profile, appears to have commenced some 140,000 years ago and lasted until about 25,000 years ago, roughly the extent of the Middle Paleolithic Period. During that time the area of the present desert provided a rich environment for hunting. The Rohri Hills, located at the Indus River margins of the desert, contain a group of sites associated with sources of chert, a type of stone that is a principal raw material for making tools and weapons. Evidence surrounding these chert bands—in an alluvial plain otherwise largely devoid of stone—suggests their development as a major factory centre during the Middle Paleolithic. The transition in this same region to a drier climate during the period from about 40,000 to about 25,000 years ago coincides with the onset of the Upper Paleolithic, which lasted until about 15,000 years ago. The basic innovation marking this stage is the production of parallel-sided blades from a prepared core. Also, tools of the Upper Paleolithic exhibit adaptations for working particular materials, such as leather, wood, and bone. The earliest rock paintings yet discovered in the region date to the Upper Paleolithic.

Other important Paleolithic sites that have been excavated include those at Hunsgi in Karnataka state, at Sanghao cave in North-West Frontier Province, Pak., and in the Vindhya Range separating the Ganges basin from the Deccan plateau. At the latter, local workers readily identified a weathered Upper Paleolithic limestone carving as a representation of a mother goddess.

Mesolithic Hunters

The progressive diminution in the size of stone artifacts that began in the Middle Paleolithic reached its climax in the small parallel-sided blades and microliths of what has been called the Indian Mesolithic. A great proliferation of Mesolithic cultures is evident throughout India, although they are known almost exclusively from surface collections of tools. Cultures of this period exhibited a wide variety of subsistence patterns, including hunting and gathering, fishing, and, at least for part of the period, some herding and small-scale agriculture. It may be inferred from numerous examples that hunting cultures frequently coexisted and interacted with agricultural and pastoral communities. These relationships must have continually varied from region to region as a result of environmental and other factors. Strikingly, such patterns of inter-action persisted in the subcontinent throughout the remainder of the prehis-toric period and long into the historic, with vestiges still discernible in some areas in the 20th century.

Thus, chronologically, the Mesolithic cultures cover an enormous span. In Sri Lanka several Mesolithic sites have been dated to as early as about 30,000 years ago, the oldest yet recorded for the period in South Asia. At the other end of the sub-continent, in caves of the Hindu Kush in northern Afghanistan, evidence of occu-pation dating to between 15,000 and 10,000 BCE represents the Epipaleolithic Stage, which may be considered to fall within the Mesolithic. The domestication of sheep and goats is thought to have begun in this region and period.

Many of the caves and rock shelters of central India contain rock paintings depicting a variety of subjects, including game animals and such human activities as hunting, honey collecting, and dancing. This art appears to have developed from Upper Paleolithic precursors and reveals much about life in the period. Along with the art have come increasingly clear indi-cations that some of the caves were sites of religious activity.

THE EARLIEST AGRICULTUR-ALISTS AND PASTORALISTS

The Indo-Iranian borderlands form the eastern extension of the Iranian plateau and in some ways mirror the environ-ment of the Fertile Crescent (the arc of agricultural lands extending from the Tigris-Euphrates river system to the Nile valley) in the Middle East. Across the pla-teau, lines of communication existed from early antiquity, which would sug-gest a broad parallelism of developments at both the eastern and western extremi-ties. During the late 20th century, knowledge of early settlements on the borders of the Indus system and Baluchistan was revolutionized by exca-vations at Mehrgarh and elsewhere.

NEOLITHIC AGRICULTURE IN THE INDUS VALLEY AND BALUCHISTAN

The group of sites at Mehrgarh provides evidence of some five or six thousand years of occupation comprising two major periods, the first from the 8th through the 6th millennium BCE and the second from the 5th through the 4th (and possibly the 3rd) millennium. The earliest evidence occurs in a mound 23 feet (7 metres) deep discovered beneath massive alluvial deposits. Two subphases of Period I are apparent from the mound artifacts.

Phase IA, dating to the 8th–7th mil-lennium BCE, was an aceramic (i.e., lacking pottery) Neolithic occupation. The main tools were stone blades, includ-ing lunates and triangles, some probably mounted in wooden hafts with bitumen mastic; a relatively small number of ground stone axes have been found. Domestication of wheat and barley appar-ently reached the area sometime during this phase, as did that of sheep and goats, although the preponderance of gazelle bones among the animal remains suggests continued dependence on hunting. Houses of mud brick date from the beginning of this phase and continue throughout the occupation. Accompaniments to the simple burial of human remains included shell or stone-bead necklaces, baskets, and occasionally young caprids (both sheep and goats) slaughtered for the purpose.

Phase 1B, dating to the 7th–6th millennium, is characterized by the emergence of pottery and improvements in agriculture. By the beginning of Phase 1B, cattle (apparently *Bos indicus,* the Indian humped variety) had come to predominate over game animals, as well as over sheep and goats. A new type of building, the small regular compartments of which identify it almost certainly as a granary, first appeared during this phase and became prevalent in Period II, indicating the frequent occurrence of crop surpluses. Burial took a more elaborate form—a funerary chamber was dug at one end of a pit, and, after inhumation, the chamber was sealed by a mud brick wall. From the latter phase of Period I also come the first small, hand-modeled female figurines of unburned clay.

The Period I evidence at Mehrgarh provides a clear picture of an early agricultural settlement exhibiting domestic architecture and a variety of well-established crafts. The use of seashells and of various semi-precious stones, including turquoise and lapis lazuli, indicates the existence of trade networks extending from the coast and perhaps also from Central Asia.

Striking changes characterize Period II. It appears that some major tectonic event took place at the beginning of the period (c. 5500 BCE), causing the deposition of great quantities of silt on the plain, almost completely burying the original mound at Mehrgarh. Nearly all features of the earlier culture persisted, though in altered form. There was an increase in the use of pottery. The granary structures proliferated, sometimes on a larger scale. The remains of several massive brick walls and platforms suggest something approaching monumental architecture. Evidence appears of several new crafts, including the first examples of the use of copper and ivory. The area of the settlement appears to have grown to accommodate an increasing population.

While the settlement at Mehrgarh merits extensive consideration, it should not be perceived as a unique site. There are indications (not yet fully explored) that other equally early sites may exist in other parts of Baluchistan and elsewhere on the Indo-Iranian borderlands.

In the northern parts of the Indus system, the earliest known settlements are substantially later than Mehrgarh. For example, at Sarai Khola (near the ruins of Taxila in the Pakistan Punjab) the earliest occupation dates from the end of the 4th millennium and clearly represents a tradition quite distinct from that of contemporary Sind or Balochistan, with ground stone axes and plain burnished red-brown pottery. The same is the case at Burzahom in the Vale of Kashmir, where deep pit dwellings are associated with ground stone axes, bone tools, and gray burnished pottery. Evidence of the "aceramic Neolithic" stage is reported at Gufkral, another site in the Kashmir region, which has been dated by radiocarbon to the 3rd millennium and later.

DEVELOPMENTS IN THE GANGES BASIN

In the hills to the south of the Ganges (Ganga) valley, a group of sites has been assigned to the "Vindhya Neolithic"; for at least one of these, Koldihwa, dates as early as the 7th millennium have been reported. The sites contain circular huts made of timber posts and thatch; associated implements and vessels include stone blades, ground stone axes, bone tools, and crude handmade pottery, often bearing the marks of cords or baskets used in shaping the clay. In one case a small cattle pen has been excavated. Rice husks occur, though whether from wild or cultivated varieties remains to be determined. There exists considerable uncertainty about the chronology of these settlements; very few radiocarbon dates penetrate further than the 2nd millennium.

EARLIEST SETTLEMENTS IN PENINSULAR INDIA

The earliest dates recorded for settlements in peninsular India belong to the opening centuries of the 3rd millennium. A pastoral character dominates the evidence. In the northern parts of Karnataka,

the nucleus from which stone-ax-using pastoralists appear to have spread to many parts of the southern peninsula has been located. The earliest radiocarbon dates obtained in this area are from ash mounds formed by the burning on these sites of great masses of cow dung inside cattle pens. These indicate that the first settlers were seminomadic and that they had large herds of Brahman (zebu) cattle. The earliest known settlements, which were located at Kodekal and Utnur, date to about 2900 BCE. Other important sites are Brahmagiri and Tekkalkota in Karnataka and Utnur and Nagarajunikonda in Andhra Pradesh. At Tekkalkota three gold ornaments were excavated, indicating exploitation of local ore deposits, but no other metal objects have been found, suggesting a relative scarcity of metals. These early sites produced distinctive burnished gray pottery, smaller quantities of black-on-red painted pottery, stone axes, and bone points, and in some instances evidence of a stone-blade industry. The axes have a generally oval section and triangular form with pointed butts. Among bone remains, those of cattle are in the majority, while those of sheep or goats are also present. Other settlements have been excavated in recent years in this region, but so far they have produced dates from the 2nd millennium, suggesting that the culture continued with little change for many centuries. Stone axes of a generally similar form have been found widely throughout the southern peninsula and may be taken as indications of the spread of pastoralists throughout the region during the 2nd millennium BCE.

EARLIEST SETTLEMENTS IN EASTERN INDIA

Archaeologists have long postulated the existence of Neolithic settlements in the eastern border regions of South Asia on the basis of widespread collections of ground stone axes and adzes, often of distinctive forms, comparable to those of Southeast Asia and south China. There is, however, little substantial evidence for the date of these collections or for the culture of the people who made them. Excavations at one site, Sarutaru, near the city of Guwahati, revealed stone axes and shouldered celts (one of the distinctive tool types of the Neolithic) in association with cord- or basket-marked pottery.

THE RISE OF URBANISM IN THE INDUS VALLEY

From about 5000 BCE, increasing numbers of settlements began to appear throughout the Indo-Iranian borderlands. These, as far as can be judged, were village communities of settled agriculturalists, employing common means of subsistence in the cultivation of wheat, barley, and other crops and in the keeping of cattle, sheep, and goats; there was a broadly common level of technology based on the use of stone for some artifacts and copper and bronze for others. Comparison and contrast of the high-quality painted pottery of the period

suggest distinct groupings among the communities.

At a somewhat later date, probably toward the middle of the 4th millennium BCE, agricultural settlements began to spread more widely in the Indus valley itself. The earliest of these provide clear links with the cultures along or beyond the western margins of the Indus valley. In the course of time, a remarkable change took place in the form of the Indus settlements, suggesting that some kind of closer interaction was developing, often over considerable distances, and that a process of convergence was under way. This continued for approximately 500 years and can now be identified as marking a transition toward the full urban society that emerged at Harappa and similar sites about 2600 BCE. For this reason, this stage has been named the Early Harappan, or Early Indus, culture.

EXTENT AND CHRONOLOGY OF EARLY HARAPPAN CULTURE

It is now clear that sites assignable to the Early Harappan Period extend over an immense area: from the Indus delta in the south, southeastward into Saurashtra; up the Indus valley to western Punjab in the northwest; eastward past Harappa to the Bahawalpur region of Pakistan; and, in the northeast, into the Indian states of Punjab and Haryana. In short, the area of the Early Harappan culture was nearly coextensive with that of the mature Indus civilization.

Radiocarbon dating of artifacts from a number of the excavated sites provides a fairly consistent chronological picture. The Early Harappan Period began in the mid-4th millennium BCE and continued until the mid-3rd millennium, when the mature Indus civilization displaced it in many regions. In some regions, notably in Punjab, the mature urban style seems never to have been fully established, and in these areas the Early Harappan style continued with little or no outward sign of mature Harappan contact until about 2000 BCE.

PRINCIPAL SITES

One of the most significant features of the Early Harappan settlements is the evidence for a hierarchy among the sites, culminating in a number of substantial walled towns. The first site to be recognized as belonging to the Early Harappan Period was Amri in 1929. In 1948 the British archaeologist Sir Mortimer Wheeler discovered a small deposit of pottery stratified below the remains of the mature Indus city at Harappa. The next site to be excavated with a view to uncovering the Early Harappan Period was Kot Diji (in present-day Sind province, Pakistan). A stone rubble wall surrounded this settlement, which appears to date to about 3000 BCE. An even earlier example is Rehman Dheri, near Dera Ismail Khan, which appears to have achieved its walled status during the last centuries of the 4th millennium. There the roughly rectangular, grid-patterned settlement was surrounded by a massive wall of mud brick. Early

Harappan Kalibangan (Kali Banga) in Rajasthan resembled Rehman Dheri in form. It later served as the basis for an expanded settlement of the mature Indus civilization. Still farther east in the eastern Punjab and in Haryana are many other Early Harappan sites. Among them several have been excavated, notably Banawali and Mitathal. Another example of a walled settlement of the period is Tharro in southern Sind. This was probably originally a coastal site, although it is now many miles from the sea. There the surrounding wall and the extant traces of houses are of local stone.

SUBSISTENCE AND TECHNOLOGY

Many of the excavated sites mentioned above have yet to be fully studied and the findings published, and knowledge of the various features of the life and economy of their inhabitants remains somewhat scanty. All the evidence indicates that the subsistence base of Early Harappan economy remained much as it had already developed at Mehrgarh some two millennia earlier; cattle, sheep, and goats constituted the principal domestic animals, and wheat and barley formed the staple crops. From Kalibangan and several other sites in Bahawalpur and Punjab comes intriguing evidence concerning the use of the plow. At the former site, excavators discovered what appeared to be a plowed field surface preserved beneath buildings from the mature Indus period. The pattern of crisscrossed furrows was virtually identical to that still employed in the region, the wider furrows in one direction being used for taller crops, such as peas, and the narrow perpendicular rows being used for oilseed plants such as those of the genus *Sesamum* (sesame). From Banawali and sites in the desiccated Sarasvati River valley came terra-cotta models of plows, supporting the earlier interpretation of the field pattern.

The evidence for the various Early Harappan crafts and their products also calls for further publication and detail before a firm picture can be obtained. Thus far, only a small number of copper tools have been found, and little can yet be confirmed regarding their sources and manufacture. A number of the settlement sites lie far from any sources of stone, and thus the regular appearance of a stone-blade industry, producing small, plain or serrated blades from prepared stone cores, implies that the raw materials must have been imported, often from considerable distances. The same assumption applies to the larger stones employed as rubbers or grinders, but in the absence of detailed research, no firm conclusions are possible. Related evidence does indicate that some contemporary sites, such as Lewan and Tarakai Qila in the Bannu basin, were large-scale factories, producing many types of tools from carefully selected stones collected and brought in from neighbouring areas. These same sites also appear to have been centres for the manufacture of beads of various semiprecious stones.

CULTURE AND RELIGION

It may be concluded on the basis of pottery decoration that major changes were taking place in the intellectual life of the whole region during the Early Harappan Period. At a number of sites the pottery bears a variety of incised or painted marks, some superficially resembling script. The significance of these marks is not clear, but most probably they represent owners' marks, applied at the time of manufacture. Although it would be an exaggeration to regard these marks as actual writing, they suggest that the need for a script was beginning to arise.

Among the painted decorations found on the pottery, some appear to carry a distinctly religious symbolism. The clearest instance of this is in the widespread occurrence of the buffalo-head motif, characterized by elongated horns and in some cases sprouting pipal (*Ficus religiosa*) branches or other plant forms. These have been interpreted as representing a "buffalo deity." A painted bowl from Lewan displays a pair of such heads, one a buffalo and the other a *Bos indicus*, each adorned with pipal foliage. Other devices from the painted pottery may also have religious significance, particularly the pipal leaves that occur as independent motifs. Other examples include fish forms and the fish-scale pattern that later appears as a common decoration on the mature Indus pottery. Throughout the region, evidence supports a "convergence" of form and decoration in anticipation of the more conservative Indus style.

INDUS RIVER

The Indus River is the great trans-Himalayan river of southern Asia. It is one of the world's longest rivers, with a length of 1,800 miles (2,900 km), and its annual average flow of 272 billion cubic yards (207 billion cubic metres) is twice that of the Nile River. The Indus rises in southwestern Tibet and flows northwest through valleys of the Himalayas. After crossing into the Kashmir region, it continues northwestward through the Indian- and Pakistani-administered areas of the region and then turns south into Pakistan. Swelled by tributaries from the Punjab region, including the Jhelum, Chenab, Ravi, Beas, and Sutlej rivers, it widens and flows more slowly. It has supplied water for irrigation on the plains of the Indus valley since ancient times.

The remains discussed above, considered collectively, suggest that four or five millennia of uninterrupted agricultural life in the Indus region set the stage for the final emergence of an indigenous Indus civilization about 2600 BCE. It could also be argued, however, that the substantial Early Harappan walled towns constituted cities. Much research, excavation, and comparative analysis are required before this fertile and provocative period can be understood.

THE INDUS CIVILIZATION

The earliest known urban culture of the Indian subcontinent is known as the Indus (or Harappan) civilization. Among the great civilizations of the ancient world—the others being Egypt, Mesopotamia, and the Huang He (Yellow River) region of China—the Indus was the most extensive.

CHARACTER AND SIGNIFICANCE

While the Indus civilization may be considered the culmination of a long process indigenous to the Indus valley, a number of parallels exist between developments on the Indus River and the rise of civilization in Mesopotamia. It is striking to compare the Indus with this better-known and more fully documented region and to see how closely the two coincide with respect to the emergence of cities and of such major concomitants of civilization as writing, standardized weights and measures, and monumental architecture. Yet nearly all the earlier writers have sensed the Indian-ness of the civilization, even when they were largely unable to articulate it. Thus, historian V. Gordon Childe wrote that:

India confronts Egypt and Babylonia by the 3rd millennium

with a thoroughly individual and independent civilization of her own, technically the peer of the rest. And plainly it is deeply rooted in Indian soil. The Indus civilization represents a very perfect adjustment of human life to a specific environment. And it has endured; it is already specifically Indian and forms the basis of modern Indian culture. (New Light on the Most Ancient East, 4th ed., 1952.)

The force of Childe's words can be appreciated even without an examination of the Indus valley script found on seals; the attention paid to domestic bathrooms, the drains, and the Great Bath at Mohenjo-daro can all be compared to elements in the later Indian civilization. The bullock carts with a framed canopy, called *ikkas*, and boats are little changed to this day. The absence of pins and the love of bangles and of elaborate nose ornaments are all peculiarly South Asian. The religion of the Indus also is replete with suggestions of traits known from later India. The significance of the bull, the tiger, and the elephant; the composite animals; the seated yogi god of the seals; the tree spirits and the objects resembling the Shiva *linga* (a phallus symbolic of the god Shiva) of later times—all these are suggestive of enduring forms in later Indian civilization.

It is still impossible to do more than guess at the social organization or the political and administrative control implied by this vast area of cultural uniformity. The evidence of widespread trade in many commodities, the apparent uniformity of weights and measures, the common script, and the uniformity—almost common currency—of the seals all indicate some measure of political and economic control and point to the great cities Mohenjo-daro and Harappa as their centres. The presence of the great granaries on the citadel mounds in these cities and of the citadels themselves suggests—partly on the analogies of the cities of Mesopotamia—the existence of priest-kings, or at least a priestly oligarchy, that controlled the economy and civil government. The intellectual mechanism of this government and the striking degree of control implicit in it are still matters of speculation. Nor can scholars yet speak with any certainty regarding relations between the cities and surrounding villages. Much more research needs to be done, on many such topics, before the full character of the Indus civilization can be revealed.

CHRONOLOGY

The first serious attempt at establishing a chronology for the Indus civilization relied on cross-dating with Mesopotamia. In this way, Cyril John Gadd cited the period of Sargon of Akkad (2334–2279 BCE) and the subsequent Isin-Larsa Period (2017–1794 BCE) as the time when trade between ancient India and Mesopotamia was at its height. Calibration of the ever-growing number of radiocarbon dates provides a reasonably consistent series from site to site. The broad picture thus obtained suggests that the mature Indus civilization emerged between 2600 and 2500 BCE and continued in full glory to about 2000 BCE. Thereafter the evidence is still somewhat unclear, but the late stage of the mature culture probably continued until about 1700 BCE, by which time it is probably accurate to speak of the Post-Urban, or Post-Harappan, stage.

EXTENT

All the earlier writers have stressed the remarkable uniformity of the products of the Harappan civilization, and for this reason they provide a definite hallmark for its settlements. The more-recent evidence suggests that, if the outermost sites are joined by lines, the area enclosed will be a little less than about 500,000 square miles (1,300,000 square km)—considerably larger than present-day Pakistan—and if, as is generally inferred, this cultural uniformity coincided with some sort of political and administrative unity, the size of the resulting "empire" is truly vast. Within this area, several hundred sites have been identified, the great majority of which are on the plains of the Indus or its tributaries or on the now dry course of the ancient Saraswati River, which flowed south of the Sutlej River and then, perhaps, southward to the Indian Ocean, east of the main course of the Indus itself. Outside the Indus system a few sites occur on the Makran Coast, the western-most of which is at Sutkagen Dor, near the present-day

frontier with Iran. These sites were probably ports or trading posts, supporting the sea trade with the Persian Gulf, and were established in what otherwise remained a largely separate cultural region. The uplands of Baluchistan, while showing clear evidence of trade and contact with the Indus civilization, appear to have remained outside the direct Harappan rule.

To the east of the Indus delta, other coastal sites are found beyond the marshy salt flats of the Rann of Kachchh (Kutch) and in the interior of the Kathiawar Peninsula (Saurashtra). These include the estuarine trading post at Lothal on the Gulf of Khambhat (Cambay), as well as many other sites, some of which are major. West of the Indus River a number of important sites are situated on the alluvial Kacchi desert region of Balochistan, Pak., toward Sibi and Quetta. East of the Indus system, toward the north, a number of sites occur right up to the edge of the Himalayan foothills, where at Alamgirpur, north of Delhi, the easternmost Harappan (or perhaps, more properly, Late Harappan) settlement has been discovered and partly excavated. If the area covered by these sites is compared with that of the Early Harappan settlements, it will be seen that there is an expansion in several directions, along the coast to both the west and the east and eastward through the Punjab toward the Ganges-Yamuna Doab.

PLANNING AND ARCHITECTURE

The Harappan sites range from extensive cities to small villages or outposts.

The two largest are Mohenjo-daro and Harappa, each perhaps originally about a mile square in overall dimensions. Each shares a characteristic layout, oriented roughly north-south with a great fortified "citadel" mound to the west and a larger "lower city" to the east. A similar layout is also discernible in the somewhat smaller town of Kalibangan, and several other major settlements appear to have shared this scheme. Other major sites include Dholavira and Surkotada near the Rann of Kachchh; Naushahro Firoz in Balochistan, Pak.; Shortughai in northern Afghanistan; Amri, Chanhu-daro, and Judeirjo-daro in Sind; and Sandhanawala in Bahawalpur. Among the smaller sites, special interest attaches to Lothal, where a number of unique and problematic features were discovered in excavations. Of all the sites, Harappa, Mohenjo-daro, Kalibangan, and Lothal have been most extensively excavated, and more can be said of their original layout and planning. Thus, they are considered in greater detail below.

At three of the excavated major sites, the citadel mound is on a north-south axis and about twice as long as it is broad.

Stupalike stone tower, Mohenjo-daro, eastern Pakistan. Frederick M. Asher

The lower city is laid out in a grid pattern of streets; at Kalibangan these were of regularly controlled widths, with the major streets running through, while the minor lanes were sometimes offset, creating different sizes of blocks. At all three sites the citadel was protected by a massive defensive wall of brick, which at Kalibangan was strengthened at intervals by square or rectangular bastions. At Kalibangan, traces of a somewhat less substantial wall around the lower town have also been discovered. In all three cases the city was situated near a river, although these courses are now extinct.

The most common building material at every site was brick, but the proportions of burned brick to unburned mud brick vary. Mohenjo-daro employs burned brick, perhaps because timber was more readily available, while mud brick was reserved for fillings and mass work. Kalibangan, on the other hand, reserved burned brick for bathrooms, wells, and drains. Most of the domestic architecture at Kalibangan was in mud brick. Brick was generally bonded in courses of alternate headers and stretchers—the so-called English bond. Stone was rarely, if ever, employed structurally. Timber was occasionally used as a lacing for brickwork, particularly in large-scale work such as the defenses or the granary at Mohenjo-daro. The common bricks were made in an open mold, but for special purposes sawed bricks were also employed. Timber was used for the universal flat roofs, and in some instances the sockets indicate square-cut beams with spans of as much as 14 feet (4.5 metres).

The houses were invariably entered from the side lanes, with the walls to the main streets presenting a blank brick facade broken only by the drainage chutes. Apart from domestic structures, a wide range of shops and craft workshops have been encountered, including potters' kilns, dyers' vats, and the shops of metalworkers, shell workers, and bead makers. There is surprisingly little evidence of public places of worship, although at Mohenjo-daro a number of possible temples were unearthed in the lower city, and other buildings of a ritual character were reported in the citadel. The size of houses varies considerably. At the one extreme are single-roomed barracks, with cooking and bathing areas formed within by partition walls, and at the other are large houses around a central courtyard or sometimes with a set of intersecting courtyards, each with its own adjoining rooms. Nearly all the larger houses had private wells. In many cases brick stairways led to what must have been upper stories or flat roofs. The bathrooms were usually indicated by the fine quality of the brickwork in the floor and by waste drains.

IMPORTANT SITES

MOHENJO-DARO

The mounds of Mohenjo-daro lie near the right bank of the Indus in the Larkana district of Sind province. The excavations revealed that the lowest level of former occupation was covered by deposits of

The Great Bath, Mohenjo-daro, eastern Pakistan. Frederick M. Asher

alluvial silt to a depth of about 30 feet (10 metres), attributable to annual flooding. The lowest levels are thus below the present-day water table and are still largely unexcavated. As noted above, the main features of the layout of Mohenjo-daro are a citadel to the west and a lower city and grid of streets to the east. Enough has been said of the general features of the lower city to make it unnecessary to say more of the considerable areas excavated in that part. The citadel, however, demands further attention. In the citadel the English

archaeologist Sir John Hubert Marshall discovered a massive platform of mud brick and clay approximately 20 feet (6 metres) in depth, above which were six main building levels. Under this platform lay the remains of the early period. It is probable, but by no means certain, that the platform was raised as protection against floods. Both it and the great brick defensive wall around the perimeter were built at the beginning of the intermediate period.

The main buildings of the citadel all apparently belong to the same period. The most striking of these is the Great Bath, which occupies a central position in the better-preserved northern half of the citadel. It is built of fine brickwork, measures 897 square feet (83 square metres), and is 8 feet (2.5 metres) lower than the surrounding pavement. The floor of the bath consists of two skins of sawed brick set on edge in gypsum mortar, with a layer of bitumen sealer sandwiched between the skins. Water was evidently supplied by a large well in an adjacent room, and an outlet in one corner of the bath led to a high corbeled drain disgorging on the west side of the mound. The bath was reached by flights of steps at either end, originally finished with timbered treads set in bitumen. The significance of this extraordinary structure can only be guessed at, but it has generally been thought that it is linked with some sort of ritual bathing. To the north and east of the bath were groups of rooms that evidently were also designed for some special function, probably associated with the group of administrators or priests who controlled not only the city

Stone board game from Harappa, now in the Harappa Museum, eastern Pakistan. Robert Harding World Imagery/Getty Images

but also the great state that it dominated. To the west of the bath a complex of brick platforms about 5 feet (1.5 metres) high and separated from each other by narrow passages formed a podium of some 150 by 75 feet (45 by 22 metres), which has been identified by Wheeler as the base of a great granary similar to that known at Harappa. Below the granary were brick loading bays. In the southern part of the mound an oblong "assembly hall" was discovered, having four rows of fine brick plinths, presumably to take wooden columns. In a room adjacent to this hall, a stone sculpture of a seated male figure was discovered, and nearby a number of large worked-stone rings, possibly of some architectural significance. It seems certain that this area was invested with some special significance and may well have been a temple or connected with some religious cult.

HARAPPA

The vast mounds at Harappa stand on the left bank of the now dry course of the Ravi River in the Punjab. They were excavated between 1920 and 1934 by the Archaeological Survey of India, in 1946 by Wheeler, and in the late 20th century by an American and Pakistani team. When first discovered, the extensive surviving brick ramparts led to the site's being described as a ruined brick castle. The lower city is partly occupied by a modern village, and it has been seriously disturbed by erosion and brick robbers. The citadel, to the west, is

roughly a parallelogram on plan, measuring approximately 1,300 by 650 feet (400 by 200 metres). Excavation there revealed a great platform of mud brick about 20 feet (6 metres) in thickness, with a massive brick wall around the perimeter. Below the defenses were discovered traces of the Early Harappan Period. The excavations were not extensive enough to reveal the layout of the interior, but about six building periods were discovered above the platform. The most interesting remains were discovered immediately north of the citadel, close to the bed of the river: there were a series of circular platforms evidently intended to hold mortars for pounding grain; a remarkable series of brick plinths, which are inferred to have formed the podium for two rows of six granary buildings, each 50 by 20 feet (15 by 6 metres) and of a different design from those at Mohenjodaro; a series of pear-shaped furnaces, apparently used for metallurgy; and two rows of single-roomed barracks, which are generally thought to have been occupied by servants. Two other discoveries at Harappa were made to the south of the citadel. There two cemeteries were found—"R. 37," belonging to the Harappan Period, and "H," dating from the Late or even Post-Harappan Period.

KALIBANGAN

Third in importance among excavated Harappan sites is Kalibangan, which stands on the left bank of the dry bed of the Saraswati River in northern Rajasthan.

Remains of the artisans' quarter excavated at Harappa, eastern Pakistan. Roger Viollet/ Getty Images

As mentioned above, an Early Harappan settlement lies beneath the later remains, and the main Harappan township has a layout strikingly similar to that of Mohenjo-daro and Harappa. In the lower town, excavation has revealed as many as nine building phases. The citadel mound is a parallelogram on a plan of about 430 feet (130 metres) on the east-west axis and 850 feet (260 metres) on the north-south. The whole site has been drastically reduced by brick robbers, but careful excavation has revealed the foundation courses of an accurately laid rhomboid central section with oblong bastions at each corner and smaller bastions on the north and south walls. The principal access was from the south via a flight of steps. Access from the north was via a narrow postern reached by a stairway, beyond which was a further rhomboid section, having an inset gateway in the northwest corner, near the riverbank. Traces of a brick wall around the lower town were also encountered. The central sector of the citadel contained a series of high brick platforms divided by narrow passages. The upper parts of these platforms had been seriously damaged, and their function is mysterious, but they do not appear to have been the foundation for a granary. The northern sector contained normal domestic housing. A cemetery was discovered a short distance to the west of the town. It may be expected that, when the excavation of this site is published, it will add greatly to knowledge of the Indus civilization.

LOTHAL

One other excavated site deserves special attention; this is Lothal, a small settlement built on low-lying ground near a tributary of the Sabarmati River on the west side of the Gulf of Khambhat. It appears to have served as a port or trading station. Its layout is distinctive: the site is roughly rectangular, measuring about 1,180 feet (360 metres) on the long north-south axis and 690 feet (210 metres) on the east-west. It was surrounded by a massive brick wall, which was probably used for flood protection. The southeastern quadrant takes the form of a great platform of brick with earth filling, rising to a height of about 13 feet (4 metres). On this were built a series of further smaller platforms with intersecting air channels, reminiscent of the granary at Mohenjo-daro, with overall dimensions of about 159 by 139 feet (48 by 42 metres). Behind this block were other buildings including a row of 12 bathrooms with connected drains, also strongly reminiscent of those

found on the citadel at Mohenjo-daro. The remaining enclosed area was evidently taken up by houses and shops. Among the significant finds were a bead maker's factory and the shops of goldsmiths and coppersmiths. The main street ran from north to south.

The most unexpected discovery at Lothal, however, was a great brick basin measuring some 718 by 121 feet (219 by 37 metres) with extant brick walls of 15 feet (4.5 metres) in height. This lay east of the settlement, alongside the platform on which the granary block stood. At one end of the basin was a small sluice or spillway with a locking device. The excavator has inferred that the basin was a dock to which ships could be brought from the nearby estuary via an artificial channel that would have been kept clear of silt by controlling the flow of water from the spillway. This view has not been universally accepted; another view is that it provided a source of fresh water for drinking or agriculture. A cemetery was found outside the perimeter of the wall, west of the site.

OTHER IMPORTANT SITES

A growing number of other sites have been excavated, each important in its own way. On the coast near Las Bela in Balochistan, materials suggesting a substantial shell-working industry have been found at Balakot. Not far from Mehrgarh, at the head of the Kacchi desert region in Balochistan, the small settlement of Naushahro Firoz provides valuable evidence of the actual transformation of Early Harappan into mature Harappan. Near the Rann of Kachchh, Surkotada is a small settlement with an oblong fortification wall of stone. Also in Kachchh is Dholavira, which appears to be among the largest Harappan settlements so far identified; a nine-year excavation at the site completed in 2001 yielded a walled Indus valley city that dated to the mid-3rd millennium BCE and covered some 3.5 acres (1.4 hectares). The Archaeological Survey of India team uncovered a sophisticated water-management system with a series of giant reservoirs—the largest 265 by 40 feet (80 by 12 metres) wide and 23 feet (7 metres) deep—used to conserve rainwater. Of excavated sites in Punjab, Banawali is an important major settlement, surrounded by massive brick defenses. One of the most surprising discoveries, far outside the central area of the Indus civilization, is Shortughai in the Amu Darya (Oxus River) valley, in northern Afghanistan. There the remains of a small Harappan colony, presumably sited so as to provide control of the lapis lazuli export trade originating in neighbouring Badakhshan, have been excavated by a French team.

POPULATION

There have been two independent estimates of the population of Mohenjo-daro. Both are based on an estimation of the original area covered and the density of the people living there, using traditional settlements in the region in the present

day for comparison. Hugh Trevor Lambrick proposed a figure of 35,000 for Mohenjo-daro and a roughly similar figure for Harappa, while Walter A. Fairservis estimated the former at about 41,250 and the latter about 23,500. These figures are probably conservative. It would be possible to produce estimates of the population for other sites along similar lines—notably for Kalibangan, of which the lower city has an area about one-fifth that of Mohenjo-daro.

AGRICULTURE AND ANIMAL HUSBANDRY

It is certain that such great concentrations of population had never been seen in the Indian subcontinent before that date. Clearly the exploitation of the Indus River floodplains and the use of the plow attested in Early Harappan times by finds in Kalibangan were matters of supreme importance. The Indus is at a minimum during the winter months and rises steadily during the spring and early summer, reaching a maximum in midsummer and then subsiding. Lambrick has shown how the traditional exploitation of the floods could provide a simple means of growing the principal crops without even plowing, manuring, or using major irrigation. The main cereals would be sown at the end of the inundation on land that had recently emerged from the floods, and the crop would be harvested in March or April. Other crops might be sown in embanked fields at the beginning of the floods so that they could receive

The Brahman or zebu (Bos indicus), *the famous humped cow of India.* AFP/Getty Images

necessary water while growing and be harvested in the autumn. Wheat samples from the Indus cities have been identified as belonging to *Triticum sphaerococcum* and two subspecies of *T. sativum—vulgare* and *compactum*. Barley is also found, of the species *Hordeum vulgare*, variety *nudum* and variety *hexastichum*. Rice is recorded in Harappan times at Lothal in Gujarat, but whether it was wild or cultivated is not yet clear. Other crops include dates, melon, sesame, and varieties of leguminous plants, such as field peas. From Chanhu-daro,

seeds of mustard (most probably *Brassica juncea*) were obtained. Finally, there is evidence that cotton was cultivated and used for textiles.

A number of domesticated animal species have been found in excavations at the Harappan cities. The Brahman or zebu (*Bos indicus*), the humped cattle of India, were most frequently encountered, though whether along with a humpless variety, such as that shown on the seals, is not clearly established. The buffalo (*B. bubalis*) is less common and may have been wild. Sheep and goats occur, as does the Indian pig (*Sus cristatus*). The camel is present, as well as the ass (*Equus asinus*). Bones of domestic fowl are not uncommon; these fowl were domesticated from the indigenous jungle fowl. Finally, the cat and the dog were both evidently domesticated. Present, but not necessarily as a domesticated species, is the elephant. The horse is possibly present but extremely rare and apparently only present in the last stages of the Harappan Period.

COMMUNICATIONS

It is clear that, to achieve the degree of uniformity of material culture evidenced in the excavations, considerable contact must have been maintained between the towns and cities of the Indus state. Such contact may have been by both land and river, just as the foreign trade must have employed both overland and sea routes. For land travel the predominant means was probably the pack bullock, camel, or ass. All these animals are still, or were until recently, used for pack transport in the more-remote country districts of the subcontinent. For travel on the flat alluvial plains, the bullock cart was probably the main vehicle. Terra-cotta models of such carts, apparently very little different from the modern Indian cart, are frequently encountered. For the transport of persons, smaller carts, with a body raised above the level of the axle and a framed canopy (much like the modern *ikka*), are known from small bronze models. Several representations of boats also occur. They are mostly of simple design without masts or sails and would be more suitable

for river travel than for sea travel. A terra-cotta model of another type of boat with a socket for mast and eye holes for rigging was discovered at Lothal. This appears to be a somewhat more seaworthy vessel. The dock basin at Lothal may have provided berth for ships of the size of the country craft that still ply between India and the Persian Gulf. Heavy pierced stones discovered in the vicinity of the dock basin at Lothal were assumed by the excavator to be similar to stones still used by the local boatmen as anchors.

CRAFT AND TECHNOLOGY

The Indus civilization exhibits a wide range of crafts and technical skills. As Childe remarked, these depended on the same basic discoveries as those exploited in Egypt or Mesopotamia, but in each case the crafts acquired a significance of their own. More-recent research at Mohenjo-daro has shown that different quarters of the lower city appeared to house the families who specialized in different crafts; such evidence strengthens the view that occupational specialization was firmly established.

Copper and bronze were the principal metals used for making tools and implements. These include flat oblong axes, chisels, knives, spears, arrowheads (of a kind that was evidently exported to neighbouring hunting tribes), small saws, and razors. All these could be made by simple casting, chiseling, and hammering. Bronze is less common than copper, and it is notably rarer in the lower levels. Four main varieties of metal have been found: crude copper lumps in the state in which they left the smelting furnace; refined copper, containing trace elements of arsenic and antimony; an alloy of copper with 2 to 5 percent of arsenic; and bronze with a tin alloy, often of as much as 11 to 13 percent. The copper and bronze vessels of the Harappans are among their finest products, formed by hammering sheets of metal. Casting of copper and bronze was understood, and figurines of men and animals were made by the lost-wax process. These too are technically outstanding, though the overall level of copper-bronze technology is not considered to have reached the level attained in Mesopotamia.

Other metals used were gold, silver, and lead. The latter was employed occasionally for making small vases and such objects as plumb bobs. Silver is relatively more common than gold, and more than a few vessels are known, generally in forms similar to copper and bronze examples. Gold is by no means common and was generally reserved for such small objects as beads, pendants, and brooches.

Other special crafts include the manufacture of faience (earthenware decorated with coloured glazes)—for making beads, amulets, sealings, and small vessels—and the working of stone for bead manufacture and for seals. The seals were generally cut from steatite (soapstone) and were carved in intaglio or incised with a copper burin (cutting tool). Beads were made from a variety of substances, but the carnelians are particularly noteworthy. They include several varieties of etched carnelian and long barrel beads made with extraordinary skill and accuracy. Shell and ivory were also worked and were used for beads, inlays, combs, bracelets, and the like.

The pottery of the Indus cities has all the marks of mass production. A substantial proportion is thrown on the wheel (probably the same kind of foot-wheel that is still found in the Indus region and to the west to this day, as distinguished from the Indian spun wheel common throughout the remaining parts of the subcontinent). The majority of the pottery is competent plain ware, well formed and fired but lacking in aesthetic appeal. A substantial portion of the pottery has a red slip and is painted with black decoration. Larger pots were probably built up on a turntable. Among the painted designs, conventionalized vegetable patterns are common, and the elaborate geometric designs of the painted pottery of Baluchistan give way to simpler motifs, such as intersecting circles or a scale pattern. Birds, animals, fish, and more-interesting scenes are comparatively rare. Of the vessel forms, a shallow platter on a tall stand (known as the offering stand) is noteworthy, as is a tall cylindrical vessel perforated with small holes over its entire length and often open at top and bottom. The function of this latter vessel remains a mystery.

Although little has survived, very great interest attaches to the fragments

THE BEGINNINGS OF INDIA'S HISTORY | 47

of cotton textiles recovered at Mohenjo-daro. These provide the earliest evidence of a crop and industry for which India has long been famous. It is assumed that the raw cotton must have been brought in bales to the cities to be spun, woven, and perhaps dyed, as the presence of dyers' vats would seem to indicate.

Stone, although largely absent from the great alluvial plain of the Indus, played a major role in Harappan material culture. Scattered sources, mostly on the periphery, were exploited as major factory sites. Thus, the stone blades found in great numbers at Mohenjo-daro originated in the flint quarries at Sukkur, where they were probably struck in quantity from prepared cores.

TRADE AND EXTERNAL CONTACTS

It has been seen above that the area covered by the Indus civilization had a remarkably uniform level of material culture. This suggests a closely knit and integrated administration and implies internal trade within the state. Evidence of the actual exportation of objects is not always easy to find, but the wide diffusion of chert blades made of the characteristic Sukkur stone and the enormous scale of the factory at the Sukkur site strongly suggest trade. Other items also appear to indicate trade, such as the almost identical bronze carts discovered at Chanhu-daro and Harappa, for which a common origin must be postulated.

The wide range of crafts and special materials employed must also have caused the establishment of economic relations with peoples living outside the Harappan state. Such trade may be considered to be of two kinds: first, the obtaining of raw materials and other goods from the village communities or forest tribes in regions adjoining the Indus culture area; and second, trade with the cities and empires of Mesopotamia. There is ample indication of the former type, even if the regions from which specific materials were derived are not easy to pinpoint. Gold was almost certainly imported from the group of settlements that sprang up in the vicinity of the goldfields of northern Karnataka, and copper could have come from several sources—principally from Rajasthan. Lead may have come from Rajasthan or elsewhere in India. Lapis lazuli was probably imported from Iran rather than directly from the mines at Badakhshan, and turquoise probably also came from Iran. Among others were fuchsite (a chromium-rich variety of muscovite) from Karnataka, alabaster from Iran, amethyst from Maharashtra, and jade from Central Asia. There is little evidence of what the Harappans gave in exchange for these materials—possibly nondurable goods such as cotton textiles and probably various types of beads. They may have also bartered tools or weapons of copper.

For the trade with Mesopotamia there is both literary and archaeological evidence. The Harappan seals were evidently used to seal bundles of merchandise, as clay seal impressions with cord or sack marks on the reverse side testify. The presence of a number of Indus seals at Ur and other Mesopotamian cities and the discovery of a "Persian Gulf" type of seal at Lothal—otherwise known from the Persian Gulf ports of Dilmun (present-day Bahrain) and Faylakah, as well as from Mesopotamia—provide convincing corroboration of the sea trade suggested by the Lothal dock. Timber and precious woods, ivory, lapis lazuli, gold, and luxury goods such as carnelian beads, pearls, and shell and bone inlays, including the distinctly Indian kidney shape, were among the goods sent to Mesopotamia in exchange for silver, tin, woolen textiles, and grains and other foods. Copper ingots appear to have been imported to Lothal from a place known as Magan (possibly in present-day Oman). Other probable trade items include products originating exclusively in each respective region, such as bitumen, occurring naturally in Mesopotamia, and cotton textiles and chickens, major products of the Indus region not native to Mesopotamia.

Mesopotamian trade documents, lists of goods, and official inscriptions mentioning Meluhha (the ancient Akkadian name for the Indus region) supplement Harappan seals and archaeological finds. Literary references to Meluhhan trade date from the Akkadian, Ur III, and Isin-Larsa periods (i.e., c. 2350–1794 BCE), but, as texts and archaeological data indicate, the trade probably started in the Early Dynastic Period (c. 2600 BCE). During the Akkadian Period, Meluhhan vessels sailed directly to Mesopotamian ports, but by the Isin-Larsa Period, Dilmun was the entrepôt for Meluhhan and Mesopotamian traders. By the subsequent Old Babylonian Period, trade between the two cultures evidently had ceased entirely.

LANGUAGE AND SCRIPTS, WEIGHTS AND MEASURES

The maintenance of so extensive a set of relations as those implicit in the size and uniformity of the Harappan state and the extent of trade contacts must have called for a well-developed means of communication. The Harappan script has long defied attempts to read it, and therefore the language remains unknown. Relatively recent analyses of the order of the signs on the inscriptions have led several scholars to the view that the language is not of the Indo-European family, nor is it close to Sumerian, Hurrian, or Elamite. If it is related to any modern language family, it appears to be the Dravidian, presently spoken throughout the southern part of the Indian peninsula; an isolated member of this group, the Brahui language, is spoken in western Pakistan, an area closer to those regions of Harappan culture. The script, which was written from right to left, is known from the 2,000-odd short inscriptions so far recovered, ranging from single characters to inscriptions of about 20 characters. There are more than 500 signs, many appearing to be compounds of two or more other signs, but it is not yet clear whether these signs are ideographic, logographic, or other. Numerous studies of the inscriptions have been made during the past decades, including those by a

Russian team under Yury Valentinovich Knorozov and a Finnish group led by Asko Parpola. Despite various claims to have read the script, there is still no general agreement.

The Harappans also employed regular systems of weights and measures. An early analysis of a fair number of the well-formed chert cuboid weights suggested that they followed a binary system for the lower denominations—1, 2, 4, 8, 16, 32, 64—and a decimal system for the larger weights—160, 200, 320, 640, 1,600, 3,200, 6,400, 8,000, and 12,800—with the unit of weight being calculated as 0.8565 gram (0.0302 ounce). However, a more recent analysis, which included additional weights from Lothal, suggests a rather different system, with weights belonging to two series. In both series the underlying principle was decimal, with each decimal number multiplied and divided by two, giving for the main series ratios of 0.05, 0.1, 0.2, 0.5, 1, 2, 5, 10, 20, 50, 100, 200, 500(?). This suggests that there is still much work to be done to understand the full complexity of the weight system. Several scales of measurement were found in the excavations. One was a decimal scale of 1.32 inches (3.35 cm) rising probably to 13.2 inches (33.5 cm), apparently corresponding to the "foot" that was widespread in western Asia; another is a bronze rod marked in lengths of 0.367 inch (0.93 cm), apparently half a digit of a "cubit" of 20.7 inches (52.6 cm), also widespread in western Asia and Egypt. Measurements from some of the structures show that these units were accurately applied in practice.

It has also been suggested that certain curious objects may have been accurately made optical squares with which surveyors might offset right angles. In view of the accuracy of so much of the architectural work, this theory appears quite plausible.

SOCIAL AND POLITICAL SYSTEM

Despite a growing body of archaeological evidence, the social and political structures of the Indus "state" remain objects of conjecture. The apparent craft specialization and localized craft groupings at Mohenjo-daro, along with the great divergence in house types and size, point toward some degree of social stratification. Trade was extensive and apparently well-regulated, providing imported raw materials for use at internal production centres, distributing finished goods throughout the region, and arguably culminating in the establishment of Harappan "colonies" in both Mesopotamia and Badakhshan. The remarkable uniformity of weights and measures throughout the Indus lands, as well as the development of such presumably civic works as the great granaries, implies a strong degree of political and administrative control over a wide area. Further, the widespread occurrence of inscriptions in the Harappan script almost certainly indicates the use of a single lingua franca. Nevertheless, in the absence of inscriptions that can be read and interpreted, it is inevitable that far less is known of these aspects of the Indus civilization than those of contemporaneous Mesopotamia.

ART

The excavations of the Indus cities have produced much evidence of artistic activity. Such finds are important, because they provide an insight into the minds, lives, and religious beliefs of their creators. Stone sculpture is extremely rare, and much of it is quite crude. The total repertoire cannot compare to the work done in Mesopotamia during the same periods. The figures are apparently all intended as images for worship. Such figures include seated men, recumbent composite animals, or—in unique instances (from Harappa)—a standing nude male and a dancing figure. The finest pieces are of excellent quality. There is also a small but notable repertoire of cast-bronze figures, including several fragments and complete examples of dancing girls, small chariots, carts, and animals. The technical excellence of the bronzes suggests a highly developed art, but the number of examples is still small. They appear to be Indian workmanship rather than imports.

The popular art of the Harappans was in the form of terra-cotta figurines. The majority are of standing females, often heavily laden with jewelry, but standing males—some with beard and horns—are also present. It has been generally agreed that these figures are largely deities (perhaps a Great Mother and a Great God), but some small figures of mothers with children or of domestic activities are probably toys. There are

Steatite seals of the Indus valley civilization (c. 2300–c. 1750 BCE); in the National Museum of India, New Delhi. P. Chandra

varieties of terra-cotta animals, carts, and toys—such as monkeys pierced to climb a string and cattle that nod their heads. Painted pottery is the only evidence that there was a tradition of painting. Much of the work is executed with boldness and delicacy of feeling, but the restrictions of the art do not leave much scope for creativity.

The steatite seals, to whose manufacture reference was made above, form the most extensive series of objects of art in the civilization. The great majority show a humpless "unicorn" or bull in profile, while others show the Indian humped bull, elephant, bison, rhinoceros, or tiger. The animal frequently stands before a ritual object, variously identified as a standard, a manger, or even an incense burner. A considerable number of the seals contain scenes of obvious mythological or religious significance. The interpretation of these seals is, however, often highly problematic. The seals were certainly more widely diffused than other artistic artifacts and show a much higher level of workmanship. Probably they functioned as amulets, as well as more-practical devices to identify merchandise.

RELIGION AND BURIAL CUSTOMS

In spite of the unread inscriptions, there is a considerable body of evidence that allows for conjecture concerning the religious beliefs of the Harappans. First, there are the buildings identified as temples or as possessing a ritual function, such as the Great Bath at Mohenjo-daro.

Then there are the stone sculptures found to a large extent associated with these buildings. Finally, there are the terra-cotta figures, as well as the seals and amulets that depict scenes with evident mythological or religious content. The interpretation of such data necessarily involves a largely subjective element, but most commentators have thought that they indicate a religious system that was already distinctly Indian. It is assumed that there was a Great God, who had many of the attributes later associated with the Hindu god Shiva, and a Great Mother, who was the Great God's spouse and shared the attributes of Shiva's wife Durga-Parvati. Evidence also exists of some sort of animal cult, related particularly to the bull, the buffalo, and the tiger. Mythological animals include a composite bull-elephant. Some seals suggest influence from or at least traits held in common with Mesopotamia; among these are the Gilgamesh (Mesopotamian epic) motif of a man grappling with a pair of tigers and the bull-man Enkidu (a human with horns, tail, and rear hooves of a bull). Among the most interesting of the seals are those that depict cult scenes or symbols; a god, seated in a yogic (meditative) posture and surrounded by beasts, with a horned headdress and erect phallus; the tree spirit with a tiger standing before it; the horned tree spirit confronted by a worshiper; a composite beast with a line of seven figures standing before it; the pipal leaf motif; and the swastika (a symbol still widely used by Hindus, Jains, and Buddhists).

Many burials have been discovered, giving clear indication of belief in an afterlife. The cemeteries excavated at Harappa, Lothal, and Kalibangan are clearly separated from the settlement and show that the predominant rite was extended inhumation, with the body lying on its back and the head generally positioned to the north. Quantities of pottery were placed in the graves, and sometimes personal ornaments adorned the bodies. Some graves took the form of brick chambers within which the body was placed. At Lothal several pairs of skeletons were found in the same grave, and it has been suggested that this is an indication of some form of suttee (a later Hindu custom in which wives end their lives after the death of the husband).

THE END OF THE INDUS CIVILIZATION

There is no general agreement regarding the causes of the breakdown of Harappan urban society. Broadly speaking, the principal theories thus far proposed fall under four headings. The first is gradual environmental change, such as a shift in climatic patterns and consequent agricultural disaster, perhaps resulting from excessive environmental stress caused by population growth and overexploitation of resources. Second, some scholars have postulated more-precipitous environmental changes, such as tectonic events leading to the flooding of Mohenjo-daro, the drying up of the Sarawati River, or

other such calamities. Third, it is conceivable that human activities, such as invasions of tribespeople from the hills to the west of the Indus valley, perhaps even Indo-Aryans, contributed to the breakdown of Indus external trade links or more directly disrupted the cities. The fourth theory posits the occurrence of an epidemic or a similar agent of devastation. It appears likely that some complex of natural forces compromised the fabric of society and that subsequent human intervention hastened its complete breakdown.

POST-HARAPPAN DEVELOPMENTS

It is still far from certain at what date the urban society broke down. The decline probably occurred in several stages, perhaps over a century or more; the period between about 2000 and 1750 BCE is a reasonable estimation. The collapse of the urban system does not necessarily imply a complete breakdown in the lifestyle of the population in all parts of the Indus region, but it seems to have involved the end of whatever system of social and political control had preceded it. After that date the cities, as such, and many of their distinctively urban traits—the use of writing and of seals and a number of the specialized urban crafts—disappear. The succeeding era, which lasted until about 750 BCE, may be considered as Post-Harappan or, perhaps better, as "Post-Urban."

THE POST-URBAN PERIOD IN NORTHWESTERN INDIA

In Pakistan's Sind province the Post-Urban phase is recognizable in the Jhukar culture at Chanhu-daro and other sites. There certain copper or bronze weapons and tools appear to be of "foreign" type and may be compared to examples from farther west (Iran and Central Asia); a different but parallel change is seen at Pirak, not far from Mehrgarh. In the Kachchh and Saurashtra regions there appears to have been a steady increase in the number of settlements, but all are small and none can compare with such undoubtedly Harappan cities as Dholavira. In this region, however, the distinctive foreign metal elements are less prominent.

An intriguing development occurs along the Saraswati valley: there the early Post-Urban stage is associated with the pottery known from the Cemetery H at Harappa. This coincides with a major reduction in both the number and size of settlements, suggesting a deterioration in the environment. In the eastern Punjab too there is a disappearance of the larger, urban sites but no comparable reduction in the number of smaller settlements. This is also true of the settlements farther east in the Ganges-Yamuna valleys. It is probably correct to conclude that, in each of these areas during the Post-Urban Period, material culture exhibited some tendency to develop regional variations, sometimes showing continuations of features already present during the Pre-Urban and Urban phases.

THE APPEARANCE OF INDO-ARYAN SPEAKERS

Scholars have traditionally agreed that a people speaking Old Indo-Aryan dialects of the Indo-Iranian branch of the Indo-European language family arrived in the Indian subcontinent during the late 3rd and 2nd millennia BCE. These newcomers purportedly came from the steppes to the north and east of the Caspian Sea, moving first southward into the southern parts of Central Asia and from there fanning out across the Iranian plateau and spreading throughout northern India, disrupting the established sedentary culture and driving its Dravidian-speaking inhabitants of the Indus civilization southward. The movement itself remains hypothetical, but evidence from cemeteries at Sibri and south of Mehrgarh, near the mouth of the Bolan Pass, shows striking parallels—including foreign copper and bronze tools and weapons and typical pottery forms—with that from cemeteries of the Sapalli-Tepe group in Tajikistan and Uzbekistan. This correspondence suggests a date of about 2000 BCE for the presence of these people on the borders of the Indus system.

However, it is even more difficult to identify traces that may be associated with the movement of Indo-Aryan speakers into the central Indus plains or to determine whether the occasional copper or bronze weapons of foreign type found in late contexts at Mohenjo-daro or Chanhu-daro are evidence of their presence there. Moreover, even if Indo-Aryans actually conquered some of the Indus cities and established hegemony over the local population, it has to be explained why they appear to have given up many of their distinctive material products while presumably retaining their distinctive speech.

One hypothesis is that between about 2000 and 1500 BCE not an invasion but a continuing spread of Indo-Aryan speakers occurred, carrying them much farther into India, to the east and south, and coinciding with a growing cultural interaction between the native population and the new arrivals. From these processes a new cultural synthesis emerged, giving rise by the end of the 2nd millennium to the conscious expressions of Aryan ethnicity found in the Rigveda, particularly in the later hymns.

A more recent and controversial theory put forward by such scholars as American Jim G. Shaffer and Indian B. B. Lal suggests that Aryan civilization did not migrate to the subcontinent but was an original ethnic and linguistic element of pre-Vedic India. This theory would explain the dbeeline of physical signs of any putative Aryan conquest and is supported by the high degree of physical continuity between Harappan and Post-Harappan society.

THE LATE 2ND MILLENNIUM AND THE REEMERGENCE OF URBANISM

Toward the end of the 2nd millennium there appears to have been a further deterioration in the environment throughout the Indus system. Many of the Post-Urban settlements seem to have been abandoned, and traces are found of temporary settlements that were probably associated with nomadic pastoral groups and distinguished by the poverty of their material culture. Along the Saraswati there is further evidence of the drying up of the Derawar oasis, with a further decline in the number and size of settlements. As yet, these events are not properly dated, but they may tentatively be assigned to a period from about 1200–800 BCE. In Saurashtra a similar if less extreme decline in the number of settlements is also evident. Even much farther south, in Maharashtra, the opening of the 1st millennium seems to have coincided with a period of desiccation, in which the flourishing agricultural settlements at sites such as Inamgaon declined; temporary encampments of pastoral nomads indicate a general deterioration in the standard of living.

To the north, in Punjab, Haryana, and the upper Gangetic plain, such deterioration is less apparent, perhaps because the proximity of the Himalayas produced a higher level of rainfall. It is in this area that a new tendency emerges—the expansion of settlements associated with the pottery known as Painted Gray Ware. This characteristic ceramic accompanied a spread of settlements toward the east into the upper Ganges-Yamuna valleys and constitutes a distinguishing feature of the process of development that, by the second quarter of the 1st millennium

BCE, gave rise to the first cities of the Ganges system. (The previous wave of urbanization appears not to have penetrated below the upper Gangetic plain.)

Another factor that coincided with, if not actually contributed to, the new process of change is the beginning and spread of iron working. The earliest dated occurrence of iron is probably that from about 1200 to 1100 BCE at Pirak in the Kacchi region. Comparably early dates are suggested at other widely scattered sites, but it probably took many years for the use of iron in almost all types of toolmaking to become common in all regions. During this period an increasingly marked contrast may be observed between the growing number of cities across the north and the relatively less-developed settlement pattern of peninsular India, where a mixture of small-scale agriculture and pastoralism coincided with the appearance of the various types of "Megalithic" graves and monuments.

PENINSULAR INDIA IN THE AFTERMATH OF THE INDUS CIVILIZATION (C. 2000–1000 BCE)

It was stated above that the earliest known settlements in peninsular India appeared early in the 3rd millennium and showed either a mixed agricultural or strongly pastoral character. From about 2000 BCE there appears to have been a general expansion of these settlements. It is sometimes suggested that this expansion may have been in some way a result of the end of the Indus civilization and that large numbers of "Harappans" migrated to the south. There is little solid evidence to support this view, and it appears rather that the development was primarily indigenous. What is particularly noteworthy is the way in which regional cultural variants occurred throughout peninsular India and often seem to be ancestral to the major cultural regions known from later historical times. In Maharashtra the excavations at Inamgaon have provided the clearest picture so far of the developments and changes that took place in one of these regions. There can be seen the variety of crops and domestic animals, the changing house types, suggestions of tribal chiefdoms, limited craft specialization, and trade. Copper and bronze artifacts, though still relatively scarce, appear alongside stone blades and axes. This mixed technology continued until the time when iron became common. Farther south, in Karnataka and Tamil Nadu, there is similar evidence, although the staple crop appears to have been millet, and wheat and barley are absent.

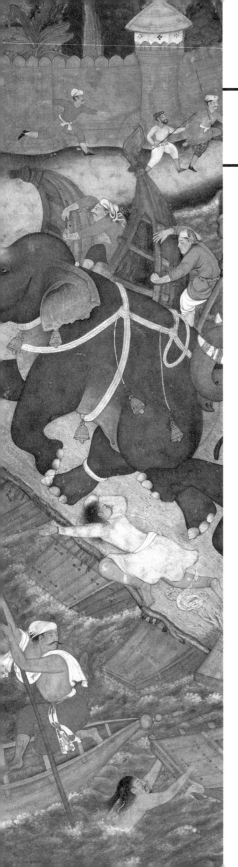

CHAPTER 2

THE DEVELOPMENT OF INDIAN CIVILIZATION FROM C. 1500 BCE TO 300 CE

The gradual decline of the Indus civilization marks the beginning of the transition, over the span of roughly 1,800 years, from prehistoric to historic times. Among many remarkable developments, the period is notable for the rise and fall of vast and small states (notably the Mauryan empire), the further spread of Indo-Aryan speakers and, later, the invasion of Alexander the Great, the emergence of great religions, and remarkable achievements in literature and the arts.

TRADITIONAL APPROACHES TO INDIAN HISTORIOGRAPHY

The European scholars who reconstructed early Indian history in the 19th century regarded it as essentially static and Indian society as concerned only with things spiritual. Indologists, such as the German Max Müller, relied heavily on the Sanskritic tradition and saw Indian society as an idyllic village culture emphasizing qualities of passivity, meditation, and otherworldliness. In sharp contrast was the approach of the Scottish historian James Mill and the Utilitarians, who condemned Indian culture as irrational and inimical to human progress. Mill first formulated a periodization of Indian history into Hindu, Muslim, and British periods, a scheme that, while still commonly used, is now controversial. During the 19th century, direct contact with Indian institutions through administration, together with the utilization of new evidence from recently deciphered inscriptions, numismatics, and local archives, provided fresh insights. Nationalist Indian historians of the early 20th century tended to exaggerate the glory of the past but nevertheless introduced controversy into historical interpretation, which in turn resulted in more precise studies of Indian institutions. In more recent times, historians have reconstructed in greater detail the social, economic, and cultural history of the subcontinent—though politics has continued to influence the study of Indian history.

A major change in the interpretation of Indian history has been a questioning of an older notion of Oriental despotism as the determining force. Arising out of a traditional European perspective on Asia, this image of despotism grew to vast proportions in the 19th century and provided an intellectual justification for colonialism and imperialism. Its deterministic assumptions clouded the understanding of early interrelationships among Indian political forms, economic patterns, and social structures.

TRENDS IN EARLY INDIAN SOCIETY

A considerable change is noticeable during this period in the role of institutions. Clan-based societies had assemblies, whose political role changed with the transformation of tribe into state and with oligarchic and monarchical governments. Centralized imperialism, which was attempted under the Mauryan empire (c. 325–185 BCE), gave way gradually to decentralized administration and to what has been called a feudalistic pattern in the post-Gupta period—i.e., from the 7th century CE. Although the village as an administrative and social unit remained constant, its relationship with the mainstream of history varied. The concept of divine kingship was known but rarely taken seriously, the claim to the status of the caste of royalty becoming more important. Because conformity to the social order had precedence over allegiance to the state, the idea of representation found expression not so much in political institutions as in caste and village assemblies. The pendulum of politics swung from large to small kingdoms, with the former attempting to establish empires—the sole successful attempt being that of the Mauryan dynasty. Thus, true centralization was rare, because local forces often determined historical events. Although imperial or near-imperial periods were marked by attempts at the evolution of uniform cultures, the periods of smaller kingdoms (often referred to as the Dark Ages by earlier historians) were more creative at the local level and witnessed significant changes in society and religion. These small kingdoms also often boasted the most elaborate and impressive monuments.

The major economic patterns were those relating to land and to commerce.

The transition from tribal to peasant society was a continuing process, with the gradual clearing of wasteland and the expansion of the village economy based on plow agriculture. Recognition of the importance of land revenue coincided with the emergence of the imperial system in the 4th century BCE; and from this period onward, although the imperial structure did not last long, land revenue became central to the administration and income of the state. Frequent mentions of individual ownership, references to crown lands, numerous land grants to religious and secular grantees in the post-Gupta period, and detailed discussion in legal sources of the rights of purchase, bequest, and sale of land all clearly indicate that private ownership of land existed. Much emphasis has been laid on the state control of the irrigation system; yet a systematic study of irrigation in India reveals that it was generally privately controlled and that it serviced small areas of land. When the state built canals, they were mainly in the areas affected by both the winter and summer monsoons, in which village assemblies played a dominant part in revenue and general administration, as, for example, in the Chola (Cola) kingdom of southern India.

The urban economy was crucial to the rise of civilization in the Indus valley (c. 2600–2000 BCE). Later the 1st millennium BCE saw an urban civilization in the Ganges (Ganga) valley and still later in coastal south India. The emergence of towns was based on administrative needs, the requirements of trade, and pilgrimage centres. In the 1st millennium CE, when commerce expanded to include trade with western Asia, the eastern Mediterranean, and Central and Southeast Asia, revenue from trade contributed substantially to the economies of the participating kingdoms, as indeed Indian religion and culture played a significant part in the cultural evolution of Central and Southeast Asia. Gold coins were issued for the first time by the Kushan dynasty and in large quantity by the Guptas; both kingdoms were active in foreign trade. Gold was imported from Central Asia and the Roman Republic and Empire and later perhaps from eastern Africa because, in spite of India's recurring association with gold, its sources were limited. Expanding trade encouraged the opening up of new routes, and this, coupled with the expanding village economy, led to a marked increase of knowledge about the subcontinent during the post-Mauryan period. With increasing trade, guilds became more powerful in the towns. Members of the guilds participated in the administration, were associated with politics, and controlled the development of trade through merchant embassies sent to places as far afield as Rome and China. Not least, guilds and merchant associations held envied and respectable positions as donors of religious institutions.

The structure of Indian society was characterized by caste. The distinguishing features of a caste society were endogamous kinship groups (*jatis*) arranged in a hierarchy of ritual ranking, based on notions of pollution and purity, with an intermeshing of service relationships and an adherence to geographic location. There was some coincidence between caste and access to economic resources. Although ritual hierarchy was unchanging, there appears to have been mobility within the framework. Migrations of peoples both within the subcontinent and from outside encouraged social mobility and change. The nucleus of the social structure was the family, with the pattern of kinship relations varying from region to region. In the more complex urban structure, occupational guilds occasionally took on *jati* functions, and there was a continual emergence of new social and professional groups.

Religion in early Indian history did not constitute a monolithic force. Even when the royalty attempted to encourage certain religions, the idea of a state religion was absent. In the main, there were three levels of religious expression. The most widespread was the worship of local cult deities vaguely associated with major deities, as seen in fertility cults, in the worship of mother goddesses, in the Shakta-Shakti cult, and in Tantrism. Less widespread but popular, particularly in the urban areas, were the more puritanical sects of Buddhism and Jainism and the *bhakti* (devotional) tradition of Hinduism. A third level included classical Hinduism and more abstract levels of Buddhism and Jainism, with an emphasis on the major deities in the case of the first and on the teachings of the founders in the case of the latter two. It was this level, endorsed by affluent patronage, that provided the base for the initial institutionalization of religion. But the three levels were not isolated; the shadow of the third fell over the first two, the more homely rituals and beliefs of which often crept into the third. This was the case particularly with Hinduism, the very flexibility of which was largely responsible for its survival. Forms of Buddhism, ranging from an emphasis on the constant refinement of doctrine on the one hand to an incorporation of magical fertility cults in its beliefs on the other, faded out toward the end of this period.

Sanskrit literature and the building of Hindu and Buddhist temples and sculpture both reached apogees in this period. Although literary works in the Sanskrit language continued to be written and temples were built in later periods, the achievement was never again as inspiring.

FROM C. 1500 TO C. 500 BCE

By about 1500 BCE an important change began to occur in the northern half of the Indian subcontinent. The Indus civilization had declined by about 2000 BCE (or perhaps as late as 1750 BCE), and the stage was being set for a second and more lasting urbanization in the Ganges valley. The new areas of occupation were contiguous with and sometimes overlapping the core of the Harappan area. There was continuity of occupation in the Punjab and Gujarat, and a new thrust toward urbanization came from the migration of peoples from the Punjab into the Ganges valley.

EARLY VEDIC PERIOD

In addition to the archaeological legacy discussed above, there remains from this period the earliest literary record of Indian culture, the Vedas. Composed in archaic, or Vedic, Sanskrit, generally dated between 1500 and 800 BCE, and transmitted orally, the Vedas comprise four major texts—the Rig-, the Sama-, the Yajur-, and the Atharvaveda. Of these, the Rigveda is believed to be the earliest. The texts consist of hymns, charms, spells, and ritual observations current among the Indo-European-speaking people known as Aryans (from Sanskrit *arya*, "noble"), who presumably entered India from the Iranian regions.

Theories concerning the origins of the Aryans, whose language is also called Aryan, relate to the question of what has been called the Indo-European homeland. In the 17th and 18th centuries CE, European scholars who first studied Sanskrit were struck by the similarity in its syntax and vocabulary to Greek and Latin. This resulted in the theory that there had been a common ancestry for these and other related languages, which came to be called the Indo-European group of languages. This in turn resulted in the notion

that Indo-European-speaking peoples had a common homeland from which they migrated to various parts of Asia and Europe. The theory stirred intense speculation, which continues to the present day, regarding the original homeland and the period or periods of the dispersal from it. The study of Vedic India is still beset by "the Aryan problem," which often clouds the genuine search for historical insight into this period.

That there was a migration of Indo-European speakers, possibly in waves, dating from the 2nd millennium BCE, is clear from archaeological and epigraphic evidence in western Asia. Mesopotamia witnessed the arrival about 1760 BCE of the Kassites, who introduced the horse and the chariot and bore Indo-European names. A treaty from about 1400 BCE between the Hittites, who had arrived in Anatolia about the beginning of the 2nd millennium BCE, and the Mitanni empire invoked several deities—Indara, Uruvna, Mitira, and the Nasatyas (names that occur in the Rigveda as Indra, Varuna, Mitra, and the Ashvins). An inscription at Bogazköy in Anatolia of about the same date contains Indo-European technical terms pertaining to the training of horses, which suggests cultural origins in Central Asia or the southern Russian steppes. Clay tablets dating to about 1400 BCE, written at Tell el-Amarna (in Upper Egypt) in Akkadian cuneiform, mention names of princes that are also Indo-European.

Nearer India, the Iranian plateau was subject to a similar migration. Comparison

VEDIC RELIGION

The ancient Vedic religion of India was contemporary with the composition of the Vedas and was the precursor of Hinduism. Often called Vedism, this religion of the Indo-European-speaking peoples who entered India sometime before 1500 BCE from the region of present-day Iran was a polytheistic system in which Indra was the highest-ranked god. It involved the worship of numerous male divinities connected with the sky and natural phenomena. Ceremonies centred on ritual sacrifice of animals and on the use of soma to achieve trancelike states. These ceremonies, simple in the beginning, grew to be so complex that only trained Brahmans could carry them out correctly. Out of Vedism developed the philosophical concepts of atman and Brahman. The spread (8th–5th century BCE) of the related concepts of reincarnation, karma, and release from the cycle of rebirth through meditation rather than sacrifice marked the end of the Vedic period and the rise of Hinduism. The Hindu initiation ceremony, upanayana, *is a direct survivor of Vedic tradition.*

of Iranian Aryan literature with the Vedas reveals striking correspondences. Possibly a branch of the Iranian Aryans migrated to northern India and settled in the Sapta Sindhu region, extending from the Kābul River in the north to the Sarasvati and upper Ganges–Yamuna Doab in the south. The Sarasvati, the sacred river at the time, is thought to have dried up during the later Vedic period. Conceived as a goddess, it was personified in later Hinduism as the inventor of spoken and written Sanskrit and the consort of Brahma, promulgator of the Vedas. It was in the Sapta Sindhu region that the majority of the hymns of the Rigveda were composed.

The Rigveda is divided into 10 *mandalas* (books), of which the 10th is believed to be somewhat later than the others. Each *mandala* consists of a number of hymns, and most *mandalas* are ascribed to priestly families. The texts include invocations to the gods, ritual hymns, battle hymns, and narrative dialogues. The 9th *mandala* is a collection of all the hymns dedicated to soma, the unidentified hallucinogenic juice that was drunk on ritual occasions.

Few events of political importance are related in the hymns. Perhaps the most impressive is a description of the battle of the 10 chiefs or kings: when Sudas, the king of the preeminent Bharatas of southern Punjab, replaced his priest Vishvamitra with Vasishtha, Vishvamitra organized a confederacy of 10 tribes, including the Puru, Yadu, Turvashas, Anu, and Druhyu, which went to war against Sudas. The Bharatas survived and continued to play an important role in historical tradition. In the Rigveda the head of a clan is called the *raja*; this term commonly has been translated as "king," but more recent scholarship has suggested "chief" as more appropriate in this early context. If such a distinction is recognized, the entire corpus of Vedic literature can be interpreted as recording the gradual evolution of the concept of kingship from earlier clan organization. Among the clans there is little distinction between Aryan and non-Aryan, but the hymns refer to a people, called the *dasyus*, who are said to have had an alien language and a dark complexion and to worship strange gods. Some *dasyus* were rich in cattle and lived in fortified places (*puras*) that were often attacked by the god Indra. In addition to the *dasyus*, there were the wealthy Panis, who were hostile and stole cattle.

The early Vedic was the period of transition from nomadic pastoralism to settled village communities intermixing pastoral and agrarian economies. Cattle were initially the dominant commodity, as indicated by the use of the words *gotra* ("cowpen") to signify the endogamous kinship group and *gavishti* ("searching for cows") to denote war. A patriarchal extended family structure gave rise to the practice of *niyoga* (levirate), which permitted a widow to marry her husband's brother. A community of families constituted a *grama*. The term *vish* is generally interpreted to mean "clan." Clan assemblies appear to have been frequent in the early stages. Various categories of assemblies are mentioned, such as *vidatha*, *samiti*, and *sabha*, although the precise distinctions between these categories are not clear. The clan also gathered for the *yajna*, the Vedic sacrifice conducted by the priest, whose ritual actions ensured prosperity and imbued the chief with valour. The chief was primarily a war leader with responsibility for protecting the clan, for which function he received a *bali* ("tribute"). Punishment was exacted according to a principle resembling the wergild of ancient Germanic law, whereby the social rank of a wronged or slain man determined the compensation due him or his survivors.

THE BEGINNING OF THE HISTORICAL PERIOD, C. 500–150 BCE

For this phase of Indian history a variety of historical sources are available. The Buddhist canon, pertaining to the period of the Buddha (c. 6th–5th century BCE) and later, is invaluable as a cross-reference for the Brahmanic sources. This also is true, though to a more limited extent, of Jain sources. In the 4th century BCE there are secular writings on political economy and accounts of foreign travelers. The most important sources, however, are inscriptions of the 3rd century BCE.

PRE-MAURYAN STATES

Buddhist writings and other sources from the beginning of this period mention 16 major states (*mahajanapada*) dominating the northern part of the subcontinent. A few of these, such as Gandhara, Kamboja, Kuru-Pancala, Matsya, Kashi, and Koshala, continued from the earlier period and are mentioned in Vedic literature. The rest were new states, either freshly created from declining older ones or new areas coming into importance, such as Avanti, Ashvaka, Shurasena, Vatsa, Cedi, Malla, Vrijji, Magadha, and Anga. The mention of so many new states in the eastern Ganges valley is attributable in part to the eastern focus of the sources and is partly the antecedent to the increasing preeminence of the eastern regions.

LOCATION

Gandhara lay astride the Indus and included the districts of Peshawar and the lower Swat and Kābul valleys. For a while its independence was terminated by its inclusion as one of the 22 satrapies of the Achaemenian Empire of Persia (c. 519 BCE). Its major role as the channel of communication with Iran and Central Asia continued, as did its trade in woolen goods. Kamboja adjoined Gandhara in the northwest. Originally regarded as a land of Aryan speakers, Kamboja soon lost its important status, ostensibly because its people did not follow the sacred Brahmanic rites—a situation that was to occur extensively in the north as the result of the intermixing of peoples and cultures through migration and trade. Kamboja became a trading centre for horses imported from Central Asia.

The Kekayas, Madras, and Ushinaras, who had settled in the region between Gandhara and the Beas River, were described as descendants of the Anu tribe. The Matsyas occupied an area

to the southwest of present-day Delhi. The Kuru-Pancala, still dominant in the Ganges–Yamuna Doab area, were extending their control southward and eastward; the Kuru capital had reportedly been moved from Hastinapura to Kaushambi when the former was devastated by a great flood, which excavations show to have occurred about the 9th century BCE. The Mallas lived in eastern Uttar Pradesh. Avanti arose in the Ujjain-Narmada valley region, with its capital at Mahishmati; during the reign of King Pradyota, there was a matrimonial alliance with the royal family at Kaushambi. Shurasena had its capital at Mathura, and the tribe claimed descent from the Yadu clan. A reference to the Sourasenoi in later Greek writings is often identified with the Shurasena and the city of Methora with Mathura. The Vatsa state emerged from Kaushambi. The Cedi state (in Bundelkhand) lay on a major route to the Deccan. South of the Vindhyas, on the Godavari River, Ashvaka continued to thrive.

The mid-Ganges valley was dominated by Kashi and Koshala. Kashi maintained close affiliations with its eastern neighbours, and its capital was later to acquire renown as the sacred city of Varanasi (Benares). Kashi and Koshala were continually at war over the control of the Ganges; in the course of the conflict, Koshala extended its frontiers far to the south, ultimately coming to comprise Uttar (northern) and Dakshina (southern) Koshala. The new states of Magadha (Patna and Gaya districts) and Anga (northwest of the delta) were also interested in controlling the river and soon made their presence felt. The conflict eventually drew in the Vrijji state (Behar and Muzaffarpur districts). For a while, Videha (modern Tirhut), with its capital at Mithila, also remained powerful. References to the states of the northern Deccan appear to repeat statements from sources of the earlier period, suggesting that there had been little further exchange between the regions.

POLITICAL SYSTEMS

The political system in these states was either monarchical or a type of representative government that variously has been called republican or oligarchic. The fact that representation in these latter states' assemblies was limited to members of the ruling clan makes the term oligarchy, or even chiefdom, preferable. Sometimes within the state itself there was a gradual change from monarchy to oligarchy, as in the case of Vaishali, the nucleus of the Vrijji state. Apart from the major states, there also were many smaller oligarchies, such as those of the Koliyas, Moriyas, Jnatrikas, Shakyas, and Licchavis. The Jnatrikas and Shakyas are especially remembered as the tribes to which Mahavira (the founder of Jainism) and Gautama Buddha, respectively, belonged. The Licchavis eventually became extremely powerful.

The oligarchies comprised either a single clan or a confederacy of clans. The elected chief or the president (*ganapati* or *ganarajya*) functioned with the assistance of a council of elders probably selected from the Kshatriya families. The most important institution was the sovereign general assembly, or *parishad*, to the meetings of which members were summoned by kettledrum. Precise rules governed the seating arrangement, the agenda, and the order of speaking and debate, which terminated in a decision. A distinction was maintained between the families represented and the others. The broad authority of the *parishad* included the election of important functionaries. An occasional lapse into hereditary office on the part of the chief may account for the tendency toward monarchy among these states. The divisiveness of factions was a constant threat to the political system.

The institutional development within these oligarchies suggests a stabilized agrarian economy. Sources mention wealthy householders (*gahapatis*) employing slaves and hired labourers to work on their lands. The existence of *gahapatis* suggests the breaking up of clan ownership of land and the emergence of individual holdings. An increase in urban settlements and trade is evident not only from references in the literary sources but also from the introduction of two characteristics of urban civilization—a script and coinage. Evidence for the script dates at least to the 3rd century BCE. The most widely used script was Brahmi, which is germane to most Indian scripts used subsequently. A variant during this period was Kharoshti, used only in northwestern India and derived from the Aramaic of western Asia. The most commonly spoken languages were Prakrit, which had its local variations in Shauraseni (from which Pali evolved), and Magadhi, in which the Buddha preached. Sanskrit, the more cultured language as compared with Prakrit, was favoured by the educated elite. Panini's grammar, the Astadhyayi, and Yaska's etymological work, the Nirukta, suggest considerable sophistication in the development of Sanskrit.

ECONOMY

Silver bent bar coins and silver and copper punch-marked coins came into use in the 5th century BCE. It is not clear whether the coins were issued by a political authority or were the legal tender of moneyers. The gradual spread in the same period of a characteristic type of luxury ware, which has come to be known as the northern black polished ware, is an indicator of expanding trade. One main trade route followed the Ganges River and crossed the Indo-Gangetic watershed and the Punjab to Taxila and beyond. Another extended from the Ganges valley via Ujjain and the Narmada valley to the western coast or, alternatively, southward to the Deccan. The route to the Ganges delta became more popular, increasing maritime contact with ports on the eastern coast of India. The expansion of trade and consequently of towns resulted in an increase in the number of artisans and merchants; some eventually formed guilds (shrenis), each of which tended to inhabit a particular part of a town. The guild system encouraged specialization of labour and the hereditary principle in professions, which was also a characteristic of caste functioning. Gradually some of the guilds acquired caste status. The practice of usury encouraged the activity of financiers, some of whom formed their own guilds and found that investment in trade proved increasingly lucrative. The changed economy is evident in the growth of cities and of an urban culture in which such distinctions as pura (walled settlement), durga (fortified town), nigama (market centre), nagara (town), and mahanagara (city) became increasingly important.

RELIGION

The changing features of social and economic life were linked to religious and intellectual changes. Orthodox traditions maintained in certain sections of Vedic literature were questioned by teachers referred to in the Upanishads and Aranyakas and by others whose speculations and philosophy are recorded in other texts. There was a sizable heterodox tradition current in the 6th century BCE, and speculation ranged from idealism to materialism. The Ajivikas and the Carvakas, among the smaller sects, were popular for a time, as were the materialist theories of the Buddha's contemporary Ajita Keshakambalin. Even though such sects did not sustain an independent religious tradition, the undercurrent of their teachings cropped up time and again in the later religious trends that emerged in India.

JAINISM

Jainism is a religion of India that teaches a path to spiritual purity and enlightenment through a disciplined mode of life founded upon the tradition of ahimsa, nonviolence to all living creatures. Beginning in the 7th–5th century BCE, Jainism evolved into a cultural system that has made significant contributions to Indian philosophy and logic, art and architecture, mathematics, astronomy and astrology, and literature. Along with Hinduism and Buddhism, it is one of the three most ancient Indian religious traditions still in existence.

While often employing concepts shared with Hinduism and Buddhism, the result of a common cultural and linguistic background, the Jain tradition must be regarded as an independent phenomenon. It is an integral part of South Asian religious belief and practice, but it is not a Hindu sect or Buddhist heresy, as earlier scholars believed.

The name Jainism derives from the Sanskrit verb ji, "to conquer." It refers to the ascetic battle that it is believed Jain renunciants (monks and nuns) must fight against the passions and bodily senses to gain omniscience and purity of soul or enlightenment. The most illustrious of those few individuals who have achieved enlightenment are called Jina (literally, "Conqueror"), and the tradition's monastic and lay adherents are called Jain ("Follower of the Conquerors"), or Jaina. This term came to replace a more ancient designation, Nirgrantha ("Bondless"), originally applied to renunciants only.

Jainism has been confined largely to India, although the recent migration of Indians to other, predominantly English-speaking countries has spread its practice to many Commonwealth nations and to the United States. Precise statistics are not available, but it is estimated that there are roughly four million Jains in India and 100,000 elsewhere.

Of all these sects, only two, Jainism and Buddhism, acquired the status of major religions. The former remained within the Indian subcontinent; the latter spread to Central Asia, China, Korea, Japan, and Southeast Asia. Both religions were founded in the 6th–5th century BCE; Mahavira gave shape to earlier ideas of the Nirgranthas (an earlier name for the Jains) and formulated Jainism (the teachings of the Jina, or Conqueror, Mahavira), and the Buddha (the Enlightened One) preached a new doctrine.

There were a number of similarities among these two sects. Religious rituals were essentially congregational. Monastic orders (the *sangha*) were introduced with monasteries organized on democratic lines and initially accepting persons from all strata of life. Such monasteries were dependent on their neighbourhoods for material support. Some of the monasteries developed into centres of education. The functioning of monks in society was greater, however, among the Buddhist orders. Wandering monks, preaching and seeking alms, gave the religions a missionary flavour. The recruitment of nuns signified a special concern for the status of women. Both religions questioned Brahmanical orthodoxy and the authority of the Vedas. Both were opposed to the sacrifice of animals, and both preached nonviolence. Both derived support in the main from the Kshatriya ruling clans, wealthy *gahapatis*, and the mercantile community; because trade and commerce did not involve killing, the principle of *ahimsa* ("noninjury") could be observed in these activities. The Jains participated widely as the middlemen in financial transactions and in later centuries became the great financiers of western India. While both religions disapproved in theory of the inequality of castes, neither directly attacked the assumptions of caste society; even so, they were able to secure a certain amount of support from lower caste groups, which was enhanced by the borrowing of rituals and practices from popular local cults. The patronage of women, especially those of royal families, was to become a noticeable feature.

MAGADHAN ASCENDANCY

Political activity in the 6th–5th century BCE centred on the control of the Ganges valley. The states of Kashi, Koshala, and Magadha and the Vrijjis battled for this control for a century until Magadha emerged victorious. Magadha's success was partly due to the political ambition of its king, Bimbisara (c. 543–491 BCE). He conquered Anga, which gave him access to the Ganges delta—a valuable asset in terms of the nascent maritime trade. Bimbisara's son Ajatashatru—who achieved the throne through patricide—implemented his father's intentions within about 30 years. Ajatashatru strengthened the defenses of the Magadhan capital, Rajagrha, and built a small fort on the Ganges at Pataligrama, which was to become the famous capital Pataliputra (modern Patna). He then attacked and annexed Kashi and Koshala. He still had to subdue the confederacy of the Vrijji state, and this turned out to be a protracted affair lasting 16 years. Ultimately the Vrijjis, including the important Licchavi clan, were overthrown, having been weakened by a minister of Ajatashatru, who was able to sow dissension in the confederacy.

The success of Magadha was not solely attributable to the ambition of Bimbisara and Ajatashatru. Magadha had an excellent geographic location controlling the lower Ganges and thus drew revenue from both the fertile plain and the river trade. Access to the delta also brought in lucrative profits from the eastern coastal trade. Neighbouring forests provided timber for building and elephants for the army. Above all, nearby rich deposits of iron ore gave Magadha a lead in technology.

Bimbisara had been one of the earliest Indian kings to emphasize efficient administration, and the beginnings of an administrative system took root. Rudimentary notions of land revenue developed. Each village had a headman who was responsible for collecting taxes and another set of officials who supervised the collection and conveyed the revenue to the royal treasury. But the full understanding of the utilization of land revenue as a major source of state income was yet to come. The clearing of land continued apace, but it is likely that the agrarian settlements were small, because literary references to journeys from one town to another mention long stretches of forest paths.

After the death of Ajatashatru (c. 459 BCE) and a series of ineffectual rulers, Shaishunaga founded a new dynasty, which lasted for about half a century until ousted by Mahapadma Nanda. The Nandas are universally described as being of low origin, perhaps Sudras. Despite these rapid dynastic changes, Magadha retained its position of strength. The Nandas continued the earlier policy of expansion. They are proverbially connected with wealth, probably because they realized the importance of regular collections of land revenue.

CAMPAIGNS OF ALEXANDER THE GREAT

The northwestern part of India witnessed the military campaign of Alexander the Great of Macedon, who in 327 BCE, in pursuing his campaign to the eastern extremities of the Achaemenian Empire, entered Gandhara. He campaigned successfully across the Punjab as far as the Beas River, where his troops refused to continue fighting. The vast army of the Nandas is referred to in Greek sources, and some historians have suggested that Alexander's Macedonian and Greek soldiers may have mutinied out of fear of this army. The campaign of Alexander made no impression on the Indian mind, for there are no references to it in Indian sources. A significant outcome of his campaign was that some of his Greek companions—such as Onesicritus, Aristobulus, and his admiral, Nearchus—recorded their impressions of India. Later Greek and Roman authors such as Strabo and Arrian, as well as Pliny and Plutarch, incorporated much of this material into their writings. However, some of the accounts are fanciful and make for better fiction than history. Alexander established a number of Greek settlements, which provided an impetus for the development of trade and communication with western Asia. Most valuable to historians was a reference to Alexander's meeting the young prince Sandrocottos, a name identified in the 18th century as Chandragupta, which provides a chronological landmark in early Indian history.

THE MAURYAN EMPIRE

The accession of Chandragupta Maurya (reigned c. 321–297 BCE) is significant in Indian history because it inaugurated what was to become the first pan-Indian empire. The Mauryan dynasty was to rule almost the entire subcontinent (except the area south of present-day Karnataka), as well as substantial parts of present-day Afghanistan.

Chandragupta Maurya

Chandragupta overthrew the Nanda power in Magadha and then campaigned in central and northern India. Greek sources report that he engaged in a conflict in 305 BCE in the trans-Indus region with Seleucus I Nicator, one of Alexander's generals, who, following the death of Alexander, had founded the Seleucid dynasty in Iran. The result was a treaty by which Seleucus ceded the trans-Indus provinces to the Maurya and the latter presented him with 500 elephants. A marriage alliance is mentioned, but no details are recorded.

The treaty ushered in an era of friendly relations between the Mauryas and the Seleucids, with exchanges of envoys. One among them, the Greek historian Megasthenes, left his observations in the form of a book, the *Indica*. Although the original has been lost, extensive quotations from it survive in the works of the later Greek writers Strabo, Diodorus, and Arrian. A major treatise on political economy in Sanskrit is the *Artha-shastra* of Kautilya (or Canakya, as he is sometimes called). Kautilya, it is believed, was prime minister to Chandragupta, although this view has been contested. In describing an ideal government, Kautilya indicates contemporary assumptions of political and economic theory, and the description of the functioning of government occasionally tallies with present-day knowledge of actual conditions derived from other sources. The date of origin of the *Artha-shastra* remains problematic, with suggested dates ranging from the 4th century BCE to the 3rd century CE. Most authorities agree that the kernel of the book was originally written during the early Mauryan period but that much of the existing text is post-Mauryan.

According to Jain sources, Chandragupta became a Jain toward the end of his reign. He abdicated in favour of his son Bindusara, became an ascetic, and traveled with a group of Jain monks to southern India, where he died, in the orthodox Jain manner, by deliberate slow starvation.

Bindusara

The second Mauryan emperor was Bindusara, who came to the throne about 297 BCE. Greek sources refer to him as Amitrochates, the Greek for the Sanskrit *amitraghata*, "destroyer of foes." This name perhaps reflects a successful campaign in the Deccan, Chandragupta having already conquered northern India. Bindusara's campaign stopped in the vicinity of Karnataka, probably because the territories of the extreme south, such as those of the Cholas, Pandyas, and Ceras, were well-disposed in their relations toward the Mauryas.

Ashoka and His Successors

Bindusara was succeeded by his son Ashoka, either directly in 272 BCE or, after an interregnum of four years, in 268 BCE (some historians say c. 265 BCE). Ashoka's reign is comparatively well documented.

He issued a large number of edicts, which were inscribed in many parts of the empire and were composed in Prakrit, Greek, and Aramaic, depending on the language current in a particular region. Greek and Aramaic inscriptions are limited to Afghanistan and the trans-Indus region.

The first major event in Ashoka's reign, which he describes in an edict, was a campaign against Kalinga in 260 BCE. The suffering that resulted caused him to reevaluate the notion of conquest by

Stupa 1 (Great Stupa), eastern gateway, Sanchi, Madhya Pradesh, India. Frederick M. Asher

violence, and gradually he was drawn to the Buddhist religion. He built a number of stupas. About 12 years after his accession, he began issuing edicts at regular intervals. In one he referred to five Greek kings who were his neighbours and contemporaries and to whom he sent envoys—these were Antiochus II Theos of Syria, the grandson of Seleucus I; Ptolemy II Philadelphus of Egypt; Antigonus II Gonatas of Macedonia; Magas of Cyrene; and Alexander (of either Epirus or Corinth). This reference has become the bedrock of Mauryan chronology. Local tradition asserts that he had contacts with Khotan and Nepal. Close relations with Tissa, the king of Sri Lanka, were furthered by the fact that Mihinda, Ashoka's son (or his younger brother according to some sources), was the first Buddhist missionary on the island.

Ashoka ruled for 37 years. After his death a political decline set in, and half a century later the empire was reduced to the Ganges valley alone. Tradition asserts that Ashoka's son Kunala ruled in Gandhara. Epigraphic evidence indicates that his grandson Dasharatha ruled in Magadha. Some historians have suggested that his empire was bifurcated. In 185 BCE the last of the Mauryas, Brihadratha, was assassinated by his Brahman commander in chief, Pushyamitra, who founded the Shunga dynasty.

FINANCIAL BASE FOR THE EMPIRE

The Mauryan achievement lay in the ability to weld the diverse parts of the subcontinent into a single political unit and to maintain an imperial system for almost 100 years. The financial base for an imperial system was provided by income from land revenue and, to a lesser extent, from trade. The gradual expansion of the agrarian economy and improvements in the administrative machinery for collecting revenue increased the income from land revenue. This is confirmed by both the theories of Kautilya and the account of Megasthenes; Kautilya maintained that the state should organize the clearing of wasteland and settle it with villages of Sudra cultivators. It is likely that some 150,000 persons deported from Kalinga by Ashoka after the campaign were settled in this manner. Megasthenes wrote that there were no slaves in India, yet Indian sources speak of various categories of slaves called *dasas*, the most commonly used designation being *dasa-bhritakas* (slaves and hired labourers). It is likely that there was no large-scale slavery for production, although slaves were used on the land, in the mines, and in the

Stupa 2, Sanchi, Madhya Pradesh, India. Frederick M. Asher

guilds, along with the hired labour. Domestic slavery was common, however.

The nature of land revenue has been a subject of controversy. Some scholars maintain that the state was the sole owner of the land, while others contend that there was private and individual ownership as well. References to private ownership would seem to be too frequent to be ignored. There also are references to the crown lands, the cultivation of which was important to the economy. Two types of taxes were levied—one on the amount of land cultivated and the other on the produce of the land. The state maintained irrigation in limited areas and in limited periods. By and large, irrigation systems were privately controlled by cultivators and landowners. There is no support for a thesis that control of the hydraulic machinery was crucial to the political control of the country.

Another source of income, which acquired increasing importance, was revenue from taxes levied on both internal and foreign trade. The attempt at improved political administration helped to break the economic isolation of various regions. Roads built to ensure quick communication with the local administration inevitably became arteries of exchange and trade.

MAURYAN SOCIETY

According to Megasthenes, Mauryan society comprised seven occupational groups: philosophers, farmers, soldiers, herdsmen, artisans, magistrates, and councillors. He defined these groups as endogamous and the professions as hereditary, which has led to their being considered as castes. The philosophers included a variety of priests, monks, and religious teachers; they formed the smallest group but were the most respected, were exempt from taxation, and were the only ones permitted to marry into the other groups. The farmers were the largest group. The soldiers were highly paid, and, if Pliny's figures for the army are correct—9,000 elephants, 30,000 cavalry, and 600,000 infantry—their support must have required a considerable financial outlay. The mention of herdsmen as a socioeconomic group suggests that, although the agrarian economy was expanding and had become central to the state income, pastoralism continued to play an important economic role. The artisans probably represented a major section of the urban population. The listing of magistrates and councillors as distinct groups is evidence of a large and recognizable administrative personnel.

MAURYAN GOVERNMENT

The Mauryan government was organized around the king. Ashoka saw his role as essentially paternal: "All men are my children." He was anxious to be in constant touch with public opinion, and to this end he traveled extensively throughout his empire and appointed a special category of officers to gauge public opinion. His edicts indicate frequent consultations with his ministers, the ministerial council being a largely advisory body. The offices of the *sannidhatri* (treasurer), who kept the account, and the *samahartri* (chief collector), who was responsible for revenue records, formed the hub of the revenue administration. Each administrative department, with its superintendents and subordinate officials, acted as a link between local administration and the central government. Kautilya believed that a quarter of the total income should be reserved for the salaries of the officers. That the higher officials expected to be handsomely paid is clear from the salaries suggested by Kautilya and from the considerable difference between the salary of a clerk (500 panas) and that of a minister (48,000 panas). Public works and grants absorbed another large percentage of state income.

The empire was divided into four provinces, each under a prince or a governor. Local officials were probably selected from among the local populace, because no method of impersonal recruitment to administrative office is mentioned. Once every five years, the emperor sent officers to audit the provincial administrations. Some categories of officers in the rural areas, such as the *rajjukas* (surveyors), combined judicial functions with assessment duties. Fines constituted the most common form of punishment, although capital punishment was imposed in extreme cases. Provinces were subdivided into districts and these again into smaller units. The village was the basic unit of administration and has remained so throughout the centuries. The headman

continued to be an important official, as did the accountant and the tax collector (*sthanika* and *gopa*, respectively). For the larger units, Kautilya suggests the maintenance of a census. Megasthenes describes a committee of 30 officials, divided into six subcommittees, who looked after the administration of Pataliputra. The most important single official was the city superintendent (*nagaraka*), who had virtual control over all aspects of city administration. Centralization of the government should not be taken to imply a uniform level of development throughout the empire. Some areas, such as Magadha, Gandhara, and Avanti, were under closer central control than others, such as Karnataka, where possibly the Mauryan system's main concern was to extract resources without embedding itself in the region.

ASHOKA'S EDICTS

It was against this background of imperial administration and a changing socioeconomic framework that Ashoka issued edicts that carried his message concerning the idea and practice of *dhamma*, the Prakrit form of the Sanskrit *dharma*, a term that defies simple translation. It carries a variety of meanings depending on the context, such as universal law, social order, piety, or righteousness; Buddhists frequently used it with reference to the teachings of the Buddha. This in part coloured the earlier interpretation of Ashoka's use of the word to mean that he was propagating

Buddhism. Until his inscriptions were deciphered in 1837, Ashoka was practically unknown except in the Buddhist chronicles of Sri Lanka—the *Mahavamsa* and *Dipavamsa*—and the works of the northern Buddhist tradition—the *Divyavadana* and the *Ashokavadana*—where he is extolled as a Buddhist emperor par excellence whose sole ambition was the expansion of Buddhism. Most of these traditions were preserved outside India in Sri Lanka, Central Asia, and China. Even after the edicts were deciphered, it was believed that they

Inscription on Ashokan pillar, Lauriya-Nandangarh, Bihar state, India.
Frederick M. Asher

corroborated the assertions of the Buddhist sources, because in some of the edicts Ashoka avowed his personal support of Buddhism. However, more-recent analyses suggest that, although he was personally a Buddhist, as his edicts addressed to the Buddhist *sangha* attest, the majority of the edicts in which he attempted to define *dhamma* do not suggest that he was merely preaching Buddhism.

Ashoka addressed his edicts to the entire populace, inscribing them on rock surfaces or on specially erected and finely polished sandstone pillars, in places where people were likely to congregate. It has been suggested that the idea of issuing such decrees was borrowed from the Persian Achaemenian emperors, especially from Darius I, but the tone and content of Ashoka's edicts are quite different. Although the pillars, with their animal capitals, have also been described as imitations of Achaemenian pillars, there is sufficient originality in style to distinguish them as fine examples of Mauryan imperial art. (The official emblem of India since 1947 is based on the four-lion capital of the pillar at Sarnath near Varanasi.) The carvings contrast strikingly with the numerous small, gray terra-cotta figures found at urban sites, which are clearly expressions of Mauryan popular art.

Ashoka defines the main principles of *dhamma* as nonviolence, tolerance of all sects and opinions, obedience to parents, respect for the Brahmans and other religious teachers and priests, liberality toward friends, humane treatment of servants, and generosity toward all. These suggest a general ethic of behaviour to which no religious or social group could object. They also could act as a focus of loyalty to weld together the diverse strands that made up the empire. Interestingly, the Greek versions of these edicts translate *dhamma* as *eusebeia* (piety), and no mention is made in the inscriptions of the teachings of the Buddha, which would be expected if Ashoka had been propagating Buddhism. His own activities under the impact of *dhamma* included attention to the welfare of his subjects, the building of roads and rest houses, the planting of medicinal herbs, the establishment of centres for tending the sick, a ban on animal sacrifices, and the curtailing of killing animals for food. He also instituted a body of officials known as the *dhamma-mahamattas*, who served the dual function of propagating the *dhamma* and keeping the emperor in touch with public opinion.

MAURYAN DECLINE

Some historians maintain that the disintegration of the Mauryan empire was an aftermath of Ashoka's policies and actions and that his pro-Buddhist policy caused a revolt among the Brahmans. The edicts do not support such a contention. It has also been said that Ashoka's insistence on nonviolence resulted in the emasculation of the army, which was consequently unable to meet the threat of invaders from the northwest. There is, however, no indication that Ashoka deliberately ignored the military wing of his administration, despite his emphasis on nonviolence.

Other explanations for the decline of the empire appear more plausible. Among these is the idea that the economy may have weakened, putting economic pressure on the empire. It has been thought that the silver currency of the Mauryas was debased as a result of this pressure. The expense required for the army and the bureaucracy must have tied up a substantial part of the income. It is equally possible that the expansion of agriculture did not keep pace with the

Lauriya-Nandangarh pillar, Bihar state, India. Frederick M. Asher

expansion of the empire, and, because many areas were nonagricultural, the revenue from the agrarian economy may not have been sufficient for the maintenance of the empire. It is extremely difficult to compute the population of the empire, but a figure of approximately 50 million can be suggested. For a population of mixed agriculturalists and others to support an empire of this size would have been extremely difficult without intensive exploitation of resources. Relatively recent excavations at urban sites show a distinct improvement in material prosperity in the post-Mauryan levels. This may be attributable to an increase in trade, but the income from trade was unlikely to have been sufficient to supplement fully the land revenue in financing the empire.

It has been argued that the Mauryan bureaucracy at the higher levels tended to be oppressive. This may have been true during the reigns of the first two emperors, from which the evidence is cited, but oppression is unlikely to have occurred during Ashoka's reign, because he was responsible for a considerable decentralization at the upper levels and for continual checks and inspections. A more fundamental weakness lay in the process of recruitment, which was probably arbitrary, with the hierarchy of officials locally recruited.

The Concept of the State

Allegiance presupposes a concept of statehood. A number of varying notions had evolved by this time to explain the evolution of the state. Some theorists pursued the thread of the Vedic monarchies, in which the clan chief became the king and was gradually invested with divinity. An alternative set of theories arising out of Buddhist and Jain thought ignored the idea of divinity and assumed instead that, in the original state of nature, all needs were effortlessly provided but that slowly a decline set in and man became evil, developing desires, which led to the notions of private property and of family and finally to immoral behaviour. In this condition of chaos, the people gathered together and decided to elect one among them (the *mahasammata*, or "great elect") in whom they would invest authority to maintain law and order. Thus, the state came into being. Later theories retained the element of a contract between a ruler and the people. Brahmanic sources held that the gods appointed the ruler and that a contract of dues was concluded between the ruler and the people. Also prevalent was the theory of *matsyanyaya*, which proposes that in periods of chaos, when there is no ruler, the strong devour the weak, just as in periods of drought big fish eat little fish. Thus, the need for a ruler was viewed as absolute.

The existence of the state was primarily dependent on two factors: *danda* (authority) and *dharma* (in its sense of the social order—i.e., the preservation of the caste structure). The *Artha-shastra*, moreover, refers to the seven limbs (*saptanga*) of the state as the king, administration, territory, capital, treasury, coercive authority, and allies. However, the importance of the political notion of the state gradually began to fade, partly because of a decline of the political tradition of the republics and the proportional dominance of the monarchical system, in which loyalty was directed to the king. The emergence of the Mauryan empire strengthened the political notion of monarchy. The second factor was that the *dharma*, in the sense of the social order, demanded a far greater loyalty than did the rather blurred idea of the state. The king's duty was to protect *dharma*, and, as long as the social order remained intact, anarchy would not prevail. Loyalty to the social order, which was a fundamental aspect of Indian civilization, largely accounts for the impressive continuity of the major social institutions over many centuries. However, it also deflected loyalty from the political notion of the state, which might otherwise have permitted more-frequent empires and a greater political consciousness. After the decline of the Mauryas, the reemergence of an empire was to take many centuries.

FROM 150 BCE TO 300 CE

The disintegration of the Mauryan empire gave rise to a number of small kingdoms, whose regional affiliations were often to be repeated in subsequent centuries. The Punjab and Kashmir regions were drawn into the orbit of Central Asian politics. The lower Indus valley became a passage for movements from the north to the west. The Ganges valley assumed a largely passive role except when faced with campaigns from the northwest. In the northern Deccan there arose the first of many important kingdoms that were to serve as the bridge between the north and the south. Kalinga was once more independent. In the extreme south the prestige and influence of the Cera, Chola, and Pandya kingdoms continued unabated. Yet in spite of political fragmentation, this was a period of economic prosperity, resulting partly from a new source of income—trade, both within the subcontinent and with distant places in Central Asia, China, the eastern Mediterranean, and Southeast Asia.

RISE OF SMALL KINGDOMS IN THE NORTH

In the adjoining area held by the Seleucids, Diodotus I, the Greek governor of Bactria, rose in rebellion against the Seleucid king Antiochus II Theos and declared his independence, which was recognized by Antiochus about 250 BCE. Parthia also declared its independence.

INDO-GREEK RULERS

A later Bactrian king, Demetrius (reigned c. 190–c. 167 BCE), took his armies into the Punjab and finally down the Indus valley and gained control of northwestern India. This introduced what has come to be called Indo-Greek rule. The chronology of the Indo-Greek rulers is based largely on numismatic evidence. Their coins were, at the start, imitations of Greek issues, but they gradually acquired a style of their own, characterized by excellent portraiture. The legend was generally inscribed in Greek, Brahmi, and Khorosti.

The best-known of the Indo-Greek kings was Menander, recorded in Indian sources as Milinda (reigned 155–130 BCE). He is featured in the Buddhist text *Milinda-panha* ("Questions of Milinda"), written in the form of a dialogue between the king and the Buddhist philosopher Nagasena, as a result of which the king is converted to Buddhism. Menander controlled Gandhara and Punjab, although his coins have been found farther south. According to one theory, he may have attacked the Shungas in the Yamuna region and attempted to extend his control into the Ganges valley, but, if he did so, he failed to annex the area. Meanwhile, in Bactria the descendants of the line of Eucratides, who had branched off from the original Bactrian line, now began to take an interest in Gandhara and finally annexed Kabul and the kingdom of Taxila. An important Prakrit inscription at Besnagar (Bhilsa district) of the late 2nd century BCE, inscribed at the instance of Heliodorus, a Greek envoy of Antialcidas of Taxila, records his devotion to the Vaishnava Vasudeva sect. Vaishnava means a worshiper of the Hindu god Vishnu, and Vasuveda is another Hindu god.

CENTRAL ASIAN RULERS

The Bactrian control of Taxila was disturbed by an intrusion of the Scythians, known in Indian sources as the Shakas (who established the Shaka satrap). They had attacked the kingdom of Bactria and subsequently moved into India. The determination of the Han rulers of China to keep the Central Asian nomadic tribes (the Xiongnu, Wu-sun, and Yuezhi) out of China forced these tribes in their search for fresh pastures to migrate southward and westward; a branch of the Yuezhi, the Da Yuezhi, moved farthest west to the Aral Sea and displaced the existing Shakas, who poured into Bactria and Parthia. The Parthian king Mithradates II tried to hold them back, but after his death (88 BCE) they swept through Parthia and continued into the Indus valley; among the early Shaka kings was Maues, or Moga (1st century BCE), who ruled over Gandhara. The Shakas moved southward under pressure from the Pahlavas (Parthians), who ruled briefly in northwestern India toward the end of the 1st century BCE, the reign of Gondophernes being remembered. At Mathura the Shaka rulers of note were Rajuvala and Shodasa. Ultimately the Shakas settled in western India and Malava and came into conflict with the kingdoms of the northern Deccan and the Ganges valley—particularly during the reigns of Nahapana, Cashtana, and Rudradaman—in the first two centuries CE. Rudradaman's fame is recorded in a lengthy Sanskrit inscription at Junagadh, dating to 150 CE.

Kujula Kadphises, the Yuezhi chief, conquered northern India in the 1st century CE. He was succeeded by his son

Vima, after whom came Kanishka, the most powerful among the Kushan kings, as the dynasty came to be called. The date of Kanishka's accession is disputed, ranging from 78 to 248. The generally accepted date of 78 is also the basis for an era presumably started by the Shakas and used in addition to the Gregorian calendar by the present-day Indian government; the era, possibly commemorating Kanishka's accession, was widely used in Malava, Ujjain, Nepal, and Central Asia. The Kushan kingdom was essentially oriented to the north, with its capital at Purusapura (near present-day Peshawar), although it extended southward as far as Sanchi and into the Ganges valley as far as Varanasi. Mathura was the most important city in the southern part of the kingdom. Kanishka's ambitions included control of Central Asia, which, if not directly under the Kushans, did come under their influence. Inscriptions fairly recently discovered in the Gilgit area further attest such Central Asian connections. Kanishka's successors failed to maintain Kushan power. The southern areas were the first to break away, and, by the middle of the 3rd century, the Kushans were left virtually with only Gandhara and Kashmir. By the end of the century they were reduced to vassalage by the king of the Persian Sāsānian dynasty.

Not surprisingly, administrative and political nomenclature in northern India at this time reflected that of western and Central Asia. The Persian term for the governor of a province, *khshathrapavan*, as used by the Achaemenians, was Hellenized into *satrap* and widely used by these dynasties. Its Sanskrit form was *kshatrapa*. The governors of higher status came to be called *maha-kshatrapa*; they frequently issued inscriptions reflecting whatever era they chose to follow, and they minted their own coins, indicating a more independent status than is generally associated with governors. Imperial titles also were taken by the Indo-Greeks, such as *basileus basileōn* ("king of kings"), similar to the Persian *shāhanshāh*, of which the later Sanskrit form was *maharatadhiraja*. A title of Central Asian derivation was the *daivaputra* of the Kushans, which is believed to have come originally from the Chinese "son of heaven," emphasizing the divinity of kingship.

OLIGARCHIES AND KINGDOMS

Occupying the watershed between the Indus and Ganges valleys, Punjab and Rajasthan were the nucleus of a number of oligarchies, or tribal republics whose local importance rose and fell in inverse proportion to the rise and fall of larger kingdoms. According to numismatic evidence, the most important politically were the Audambaras, Arjunayanas, Malavas, Yaudheyas, Shibis, Kunindas, Trigartas, and Abhiras. The Arjunayanas had their base in the present-day Bharatpur-Alwar region. The Malavas appear to have migrated from the Punjab to the Jaipur area, perhaps after the Indo-Greek invasions; they are associated with the Malava era, which has been identified with the Vikrama era, also known as the

Krita era and dating to 58 BCE. It is likely that southern Rajasthan as far as the Narmada River and the Ujjain district was named Malwa after the Malavas. Yaudheya evidence is scattered over many parts of the Punjab and the adjoining areas of what is now Rajasthan and Uttar Pradesh, but during this period their stronghold appears to have been the Rohtak district, north of Delhi; the frequent use of the term *gana* ("group") on Yaudheya coins indicates an adherence to the tribal tradition. References to Shaiva (Shiva-related) deities, especially Karttikeya or Skanda, the legendary son of Shiva, are striking. The Shibis also migrated from the Punjab to Rajasthan and settled at Madhyamika (near Chitor, now Chittaurgarh).

Coins of the Kunindas locate them in the Shiwalik Range between the Yamuna and the Beas rivers. The Trigartas have been associated with the Chamba region of the upper Ravi River, but they also may have inhabited the area of Jalandhara in the plains. The Abhiras lived in scattered settlements in various parts of western and central India as far as the Deccan. Most of these tribes claimed descent from the ancient lineages of the Puranas, and some of them were later connected with the rise of Rajput dynasties.

In addition to the oligarchies, there were small monarchical states, such as Ayodhya, Kaushambi, and the scattered Naga kingdoms, the most important of which was the one at Padmavati (Gwalior). Ahicchatra (now the Bareilly district of Uttar Pradesh) was ruled by kings who bore names ending in the suffix -*mitra*.

THE SHUNGA KINGDOM

Magadha was the nucleus of the Shunga kingdom, which succeeded the Mauryan. The kingdom extended westward to include Ujjain and Vidisha. The Shungas came into conflict with Vidarbha and with the Yavanas, who probably were Bactrian Greeks attempting to move into the Ganges valley. (The word *yavana* derives from the Prakrit *yona*, suggesting that the Ionians were the first Greeks with whom the Persians and Indians came into contact. In later centuries the name Yavana was applied to all peoples coming from western Asia and the Mediterranean region, which included the Romans, Persians, and Arabs.) The Shunga dynasty lasted for about one century and was then overthrown by the Brahman minister Vasudeva, who founded the Kanva dynasty, which lasted 45 years and following which the Magadha area was of greatly diminished importance until the 4th century CE.

KALINGA

Kalinga rose to prominence under Kharavela, dated with some debate to the 1st century BCE. Kharavela boasts, perhaps exaggeratedly for a pious Jain, of successful campaigns in the western Deccan and against the Yavanas and Magadha and of a triumphal victory over the Pandyas of southern India.

THE ANDHRAS AND THEIR SUCCESSORS

The Andhras are listed among the tribal peoples in the Mauryan empire. Possibly they rose to being local officials and then, on the disintegration of the empire, gradually became independent rulers of the northwestern Deccan. It cannot be ascertained for certain whether the Andhras arose in the Andhra region (i.e., the Krishna-Godavari deltas) and moved up to the northwestern Deccan or whether their settling in the delta gave it their name. There is also controversy as to whether the dynasty became independent at the end of the 3rd century BCE or at the end of the 1st century BCE. Their alternative name, Satavahana, is presumed to be the family name, whereas Andhra was probably that of the tribe. It is likely that Satavahana power was established during the reign of Shatakarni I, with the borders of the kingdom reaching across the northern Deccan; subsequent to this the Satavahana dynasty suffered an eclipse in the 1st century CE, when it was forced out of the northern Deccan by the Shakas and resettled in Andhra. In the 2nd century CE the Satavahanas reestablished their power in the northwestern Deccan, as evidenced by Shaka coins from this region overstruck with the name Gautamiputra Shatakarni. That the Andhras did not control Malava and Ujjain is clear from the claim of the Shaka king Rudradaman to these regions. The last of the important Andhra kings was Yajnashri Shatakarni, who ruled at the end of the 2nd century CE and asserted his authority over the Shakas. The 3rd century saw the decline of Satavahana power, as the kingdom broke into small pockets of control under various branches of the family.

The Satavahana feudatories then rose to power. The Abhiras were the successors in the Nashik area. The Iksvakus succeeded in the Krishna-Guntur region. The Cutu dynasty in Kuntala (southern Maharashtra) had close connections with the Satavahanas. The Bodhis ruled briefly in the northwestern Deccan. The Brihatphalayanas came to power at the end of the 3rd century in the Masulipatam area. In these regions the Satavahana pattern of administration continued; many of the rulers had matronymics (names derived from that of the mother or a maternal ancestor); many of the royal inscriptions record donations made to Buddhist monks and monasteries, often by princesses, and also land grants to Brahmans and the performance of Vedic sacrifices by the rulers.

SOUTHERN INDIAN KINGDOMS

Significant, historically attested contact between the north and the Tamil regions can be reasonably dated to the Mauryan period. Evidence on the early history of the south consists of the epigraphs of the region, the Tamil *cankam* (*sangam*) literature, and archaeological data.

Inscriptions in Brahmi (recently read as Tamil Brahmi) date to between the 2nd century BCE and the 4th century CE. Most of the inscriptions record donations made by royalty or by merchants and artisans to Buddhist and Jain monks. These are useful in corroborating evidence from the *cankam* literature, a collection of a large number of poems in classical Tamil that, according to tradition, were recited at three assemblies of poets held at Madurai. Included in this literature are the Eight Anthologies (*Ettutokai*) and Ten Idylls (*Pattupattu*). The grammatical work *Tolkappiyam* also is said to be of the same period. The literature probably belongs to the same period as the inscriptions, although some scholars suggest an earlier date. The historical authenticity of sections of the *cankam* literature has been confirmed by archaeological evidence.

Tamilakam, the abode of the Tamils, was defined in *cankam* literature as approximately equivalent to the area south of present-day Chennai (Madras). Tamilakam was divided into 13 *nadus* (districts), of which the region of Madurai was the most important as the core of the Tamil speakers. The three major chiefdoms of Tamilakam were those of the Pandya dynasty (Madurai), the Ceras (Cheras; Malabar Coast and the hinterland), and the Cholas (Thanjavur and the Kaveri valley), founders of the Chola dynasty. The inscriptions of the Pandyas, recording royal grants and other grants made by local citizens, date to the 2nd century BCE. The chief Nedunjeliyan (early 3rd century CE) is celebrated by the poets of the *cankam* as the victor in campaigns against the Ceras and the Cholas. Cera inscriptions of the 2nd century CE

referring to the Irrumporai clan have been found near Karur (Tiruchchirapalli district), identified with the Korura of Ptolemy. *Cankam* literature mentions the names of Cera chiefs who have been dated to the 1st century CE. Among them, Nedunjeral Adan is said to have attacked the Yavana ships and held the Yavana traders to ransom. His son Shenguttuvan, much eulogized in the poems, also is mentioned in the context of Gajabahu's rule in Sri Lanka, which can be dated to either the first or last quarter of the 2nd century CE, depending on whether he was the earlier or the later Gajabahu. Karikalan (late 2nd century CE) is the best known of the early Chola chiefs and was to become almost a kind of eponymous ancestor to many families of the south claiming Chola descent. The early capital was at Uraiyur, in an area that stretched from the Vaigai River in the south to Tondaimandalam in the north. The three chiefdoms were frequently at war; in addition there were often hostilities with Sri Lanka. Mention is also made of the ruler of Tondaimandalam with its capital at Kanchipuram. There is also frequent mention of the minor chieftains, the Vel, who ruled small areas in many parts of the Tamil country. Ultimately all the chiefdoms suffered at the hands of the Kalvar, or Kalabras, who came from the border to the north of Tamilakam and were described as evil rulers, but they were overthrown in the 5th century CE with the rise of the Chalukyas (Calukyas) and Pallava dynasties.

Cankam literature reflects the indigenous cultural tradition as well as elements of the intrusion of the northern Sanskritic tradition, which by now was beginning to come into contact with these areas, some of which were in the process of change from chiefdoms to kingdoms. In poems praising the chiefs, heroism in raids and gift-giving are hailed as the main virtues. The predominant economy remained pastoral-cum-agrarian, with an increasing emphasis on agriculture. The Tamil poems divide the land into five ecological zones, or *tinais*. Among the poems that make reference to social stratification, one uses the word *kudi* ("group") to denote caste. Each village had its *sabha,* or council, for administering local affairs, an institution that was to remain a fixture of village life. Religious observance consisted primarily in conducting sacrifices to various deities, among whom Murugan was preeminent.

Trade with the Yavanas and with the northern parts of the subcontinent provided considerable economic momentum for the southern Indian states. Given the terrain of the peninsula and the agricultural technology of the time, large agrarian-based kingdoms like those of northern India were not feasible, although the cultivation of rice provided a base for economic change. Inevitably, trade played more than a marginal role, and overseas trade became a major economic activity. Almost as soon as the Roman trade began to decline, the Southeast Asian trade commenced; in subsequent centuries this became the focus of maritime interest.

CONTACTS WITH THE WEST

Numerous sources from the 1st millennium BCE mention trade between western Asia and the western coast of India. Hebrew texts refer to the port of Ophir, sometimes identified with Sopara, on the west coast. Babylonian builders used Indian teak and cedar in the 7th and 6th centuries BCE. The Buddhist *jataka* literature mentions trade with Baveru (Babylon). After the decline of Babylon, Arab merchants from southern Arabia apparently continued the trade, probably supplying goods to Egypt and the eastern Mediterranean. The discovery of the regular seasonal monsoon winds, enabling ships to sail a straight course across the Arabian Sea, made a considerable difference to shipping and navigation on the route from western Asia to India. Unification of the Mediterranean and western Asian world at the turn of the Christian era under the Roman Empire brought Roman trade into close contact with India—overland with northern India and by sea with peninsular India. The emperor Augustus received two embassies—almost certainly trade missions—from India in 25–21 BCE.

The *Periplus Maris Erythraei* ("Navigation of the Erythrean [i.e., Red] Sea"), an anonymous Greek travel book written in the 1st century CE, lists a series of ports along the Indian coast, including Muziris (Cranganore), Colchi (Korkai), Poduca, and Sopatma. An excavation at Arikamedu (near present-day Puducherry [Pondicherry]) revealed a Roman trading settlement of this period, and elsewhere too the presence of Roman pottery, beads, intaglios, lamps, glass, and coins point to a continuous occupation, resulting even in imitations of some Roman items. It would seem that textiles were prepared to Roman specification and exported from such settlements. Graffiti on pottery found at a port in the Red Sea indicates the presence of Indian traders.

Large hoards of Roman coins substantiate other evidence. The coins are mainly of the emperors Augustus (reigned 27 BCE–14 CE), Tiberius (reigned 14–37), and Nero (reigned 54–68). Their frequency suggests that the Romans paid for the trade in gold coins. Many are overstruck with a bar, which may indicate that they were used as bullion in India; certainly, the Roman savant Pliny the Elder complained that the Indian luxury trade was depleting the Roman treasury. The coins are found most often in trading centres or near the sources of semiprecious stones, especially quartz and beryl. *Cankam* literature attests the prosperity of Yavana merchants trading in towns such as Kaveripattinam (in the Kaveri delta). The *Periplus* lists the major exports of India as pepper, precious stones, pearls, tortoise shells, ivory, such aromatic plants as spikenard (*Nardostachys jatamansi*) and malabathrum (*Cinnamomum malabathrum*), and silk and other textiles. For these the Romans traded glass, copper, tin, lead, realgar (a red pigment), orpiment (a gold pigment), antimony, and wine, or else they paid in gold coins.

The maritime trade routes from the Indian ports were primarily to the Persian Gulf and the Red Sea, from where they went overland to the eastern Mediterranean and to Egypt, but Indian merchants also ventured out to Southeast Asia seeking spices and semiprecious stones. River valleys and the Mauryan roads were the chief routes within India. Greek sources refer to a royal highway built by the Mauryas, connecting Taxila with Pataliputra and terminating at Tamralipti, the main port in the Ganges delta. On the western coast the major port of Bhrigukaccha (modern Bharuch) was connected with the Ganges valley via Rajasthan or, alternatively, Ujjain. From the Narmada valley there were routes going into the northwestern Deccan and continuing along rivers flowing eastward to various parts of the peninsula. Goods were transported mainly in caravans of oxen and donkeys—but only in the dry seasons, the rains creating impossible conditions for travel. Coastal and river shipping was clearly cheaper than overland transport. The main northern route connected Taxila with Kābul and Kandahār and from there branched off in various directions, mainly linking up with routes across Persia to the Black Sea ports and the eastern Mediterranean. The route connecting China with Bactria via Central Asia, which would shortly become famous as the Silk Road, linked the oases of Kashgar, Yarkand, Khotan, Miran, Kucha, Karashahr, and Turfan, in all of which Indian merchants established trading stations. The Central Asian route brought Chinese goods in large quantities into the Indian and western Asian markets. It is thought that the prosperity resulting from this trade enabled the Kushans to issue the first Indian gold coins. Another consequence was the popularity of horsemanship.

SOCIETY AND CULTURE

The commercial economy played a central role during this period. Circuits of exchange developed at various levels among groups throughout the subcontinent. In some regions these patterns extended to external trade. Agrarian expansion was not arrested, and land revenue continued to be a major source of income, but profit from trade made a substantial difference to the urban economy, noticeably improving the standard of living and registering a growth in the number and size of towns.

GUILDS

The social institution most closely related to commercial activity was the *shreni,* or guild, through which trade was channeled. The guilds were registered with the town authority, and the activities of guild members followed strict guidelines called the *shreni-dharma.* The wealthier guilds employed slaves and hired labourers in addition to their own artisans, though the percentage of such slaves appears to have been small. Guilds had their own seals and insignia.

They often made lavish donations to Buddhist and Jain monasteries, and some of the finest Buddhist monuments of the period resulted from such patronage. In some areas, such as the Deccan, members of the royal family invested money with a particular guild, and the accruing interest became a regular donation to the Buddhist sangha. This must also have enhanced the political prestige of the guild.

FINANCE

Increasing reliance on money in commerce greatly augmented the role of the financier and banker. Sometimes the wealthier guilds offered financial services, but the more usual source of money was the merchant financier (*shresthin*). Coinage proliferated in the various kingdoms, and minting attained a high level of craftsmanship. The most widely used coins were the gold *dinaras* and *suvarnas,* based on the Roman denarius (124 grains [about 8 grams]); a range of silver coins, such as the earlier *karshapana* (or *pana;* 57.8 grains [3.75 grams]) and the *shatamana;* an even wider range of copper coins, such as the *masa, kakani,* and a variety of unspecified standards; and other coins issued in lead and potin, particularly in western India. Usury was an accepted part of the banker's trade, with 15 percent being the typical interest rate, although this varied according to the enterprise for which the money was borrowed. Expanding trade also introduced a multiplicity of weights and measures.

IMPACT OF TRADE

Foreign trade probably had its greatest economic impact in the south, but the interchange of ideas appears to have been more substantial in the north. This latter effect may have been attributable to the north's longer association with western Asia and the colonial Hellenic culture. Greek, along with Aramaic, was widely spoken in Afghanistan and was doubtless understood in Taxila. The spurt of geographic studies in the Mediterranean produced works with extensive descriptions of the trade with India; these include Strabo's *Geography*, Ptolemy's *Geography*, Pliny's *Natural History*, and the *Periplus Maris Erythraei*. The most obvious and visible impact occurred in Gandhara art, which depicted Indian themes influenced by Hellenistic and Roman styles, an attractive hybrid that influenced the development of Buddhist iconography. The more prized among objects were the ivory carvings that reached Afghanistan from central India.

RELIGIOUS PATRONAGE

If art remains are an index to patronage, then Buddhism seems to have been the most-favoured religion, followed by Shaivism and the Bhagavata cult. Buddhist centres generally comprised a complex of three structures—the monastery (*vihara*), the hall of worship (*caitya*), and the sacred tumulus (*stupa*)—all of which were freestanding structures in the north but were initially rock-cut

monuments in the Deccan. The Jains found more patrons in the Deccan. Literary sources of the period mention Hindu temples, but none of comparable antiquity have been found. Apart from the Gandhara style of sculpture, a number of indigenous centres in other parts of India, such as Mathura, Karli, Nagarjunakonda, and Amaravati, portrayed Buddhist legends in a variety of

Head of Buddha in gray schist, 2nd–3rd century CE, *showing Hellenistic influences; from Gandhara, northwestern Pakistan.* Courtesy of the trustees of the British Museum

local stones. The more popular medium was terra-cotta, by then changed from gray to red, depicting not only ordinary men and women and animal figures but also large numbers of mother goddesses, indicating the continued popular worship of these deities.

The practice of Buddhism was itself undergoing change. Affluent patronage endowed the large monasteries with land and slaves. Association with royalty gave Buddhism access to power. Under the proselytizing consciousness that had gradually evolved, Buddhist monks traveled as missionaries to Central Asia and China, western Asia, and Southeast Asia. New situations inevitably led to the need for new ideas, as is most clearly seen in the contact of Buddhism with Christianity

Central nave of the Buddhist caitya *(holy place) at Karli, near Pune, Maharashtra, India.* Holle Bildarchiv

and Zoroastrianism in Central Asia. Arguments over the original teaching of the Buddha had already resulted in a series of councils called to clarify the doctrine. The two main sects were the Theravada, centred at Kaushambi, which compiled the Pali canon on Buddhist teachings, and the Sarvastivada, which arose at Mathura, spread northward, and finally established itself in Central Asia, using Sanskrit as the language for preserving the Buddhist tradition. A council held in Kashmir during the reign of Kanishka ratified the separation of the two main schools of Buddhism—the Mahayana ("Greater Vehicle") and the Theravada (or Hinayana, "Lesser Vehicle"). The impressive dominance of Buddhism did not arise without hostility from the patrons of other religions.

Jainism had by now also split into two groups: the Digambara ("Sky-Clad"—i.e., naked), the more orthodox, and the Shvetambara ("White-Clad"), the more liberal. The Jains were not as widespread as the Buddhists, their main centres being in western India, Kalinga for a brief period, and the Mysore (modern Karnataka) and Tamil country.

Brahmanism also underwent changes with the gradual fading out of some of the Vedic deities. The two major gods were Vishnu and Shiva, around whom there emerged a monotheistic trend perhaps best expressed in the *Vaishnava Bhagavadgita*, which most authorities would date to the 1st century BCE. The doctrine of karma and rebirth, emphasizing the influence of actions performed either in this life or in former lives on present and future lives, became central to Hindu belief and influenced both religious and social notions. Vedic sacrifices were not discontinued but gradually became symbols of such ceremonial occasions as royal consecrations. Sacrificial ritual was beginning to be replaced by the practice of *bhakti,* a form of personal devotion whereby the worshiper shares in the grace of the deity.

LITERATURE

Popular epics, such as the *Mahabharata* and the *Ramayana*, were injected with didactic sections on religion and morality and elevated to the status of sacred literature. Their heroes, Krishna and Rama, were incorporated into Vaishnavism as avatars (incarnations) of Vishnu. The concept of incarnations was useful in subsuming local deities and cults.

The epics also served as a treasury of stories, which provided themes and characters for countless poems and plays. The works of the dramatist Bhasa, notably *Svapnavasavadatta* and *Pratijnayaugandharayana*, were foundational to the Sanskrit drama. Ashvaghosa, another major dramatist who wrote in Sanskrit, based his works on Buddhist

Ladies in conversation, detail from a folio from a manuscript of the Mahabharata, 1516. P. Chandra

themes. The popularity of drama necessitated the writing of a work on dramaturgy, the *Natyashastra* ("Treatise on Dramatic Art") of the sage-priest Bharata. The composition of *Dharma-shastras* (collections of treatises on sacred duties), among which the most often quoted is ascribed to Manu, became important in a period of social flux in which traditional social law and usage were important as precedent. A commentary on the earlier Sanskrit grammar of Panini was provided by the *Mahabhasya* of Patanjali, timely because even the non-Indian dynasties of the north and west made extensive use of Sanskrit. Of the sciences, astronomy and medicine were foremost, both reflecting the interchange of ideas with western Asia. Two basic medical treatises, composed by Caraka and Sushruta, date to this period.

ASSIMILATION OF FOREIGNERS

The presence of foreigners, most of whom settled in Indian cities and adopted Indian habits and behaviour in addition to religion, became a problem for social theorists because the newcomers had to be fitted into caste society. It was easier to accommodate a group rather than an individual into the social hierarchy, because the group could be given a *jati* status. Technically, conversion to Hinduism was difficult because one had to be born into a particular caste, and it was karma that determined one's caste. The theoretical definition of caste society continued as before, and the four varnas were referred to as the units of society. The assimilation of local cults demanded the assimilation of cult priests, who had to be accommodated within the Brahmanic hierarchy. The Greeks and the Shakas, clearly of non-Indian origin and initially the ruling group, were referred to as "fallen Kshatriyas." The Vaishya and Sudra groups did not pose such a serious problem, because their vague definition gave them social mobility. It is likely that in such periods of social change some lower-caste groups may have moved up the ladder of social hierarchy.

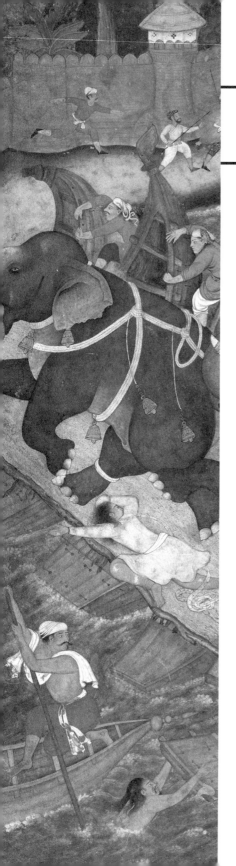

CHAPTER 3

DEVELOPMENTS FROM 300 TO C. 1200 CE

T he period between 300 and 1200 was a time of many changes. Great civilizations rose and fell. Some of India's most impressive works of art were created. Philosophy and religion developed. Islam entered the mix of cultures that would enrich the subcontinent.

FROM 300 TO 750 CE

Historians once regarded the Gupta period (c. 320–540) as the classical age of India, the period during which the norms of Indian literature, art, architecture, and philosophy were established. It was also thought to have been an age of material prosperity, particularly among the urban elite, and of renascent Hinduism. Some of these assumptions have been questioned by more-extensive studies of the post-Mauryan, pre-Gupta period. Archaeological evidence from the earlier Kushan levels suggests greater material prosperity, to such a degree that some historians argue for an urban decline in the Gupta period. Much of Gupta literature and art derived from that of earlier periods, and renascent Hinduism is probably more correctly dated to the post-Gupta time. The Gupta realm, although less extensive than that of the Mauryas, did encompass the northern half and central parts of the subcontinent. The Gupta period also has been called an imperial age, but the administrative centralization so characteristic of an imperial system is less apparent than during the Mauryan period.

NORTHERN INDIA
UNDER THE GUPTAS

The Guptas, a comparatively unknown family, came from either Magadha or eastern Uttar Pradesh. The third king, Chandra Gupta I (reigned c. 320–c. 330), took the title of *maharajadhiraja*. He married a Licchavi princess—an event celebrated in a series of gold coins. It has been suggested that, if the Guptas ruled in Prayaga (present-day Allahabad in eastern Uttar Pradesh), the marriage alliance may have added Magadha to their domain. The Gupta era began in 320, but it is not clear whether this date commemorated the accession of Chandra Gupta or the assumption of the status of independence.

Chandra Gupta appointed his son Samudra Gupta (reigned c. 330–c. 380) to succeed him about 330, according to a long eulogy to Samudra Gupta inscribed on a pillar at Allahabad. The coins of an obscure prince, Kacha, suggest that there may have been contenders for the throne. Samudra Gupta's campaigns took him in various directions and resulted in many conquests. Not all the conquered regions were annexed, but the range of operations established the military prowess of the Guptas. Samudra Gupta acquired Pataliputra (present-day Patna), which was to become the Gupta capital. Proceeding down the eastern coast, he also conquered the states of Dakshinapatha but reinstated the vanquished rulers.

Among those he rendered subservient were the rulers of Aryavarta, various forest chiefs, the northern oligarchies, and border states in the east, in addition to Nepal. More-distant domains brought within Samudra Gupta's orbit were regarded as subordinate; these comprised the "king of kings" of the northwest, the Shakas, the Murundas, and the inhabitants of "all the islands," including Sinhala (Sri Lanka), all of which are listed in the inscription at Allahabad. It would seem that the campaign extended Gupta power in northern and eastern India and virtually eliminated the oligarchies and the minor kings of central India and the Ganges valley. The identity of the islands remains problematic, as they could either have been the ones close to India or those of Southeast Asia, with which communication had increased. The Ganges valley and central India were the areas under direct administrative control. The campaign in the eastern coastal areas may have been prompted by the desire to acquire the trading wealth of these regions. The grim image of Samudra Gupta as a military conqueror is ameliorated, however, by references to his love of poetry and by coins on which he is depicted playing the lyre.

Samudra Gupta was succeeded about 380 by his son Chandra Gupta II (reigned c. 380–c. 415), though there is some evidence that there may have been an intermediate ruler. Chandra Gupta II's major campaign was against the Shaka rulers of Ujjain, the success of which was celebrated in a series of silver coins. Gupta interest lay not merely in the political control of the west but in the wealth the area derived from trade with western and southeastern Asia. Gupta territory adjoining the northern Deccan was secured through a marriage alliance with the Vakataka dynasty, the successors of the Satavahanas in the area. Although Chandra Gupta II took the title of Vikramaditya ("Sun of Valour"), his reign is associated more with cultural and intellectual achievements than with military campaigns. His Chinese contemporary Faxian, a Buddhist monk, traveled in India and left an account of his impressions.

The first hint of a fresh invasion from the northwest comes in the reign of Chandra Gupta's son and successor, Kumara Gupta (reigned c. 415–455). The threat was that of a group known in Indian sources as the Hunas, or Huns, though it is not clear whether this group had any relations to the Huns of European history. They were in any event a branch of a Central Asian group known as the Hephthalites. Skanda Gupta (c. 455–467), who succeeded Kumara Gupta, and his successors all had to face the full-fledged invasion of the Hunas. Skanda Gupta managed to rally Gupta strength for a while, but after his death the situation deteriorated. Dissensions within the royal family added to the problem. Gupta genealogies of this period show considerable variance in their succession lists. By the mid-6th century, when the dynasty apparently came to an end, the kingdom had dwindled to a small size. Northern India and parts of central India were in the hands of the Hunas.

Administratively, the Gupta kingdom was divided into provinces called *deshas* or *bhuktis*, and these in turn into smaller units, the *pradeshas* or *vishayas*. The provinces were governed by *kumaramatyas*, high imperial officers or members of the royal family. A decentralization of authority is evident from the composition of the municipal board (*adhishthana-adhikarana*), which consisted of the guild president (*nagara-shreshthin*), the chief merchant (*sarthavaha*), and representatives of the artisans and of the scribes. During that period the term *samanta*, which originally meant neighbour, was beginning to be applied to intermediaries who had been given grants of land or to conquered feudatory rulers. There was also a noticeable tendency for some of the higher administrative offices to become hereditary. The lack of firm control over conquered areas led to their resuming independence. The repeated military action that this necessitated may have strained the kingdom's resources.

The coming of the Hunas brought northern India once more into close contact with Central Asia, and a number of Central Asian tribes migrated into India. It has been suggested that the Gurjaras, who gradually spread to various parts of northern India, may be identified with the Khazars, a Turkic people of Central Asia. The Huna invasion challenged the stability of the Gupta kingdom, even though the ultimate decline may have been caused by internal factors. A severe blow was the resultant disruption of the Central Asian trade and the decline in the income that northern India had derived from it. Some of the north Indian tribes migrated to other regions, and this movement of peoples effected changes in the social structure of the post-Gupta period. The rise of Rajput families and "Kshatriya" dynasties is associated by some scholars with tribal chiefs in these new areas.

The first Huna king in India was Toramana (early 6th century), whose inscriptions have been found as far south as Eran (Madhya Pradesh). His son Mihirakula, a patron of Shaivism, is recorded in Buddhist tradition as uncouth and extremely cruel. The Gupta rulers, together with Yashodharman of Malava, seem to have confronted Mihirakula and forced him back to the north. Ultimately his kingdom was limited to Kashmir and Punjab with its capital at Shakala (possibly present-day Sialkot). Huna power declined after his reign.

SUCCESSOR STATES TO THE GUPTAS

Of the kingdoms that arose as inheritors of the Gupta territory, the most important were those of Valabhi (Saurashtra and Kathiawar); Gujarata (originally the area near Jodhpur), believed to be the nucleus of the later Pratihara kingdom; Nandipuri (near Bharuch); Maukhari (Magadha); the kingdom of the later Guptas (in the area between Malava and Magadha); and those of Bengal, Nepal, and Kamarupa (in the Assam Valley). Orissa (Kongoda) was under the Mana and Shailodbhava dynasties before being conquered by Shashanka, king of Gauda (lower Bengal). In the early 7th century Shashanka annexed a substantial part of the Ganges valley, where he came into conflict with the Maukharis and the rising Puspabhuti (Pushyabhuti) dynasty of Thanesar (north of Delhi).

The Puspabhuti dynasty aspired to imperial status during the reign of Harsha (Harsavardhana). Sthanvishvara (Thanesar) appears to have been a small principality, probably under the suzerainty of the Guptas. Harsha came to the throne in 606 and ruled for 41 years. The first of the major historical biographies in Sanskrit, the *Harshacarita* ("Deeds of Harsha"), was written by Bana, a celebrated author attached to his court, and contains information on Harsha's early life. A fuller account of the period is given by the Chinese Buddhist pilgrim Xuanzang, who traveled through India and stayed for some time at a monastery at Nalanda. Harsha acquired Kannauj (in Farrukhabad district), which became the eponymous capital of his large kingdom. He waged a major but unsuccessful campaign against Pulakeshin II, a king of the Chalukya dynasty of the northern Deccan, and was confined to the northern half of the subcontinent. Nor was his success spectacular in western India against Valabhi, Nandipuri, and Sind (lower Indus valley). In his eastern campaign, however, Harsha met with little resistance (Shashanka having died in 636) and acquired Magadha, Vanga, and Kongoda (Orissa). His alliance with Bhaskaravarman of Kamarupa (Assam) proved helpful. Although Harsha failed to build an empire, his kingdom was of no mean size, and he earned the reputation of being the preeminent ruler of the north. He is remembered as the author of three Sanskrit plays—*Ratnavall, Priyadarshika,* and *Nagananda*—the theme of the last indicating his interest in Buddhist thought. The Tang emperor of China, Taizong, sent a series of embassies to Harsha, establishing closer ties between the two realms. After the death of Harsha, the kingdom of Kannauj entered a period of decline until the early 8th century, when it revived with the rise of Yashovarman, who is eulogized in the Prakrit poem Gaudavadha ("The Slaying of [the King of] Gauda") by Vakpati. Yashovarman came into conflict with Lalitaditya, the king of Kashmir of the Karkota dynasty, and appears to have been defeated.

In the 8th century the rising power in western India was that of the Gurjara-Pratiharas. The Rajput dynasty of the Guhilla had its centre in Mewar (with Chitor as its base). The Capa family was associated with the city of Anahilapataka (present-day Patan) and are involved in early Rajput history. In the Haryana region the Tomara Rajputs (Tomara dynasty), originally feudatories of the Gurjara-Pratiharas, founded the city of Dhillika (modern Delhi) in 736. The political pattern of this time reveals a rebirth of regionalism and of new political and economic structures.

In the early 8th century a new power base was established briefly with the arrival of the Arabs in Sind. Inscriptions of the western Indian dynasties speak of controlling the tide of the *mleccha*, which has been interpreted in this case to mean the

Arabs; some Indian sources use the term *yavana*. The conquest of Sind marked the easternmost extent of Arab territorial control. A 13th-century Persian translation of a chronicle from Sind, the *Chach-nāmeh*, gives an account of these events. The initial naval expedition met with failure, so the Arabs conducted an overland campaign. The Arab hold on Sind was loose at first, and the local chiefs remained virtually independent, but by 724 the invaders had established direct rule, with a governor representing the Muslim caliph. Arab attempts to advance into Punjab and Kashmir, however, were checked. The Indians did not fully comprehend the magnitude of Arab political and economic ambitions. Along the west coast, the Arabs were seen as familiar traders from western Asia. The possible competition with Indian trade was not realized.

THE DECCAN

In the Deccan the Vakataka dynasty was closely tied to the Guptas. With a nucleus in Vidarbha, the founder of the dynasty, Vindhyashakti, extended his power northward as far as Vidisha (near Ujjain). At the end of the 4th century, a collateral line of the Vakatakas was established by Sarvasena in Vatsagulma (Basim, in Akola district), and the northern line helped the southern to conquer Kuntala (southern Maharashtra). The domination of the northern Deccan by the main Vakataka line during this period is clearly established by the matrimonial alliances not only with the Guptas but also with

DECCAN

The entire southern peninsula of India south of the Narmada River is marked centrally by a high triangular tableland called the Deccan. The name derives from the Sanskrit daksina *("south"). The plateau is bounded on the east and west by the Ghats ranges, escarpments that meet at the plateau's southern tip. Its northern extremity is the Satpura Range. The Deccan's average elevation is about 2,000 feet (600 metres), sloping generally eastward. Its principal rivers—the Godavari, Krishna, and Kaveri (Cauvery)—flow from the Western Ghats eastward to the Bay of Bengal. The plateau's climate is drier than that on the coasts and is arid in places.*

The Deccan's early history is obscure. There is evidence of prehistoric human habitation; low rainfall must have made farming difficult until the introduction of irrigation. The plateau's mineral wealth led many lowland rulers, including those of the Mauryan (4th–2nd century BCE) and Gupta (4th–6th century CE) dynasties, to fight over it. From the 6th to the 13th century, the Chalukya, Rashtrakuta, Later Chalukya, Hoysala, and Yadava families successively established regional kingdoms in the Deccan, but they were continually in conflict with neighbouring states and recalcitrant feudatories. The later kingdoms also were subject to looting raids by the Muslim Delhi sultanate, which eventually gained control of the area.

In 1347 the Muslim Bahmani dynasty established an independent kingdom in the Deccan. The five Muslim states that succeeded the Bahmani and divided its territory joined forces in 1565 at the Battle of Talikota to defeat Vijayanagar, the Hindu empire to the south. For most of their reigns, however, the five successor states formed shifting patterns of alliances in an effort to keep any one state from dominating the area and, from 1656, to fend off incursions by the Mughal Empire to the north. During the Mughal decline in the 18th century, the Marathas, the nizam of Hyderabad, and the Arcot nawab vied for control of the Deccan. Their rivalries, as well as conflicts over succession, led to the gradual absorption of the Deccan by the British. When India became independent in 1947, the princely state of Hyderabad resisted initially but joined the Indian union in 1948.

other peninsular dynasties such as the Visnukundins and the Kadambas. The Vakatakas were weakened by attacks from Malava and Koshala in the 5th century. Ultimately, the Chalukyas (Calukyas) of Vatapi (present-day Badami) ended their rule.

Of the myriad ruling families of the Deccan between the 4th and 7th centuries—including the Nalas, the Kalacuris, the Gangas, and the Kadambas—the most significant were the Chalukyas, who are associated with Vatapi in the 6th century. The Chalukyas controlled large parts of the Deccan for two centuries. There were many branches of the family, the most important of which were the Eastern Chalukyas, ruling at Pishtapura (modern Pithapuram in the Godavari River delta) in the early 7th century; the Chalukyas of

Vemulavada (near Karimnagar, Andhra Pradesh); and the renascent Later Chalukyas of Kalyani (between the Bhima and Godavari rivers), who rose to power in the 10th century. Chalukya power reached its zenith during the reign of Pulakeshin II (610–642), a contemporary of Harsha. The early years of Pulakeshin's reign were taken up with a civil war, after which he had to reconquer lost territories and reestablish his control over recalcitrant feudatories. Pulakeshin then campaigned successfully in the south against the Kadambas, the Alupas, and the Gangas. Leading his armies north, he defeated the Latas, Malavas, and Gurjaras. Pulakeshin's final triumph in the north was the victory over Harsha of Kannauj. Pulakeshin then turned his attention to the eastern Deccan and conquered southern Koshala, Kalinga, Pishtapuram, and the Vishnukundin kingdom. He started the collateral branch of the Eastern Chalukyas based at Pishtapuram with his younger brother Vishnuvardhana as the first king. Pulakeshin then launched another major campaign against the powerful southern Indian kingdom of the Pallavas, in which he defeated their king Mahendravarman I—thus inaugurating a conflict between the two kingdoms that was to continue for many centuries. Pulakeshin II sent an embassy to the court of the Sāsānian Persian king Khosrow II. Good relations between the Persians and the Indians of the Deccan were of great advantage to the Zoroastrians of Persia, who, fleeing from the Islamic persecution in subsequent centuries, sought asylum in India and settled along the west coast of the Deccan. Their descendants today constitute the Parsi community.

Control over both coasts enhanced the Chalukya king's already firm hold on the Deccan. The major river valleys of the plateau—the Narmada, Tapi (Tapti), Godavari with its tributaries, and Krishna—were in Chalukya hands, as were the valuable routes in the valleys. This amounted to control of the west coast trade with western Asia and the Kalinga and Andhra trade on the east coast with Southeast Asia. The centuries-long conflict between the northern and the southern Deccan, of which the Chalukya-Pallava conflict was but a facet, also had geographic, political, and economic causes. Any southern Indian power seeking to expand would inevitably try to move up the east coast, which was not only the most fertile area of the peninsula but was also wealthy from the income of trade with Southeast Asia. Therefore, control of the northern Deccan required control of the east coast as well. With the major maritime activity gradually concentrating on Southeast Asian trade, in which even the west coast had a large share, the control of both coasts was of considerable economic advantage. It was along the east coast, therefore, that the conflict between the two regions often erupted. The next 100 years of Chalukya power witnessed the continuation of this conflict, weakening both contenders. Ultimately, in the mid-8th century, a feudatory of the Chalukyas, Dantidurga of the Rashtrakuta dynasty, rose to importance and established himself in place of the declining Chalukya dynasty. The Eastern Chalukyas, who had managed to avoid involvement in the conflict, survived longer and came into conflict with the Rashtrakutas. Another branch of the Chalukyas established itself at Lata in the mid-7th century and played a prominent role in obstructing the Arab advance.

SOUTHERN INDIA

The southern part of the peninsula split into many kingdoms, each fighting for supremacy. Cera power relied mainly on a flourishing trade with western Asia. The Cholas retired into insignificance in the Uraiyur (Tiruchchirappalli) area. The Pandyas were involved in fighting the rising power of the Pallavas, and occasionally they formed alliances with the Deccan kingdoms.

The origin of the Pallava dynasty is obscure. It is not even clear whether the early Pallavas of the 3rd century were the ancestors of the later Pallavas of the 6th century, who are sometimes distinguished by the title "imperial." It would seem, though, that their place of origin was Tondaimandalam, with its centre at Kanchipuram (ancient Kanci). Prakrit copperplate charters issued by the early kings from Kanchipuram often mention places just to the north in Andhra Pradesh, suggesting that the dynasty may have migrated to the Kanchipuram area. The Sanskrit and Tamil epigraphic records of the later kings of the dynasty indicate that the later Pallavas became dominant

in the 6th century after a successful attack against the Kalabhras, which extended their territory as far south as the Kaveri River. The Pallavas reached their zenith during the reign of Mahendravarman I (c. 600–630), a contemporary of Harsha and Pulakeshin II. Among the sources of the period, Xuanzang's account serves as a link, as he traveled through the domains of all three kings. The struggle for Vengi between the Pallavas and the Chalukyas became the immediate pretext for a long, drawn-out war, which began with the defeat of the Pallavas. Apart from his campaigns, Mahendravarman was a writer and artist of some distinction. The play associated with him, *Mattavilasaprahasana,* treats in a farcical manner the idiosyncrasies of Buddhist and Shaiva ascetics.

Mahendravarman's successor, Narasimhavarman I (reigned c. 630–668), also called Mahamall or Mamalla, avenged the Pallava defeat by capturing Vatapi. He sent two naval expeditions from Mahabalipuram to Sri Lanka to assist the king Manavamma in regaining his throne. Pallava naval interests laid the foundation for extensive reliance on the navy by the succeeding dynasty, the Cholas. Toward the end of the 8th century, the Gangas and the Pandyas joined coalitions against the Pallavas. As the Chalukyas declined under pressure from the Rashtrakutas, the Pandyas gradually took on the Pallavas and, by the mid-9th century, advanced as far as Kumbakonam. This defeat was avenged, but, by the end of the 9th century, Pallava power had ceased to be significant.

SOCIETY AND CULTURE

Some of the Pallava kings took an interest in the Alvars and Nayanars, the religious teachers who preached a new form of Vaishnavism and Shaivism based on the *bhakti* (devotional) cults. Among the Shaivas were Appar (who is said to have converted Mahendravarman from Jainism) and Manikkavacakar. Among the Vaishnavas were Nammalvar and a woman teacher, Andal. The movement aimed at preaching a popular Hinduism, in which Tamil was preferred to Sanskrit, and emphasized the role of the peripatetic teacher. Women were encouraged to participate in the congregations. The Tamil devotional cult and similar movements elsewhere were in a sense competitive with Buddhism and Jainism, both of which suffered a gradual decline in most areas. Jainism found a foothold in Karnataka, Rajasthan, and Gujarat. Buddhism flourished in eastern India, with major monastic centres at Nalanda, Vikramashila, and Paharpur that attracted vast numbers of students from India and abroad. Tibetan and eastern Indian cults, particularly the Tantric cults, influenced the development of Vajrayana ("Thunderbolt Vehicle") Buddhism. The widespread Shakti cult associated with Hindu practice was based on the notion that the male can be activated only by union with the female. Thus, the gods were given consorts—Lakshmi (or Shri) for Vishnu; Parvati, Kali, and Durga for Shiva—and ritual was directed toward the worship of the mother goddess. Much of the ritual was derived from the earlier fertility cults and local rites and beliefs that were assimilated into Hinduism.

During the same period, orthodox Brahmanism received encouragement, especially from the royal families. Learned Brahmans were given endowments of land. The performance of Vedic sacrifices for purposes of royal legitimacy gave way to the keeping of genealogies, which the Brahmans now controlled. The new Brahmanism acquired a locality and an institution in

Sandstone sculpture of the Buddha, 5th century CE, from Sarnath, Uttar Pradesh, India; in the Indian Museum, Kolkata. P. Chandra

the form of the temple. The earliest remains of a Hindu temple, discovered at Sanchi, date to the Gupta period. These extremely simple structures consisted of a shrine room, called a *garbhagrha* ("womb house," or sanctum sanctorum), which contained an image of the deity and opened onto a porch. Over the centuries, additional structures were added until the temple complexes covered many acres. In the peninsula the early rock-cut temples imitated Buddhist models. Although the Chalukyas did introduce freestanding temples, most of their patronage extended to rock-cut monuments. The Pallavas also began with rock-cut temples, as at Mahabalipur, but, when they took to freestanding temples, they produced the most-impressive examples of their time.

As temples and monasteries became larger and more complex, the decorative arts of mural painting and sculpture flourished. Early examples of mural painting occur at Bagh and Sittanvasal (now in Tamil Nadu), and the tradition reached its apogee in the murals at the Ajanta Caves (Maharashtra) during the Vakataka and Chalukya periods. The fashion for murals in Buddhist monasteries spread from India to Afghanistan and Central Asia and ultimately to China. Equally impressive was the Buddhist sculpture at Sarnath, in Uttar Pradesh. It is possible that the proliferation of Buddhist images led to the depiction of Hindu deities in iconic form.

Temples were richly endowed with wealth and land, and the larger institutions could accommodate colleges of higher learning (*ghatikas* and

Fresco of a court scene from Cave I, Ajanta, Maharashtra, India, 600–700 CE. V. Panjabi—Shostal/EB Inc.

mathas), primarily for priests. These colleges became responsible for much of the formal education, and inevitably the use of Sanskrit became widespread. There was an appreciable development of Hindu philosophy, which now recognized six major systems (*darshans*): Nyaya, Vaishesika, Samkhya, Yoga, Mimamsa, and Vedanta. Indicative of the growing domination of Brahmanic intellectual life, the ancient Puranas were now written substantially in their present form under Brahmanic influence.

The flowering of classical Sanskrit literature is indicated by the plays and poems of Kalidasa (*Abhijnanashakuntala, Malavikagnimitra, Vikramorvashiya, Raghuvamsha, Meghaduta*), although Kalidasa's precise date is uncertain. In the south the propagation of Sanskrit resulted in the *Kiratarjuniya,* an epic written by Bharavi (7th century); in Dandin's *Dashakumaracarita,* a collection of popular stories (6th century); and in Bhavabhuti's play *Malatimadhava.* Tamil literature flourished as well, as evidenced by two didactic works, the *Tirukkural* (by Tiruvalluvar) and *Naladiyar,* and by the more lyrical *Silappadikaram* and *Manimekhalai,* two Tamil epics. Representing a less common genre of literature in the Gupta period was the *Kama-sutra* of Vatsyayana, a manual on the art of love. This was a collation and revision of earlier texts and displays a remarkable sophistication and urbanity. It was a period of literary excellence, though in the other arts such levels of excellence came later. Not all the

achievements can be associated with the Gupta dynasty.

The monasteries and temples were centres of formal learning, and the guilds were centres of technical knowledge. The mixture of the theoretical and practical, however, sometimes occurred, as in the case of medicine, particularly veterinary science. Advances in metallurgy are attested in such objects as the Sultanganj Buddha and a famous iron pillar now at Mehrauli (Delhi). Gold and silver coins of the Gupta period exhibit a refinement that was not to be surpassed for many centuries. Mathematics was particularly advanced, probably more so than anywhere in the world at the time. Indian numerals were later borrowed by the Arabs and introduced to Europe as Arabic numerals. The use of the cipher and the decimal system is confirmed by inscriptions. With advances in mathematics there was comparable progress in astronomy. Aryabhata I, writing in 499, calculated π (pi) to 3.1416 and the solar year to 365.3586... days and stated that the earth was spherical and rotated on its axis. That European astronomy was also known is suggested by the 6th-century astronomer Varahamihira, who mentions the Romaka Siddhanta ("School of Rome") among the five major schools of astronomy.

Legal texts and commentaries were abundant—the better-known being those of Yajnavalkya, Narada, Brihaspati, Katyayana. Earlier texts relating to social problems and property rights received particular attention. The post-Gupta period saw considerable and lasting social change, which resulted not only from outside influences but also from the interaction of the elite Sanskritic culture with more-parochial non-Sanskritic cultures. The expanding village economy opened up new areas geographically, and the increasing importance of guilds in the towns indicated fresh perspectives on social life. These activities also incorporated new groups and cultures into the existing norms of Indian society.

FROM 750 TO C. 1200

In both North and South India, smaller kingdoms strove to dominate their neighbours. Yet despite the depredations of war, this period proved to be culturally rich and productive for much of the subcontinent. New influences flowed into the subcontinent from the sophisticated empires of Anatolia (Turkey).

NORTHERN INDIA

The 8th century was a time of struggle for control over the central Ganges valley—focusing on Kannauj—among the Gurjara-Pratihara, the Rashtrakuta, and the Pala dynasties.

THE TRIPARTITE STRUGGLE

The Pratiharas rose to power in the Avanti-Jalaor region and used western India as a base. The Chalukyas fell about 753 to one of their own feudatories, the Rashtrakutas under Dantidurga, who established a dynasty. The Rashtrakuta

interest in Kannauj probably centred on the trade routes from the Ganges valley. This was the first occasion on which a power based in the Deccan made a serious bid for a pivotal position in northern India. From the east the Palas also participated in the competition. They are associated with Pundravardhana (near Bogra, Bangl.), and their first ruler, Gopala (reigned c. 750–770), included Vanga in his kingdom and gradually extended his control to the whole of Bengal.

Vatsaraja, a Pratihara ruler who came to the throne about 778, controlled eastern Rajasthan and Malava. His ambition to take Kannauj brought him into conflict with the Pala king, Dharmapala (reigned c. 770–810), who had by this time advanced up the Ganges valley. The Rashtrakuta king Dhruva (reigned c. 780–793) attacked each in turn and claimed to have defeated them. This initiated a lengthy tripartite struggle. Dharmapala soon retook Kannauj and put his nominee on the throne. The Rashtrakutas were preoccupied with problems in the south. Vatsaraja's successor, Nagabhata II (reigned c. 793–833), reorganized Pratihara power, attacked Kannauj, and for a short while reversed the situation. However, soon afterward he was defeated by the Rashtrakuta king Govinda III (reigned 793–814), who in turn had to face a confederacy of southern powers that kept him involved in Deccan politics, leaving northern India to the Pratiharas and Palas. Bhoja I (reigned c. 836–885) revived the power of the Pratiharas by bringing Kalanjara, and possibly Kannauj as well, under Pratihara control. Bhoja's plans to extend the kingdom, however, were thwarted by the Palas and the Rashtrakutas. More serious conflict with the latter ensued during the reign of Krishna II (reigned c. 878–914).

An Arab visitor to western India, the merchant Sulaymān, referred to the kingdom of Juzr (which is generally identified as Gurjara) and its strong and able ruler, who may have been Bhoja. Of the successors of Bhoja, the only one of significance was Mahipala (reigned c. 908–942), whose relationship with the earlier king remains controversial. Rajashekhara, a renowned poet at his court, implies that Mahipala restored the kingdom to its original power, but this may be an exaggeration. By the end of the 10th century the Pratihara feudatories—Cauhans (Cahamanas), Chandelas (Candellas), Guhilas, Kalacuris, Paramaras, and Chalukyas (also called Solankis)—were asserting their independence, although the last of the Pratiharas survived until 1027. Meanwhile Devapala (reigned c. 810–850) was reasserting Pala authority in the east and, he claimed, in the northern Deccan. At the end of the 9th century, however, the Pala kingdom declined, with feudatories in Kamarupa (modern Assam) and Utkala (Orissa) taking independent titles. Pala power revived during the reign of Mahipala (reigned c. 988–1038), although its stronghold now was Bihar rather than Bengal. Further attempts to recover the old Pala territories were made by Ramapala, but Pala power gradually declined. There was a brief revival of power in Bengal under the Sena dynasty (c. 1070–1289).

In the Rashtrakuta kingdom, Amoghavarsa (reigned c. 814–878) faced a revolt of officers and feudatories but managed to survive and reassert Rashtrakuta power despite intermittent rebellions. Campaigns in the south against Vengi and the Gangas kept Amoghavarsa preoccupied and prevented him from participating in northern politics. The Rashtrakuta capital was moved to Manyakheta (Andhra Pradesh), doubtlessly to facilitate southern involvements, which clearly took on more-important dimensions at this time. Sporadic campaigns against the Pratiharas, the Eastern Chalukyas, and the Cholas, the new power of the south, continued. Indra III (reigned 914–927) captured Kannauj, but, with mounting political pressures from the south, his control over the north was inevitably short-lived. The reign of Krishna III (reigned c. 939–968) saw a successful campaign against the Cholas, a matrimonial alliance with the Gangas, and the subjugation of Vengi. Rashtrakuta power declined suddenly, however, after the reign of Indra, and this was fully exploited by the feudatory Taila.

Taila II (reigned 973–997), who traced his ancestry to the earlier Chalukyas of Vatapi, ruled a small part of Bijapur. Upon the weakening of Rashtrakuta power, he defeated the king, declared his independence, and founded what has come to be called the Later Chalukya dynasty. The kingdom included much of Karnataka,

Konkan, and the territory as far north as the Godavari River. By the end of the 10th century, the Later Chalukyas clashed with the ambitious Cholas. The Chalukyas' capital was subsequently moved north to Kalyani (near Bidar, in Karnataka). Campaigns against the Cholas took a more serious turn during the reign of Someshvara I (reigned 1043–68), with alternating defeat and victory. The Later Chalukyas, however, by and large retained control over the western Deccan despite the hostility of the Cholas and of their own feudatories. In the middle of the 12th century, however, a feudatory, Bijjala (reigned 1156–67) of the Kalacuri dynasty, usurped the throne at Kalyani. The last of the Chalukya rulers, Someshvara IV (reigned 1181–c. 1189), regained the throne for a short period, after which he was overthrown by a feudatory of the Yadava dynasty.

On the periphery of the large kingdoms were the smaller states such as Nepal, Kamarupa, Kashmir, and Utkala (Orissa) and lesser dynasties such as the Shilaharas in Maharashtra. Nepal had freed itself from Tibetan suzerainty in the 8th century but remained a major trade route to Tibet. Kamarupa, with its capital at Pragjyotisapura (near present-day Gawahati), was one of the centres of the Tantric cult. In 1253 a major part of Kamarupa was conquered by the Ahom, a Shan people. Politics in Kashmir were dominated by turbulent feudatories seeking power. By the 11th century Kashmir was torn between rival court factions, and the oppression by Harsha accentuated the suffering of the people. Smaller states along the Himalayan foothills managed to survive without becoming too embroiled in the politics of the plains.

THE RAJPUTS

In Rajasthan and central India there arose a number of small kingdoms ruled by dynasties that came to be called the Rajputs (from Sanskrit *raja-putra*, "son of a king"). The name was assumed by royal families that claimed Kshatriya status and linked their lineage either with the Suryavamshi (solar) or the Candravamshi (lunar), the royal lineages of the *itihasa-purana* tradition, or else with the Agnikula (fire lineage), based on a lesser myth in which the eponymous ancestor arises out of the sacrificial fire. The four major Rajput dynasties—Pratihara, Paramara, Cauhan, and Chalukya—claimed Agnikula lineage. The references in Rajput genealogies to supernatural ancestry suggest either an obscure origin—perhaps from semi-Hinduized local tribes who gradually acquired political and economic status—or else a non-Indian (probably Central Asian) origin.

The Chalukyas of Gujarat had three branches: one ruling Mattamayura (the Malava-Cedi region), one established on the former kingdom of the Capas at Anahilapataka (present-day Patan), and the third at Bhrigukaccha (present-day Bharuch) and Lata in the coastal area. By the 11th century they were using Gujarat as a base and attempting to annex neighbouring portions of

Rajasthan and Avanti. Kumarapala (reigned c. 1143–72) was responsible for consolidating the kingdom. He is also believed to have become a Jain and to have encouraged Jainism in western India. Hemacandra, an outstanding Jain scholar noted for his commentaries on political treatises, was a well-known figure at the Chalukya court. Many of the Rajput kingdoms had Jain statesmen, ministers, and even generals, as well as Jain traders and merchants. By the 14th century, however, the Chalukya kingdom had declined.

Adjoining the kingdom of the Chalukyas was that of the Paramaras in Malava, with minor branches in the territories just to the north (Mount Abu, Banswara, Cungarpur, and Bhinmal). The Paramaras emerged as feudatories of the Rashtrakutas and rose to eminence during the reign of Bhoja. An attack by the Chalukyas weakened the Paramaras in 1143. Although the dynasty was later re-established, it remained weak. In the 13th century the Paramaras were threatened by both rising Yadava power in the Deccan and the Turkish kingdom at Delhi; the latter conquered the Paramaras in 1305.

The Kalacuris of Tripuri (near Jabalpur) also began as feudatories of the Rashtrakutas, becoming a power in central India in the 11th century during the reigns of Gangeyadeva and his son Lakshmikarna, when attempts were made to conquer territories as far afield as Utkala (Orissa), Bihar, and the Ganges-Yamuna Doab. There they came into conflict with the Turkish governor of the Punjab, who briefly had extended his territory as far as Varanasi. To the west there were conflicts with Bhoja Paramara, and the Kalacuris declined at the end of the 12th century.

The Chandelas, whose kingdom comprised mainly Bundelkhand, were feudatories of the Pratiharas. Among the important rulers was Dhanga (reigned c. 950–1008), who issued a large number of inscriptions and was generous in donations to Jain and Hindu temples. Dhanga's grandson Vidyadhara (reigned 1017–29), often described as the most powerful of the Candela kings, extended the kingdom as far as the Chambal and Narmada rivers. There he came into direct conflict with the Turkic conqueror Maḥmūd of Ghazna when the latter swept down from Afghanistan in a series of raids. But the ensuing battles were indecisive. The Chandelas also had to face the attacks of the Cauhans, who were in turn being harassed by the Turks. The Turkish kingdom at Delhi encroached into Bundelkhand, but the Chandelas survived until the 16th century as minor chieftains.

The Gahadavalas rose to importance in Varanasi and extended their kingdom up the Gangetic plain, including Kannauj. The king Jayacandra (12th century) is mentioned in the poem *Prithviraja-raso* by Candbardai, in which his daughter, the princess Sanyogita, elopes with the Cauhan king Prithviraja. Jayacandra died in battle against the Turkish leader, Mu'izz al-Dīn Muḥammad ibn Sām (Muḥammad of Ghūr), and his kingdom was annexed.

Inscriptional records associate the Cauhans with Lake Shakambhari and its environs (Sambhar Salt Lake, Rajasthan). Cauhan politics were largely campaigns against the Chalukyas and the Turks. In the 11th century the Cauhans founded the city of Ajayameru (Ajmer) in the southern part of their kingdom, and in the 12th century they captured Dhillika (Delhi) from the Tomaras and annexed some Tomara territory along the Yamuna River. Prithviraja III has come down both in folk and historical literature as the Cauhan king who resisted the Turkish attacks in the first battle at Taraori (Tarain) in 1191. Prithviraja, however, was defeated at a second battle in the same place in 1192; the defeat ushered in Turkish rule in northern India.

THE COMING OF THE TURKS

The establishment of Turkish power in India is initially tied up with politics in the Punjab. The Punjab was ruled by Jayapala of the Hindu Shahi family (Shahiya), which had in the 9th century wrested the Kābul valley and Gandhara from a Turkish Shah. Political and economic relations were extremely close between the Punjab and Afghanistan. Afghanistan in turn was closely involved with Central Asian politics. Sebüktigin, a Turk, was appointed governor of Ghazna in 977. He attacked the Hindu Shahis and advanced as far as Peshawar. His son Maḥmūd succeeded to the Ghazna principality in 998. Maḥmūd went to war with the Shahiya dynasty, and, almost every year until his death in 1030, he led raids against the rich temple towns in northern and western India, using the wealth obtained from the raids to finance successful campaigns in Central Asia and build an empire there. He acquired a reputation as an iconoclast as well as a patron of culture and was responsible for sending to India the scholar al-Bīrūnī, whose study *Ta'rīkh al-Hind* ("The History of India") is a source of valuable information. Maḥmūd left his governors in the Punjab with a rather loose control over the region.

In the 12th century the Ghūrid Turks were driven out of Khorāsān and later out of Ghazna by the Khwārezm-Shah dynasty. Inevitably the Ghūrids sought their fortune in northern India, where the conflict between the Ghaznavids and the local rulers provided an excellent opportunity. Muḥammad of Ghūr advanced into the Punjab and captured Lahore in 1185. Victory in the second battle of Taraori consolidated Muḥammad's success, and he left his *mamlūk* (slave) general, Quṭb-al-Dīn Aybak, in charge of his Indian possessions. Muḥammad was assassinated in 1206 on his way back to Afghanistan. Quṭb al-Dīn remained in India and declared himself sultan of Delhi, the first of the Mamlūk dynasty.

THE DECCAN AND THE SOUTH

In the northern Deccan the decline of the Later Chalukyas brought about the rise of their feudatories, among them the Yadava dynasty (also claiming descent from the Yadu tribe) based at Devagiri (Daulatabad), whose kingdom (Seunadesha) included the broad swaths of what is now Maharashtra state. The kingdom expanded during the reign of Simhana (reigned c. 1210–47), who campaigned against the Hoysala in northern Karnataka, against the lesser chiefs of the western coast, and against the Kakatiya kingdom in the eastern Deccan. Turning northward, Simhana attacked the Paramaras and the Chalukyas. The Yadavas, however, facing the Turks to the north and the powerful Hoysalas to the south, declined in the early 14th century.

In the eastern Deccan the Kakatiya dynasty was based in parts of what is now Andhra Pradesh state and survived until the Turkish attack in the 14th century. The Eastern Chalukyas ruled in the Godavari River delta, and in the 13th century their fortunes were tied to those of the Cholas. The Eastern Gangas, ruling in Kalinga, came into conflict with the Turks advancing down the Ganges River valley to the delta during the 13th century.

THE CHOLAS

The Cholas (Colas) were by far the most important dynasty in the subcontinent at this time, although their activities mainly affected the peninsula and Southeast Asia. The nucleus of Chola power during the reign of Vijayalaya in the late 9th century was Thanjavur, from which the Cholas spread northward, annexing in the 10th century what remained of Pallava territory. To the south they came up

against the Pandyas. Chola history can be reconstructed in considerable detail because of the vast number of lengthy inscriptions issued not only by the royal family but also by temple authorities, village councils, and trade guilds. Parantaka I (reigned 907–953) laid the foundation of the kingdom. He took the northern boundary up to Nellore (Andhra Pradesh), where his advance was stopped by a defeat at the hands of the Rashtrakuta king Krishna III. Parantaka was more successful in the south, where he defeated both the Pandyas and the Gangas. He also launched an abortive attack on Sri Lanka. For 30 years after his death, there was a series of feeble reigns that did not strengthen the Chola position. There then followed two outstanding rulers who rapidly reinstated Chola power and ensured the kingdom its supremacy. These were Rajaraja I and Rajendra.

Rajaraja (reigned 985–1014) began establishing power with attacks against the Pandyas and Illamandalam of Sri Lanka. Northern Sri Lanka became a province of the Chola kingdom. A campaign against the Gangas and Chalukyas extended the Chola boundary north to the Tungabhadra River. On the eastern coast the Cholas battled with the Chalukyas for the possession of Vengi. A marriage alliance gave the Cholas an authoritative position, but Vengi remained a bone of contention. A naval campaign led to the conquest of the Maldive Islands, the Malabar Coast, and northern Sri Lanka, all of which were essential to the Chola control over trade with Southeast Asia and with Arabia and eastern Africa. These were the transit areas, ports of call for the Arab traders and ships to Southeast Asia and China, which were the source of the valuable spices sold at a high profit to Europe.

Rajaraja I's son Rajendra participated in his father's government from 1012, succeeded him two years later, and ruled until 1044. To the north he annexed the Raichur Doab (the interfluve between the Krishna and Tungabhadra rivers in Karnataka) and moved into Manyakheta in the heart of Chalukya territory. A revolt against Mahinda V of Sri Lanka gave Rajendra the excuse to conquer southern Sri Lanka as well. In 1021–22 the now-famous northern campaign was launched. The Chola army campaigned along the east coast as far as Bengal and then north to the Ganges River—almost the exact reverse of Samudra Gupta's campaign to Kanchipuram in the 4th century CE. The most spectacular campaign, however, was a naval campaign against the Srivijaya empire in Southeast Asia in 1025. The reason for the assault on Srivijaya and neighbouring areas appears to have been the interference with Indian shipping and mercantile interests seeking direct trading connections with southern China. The Chola victory reinstated these connections, and throughout the 11th century Chola trading missions visited China.

THE HOYSALAS AND PANDYAS

The succession after Rajendra is confused until the emergence of Kulottunga I (reigned 1070–1122), but his reign was the last of any significance. The 12th and 13th centuries saw a gradual decline in Chola power, accelerated by the rise of the Hoysalas to the west and the Pandyas to the south.

The Hoysalas began as hill chieftains northwest of Dorasamudra (modern Halebid), feudatory to the Chalukyas. Vishnuvardhana consolidated the kingdom in the 12th century. The Hoysalas were involved in conflict with the Yadava kingdom, which was seeking to expand southward, particularly during the reign of Ballala II (reigned 1173–1220). Hostilities also developed with the Cholas to the east. The armies of the Turks eroded the Hoysala kingdom until, in the 14th century, it gave way to the newly emerging Vijayanagar empire. In the 13th century the Pandyas became the dominant power in the south, but their supremacy was brief because they were attacked in the 14th century by Turkish armies. Information on the dynasty is supplemented by the colourful account of Venetian traveler Marco Polo, who visited the region in 1288 and 1293.

SOCIETY AND CULTURE

Apart from the political events of the time, a common development in the subcontinent was the recognizable decentralization of administration and revenue collection. From the Chola kingdom there are long inscriptions on temple walls referring to the organization and functioning of village councils. Villages that had been donated to Brahmans had councils called *sabhas*; in the non-Brahman villages the council was called the ur. Eligibility qualifications generally relating to age and ownership of property were indicated, along with procedural rules. The council was divided into various committees in charge of the different aspects of village life and administration. Among the responsibilities of the council was the collection of revenue and the supervision of irrigation. References to village bodies and local councils also occur in inscriptions from other regions. A more recent and much-contested view held by some historians holds that the Chola state was a segmentary state with control decreasing from the centre outward and a ritual hierarchy that determined the relations between the centre and the units of the territory. The nature of the state during this period has been the subject of widespread discussion among historians.

In the Deccan the rise and fall of dynasties was largely the result of the feudatory pattern of political relationships. The same held true of northern India and is seen both in the rise of various Rajput dynasties and in their inability to withstand the Turkish invasions. There is considerable controversy among historians as to whether it would be accurate to describe the feudatory pattern as feudalism per se. Some argue that, although it was not identical to the classic example of feudalism in western Europe, there are sufficient similarities to allow the use of the term. Others contend that the

dissimilarities are substantial, such as the apparent absence of an economic contract involving king, vassal, and serf. In any event, the patterns of land relations, politics, and culture changed considerably, and the major characteristic of the change consists of forms of decentralization.

The commonly used term for a feudatory was *samanta*, which designated either a conquered ruler or a secular official connected with the administration who had been given a grant of land in lieu of a salary and who had asserted ownership over the land and gradually appropriated rights of ruling the area. There were various categories of *samantas*. As long as a ruler was in a feudatory status, he called himself *samanta* and acknowledged his overlord in official documents and charters. Independent status was indicated by the elimination of the title of *samanta* and the inclusion instead of royal titles such as *maharaja* and *maharatadhiraju*. The feudatory had certain obligations to the ruler. Although virtually in sole control administratively and fiscally over the land granted to him, he nevertheless had to pay a small percentage of the revenue to the ruler and maintain a specified body of troops for him. He was permitted the use of certain symbols of authority on formal occasions and was required, if called upon, to give his daughter in marriage to his suzerain. These major administrative and economic changes, although primarily concerning fiscal arrangements and revenue organization, also had their impact on politics and culture. The grantees or intermediaries in a hierarchy of grants were not merely secular officials but were often Brahman beneficiaries who had been given grants of land in return for religious services rendered to the state. The grants were frequently so lucrative that the Brahmans could marry into the families of local chiefs, which explains the presence of Brahman ancestors in the genealogies of the period.

THE ECONOMY

Cultivation was still carried out by the peasants, generally Sudras, who remained tied to the land. Since the revenue was now to be paid not to the king but to the *samanta*, the peasants naturally began to give more attention to his requirements. Although the *samantas* copied the lifestyle of the royal court, often to the point of setting up miniature courts in imitation of the royal model, the system also encouraged parochial loyalties and local cultural interests. One manifestation of this local involvement was a sudden spurt of historical literature such as Bilhana's *Vikramankadevacarita,* the life of the Chalukya king Vikramaditya VI, and Kalhana's *Rajatarangini,* a history of Kashmir.

The earlier decline in trade was gradually reversed in this period, with trade centres emerging in various parts of the subcontinent. Some urban centres developed from points of exchange for agrarian produce, whereas others were involved in long-distance trade. In some cases, traders from elsewhere settled in India, such as the Arabs on the Malabar Coast; in other cases Indian traders went to distant lands. Powerful trading guilds could enjoy political and military support, as was the case during the Chola monarchy. Even the rich Hindu temples of southern India invested their money in trade. Pala contacts were mainly with Srivijaya, and trade was combined with Buddhist interests. The monasteries at Nalanda and Vikramashila maintained close relations. By now eastern India was the only region with a sizable Buddhist presence. The traditional trade routes were still used, and some kingdoms drew their revenue from such routes as those along the Aravalli Range, Malava, and the Chambal and Narmada valleys. Significantly, the major technological innovation, the introduction of the *sāqiyah* (Persian wheel), or *araghatta*, as an aid to irrigation in northern India, pertains to agrarian life and not to urban technology.

SOCIAL MOBILITY

Historians once believed that the post-Gupta period brought greater rigidity in the caste structure and that this rigidity was partially responsible for the inability of Indians to face the challenge of the Turks. This view is now being modified. The distinctions, particularly between the Brahmans and the other castes, were in theory sharper, but in practice it now appears that social restrictions were not so rigid. Brahmans often lived off the land and founded dynasties. Most of the groups claiming Kshatriya status had only recently acquired it. The conscious reference to being Kshatriya, a characteristic among Rajputs, is a noticeable feature in post-Gupta politics. The fact that many of these dynasties were of obscure origin suggests some social mobility: a person of any caste, having once acquired political power, could also acquire a genealogy connecting him with the traditional lineages and conferring Kshatriya status. A number of new castes, such as the Kayasthas (scribes) and Khatris (traders), are mentioned in the sources of this period. According to the Brahmanic sources, they originated from intercaste marriages, but this is clearly an attempt at rationalizing their rank in the hierarchy. Many of these new castes played a major role in society. The hierarchy of castes did not have a uniform distribution throughout the country. But the preeminent position of the Brahman was endorsed not merely by the fact that many had lands and investments but also by the fact that they controlled education. Formal learning was virtually restricted to the institutions attached to the temples. Technical knowledge was available in the various artisan guilds. Hierarchy existed, however, even among the Brahmans; some Brahman castes, who had perhaps been tribal priests before being assimilated into the Sanskritic tradition, remained ordinary village priests catering to the day-to-day religious functions.

RELIGION

The local nucleus of the new culture led to a large range of religious expression, from the powerful temple religion of Brahmanism to a widespread popular bhakti religion and even more widespread fertility cults. The distinctions between the three were not clearly demarcated in practice; rites and concepts from each flowed into the other. The formal worship of Vishnu and Shiva had the support of the elite. Temples dedicated to Vaishnava and Shaiva deities were the most numerous. But also included were some of the chief deities connected with the fertility cult, and the mother goddesses played an important role. The Puranas had been rewritten to incorporate popular religion; now the *upa-puranas* were written to record rites and worship of more-localized deities. Among the more-popular incarnations of Vishnu was Krishna, who, as the cowherd deity, accommodated pastoral and erotic themes in worship. The love of Krishna and Radha was expressed in sensitive and passionate poetry.

The introduction of the erotic theme in Hinduism was closely connected with the fertility cult and Tantrism. The latter, named for its scriptures, the Tantras, influenced both Hindu and Buddhist ritual. Tantrism, as practiced by the elite, represented the conversion of a widespread folk religion into a sophisticated one. The emphasis on the mother goddess, related to that expressed in the Shakti (Śakti) cult, strengthened the status of the female deities. The erotic aspect also was related to the importance of ritual coition in some Tantric rites. The depiction of erotic scenes on temple walls therefore had a magico-religious context.

Vajrayana Buddhism, current in eastern India, Nepal, and Tibet, shows evidence of the impact of Tantrism. The goddess Tara emerges as the saviour and is in many ways the Buddhist counterpart of Shakti. Buddhism was on the way out—the Buddha had been incorporated as an avatar of Vishnu—and had lost much of its popular appeal, which had been maintained by the simple habits of the monks. The traditional source of Buddhist patronage had dwindled with declining trade. Jainism, however, managed to maintain some hold in Rajasthan, Gujarat, and Karnataka. The protest aspect of both

Ramanuja, bronze sculpture, 12th century, from a Vishnu temple in Tamil Nadu state, India. Courtesy of the Institut Français d'Indologie, Pondicherry

Buddhism and Jainism, especially the opposition to Brahmanic orthodoxy, had now been taken over by the Tantrists and the *bhakti* cults. The Tantrists expressed their protest through some rather extreme rites, as did some of the heretical sects such as the Kalamukhas and Kapalikas. The *bhakti* cults expressed the more-puritanical protest of the urban groups, gradually spreading to the rural areas. Preeminent among the *bhakti* groups during this period were the Lingayats, or Virashaivas, who were to become a powerful force in Karnataka, and the Pandharpur cult in Maharashtra, which attracted such preachers as Namadeva and Jnaneshvara.

LITERATURE AND THE ARTS

It was also in the *matha* (monastery) and the *ghatika* (assembly hall), attached to the temples, that the influential philosophical debates were conducted in Sanskrit. Foremost among the philosophers were Shankara (8th–9th century), Ramanuja (d. 1137), and Madhva (13th century). The discussions centred on religious problems, such as whether knowledge or devotion was the more effective means of salvation, and problems of metaphysics, including that of the nature of reality.

Court literature, irrespective of the region, continued to be composed in Sanskrit, with the many courts competing for the patronage of the poets and the dramatists. There was a revival of interest in earlier literature, generating copious commentaries on prosody, grammar, and technical literature. The number of lexicons increased, perhaps necessitated by the growing use of Sanskrit by non-Sanskrit speakers. Literary style tended to be pedantic and imitative, although there were notable exceptions, such as Jayadeva's lyrical poem on the love of Radha and Krishna, the *Gitagovinda*. The *bhakti* teachers preached in the local languages, giving a tremendous stimulus to literature in these languages. Adaptations of the *Ramayana*, *Mahabharata*, and Bhagavadgita were used regularly by the

Kailasa Temple, Ellora Caves, Maharashtra state, India. Frederick M. Asher

bhakti teachers. There was thus a gradual breaking away from Sanskrit and the Prakrit languages via the Apabhrahmsha language and the eventual emergence and evolution of such languages as Kannada, Telugu, Marathi, Gujarati, Bengali, and Oriya and of the Bihari languages.

The period was rich in sculpture, in both stone and metal, each region registering a variant style. Western India and Rajasthan emphasized ornateness, with the Jain temples at Mount Abu attaining a perfection of rococo. Nalanda was the centre of striking but less-ornate images in black stone and of Buddhist bronze icons. Central Indian craftsmen used the softer sandstone. In the peninsula the profusely sculptured rock-cut temples such as the Kailasa at the Ellora Caves, under Chalukya and Rashtrakuta patronage, displayed a style of their own. The dominant style in the south was that of Chola sculpture, particularly in bronze. The severe beauty and elegance of these bronze images, mainly of Shaiva and Vaishnava deities and saints, remains unsurpassed. A new genre of painting that rose to popularity in Nepal, eastern India, and Gujarat was the illustration of Buddhist and Jain manuscripts with miniature paintings.

Temple architecture was divided into three main styles—*nagara*, *dravida*, and *vasara*—which were distinguished by the ground plan of the temple and by the shape of the *shikhara* (tower) that rose over the *garbhagrha* (cubical structure)

Surya temple, Osian, Rajasthan state, India. Frederick M. Asher

and that became the commanding feature of temple architecture. The north Indian temples conformed to the *nagara* style, as is seen at Osian (Rajasthan state); Khajuraho (Madhya Pradesh state); and Konarka, Bhubaneshwar, and Puri (Orissa state). The Orissa temples, however, remain nearest to the original archetype. South Indian temple architecture, or *dravida*, style—with its commanding *gopuras* (gateways)—can be seen in the Rajarajeshvara and the Gangaikondacolapuram temples. The Deccani style, *vasara*, tended to be an intermixture of the northern and the southern, with early examples at Vatapi, Aihole, and Pattadakal and, later, at Halebid, Belur, and Somnathpur in the vicinity of Mysore. The wealth of the temples made them the focus of attack from plunderers.

The question that is frequently posed as to why the Turks so easily conquered northern India and the Deccan has in

Citragupta temple, at Khajuraho, Madhya Pradesh state, India, 11th century. P. Chandra

part to do with what might be called the medieval ethos. A contemporary observed that the Indians had become self-centred and unaware of the world around them. This was substantially true. There was little interest in the politics of neighbouring countries or in their technological achievements. The medieval ethos expressed itself not only in the "feudatory" attitude toward politics and the parochial concerns that became dominant and prevented any effective opposition to the Turks but also in the trappings of chivalry and romanticism that became central to elite activity.

It has been generally held that the medieval period of Indian history began with the arrival of the Turks (dated to either 1000 or 1206 CE), because the Turks brought with them a new religion, Islam, which changed Indian society at all levels. Yet the fundamental changes that took place about the 8th century, when the medieval ethos was introduced, would seem far more significant as criteria.

CHAPTER 4

NORTHERN INDIA IN THE EARLY MUSLIM PERIOD

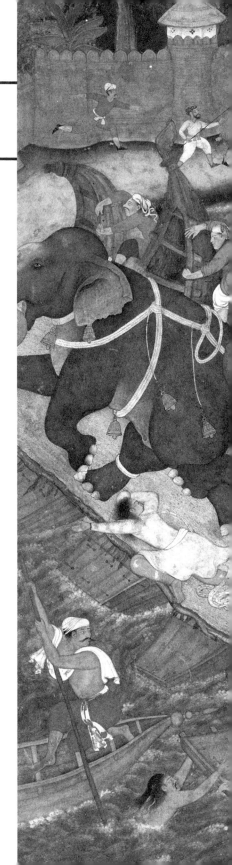

The first Muslim raids in the subcontinent were made by Arabs on the western coast and in Sind during the 7th and 8th centuries, and there had been Muslim trading communities in India at least since that time. The significant and permanent military movement of Muslims into northern India, however, dates from the late 12th century and was carried out by a Turkish dynasty that arose indirectly from the ruins of the 'Abbāsid caliphate. The road to conquest was prepared by Sultan Maḥmūd of Ghazna (now Ghaznī, Afg.), who conducted more than 20 raids into north India between 1001 and 1027 and established in the Punjab the easternmost province of his large but short-lived empire. Maḥmūd's raids, though militarily successful, primarily had as their object taking plunder rather than conquering territory.

THE DELHI SULTANATE

The decline of the Ghaznavids after 1100 was accentuated by the sack of Ghazna by the rival Shansabānīs of Ghūr in 1150–51. The Ghūrids, who inhabited the region between Ghazna and Herāt, rose rapidly in power during the last half of the 12th century, partly because of the changing balance of power that resulted from the westward movement of the non-Muslim Qara Khiṭāy (Karakitai) Turks into the area dominated by the Seljuq Turks, who had been the principal power in Iran and

The tomb of Ghiyāth al-Dīn, Delhi. Frederick M. Asher

parts of Afghanistan during the previous 50 years. The Seljuq defeat in 1141 led to a struggle for power among the Qara Khiṭāy, the Khwārezm-Shahs, and the Ghūrids for control of parts of Central Asia and Iran. By 1152 Ghazna had been captured again by the Ghūrid ruler, 'Alā' al-Dīn. After his death the Ghūrid territory was partitioned principally between his two nephews, Ghiyāth al-Dīn Muḥammad and Mu'izz al-Dīn Muḥammad ibn Sām, commonly called Muḥammad of Ghūr. Ghiyāth al-Dīn ruled over Ghūr from Fīrūz-Kūh and looked toward Khorāsān,

while Muḥammad of Ghūr was established in Ghazna and began to try his luck in India for expansion. The Ghūrid invasions of north India were thus extensions of a Central Asian struggle.

Almost all of north India was, however, already in contact with Ghūr through extensive trade, particularly in horses. The Ghūrids were well known as horse breeders. Ghūr also had a reputation for supplying Indian and Turkish slaves to the markets of Central Asia. Muslim merchants and saints had settled much beyond Sind and the Punjab in a number of towns in what are now Uttar Pradesh and Bihar. The Ghūrids also were familiar with the fabulous wealth of western and central India. They therefore followed a route into India through the Gumal Pass, with an eye set eventually on Gujarat. It was only after suffering a severe defeat at the hands of the Chalukya army of Gujarat that they turned to a more northerly route through the Khyber Pass.

THE TURKISH CONQUEST

By 1186 the Ghūrids had destroyed the remnants of Ghaznavid power in the northwest and were in a favourable military position to move against the northern Indian Rajput powers. The conquest of the Rajputs was not easy, however. The Cauhans (Cahamanasa) under Prithviraja defeated Muḥammad of Ghūr in 1191 at Taraori, northwest of Delhi, but his forces returned the following year to defeat and kill the Rajput king on the same battlefield. The victory opened the road to Delhi, which was conquered in 1193 but left in the hands of a tributary Hindu king. Muḥammad of Ghūr completed his conquests with the occupation of the military outposts of Hansi, Kuhram, Sursuti, and Sirhind and then returned to Ghazna with a large hoard of treasure, leaving his slave and lieutenant, Quṭb al-Dīn Aybak, in charge of consolidation and further expansion.

Quṭb al-Dīn displaced the Cauhan chief and made his headquarters at Delhi in 1193, when he began a campaign of expansion. By 1202 he was in control of Varanasi, Badaun, Kannauj, and Kalinjar.

In the meantime, an obscure adventurer, Ikhtiyār al-Dīn Muḥammad Bakhtiyār Khaljī of the Ghūrid army, conquered Nadia, the capital of the Sena kings of Bengal (1202). Within two years Bakhtiyār embarked on a campaign to conquer Tibet in order to plunder the treasure of its Buddhist monasteries, and in 1206 he attacked Kamarupa (Assam) to gain control of Bengal's traditional trade route leading to Southeast Asian gold and silver mines. The attempt, however, proved disastrous. Bakhtiyār managed to return to Bengal with a few hundred men, and there he died.

The availability of a large number of military adventurers from Central Asia who would follow commanders with reputations for success was one of the important elements in the rapid Ghūrid conquest of the major cities and forces of the north Indian plain. Other factors were important as well; better horses contributed to the success of mobile tactics, and the Ghūrids also made better use of metal for weapons, armour, and stirrups than did most of their adversaries. Perhaps most important was the tradition of centralized organization and planning, which was conducive to large-scale military campaigns and to the effective organization of postcampaign occupation forces. While the Rajputs probably saw the Ghūrids as an equal force competing for paramount power in north India, the Ghūrids had in mind the model of the successor states to the 'Abbāsid caliphate, the old Iranian Sāsānid empire, and particularly the vast centralized empire of Maḥmūd of Ghazna.

Soon, however, the Ghūrid possessions were insecure everywhere. In 1205 Sultan Muḥammad of Ghūr suffered a severe defeat at Andkhvoy (Andkhui) at the hands of the Khwārezm-Shah dynasty. News of the defeat precipitated a rebellion by some of the sultan's followers in the Punjab, and, although the rebellion was put down, Muḥammad of Ghūr was assassinated at Lahore in 1206. The Ghūrids at the time held the major towns of the Punjab, of Sind, and of much of the Gangetic Plain, but almost all the land outside the cities still was subject to some form of control by Hindu chiefs. Even in the Ganges–Yamuna Doab, the Gahadavalas held out against the Turks. Most significantly, the chiefs of Rajasthan had not been permanently subdued.

THE EARLY TURKISH SULTANS

When Quṭb al-Dīn Aybak assumed authority over the Ghūrid possessions in India, he moved from the neighbourhood of Delhi to Lahore. There he set up guard against another of Muḥammad of Ghūr's slaves, Tāj al-Dīn Yildiz of Ghazna, who also claimed his former master's Indian possessions. In 1208 Quṭb al-Dīn defeated his rival and captured Ghazna but soon was driven out again. He died in 1210 in a polo accident, having made no effort to extend his Indian conquests, but he had managed

to establish the foundation of an Indian Muslim state.

Quṭb al-Dīn was the first ruler in what has become known, perhaps unreasonably, as the Slave dynasty (only he actually attained a freed status after becoming ruler). Slavery was, however, an integral part of the political system. As practiced in eastern Muslim polities of this period, the institution of slavery provided a nucleus of well-trained and loyal military followers (the *mamlūks*) for important political figures; indeed, one of

Quṭb Mīnār (1199)—a minaret built for Quṭb al-Dīn Aybak—and the Alai Darwaza domed gateway (1311) at Quwat al-Islam Mosque complex, Delhi.
Frederick M. Asher

SLAVE DYNASTY

The Slave dynasty constituted a line of sultans at Delhi that lasted for nearly a century (1206–90). Their family name was Mui'zzī.

The dynasty was founded by Quṭb al-Dīn Aibak, a favourite slave of the Muslim general and later sultan Muḥammad of Ghūr. Quṭb al-Dīn had been among Muḥammad's most trusted Turkish officers and had overseen his master's Indian conquests. When Muḥammad was assassinated in 1206, Quṭb took power in Lahore. He managed to consolidate his position in a seesawing war with a rival Slave ruler, Tāj al-Dīn Yildiz, during which he captured and lost Ghazna. He was eventually confined to being a purely Indian sovereign. He died in 1210 as a result of a polo accident, and the crown shortly passed to Iltutmish, his son-in-law.

By the time of Iltutmish's accession, the family's holdings had been severely reduced. Iltutmish, the greatest of the Slave kings, defeated and put to death Yildiz (1216), restored the Bengal governor to obedience, and added considerable new territory to the empire, including the Lower Sindh.

After the death of Iltutmish, his able daughter Raziyya attempted to serve as sultan but was defeated by opposing Turkish Slave nobles. After 1246 the sultanate was controlled by Ghiyās al-Dīn Balban, who was to be sultan himself from 1266 to 1287. Under Balban the Delhi sultanate fought off several Mongol invasions. The Slave dynasty ended when Jalāl al-Dīn Fīrūz Khaljī staged a successful coup on June 13, 1290, and brought the Khaljīs to power.

the principal objects of this form of slavery was to train specialists in warfare and government, usually Turks, whose first loyalty would be to their masters. Slave status was honourable and was a principal avenue to wealth and high position for talented individuals whose origins were outside the ruling group. It has been observed that a slave was a better investment than a son, whose claim was not based upon proved efficiency. Yet, slaves with high qualifications could get out of control, and often slaves or former slaves controlled their masters as much as they were controlled by them. The beneficial results for the sultanate of this type of political interaction were that some men of talent had room to rise within the system and thus were less tempted to tear it down and that the responsibilities of government tended to rest in the hands of capable men, whether or not they were the actual rulers.

The sultans thus not only kept a close watch over the slave market but also commissioned slave merchants as state agents. Sultan Shams al-Dīn Iltutmish (reigned 1211–36), son-in-law and successor to Aybak, who was himself a *mamlūk*, sent a merchant to Samarkand, Bukhara, and Tirmiz to purchase young slaves on his behalf.

Consolidation of Turkish Rule

During his reign, Iltutmish was faced with three problems: defense of his western frontier, control over the Muslim nobles within India, and subjugation of the many Hindu chiefs who still exercised a large measure of independent rule. His relative success in all three areas gives him claim to the title of founder of the independent Delhi sultanate. His reign opened with a factional dispute in which he and his Delhi-based supporters defeated and killed the rival claimant to the throne, Quṭb al-Dīn's son, and put down a revolt by a portion of the Delhi guards. In the west Iltutmish was passive at first and even accepted investiture from his old rival, Yildiz, but, when Yildiz was driven from Ghazna into the Punjab by the Khwārezm-Shah 'Alā' al-Dīn Muḥammad in 1215, Iltutmish was able to defeat and capture him at Taraori. Iltutmish might have faced a threat himself from the Khwārezm-Shah had it not been for the latter's conflict with the Mongol armies of Genghis Khan. Again Iltutmish waited while refugees, including the heir to the Khwārezm-Shahī throne, poured into the Punjab and while Nāṣir al-Dīn Qabācha, another of Muḥammad of Ghūr's former slaves, maintained a perilous hold on Lahore and Multan. Iltutmish's political talents were pushed to the maximum as he tried desperately to avoid a direct confrontation with the armies of Genghis Khan. He refused aid to the Khwārezm-Shah heir against the Mongols and yet would not attempt to capture him. Fortunately, the Mongols were content to send raiding parties no further than the Salt Range (in the northern Punjab region), which Iltutmish wisely ignored, and eventually the Khwārezm-Shah prince fled from India after causing enormous destruction within Qabācha's domains. Thus, Iltutmish's cause was advanced, and in 1228 he was able to drive Qabācha from the Punjabi cities of Multan and Uch and, by establishing his frontier east of the Beas River, to avoid a direct confrontation with the Mongols. He was not able to gain effective control of the western Punjab, however, largely because the area was subject to raids by hill tribes.

In the east in 1225, Iltutmish launched a successful campaign against Ghiyāth al-Dīn 'Iwāz Khaljī, one of Bhaktiyār Khaljī's lieutenants, who had assumed sovereign authority in Lakhnauti (northern Bengal) and was encroaching on the province of Bihar. 'Iwāz Khaljī was defeated and slain in 1226, and in 1229 Iltutmish invaded Bengal and slew Balka, the last of the Khaljī chiefs to claim independent power. Iltutmish's campaigns in Rajasthan and central and western India were ultimately less successful, although he temporarily captured Ranthambhor (1226), Mandor (Mandawar; 1227), and Gwalior (1231) and plundered Bhilsa and Ujjain in Malwa (1234–35). His generals suffered defeats, however, at the hands of the Cauhans of Bundi, the Chalukyas of Gujarat, and the Chandelas (Candellas) of Narwar.

By 1236, the year Iltutmish died, the Delhi sultanate was established as clearly the largest and most powerful of a number of competing states in north India. Owing to Iltutmish's able leadership, Delhi was no longer subordinate to Ghazna, nor was it to remain simply a frontier outpost; it was to become, rather, a proud centre of Muslim power and culture in India. Iltutmish made clear, however, to what extent Islam and Islamic law (Sharī'ah) could determine the contour of politics and culture in the overwhelmingly non-Muslim Indian environment. Early in his reign, a party of theologians approached him with the plea that the infidel Hindus be forced, in accordance with Islamic law, to accept Islam or face death. On behalf of the sultan, his *wazīr* (vizier) told the divines that this was impractical, since the Muslims were as few as grains of salt in a dish of food. Despite the Islamic proscription against women rulers, Iltutmish nominated his daughter Raziyyah (Raziyyat al-Dīn) to be his successor. By refusing shelter to the Muslim Jalāl al-Dīn Mingburnu (the last Khwārezm-Shah) against the pagan Genghis Khan, he politely asserted that the Turkish power in Delhi, even though a sequel to a Central Asian social and political struggle, was no longer to involve itself in the power politics of countries of the Islamic East. Iltutmish legitimated his ambition by obtaining a letter of investiture from the 'Abbāsid caliph in Baghdad, whose name appeared in Hindi on the bullion currency so that the people on the streets might perceive the nature of the new regime.

Iltutmish seems to have enjoyed support among his nobles and advisers for his assertion that the legal structure of the state in India should not be based strictly on Islamic law. Gradually, a judicious balance between the dictates of Sharī'ah and the needs of the time emerged as a distinctive feature of the Turkish rule. The Muslim constituency, however, could not adjust to the idea of being ruled by a woman, and Raziyyah (reigned 1236–40) fairly quickly succumbed to powerful nobles (the Shamsī), who once had been Iltutmish's slaves.

Still, the new state had enough internal momentum to survive severe factional disputes during the 10 years following Iltutmish's death, when four of Iltutmish's children or grandchildren were in turn raised to the throne and deposed. This momentum was maintained largely through the efforts of Iltutmish's personal slaves, who came to be known as the Forty (Chihilgān), a political faction whose membership was characterized by talent and by loyalty to the family of Iltutmish.

The political situation had changed by 1246, when Ghiyāth al-Dīn Balban, a junior member of the Forty, had gained enough power to attain a controlling position within the administration of the newest sultan, Nāṣir al-Dīn Maḥmūd (reigned 1246–66). Balban, acting first as *nā'ib* ("deputy") to the sultan and later as sultan (reigned 1266–87), was the most important political figure of his time. The period was characterized by almost continuous struggles to maintain Delhi's position against the revived power of the Hindu chiefs (principally Rajputs) and by vigilance against the strife-ridden but still dangerous Mongols in the west. Even in the central regions of the state, sultanate rule was sometimes challenged by discontented Muslim nobles.

During the first 10 years of Nāṣir al-Dīn Maḥmūd's reign, Balban's campaigns against the Hindu chiefs were only partially successful. By 1266, when he assumed the sultanate, his military strategy was to work outward from the capital. First, he cleared the forests of Mewatis (Mina); then he restored order in the Doab and at Oudh (present-day Ayodhya) and suppressed a revolt in the region of the cities of Badaun and Amroha with particular viciousness. Having established the security of his home territory, Balban then chose to consolidate his rule over the provincial governors rather than to embark upon expeditions against Hindu territories. Thus, he reacted vigorously and effectively against an attempt to establish an independent state in Bengal in the 1280s.

Balban sought to raise the prestige of the institution of the sultanate through the use of ceremony, the strict administration of justice, and the formulation of a despotic view of the relationship between ruler and subject. Probably the most significant aspect of his reign was this elevation of the position of the sultan, which made possible the reorganization and strengthening of the army and the imposition of a tighter administrative apparatus. Iltutmish had enforced the centre's control over the nobles in the districts (iqṭā's and wilāyahs) by subjecting them to periodic transfers. Balban's government began to investigate what was actually collected and spent within the iqṭā'. He appointed a new category of officials, the khwājas, to estimate both the income of the iqṭā' holders and the expenses they incurred in maintaining their troops. Any surplus (fawāḍil) was to be remitted to the sultan's treasury. Balban's policy of consolidation, the success of which owed much to the death or incapacity of most of the Forty and to the lack of rival claimants to the throne, strengthened sultanate rule so that his successors could undertake a number of successful expansionist campaigns after 1290.

THE KHALJĪS

Balban's immediate successors, however, were unable to manage either the administration or the factional conflicts between the old Turkish nobility and the new forces, led by the Khaljīs; after a struggle between the two factions, Jalāl al-Dīn Fīrūz Khaljī assumed the sultanate in 1290. During his short reign (1290–96), Jalāl al-Dīn suppressed a revolt by some of Balban's officers, led an unsuccessful expedition against Ranthambhor, and defeated a substantial Mongol force on the banks of the Sind River in central India. In 1296 he was assassinated by his ambitious nephew and successor, 'Alā' al-Dīn Khaljī (reigned 1296–1316).

The Khaljī dynasty was not recognized by the older nobility as coming from pure Turkish stock (although they were Turks), and their rise to power was aided by impatient outsiders, some of them Indian-born Muslims, who might expect to enhance their positions if the hold of the followers of Balban and the Forty were broken. To some extent then, the Khaljī usurpation was a move toward the recognition of a shifting balance of power, attributable both to the developments outside the territory of the Delhi sultanate, in Central Asia and Iran, and to the changes that followed the establishment of Turkish rule in northern India.

In large measure, the dislocation in the regions beyond the northwest assured the establishment of an independent Delhi sultanate and its subsequent consolidation. The eastern steppe tribes' movements to the west not only ended the threat to Delhi from the rival Turks in Ghazna and Ghūr but also forced a number of the Central Asian Muslims to migrate to northern India, a land that came to be known as Hindustan. Almost all the high nobles, including the famous Forty in the 13th century, were of Central Asian origin; many of them were slaves purchased from the Central Asian bazaars. The same phenomenon also led to the destabilization of the core of the Turkish *mamlūks*. With the Mongol plunder of Central Asia and eastern Iran, many more members of the political and religious elite of these regions were thrown into north India, where they were admitted into various levels of the military and administrative cadre by the early Delhi sultans.

CENTRALIZATION AND EXPANSION

During the reign of 'Alā' al-Dīn Khaljī, the sultanate briefly assumed the status of an empire. In order to achieve his goals of centralization and expansion, 'Alā' al-Dīn needed money, a loyal and reasonably subservient nobility, and an efficient army under his personal control. He had earlier, in 1292, partly solved the problem of money when he conducted a lucrative raid into Bhilsa in central India. Using that success to build his position and a fresh army, he led a brilliant and unauthorized raid on the fabulously wealthy Devagiri (present-day Daulatabad), the capital of the Yadavas, in the Deccan early in 1296. The wealth of Devagiri not only financed his usurpation but provided a good foundation for his state-building plans. 'Alā' al-Dīn already had the support of many of the disaffected Turkish nobles, and now he was able to purchase the support of more with both money and promotion.

TAXATION AND DISTRIBUTION OF REVENUE RESOURCES

Centralization and heavy agrarian taxation were the principal features of 'Alā' al-Dīn's rule. The sultan and his nobles depended in the 13th century largely on tribute extorted from the subjugated local potentates and on plunder from the unpacified areas. The sultanate thus had no stable economic base; the nobles were often in debt for large sums of money to the moneylenders of Delhi. 'Ala' al-Dīn Khaljī altered the situation radically, implementing the principles of the *iqtā'* (revenue district) and the *kharāj* (land tax) in their classic sense. The *iqtā'*, formerly loosely used to mean a transferable revenue assignment to a noble, now combined the two functions of collection and distribution of the sultan's claim to the bulk of the surplus agrarian product in the form of *kharāj*.

'Ala' al-Dīn imposed a land tax set at half the produce (in weight or value) on each individual peasant's holding, regardless of size. It was to be supplemented by a house and cattle tax. The revenue resources so created, divided into iqtā's, or different territorial units, were distributed among the nobles. But the nobles had no absolute control of their iqtā's. They had to submit accounts of their income and expenditure and send the balances to the sultan's treasury. The sultan had prepared an estimate of the produce of each locality by measuring the land. A set of officers in each iqtā', separate from the assignee, ensured the sultan's control over it. The khālisah, the territory whose revenues accrued directly to the sultan's own treasury, was expanded significantly, enabling the sultan to pay a much larger number of his soldiers and cavalry troops in cash. Through these measures the sultan struck hard at all the others—his officials and the local rural potentates—who shared economic and political power with him.

The magnitude and mechanism of agrarian taxation enabled the sultan to achieve two important objectives: (1) to ensure supplies at low prices to grain carriers and (2) to fill the state granaries with a buffer stock, which, linked with his famous price regulations, came as a solution to the critical financial problem of maintaining a large standing army. Following their occupation of Afghanistan, the Chagatai Mongols began to penetrate well beyond the Punjab, necessitating a comprehensive defense program for the sultanate, including the capital, Delhi, which underwent a two-month siege in 1303. Besides fortifying the capital and supplying the frontier towns and forts with able commanders, marshaling a large army was the task of the hour. Further, the vast expenditure was to be financed by means of the existing resources of the state. 'Ala' al-Dīn planned to compensate for the low cash payments to his soldiers by a policy of market control. The policy enhanced the purchasing power of the soldiers and enabled them to live in tolerable comfort.

EXPANSION AND CONQUESTS

The result of 'Ala' al-Dīn's reforms and his energetic rule was that the sultanate expanded rapidly and was subject to a more unified and efficient direction than during any other period. 'Ala' al-Dīn began his expansionist activities with the subjugation of Gujarat in 1299. Next he moved against Rajasthan and then captured Ranthambhor (1301), Chitor (1303), and Mandu (1305), later adding Siwan (1308) and Jalor (1312). The campaigns in Rajasthan opened the road for further raids into south India.

These raids were intended to result not in occupation of the land but rather in the formal recognition by Hindu kings of 'Alā' al-Dīn's supremacy and in the collection of huge amounts of tribute and booty, which were used to finance his centralizing activities in the north. 'Alā' al-Dīn's lieutenant Malik Kāfūr again subdued the Yadava kingdom of Devagiri in 1307 and two years later added the Kakatiya kingdom of Telingana. In 1310–11 Malik Kāfūr plundered the Pandya kingdom in the far south, and in 1313 Devagiri was again defeated and finally annexed to the sultanate.

'Alā' al-Dīn also managed to fend off a series of Mongol attacks—at least five during the decade 1297–1306. After 1306 the invasions subsided, probably as much because of an intensification of internal Mongal rivalries as of the lack of their success in India.

Ambition, a talent for ruling, and the gold of southern India carried 'Alā' al-Dīn a long way, but it is also significant that he was one of the first rulers to deliberately expand political participation within the sultanate government. Not only did he partly open the gates to power for the non-Turkish Muslim nobility—some of whom were even converted Hindus—but he also at least made gestures toward the inclusion of Hindus within the political world he viewed as legitimate. Both 'Alā' al-Dīn and his son married into the families of important Hindu rulers, and several such rulers were received at court and treated with respect.

THE URBAN ECONOMY

The expansion and centralization of the Khaljī sultanate paralleled economic and technological developments of the late 13th and early 14th centuries. Delhi in the 13th century became one of the largest cities in the whole of the Islamic world, and Multan, Lahore, Anhilwara, Kar, Cambay (Khambhat), and Lakhnauti emerged as major urban centres. The repeated Mongol invasions certainly affected the fortunes of some northwestern cities, but on the whole the period was marked by a flourishing urban economy and corresponding expansion in craft production and commerce. Advancements in the textile industry included the introduction of the wooden cotton gin and the spinning wheel and, reportedly, of the treadle loom and sericulture (the raising of silkworms). In construction technology, cementing lime and vaulted roofing radically changed the face of the city. The production of paper gave rise to increased record keeping in government offices and to widespread use of bills of exchange (*hundis*).

An expanding trade in textiles and horses provided constant nourishment to the economies of these towns. Bengal and Gujarat were the production centres for both coarse cloths and fine fabrics. Since cavalry came to be the mainstay of the political and military system of the Delhi sultans, horses were imported in large numbers beginning in the early years of the 13th century. Earlier in the 12th century the Hindu kings also kept large standing armies that included cavalry. The Turks, however, had far superior horsemen. Iron stirrups and heavy armour, for both horses and horsemen, came into common use during the period, with significant impact on warfare and military organization. The Battles of Taraori, between Prithviraja III Cauhan and Muḥammad of Ghūr, were mainly engagements of cavalrymen armed with bows and spears; superior Ghūrid tactics were decisive.

The Multanis and Khorāsānīs, in the main, controlled the long-distance overland trade. Trade between the coastal ports and northern India was in the hands of Marwaris and Gujaratis, many of whom were Jains. A measure of commercial expansion was the emergence and increasing role of the dallals, or brokers, who acted as middlemen in transactions for which expert knowledge was required, such as the sale of horses, slaves, and cattle. 'Alā' al-Dīn Khaljī extended a large loan to the Multanis for bringing goods from afar into Delhi. By the mid-13th century a stable equation between gold and silver was attained, resulting in a coinage impressive in both quality and volume. Northern Indian merchants now benefited from the unification of the Central Asian steppes, which from 1250 until about 1350 (following an initially quite destructive Mongol impact) opened up a new and secure trade route from India to China and the Black Sea. Further, there arose a chain of sea emporia all along the Indian Ocean coast. It was, however, plunder and tribute from Gujarat, the Deccan, eastern and central India, and Rajasthan—combined with regular taxation in the Indo-Gangetic Plain—that sustained the economy and the centralizing regime of Delhi.

THE TUGHLUQS

Within five years of 'Alā' al-Dīn's death (1316), the Khaljīs lost their power. The succession dispute resulted in the murder of Malik Kāfūr by the palace guards and in the blinding of 'Alā' al-Dīn's six-year-old son by Quṭb al-Dīn Mubārak Shah, the sultan's third son, who assumed the sultanate (reigned 1316–20). Quṭb al-Dīn suppressed revolts in Gujarat and Devagiri and conducted another raid on Telingana. He was murdered by his favourite general, a Hindu convert named Khusraw Khan, who had built substantial support among a group of Hindus outside the traditional nobility. Opposition to Khusraw's rule arose immediately, led by Ghāzī Malik, the warden of the western marches at Deopalpur, and Khusraw was defeated and slain after four months.

Ghāzī Malik, who ascended the throne as Ghiyāth al-Dīn Tughluq (reigned 1320–25), had distinguished himself prior to his accession by his successful defense of the frontier against the Mongols. His reign was brief but eventful. He captured Telingana, conducted raids in Jajnagar, and reconquered Bengal, which had been independent under Muslim kings since the death of Balban. While returning from the Bengal campaign, the sultan was killed when a wooden shelter collapsed on him at Afghanpur, near Delhi. Although some historians have argued that Muḥammad ibn Tughluq plotted his father's death, the case never has been proved.

The reign (1325–51) of Muḥammad ibn Tughluq marked both the high point of the sultanate and the beginning of its decline. The period from 1296 to 1335 can be seen as one of nearly continuous centralization and expansion. There were few places in the subcontinent where the sultan's authority could be seriously challenged. Muḥammad ibn Tughluq, however, was unable to maintain the momentum of consolidation. By 1351 southern India had been lost and much of the north was in rebellion.

Reversal and Rebellion

Muḥammad ibn Tughluq faced serious problems resulting from expansion into southern India. Eschewing the Khaljī policy of maintaining Hindu tributary states in the south, Muḥammad ibn Tughluq, while still a prince, had begun to bring southern Hindu powers under the direct control of the sultanate, a policy he continued as sultan. Direct Muslim rule in the south, however, did not necessarily signify control from Delhi. In an effort both to settle other Muslim nobles in the south and to maintain his control over them, the sultan made Daulatabad (Devagiri) his second capital in 1327.

Muḥammad ibn Tughluq moved to Daulatabad to ensure an effective control over the wealthy and fertile Deccan and Gujarat and possibly also to gain access to the western and southern ports. Gujarat, the Coromandel Coast, and Bengal were the core areas of India's overseas trade. Huge supplies of textiles and other goods, including glass and metal objects manufactured in these regions, were exported to the Middle East, Africa, and East and Southeast Asia in exchange for horses, precious metals, extracted goods, and raw materials. Muḥammad ibn Tughluq also planned to face the Mongols by positioning and equipping himself at a safe distance from the northwest.

However, no sooner was the sultan established at Daulatabad than trouble broke out in the north, on the western border, and in Bengal. Muḥammad ibn Tughluq had to move back to Delhi to crush the rebellions by his nobles. He also was less successful against an invasion by the Mongols, who had come almost to the gates of Delhi. On the other hand, by 1335 the Muslim governor of Ma'bar, the southernmost province of the sultanate, declared his independence and founded the sultanate of Madura while Muḥammad ibn Tughluq was busy quelling a rebellion in Lahore. Soon rebellions by Hindu chiefs had resulted in the formation of several new states, the most important of which was Vijayanagar. During the next few years, while the sultan shuttled to and fro in an attempt to put down rebellions in practically every province, he lost control of the rest of his south Indian possessions after successful rebellions in Gulbarga (1339), Warangal (1345–46), and Daulatabad, which led to the founding of the Bahmani sultanate (1347). Muḥammad ibn Tughluq spent the last five years of his life trying to suppress yet another rebellion in Gujarat and thus could not make an attempt to regain Daulatabad.

Muḥammad ibn Tughluq's successor, his cousin Fīrūz Shah (reigned 1351–88), campaigned in Bengal (1353–54 and 1359), Orissa (1360), Nagarkot (1361), Sind (1362 and 1366–67), Etawah (1377), and Katehr (1380). Fīrūz was unable to recover Bengal for the sultanate, and Sind was no more than a tribute-paying vassal during his reign. Fīrūz also showed no interest in reconquering the southern provinces. He refused to accept an invitation (c. 1365) from a Bahmani prince to intervene in the politics of the Deccan.

Fīrūz has been noted in particular for his conciliatory attitude toward the two main influential Muslim groups of the period—the religious leaders and the nobility. While 'Alā' al-Dīn Khaljī had kept religion and religious leaders apart from his political plans and Muḥammad ibn Tughluq had incurred the enmity of at least some Sufis because of his refusal to give them what they regarded as proper support, Fīrūz rewarded Sufis and other religious leaders generously and listened to their counsel. He also created charities to aid poor Muslims, built colleges and mosques, and abolished taxes not recognized by Muslim law.

Balban, 'Alā' al-Dīn, and Muḥammad ibn Tughluq all had made attempts to check the power of the nobility and the religious leaders; the latter two also had realized the necessity of allowing a certain amount of mobility both into and within the army and civil administration for groups that had come to represent significant and articulated interests. Such a policy also enhanced the power of the sultans over all the nobility, because it removed old nobles and provided grateful new ones. Judging by the revolts during his reign, however, Muḥammad ibn Tughluq's policy toward his nobility was too autocratic to succeed. Fīrūz adopted policies that gave his nobles much more autonomy. The result was that the sultan lost both an important means of leverage and a means of adjusting to new political circumstances. Fīrūz also made little or no attempt to pay officers in cash (rather than in assignments of land revenue), granted hereditary appointments, and extended the system of revenue farming. All these measures, which reversed policies adopted by one or more of the strong rulers of the previous several decades, tended to decrease Fīrūz's control over his nobility and over the revenue system.

SOCIETY AND THE STATE UNDER THE TUGHLUQS

The Tughluq rule roughly coincided with an important and interesting development in the Hindu countryside, which, to a degree, was a reaction to 'Alā' al-Dīn Khaljī's harsh measures. If, on the one hand, his new policy of taxation cut into the power of the erstwhile ruling chiefs who had escaped regular payment by offering tribute only under military pressure, it meant, on the other hand, a heavy loss of revenue for the small landlords and village headmen. The latter were also often subjected to severe corporal torture. The power of the Delhi regime, however, suffered an obvious setback after that. The former rural elite began to reappear, consolidated into the great Rajput caste spread over much of northern India. Incorporating such groups as the Cauhans and the Gahadawalas as subcastes and clans, the Rajputs claimed power and perquisites, at least at the local level. The first appearance of the generic term *zamindar*, which denoted first superior rights over land and its produce and later came to represent the local power-mongers themselves, dates to this period. The new caste cohesion also created a sense of unity between the village elite and the peasantry, which in turn added to their strength; at certain levels, the two classes became virtually undifferentiated.

The Tughluqs thus had to handle the rural classes with care and diplomatic skill. Ghiyāth al-Dīn Tughluq modified 'Alā' al-Dīn Khaljī's system by exempting the village headmen from paying taxes on their cultivation and cattle, but he confirmed the Khaljī sultan's injunctions that the headmen were not to levy anything in addition to the existing land tax on the peasantry. As Muḥammad ibn Tughluq adopted a stern policy, he provoked rebellion by the rural chiefs and the peasants, but,

interestingly, he was also the first Indian ruler in recorded history to advance loans (*taccavi*) to the villagers for rehabilitation following a disastrous famine. He also proposed a grand scheme for improving cropping patterns and extending cultivation. Fīrūz Tughluq created the biggest network of canals known in premodern India, wrote off the loans granted earlier to the peasants by Muḥammad ibn Tughluq, and, more significantly, enforced a policy of fixed tax, as opposed to the former proportional one, thus guaranteeing in normal times a larger share of surplus to the intermediaries.

The desire of the Tughluq sultans for warmer relations with society as a whole was further illustrated by a generally appreciative approach to local social and religious practices. A few Hindus and Jains had held state positions under the Khaljīs; under the Tughluqs the non-Muslim Indians rose to high and extremely responsible offices, including the governorships of provinces. Muḥammad ibn Tughluq was the first Muslim ruler to make planned efforts to induct Hindus into administration. He also conducted several discourses with Indian scholars and saints. Fīrūz showed keen interest in Indian culture, commissioning Persian translations (Persian being the court language) of some important Sanskrit texts and placing an Ashokan pillar in a prominent position on the roof of his palace.

While all these developments indicated the sultans' broadly tolerant and catholic policies, they demonstrated at the same time the strength of the locality. What was then emerging was a kind of tacit sharing of power between the local Hindu magnates and the essentially town-based Muslim aristocracy as a crucial source of political stability. Significantly, by the time of the Tughluqs, a theory of Islamic power, different from the universal Islamic theory of state, had also begun to emerge. The Turkish state was, in a formal sense, Islamic. The sultans could not allow open violation of Sharī'ah. They appointed Muslim divines ('ulamā') to profitable offices and granted revenue-free lands to many of them. But the policy of the state was based increasingly upon the opinion of the sultans and their advisers and not on any religious texts as interpreted by the 'ulamā'. In view of practical needs and worldly considerations (jahāndārī), the sultans supplemented Sharī'ah by framing their own state laws (thawābit). These regulations in cases of conflict overrode the universal Muslim law.

Accommodation and tolerance afforded a most secure course in such a situation; however, the threat from the locality, as well as from the Muslim nobles in control of the provinces, sometimes compelled the sultans to assert their Islamic connections rather forcefully. By doing so, the sultans also intended to strike a balance between the demands of orthodoxy and the needs of the state. Ghiyth al-Dīn Tughluq's success against Khusraw Khan was presented as the regeneration of Islam in India. Muḥammad ibn Tughluq had removed the name of the

'Abbāsid caliph from his coins, but, when he faced rebellion from every side, he searched for a caliph who could give him some moral authority to deal at least with his refractory Muslim officers. Fīrūz inherited a more difficult situation. Like his predecessor, he obtained a letter of investiture from the caliph. Further, he took several measures to align the state with Sunnite orthodoxy. In addition to giving important concessions to the 'ulamā', he banned unorthodox practices, persecuted heretical sects, and refused to exempt the Brahmans from the payment of jizyah, or poll tax on non-Muslims, on the ground that this was not provided for in the Sharī'ah. Muḥammad ibn Tughluq's largesse toward the Muslim foreigners was legendary. Fīrūz generously funded pious works within his territory and in other parts of the Islamic world.

The Tughluqs did not fare well in the face of an imminent crisis of the central treasury. With the loss of Bengal and the southern provinces, Delhi was disconnected from the important supply lines of its gold and silver. This in turn affected its capacity to import horses and soldiers. Cavalry, the backbone of the sultanate army, was thus severely crippled. Good warhorses were extremely expensive; in the mid-14th century an ordinary Central Asian steed cost 100 silver tangas, an exceptional one 500 silver tangas, while a fine Arabian or Persian racehorse cost as much as 1,000 to 4,000 silver tangas. The sultans' liberal support of the various holy centres and eminent individuals of the Islamic East also contributed to the shortage of precious metals. In response, Muḥammad ibn Tughluq attempted to reduce the weight of his coins and experimented with token money. His proposed expeditions to Khorāsān and the Himalayas were possibly aimed at locating new sources of horses and precious metals. Fīrūz Tughluq addressed the crisis by withdrawing the practice of cash payment to the soldiers and by building an army from among the huge corps of slaves (*mamlūks*) plundered from throughout the sultanate. The slaves were, however, no match for the mounted archers from the countries northwest of the subcontinent.

Thus, Fīrūz's weak policy toward his nobility, his light hand on the reins of administration, the resultant inefficiency and corruption among his ranks, and, indeed, his predecessor Muḥammad ibn Tughluq's failure could be explained only in part in terms of these leaders' personal proclivities. Both were overwhelmed by social and economic circumstances.

DECLINE OF THE SULTANATE

By 1388, when Fīrūz Tughluq died, the decline of the sultanate was imminent; subsequent succession disputes and palace intrigues only accelerated its pace. The sons and grandsons of Fīrūz, supported by various groups of nobles, began a struggle for the throne that rapidly diminished the authority of Delhi and provided opportunities for Muslim nobles and Hindu chiefs to enhance their autonomy. By 1390 the governor of

Gujarat had declared his independence, and between 1391 and 1394 the important Rajput chiefs of Etawah rebelled and were defeated four times. By 1394 there were two sultans, both residing in or near Delhi. The result was bitter civil war for three years; meanwhile, the disastrous invasion of Timur (the Tamerlane of Western literature) drew nearer.

Timur invaded India in 1398, when he was in possession of a vast empire in the Middle East and Central Asia, and dealt the final blow to the effective power and prestige of the Delhi sultanate. In a well-executed campaign of four months—during which many of the disunited Muslim and Hindu forces of northern India either were bypassed or submitted peacefully while Rajputs and Muslims fighting together were slaughtered at Bhatnagar—Timur reached Delhi and, in mid-December, defeated the army of Sultan Maḥmūd Tughluq and sacked the city. It is said that Timur ordered the execution of at least 50,000 captives before the battle for Delhi and that the sack of the city was so devastating that practically everything of value was removed—including those inhabitants who were not killed.

Timur's invasion further drained the wealth of the Delhi sultanate. Billon tanga then replaced the relatively pure silver coins as the standard currency of trade in almost the entire northern part of India. Bengal, which imported silver from Myanmar (Burma) and China, was, however, an obvious exception. The silver and gold coins struck in the period of the last Tughluqs and their successors in

Delhi in the 15th and early 16th centuries were mainly commemorative issues.

THE POST-DELHI SULTANATE PERIOD

During the 15th and early 16th centuries, no paramount power enjoyed effective control over most of north India and Bengal. Delhi became merely one of the regional principalities of north India, competing with the emerging Rajput and Muslim states.

THE RISE OF REGIONAL STATES

Gujarat, Malwa, and Jaunpur soon became powerful independent states; old and new Rajput states rapidly emerged; and Lahore, Dipalpur, Multan, and parts of Sind were held by Khizr Khan Sayyid for Timur (and later for himself). Khizr Khan also took over Delhi and a small area surrounding it after the last of the Tughluqs died in 1413, and he founded the dynasty known as the Sayyid. The Sayyids ruled the territory of Delhi until 1451, trying to obtain tribute and recognition of suzerainty from the nearby Rajput rulers and fighting almost continuously against neighbouring states to preserve their kingdom intact. The last Sayyid ruler, 'Alā' al-Dīn 'Ālam Shah (reigned 1445–51), peacefully surrendered Delhi to his nominal vassal, the Afghan Bahlūl Lodī (reigned 1451–89), and retired to the Badaun district, which he retained until his death in 1478. Before he moved to Delhi, Bahlūl Lodī had already carved

out a kingdom in the Punjab that was larger than that of the Sayyid sultans.

Meanwhile, the neighbouring kingdom of Jaunpur developed into a power equal to Delhi during the reign (1402–40) of Ibrāhīm Sharqī. Ibrāhīm's successor, Maḥmūd, conducted expansionist campaigns against Bengal and Orissa and, in 1452, initiated a conflict with the Lodī sultans of Delhi that lasted at least until the defeat and partial annexation of Jaunpur by Bahlūl Lodī in 1479.

The lack of unified rule has led some historians to describe the period as one of political anarchy and confusion, in which the inhabitants suffered because there was no strong guiding hand. Such a conclusion is far from certain, however, even for the central areas of the Gangetic Plain, where many battles were fought. In areas where effective regional rule was either restored or developed—as in Rajasthan, Orissa, Bengal, Gujarat, Malwa, Jaunpur, and various smaller states in the north, as well as in the large and small states of the Deccan—the quality of life may well have been comparable or superior to that of earlier centuries for cultivators, townspeople, landholders, and nobles. Although contemporary sources are scarce, the information available does not indicate a significant decline in total cultivation or trade (despite some alteration of trade routes). To the contrary, Gujarat and Bengal, in addition to their fertile tracts and rich handicrafts, carried on a brisk overseas trade. The Gujarati traders had a big role in the trade of the Middle East and Africa; Chittagong in Bengal was a flourishing port for trade with China and for the reexport of Chinese goods to other parts of the world.

STRUGGLE FOR SUPREMACY IN NORTHERN INDIA

These regional states had enough vigour and strength to balance and check the growth of each other's power. With the Lodī conquest of Jaunpur, however, Delhi appeared to reestablish its hegemony over northern India. Bahlūl (reigned 1451–89) and his two successors, Sikandar (reigned 1489–1517) and Ibrāhīm (reigned 1517–26), continued intermittently to expand their control over the surrounding territory. Bahlūl pacified the Ganges–Yamuna Doab and subdued Etawah, Chandwar, and Rewari. Sikandar completed the pacification of Jaunpur (1493), campaigned into Bihar, and founded the city of Agra in 1504 as a base from which to launch his attempt to control Malwa and Rajasthan.

By the time of Sikandar's death, the Afghans could claim a somewhat uneven control over the Punjab and most of the Gangetic Plain down to Bihar. Still, the question of Lodī hegemony in north India was far from settled. Rana Sanga of Mewar did not simply check the Lodī encroachments into central India but also repulsed a Lodī attempt to invade Mewar and threatened to move toward Bayana and Agra. Eastern Malwa, including Chanderi (at that time in possession of a Rajput leader, Medini Rai), passed under his overlordship. Rana Sanga defeated the Khalji sultan of Malwa and

took him prisoner in Chitor. The rana was thus emerging as another formidable Rajput contender for supremacy in north India. Meanwhile, Bābur, a descendant of Timur, was knocking at the gates of India.

Ibrāhīm Lodī was more autocratic than his predecessor, and he was ultimately less able to control his skittish nobility, which had swelled significantly following the immigration into India of a considerable number of Afghans. They tended to see the Lodī sultans as merely first among equals. Ibrāhīm soon faced an Afghan rebellion in the east under the leadership of his brother Jalāl Khan, and, while Ibrāhīm put down this and other Afghan revolts in the region, the groundwork for the final disaster was laid in the west. Dawlat Khan Lodī, governor of the Punjab, and 'Ālam Khan Lodī, Ibrāhīm's uncle, appealed to Bābur, the Mughal ruler of Kābul, to aid them in their attempt to overthrow the sultan. The adventurous Bābur was at that time probably thinking only of annexing the Punjab, but, as his previous history had demonstrated, he was quick to take advantage of political opportunities. In 1524 he led an expedition to Lahore and defeated Ibrāhīm's army. Bābur then passed over his Afghan allies and appointed his own officials in the Punjab. After his allies had indignantly left him, he went on to defeat and kill Ibrāhīm at the first of three important battles at Panipat, near Delhi, in 1526. The Afghan sultanate underwent a short revival under the Sūrs in 1540–55, only to be replaced by the Mughals again under Humāyūn and then Akbar the Great.

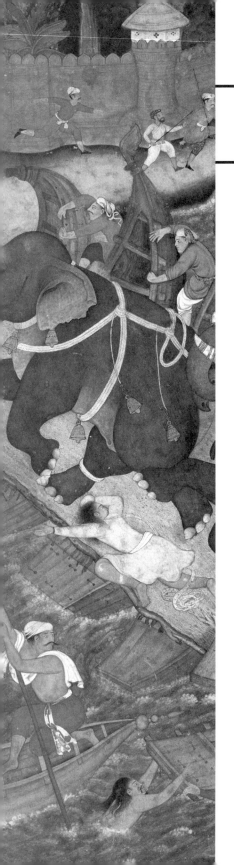

CHAPTER 5

Southern India in the Early Muslim Period

Sultanate rule in most of southern India existed for only a few years and was firmly established only in the northern Deccan, with Daulatabad as its centre. The forced withdrawal of the sultanate forces from the Deccan between 1330 and 1347 was partly the result of resistance offered by Hindu chiefs and some Muslim nobles. Members of those two groups established several rebel principalities and the two strongest states of the south—the Muslim-ruled Bahmani kingdom and the Hindu-ruled Vijayanagar empire.

THE MUSLIM STATES OF SOUTHERN INDIA, C. 1350–1680

Ma'bar, the first among the rebel states to emerge in south India, was founded at Madurai by the erstwhile Tughluq general Jalāl al-Dīn Aḥsan Shah in 1335. Lasting only 43 years, with seven rulers in quick succession, Ma'bar covered the mainly Tamil region between Nellore and Quilon and contributed to the commercial importance of south India by encouraging Muslim traders from the Middle East and even attempting to sponsor an expedition to the Maldives. The Ma'bar wars with the Hoysala dynasty of Karnataka took place in the lower Kaveri region and were fought for control over a series of fortified trading stations between the coast and the interior. The Vijayanagar invasion under Prince

Kumara Kampana dealt a severe blow to Ma'bar's commercial importance in 1347; Vijayanagar completed the conquest in 1377–78 under Harihara II.

THE BAHMANI SULTANATE

A revolt by a group of Muslim nobles against Muḥammad ibn Tughluq that began in Daulatabad in 1345 culminated in the foundation of the Bahmani sultanate by Ḥasan Gaṅgū, who ascended the throne of Daulatabad as 'Alā' al-Dīn

Tomb of 'Alā' al-Dīn Bahmani, Bidar, Karnataka, India. Frederick M. Asher

Bahman Shah in 1347 and soon moved his capital to the more centrally located Gulbarga on the Deccan plateau. Much of the political and military history of the Bahmani sultanate can be described as a generally effective attempt to gain control of the Deccan and a less successful effort to expand outward from it. The initial period of consolidation was followed by a much longer period of intermittent warfare against Malwa and Gujarat in the north, Orissa and the Reddi kingdoms of Andhra in the east, and Vijayanagar in the south.

The rise of Bahmani, Vijayanagar, and other subregional kingdoms signified a new trend in the political and military history of southern India, with the emergence of fortified warrior strongholds under Muslim and Hindu chiefs and of advanced military technology, including artillery and heavy cavalry. Control over such strongholds was thus essential to Bahmani's military supremacy.

BAHMANI CONSOLIDATION OF THE DECCAN

Bahman Shah spent most of his reign consolidating a kingdom in the Deccan and strengthening his hold over those Muslim nobles who chose to remain there rather than to join Muḥammad ibn Tughluq in northern India. He adopted the four territorial divisions (ṭarafs) established by Muḥammad ibn Tughluq for his own administration and established departments and appointed functionaries similar to those of the Delhi

Jāmiʿ Masjid ("Congregational Mosque"), Gulbarga Fort, Karnataka, India. Photographer: John Henry Rice; Courtesy: Encyclopædia Britannica, Inc.

sultanate. Working outward from his capital, he was able to establish his authority over the western half of the Deccan plateau and to impose an annual tribute upon the Hindu state of Warangal, which had also emerged from the breakup of the Deccan portion of the Tughluq empire. Often, however, the tribute was not paid, and a number of wars were fought over the question of whether the Bahmanis could maintain a superior position in relation to their eastern neighbours, including also the Reddi kingdoms of Rajahmundry and Kondavidu, in the following years.

Muḥammad Shah I (reigned 1358–75), son and successor of Bahman Shah, began the struggle with Vijayanagar that was to outlast the Bahmani sultanate and continue, as a many-sided conflict, into the 17th century. There were at least 10 wars during the period 1350–1500, most of which were concerned with control over the Tungabhadra-Krishna Doab. The doab had been an area of contention long before the foundation of either the

Bahmani kingdom or Vijayanagar. Claims and counterclaims of victory show that neither side gained effective and lasting control over the doab, and the struggle extended eventually into the Konkan and Andhra regions. In his wars against Vijayanagar and Telingana (Warangal), Muḥammad Shah made use of newly organized artillery to defeat an army much larger than his own. His two wars with Vijayanagar gained him little, but his attack on Telingana in 1363 brought him a large indemnity, including the turquoise throne and the town of Golconda with its dependencies; in 1365 his rapid response to a rebellion by the governor of Daulatabad and some Maratha and other chieftains of Berar and Baglana led to a quick victory. The sultan devoted the last decade of his reign to consolidating his hold over the territories in his possession. Institutional and geographic consolidation under Muḥammad Shah laid a solid foundation for the kingdom. His legacy was soon disturbed, however, when his son and successor, 'Alā' al-Dīn Mujāhid (reigned 1375–78), was assassinated by his cousin Dā'ūd while returning from a campaign in Vijayanagar. Dā'ūd was in turn murdered by 'Alā' al-Dīn's partisans, who then set Dā'ūd's brother Muḥammad II (reigned 1378–97) on the throne and blinded Dā'ūd's son. These political difficulties enabled Vijayanagar to take away Goa and other territory along the western coast, but the rest of Muḥammad II's reign was peaceful, and the sultan spent much of his time building his court as a centre of culture and learning.

Several political and cultural tendencies that emerged at this time had significant effects on the development of the Bahmani state and its successors. Although the state had been organized by a group of dissident nobles from the Delhi sultanate, differences in both the culture and the political affiliation of the nobilities developed, largely because of differences in recruiting patterns. Soon after the foundation of the Bahmani state, large numbers of Arabs, Turks, and particularly Persians began to immigrate to the Deccan, many of them at the invitation of Sultan Muḥammad I, and there they had a strong influence on the development of Muslim culture during subsequent generations. The new settlers (āfāqīs) also had a political effect, as they soon began competing successfully for important positions within the political hierarchy. The original rebels from the Delhi sultanate and their descendants, who came to be called dakhnīs (i.e., Deccanis—from the Deccan), thought of themselves as the old nobility and thus resented the success of the newcomers. The situation was comparable to that of the Delhi sultanate, in which a party of entrenched nobles had tried to protect their privileged position against newcomers who were developing claims to power. Thus, the distribution of high offices among Persian newcomers by Sultan Ghiyāth al-Dīn (Muḥammad II's oldest son, who ruled for about two months) in 1397 was seen as a threat by the old nobles and Turks and was probably a major reason for his assassination.

Tomb of Fīrūz Shah Bahmani, Gulbarga, Karnataka, India. Photographer: John Henry Rice; Courtesy: Encyclopædia Britannica, Inc.

Later the addition of Hindu converts and Hindus to the nobility complicated the situation further, as it had in the north, but the division between Deccanis and *āfāqīs* (hereinafter called newcomers) was most significant and contributed to the disintegration of the Bahmani state.

Muḥammad II's peaceful reign was followed by a year of succession disputes caused both by party conflicts and by dynastic rivalries. When Muḥammad's cousins Aḥmad and Fīrūz finally gained control, Fīrūz succeeded as Fīrūz Shah

Bahmani. His reign (1397–1422) was a period of notable cultural activity in the Bahmani sultanate, as well as one of continued development of the trend toward wider political participation. Noted for his intelligence and learning, Fīrūz established on the Bhima River his new capital, Firuzabad, as the greatest centre of Muslim culture in India at a time when the Delhi sultanate was rapidly dissolving. Perhaps in an effort to balance the continuing influx of Persians, as well as to strengthen his own position as a ruler who was above all the nobles and who recognized the realities of political power, Fīrūz gave a number of high offices to Hindus (Brahmans) and married several Hindu women, including the daughter of the king of Vijayanagar. Thus, the parallel with the earlier development of the Delhi sultanate nobility continued. The fact that Hindus were becoming politically more significant at a time when the military rivalry with Vijayanagar was renewed suggests a political rather than a religious motivation for that rivalry.

Fīrūz stopped an invasion in the north by the Gond raja of Kherla in Madhya Pradesh and conducted two moderately successful campaigns against Vijayanagar. The first brought him a tribute payment and temporary military control over the Raichur Doab, while the second ended with his marriage to the Vijayanagar king's daughter and the establishment of an apparently amicable relationship between the two rulers. The peace lasted for only 10 years, however, and a third war (1417–20) ended in a disastrous defeat for Fīrūz by the united forces of Vijayanagar and Fīrūz's former allies, the Velama faction of the Reddi ruling group in Andhra. The Vemas of Kondavidu, once hostile, now joined the sultan. Fīrūz's position was so weakened by the defeat that he was forced to abdicate in favour of his brother Aḥmad, who had the support of most of the army.

One of the first acts of the new sultan, Shihāb al-Dīn Aḥmad I (reigned 1422–36), was to move the capital from Gulbarga to Bidar, which was surrounded by more fertile ground and had become more centrally located now that some territory had been gained to the southeast, in Telingana. Perhaps, also, the move signified Aḥmad's expansionist ambitions, for in 1425 he defeated and killed the Velama ruler of Warangal and finally annexed most of Telingana, bringing his eastern border to the edge of Orissa. During the next decade, however, rebellions forced Aḥmad to allow local chieftains to rule as tributaries throughout much of the area.

EXTERNAL AND INTERNAL RIVALRIES

Although the Bahmani state had been threatened from the north earlier, it was during Aḥmad's reign that conflicts first broke out with the northern neighbours Malwa and Gujarat. The breakdown of centralized authority within the Delhi sultanate and the consequent rise of provincial kingdoms meant that new rivalries could develop on a regional basis, and the Bahmani sultans found themselves contending with two of the successor states of the Delhi sultanate in an arena where their expansionist ambitions had some chance of success. A border dispute with Malwa led to a Bahmani victory and a short-lived recognition of the chieftainship of Kherla as a Bahmani protectorate. Aḥmad I then forged an alliance with another northern neighbour, Khandesh, which acted as a buffer between Bahmani and the kingdoms of Malwa and Gujarat. On the pretext of giving aid to a Hindu chieftain who had revolted against

Gujarat, he sent unsuccessful expeditions into Gujarat in 1429 and 1430. The latter defeat was especially significant, as it partly stemmed from rivalries between the Deccani officers and the newcomers from the Middle East, a friction that appears to have become gradually more intense from this point until the decline of the Bahmani sultanate.

Toward the close of his reign, Aḥmad I named his eldest son as his successor and gave him full charge of the administration; he parceled out the provinces (ṭarafs) among his other sons, exacting from them promises that they would be loyal to the new sultan, ʿAlāʾ al-Dīn Aḥmad II (reigned 1436–58). Even though Aḥmad II had to face a rebellion by one of his brothers, a precedent was set for a rule of primogeniture, which seemed to alleviate the problem of succession disputes for the rest of the century. Unfortunately for later Bahmani rulers, rivalries among the nobility were to prove just as detrimental to the fortunes of the dynasty as family disputes were in many other dynasties of the period.

Aḥmad II proved to be a weaker ruler than his father had been, and during his reign the conflicts among the nobles intensified. Two short wars with Vijayanagar in 1436 and 1443–44 were confined to Tungabhadra-Krishna Doab and signified little except the arrival of a new power, the Hindu Gajapati king of Orissa, who allied himself with the Bahmani ruler in the second campaign. Perhaps more significant in its ultimate effect was the Bahmani victory over Khandesh in 1438. The force in that campaign was composed exclusively of newcomers, who had convinced the sultan that Deccani treachery had been responsible for the defeat in Gujarat in 1430. The newcomers thereby gained considerable influence with the sultan but at the same time intensified the resentment of the Deccanis, who retaliated in 1446 by massacring a large number of them, with the malleable sultan's tacit permission. Later, when the sultan was convinced that the newcomers had been unjustly killed, he punished many of the responsible Deccanis and promoted the surviving newcomers. During the last years of his reign, Aḥmad had to face a rebellion in Telingana led by his son-in-law and supported by the sultan of Malwa. It was at this time that Maḥmūd Gāwān, a newly arrived noble from Persia, displayed his military and diplomatic skills by persuading the rebels to desist and the sultan to pardon them.

Under the successors of Aḥmad II, Bahmani faced continuous disturbances, such as further rebellion in Telingana and three serious onslaughts by Maḥmūd Khaljī of Malwa; the Gajapati king of Orissa joined the fray by making inroads into the heart of the Bahmani kingdom. Humāyūn (reigned 1458–61) and Niẓām al-Dīn Aḥmad III (reigned 1461–63) sought the help of Muḥammad Begarā of Gujarat against Malwa and warded off the invasions.

VIZIERATE OF MAḤMŪD GĀWĀN

The most notable personality of the period was Maḥmūd Gāwān, who was a leading administrator during the reigns of Humāyūn and his son Aḥmad III and was vizier (chief minister) under Muḥammad III (reigned 1463–82). During Maḥmūd Gāwān's ascendancy, the Bahmani state achieved both its greatest size and greatest degree of centralization, and yet, partly because of the attempts at centralization and partly because of the continuing rivalry between the Deccanis and the newcomers, the period ended with Maḥmūd Gāwān's assassination and the rapid dissolution of the effective power of the Bahmani state.

After Maḥmūd Gāwān's installation as vizier in 1463, a series of Bahmani campaigns resulted in the subjugation in the west of most of the Konkan, including several forts (e.g., Khelna, Belgaum, and Kolhapur) and the important port of Goa, which was then under Vijayanagar control. This not only guaranteed the safety of Muslim merchants and pilgrims from piratical attacks but also gave Bahmani virtual command over the west coast trade, at least until the arrival of the Portuguese. In the north the frontier with Malwa was maintained more or less as it was, although Bahmani agreed to return Kherla's status as a fief of Malwa. An alliance with Vijayanagar proved effective in defeating Orissa in 1470. Later, campaigns in the east brought some advantages against the rival claimants to the Orissa throne, who sought Bahmani's help against one another. In 1481 Muḥammad III, with Maḥmūd Gāwān, succeeded in taking Kondapalli from Saluva Narasimha, the Vijayanagar general, and the sultan quickly marched south as far as Kanchipuram in a show of prowess.

As vizier, Maḥmūd Gāwān attempted to enhance the central authority—ostensibly of the crown but possibly his own as well—through a series of administrative reforms and political maneuvers. Up to the 1470s the kingdom had been divided into four provinces, centring around the cities of Daulatabad, Mahur, Bidar, and Gulbarga, respectively. The governors of the four provinces had control over almost all aspects of civil and military administration within their territorial jurisdictions. Administration was thus decentralized from the beginning, but the relative power of the provincial governors as compared with the centre potentially became even greater as the state expanded and each of the four provinces grew larger. To decrease the power of the governors, Maḥmūd Gāwān divided each of the overgrown provinces into two, under separate governors, reduced the military control of the governors by bringing all forts but one in each province directly under the control of the sultan, and tightened central control over the employment and payment of troops within the provinces. In addition, he introduced a system of measurement and valuation of agricultural land and created a large block of crown land within each province. Perhaps the most significant of all of Maḥmūd Gāwān's measures was his policy of balancing important appointments between Deccanis and newcomers in order to reduce disputes among the nobility and to keep himself, as vizier, above party conflicts.

Unfortunately for Maḥmūd Gāwān and for the Bahmani dynasty, party strife had developed to such an extent that a group of Deccani nobles—motivated by hostility toward the chief minister as a newcomer, as well as by dislike of his efforts toward centralization—falsified evidence to make Maḥmūd Gāwān appear a traitor and convinced Muḥammad III to execute him in 1481. The execution was widely disapproved of by the newcomers and even by some of the Deccani nobles, many of whom sided with Yūsuf ʿĀdil Khan, previously Maḥmūd Gāwān's chief supporter. Most of the newcomers returned to their provinces and refused to come to the capital, and the sultan was left with only the support of the conspirators. When he died in 1482 (of grief over his error in judgment, the chronicles report), the leader of the conspirators, Malik Nā'ib, was able to make himself regent for Muḥammad's minor son, Shihāb al-Dīn Maḥmūd (reigned 1482–1518).

BAHMANI DECLINE

Maḥmūd's reign hastened the disintegration of the Bahmani kingdom. An abortive attempt to assassinate Yūsuf ʿĀdil Khan resulted in the Khan's agreement to retire to Bijapur and leave Malik Nā'ib and the conspirators in charge at Bidar. Now the lack of institutionalized central power brought group conflicts to the fore. Malik Nā'ib, never popular even with a number of the Deccanis, was put to death in 1486 by the Abyssinian governor of Bihar, and the sultan subsequently began to rely on

the newcomers for support. An attempt on Maḥmūd's life in 1487 by a group of Deccanis strengthened the sultan's reliance on the newcomers and led to the slaughter of a great many Deccanis. But by this time it began to become apparent that the power of the sultan was less than that of several of his nobles, and, although he continued to be a valuable pawn for the provincial governors to try to control, his power to rule was nearly gone. The provincial governors and their followers could not be controlled, nor did they believe that maintaining the centralized Bahmani state would any longer be in their best interests. Consequently, the governors were usually unwilling to aid the sultan when he attempted to put down rebellions by other governors or by powerful nobles.

One of the first revolts was that of the *kotwal* (superintendent of police) of Bidar, Qāsim Barīd, a Turkish noble who defeated the army sent against him by the sultan and then forced Maḥmūd to make him chief minister of the state. Qāsim Barīd's attempt to reimpose central authority was opposed by most of the chief nobles, however, who defeated him once and then refused to recognize his authority. Next, Malik Aḥmad Niẓām al-Mulk, the son of Malik Nā'ib, began to carve out a territory for himself by conquering Maratha forts along the western coast. He defeated the two armies sent against him by the sultan, whom he forced to recognize his conquests, and in 1490 he assumed a practical independence and established his capital at

Ahmadnagar. Yūsuf 'Ādil Khān of Bijapur and Faṭḥ Allāh 'Imād al-Mulk of Berar had demonstrated their sympathy for Malik Aḥmad's activities and soon emulated him. Although the three governors still did not assume the insignia of royalty, it was clear by the end of 1490 that Sultan Maḥmūd and the chief minister, Qāsim Barīd, could not command any of them.

SUCCESSORS TO THE BAHMANI

During the 1490s the rivalries intensified among the former provincial governors, other high nobles, and Qāsim Barīd, who was the effective head of the government at the Bahmani capital. Each began to form temporary alliances and to fight battles with other nobles in order to enhance his own position. Gradually the five successor states to the Bahmani sultanate took shape, as lesser nobles were defeated and their territories were incorporated by the provincial governors or retained by Bidar. Bijapur (1490), Ahmadnagar (1490), and later Golconda (1512) emerged as the most successful of these states. Although a Bahmani sultan still remained as a puppet ruler until at least 1538, effective control of the Bidar government passed into the hands of Qāsim Barīd's son Amīr Barīd upon his father's death in 1505, thus establishing what proved to be a dynastic claim for the Barīd Shāhī dynasty of Bidar.

Ironically, the conflict between Deccanis and newcomers, which had done so much to destroy the unity of the sultanate, was of little importance after 1492. The major rivalry of the next decade was between two newcomers, Qāsim Barīd and Yūsuf 'Ādil Khan. (Qāsim Barīd, however, was supported by the Deccanis of Bidar in his struggle with another Deccani, Malik Aḥmad of Ahmadnagar.) The shift resulted from the fact that there were no longer parties of nobles but rather semi-independent states whose rulers were attempting to establish and expand their authority. Political expediency dictated the shifting alliances among these regional chiefs, who were no longer representatives of factional politics but were potential rulers of independent states. The primary goals of territorial integrity and military supremacy offered sufficient rationale for one or the other of these chiefs to seek even the alliance of their traditional enemy Vijayanagar, particularly in the conflicts between Bijapur and Ahmadnagar.

One issue that occasionally united the Bahmani successor states was the desire to profit at the expense of Vijayanagar. Sultan Maḥmūd II proposed in 1501 that a policy of an annual jihad, or holy war, against the Hindu kingdom be adopted by the Muslim nobles. A number of relatively successful raids were undertaken during the next few years, but in 1509 the new ruler of Vijayanagar, Krishna Deva Raya, repulsed the Muslims, who suffered substantial losses. Later the political ambitions of Bijapur and Ahmadnagar prompted a series of successful interventions by Vijayanagar under Rama Raya, a regent who finally usurped the Vijayanagar throne and played a significant role in

Deccan politics. The excesses of Rama Raya, carried out on the pretext of assisting Bijapur against Ahmadnagar in their wars, led to a temporary but fruitful coalition among the five successor states and the crushing defeat of Vijayanagar's powerful forces at the Battle of Talikota in 1565, which, though it did not destroy the Hindu kingdom, ultimately helped the expansionist ambitions of Bijapur and Golconda.

During the 16th century the strongest and best-organized of the Bahmani successor states was Ahmadnagar (Niẓām Shāhī), followed by Bijapur (ʿĀdil Shāhī) and then Golconda. All three were much larger and more important than Berar and Bidar, and all three either began with or soon came to accept the Shīʿite form of Islam (the religion of the Persian newcomers) as the official faith of their rulers. During the 16th century the three major states formed shifting patterns of alliances, which sometimes (both before and after 1565) also included Vijayanagar, while the two smaller Muslim states ranged themselves on one side or the other in order to protect their independence. The goal of military campaigns normally was to humble the adversary without doing irreparable harm, for all three major Muslim states feared the supremacy of any one state, and a tripartite division of territory seemed more likely to ensure the continued independence of all.

Bijapur and Ahmadnagar were drawn into a series of conflicts over the forts in the Maratha region and the Konkan coast. A treaty between the two in 1571, however, reveals their interest in restoring a balance in the political situation by recognizing the right of Ahmadnagar to annex Berar and Bidar in return for recognition of Bijapur's right to occupy extensive territories in the south, particularly portions of Vijayanagar. Ahmadnagar did not annex Bidar, owing to intervention by Ibrāhīm Quṭb Shah of Golconda, but it did acquire Berar in 1574. Bijapur was unable to take full advantage of the opportunities for expansion to the south during the 1570s because of factional disputes among the nobles, as well as Golconda's interests in the Vijayanagar-controlled areas. Thus, Ahmadnagar managed to retain a slightly superior position.

The tide began to turn in the 1580s, however, with the establishment of a stable regency at Bijapur, fortified by a series of marriage alliances with other royal lines in the Deccan and by the political deterioration of Ahmadnagar under the rule of the slightly mad Murtaḍā Niẓām Shah. Murtaḍā's murder in 1588, by a son who was more insane than he, set off a chain of events that resulted in simultaneous invasions by Bijapur from the south and by Murtaḍā's brother Burhān, who had the support of the Mughal emperor Akbar, from the north. Burhān defeated the army of Ahmadnagar, recalled the foreign nobles (as the newcomers of Bahmani times were by then designated) who had been expelled from the kingdom, and assumed the throne in 1591. Campaigns against Bijapur and against the Portuguese at Chaul (just south of present-day Mumbai [Bombay]), as well as a bitter rivalry between the

Quṭb Shāhī tombs, Golconda, Andhra Pradesh, India. Frederick M. Asher

Deccani and foreign nobles, further weakened Ahmadnagar at a time when Akbar's growing interest indicated grave danger. The deaths of both Burhān and his son in 1595 were followed by increased factionalism and eventually by civil war as rival claimants to the throne were put forward. When one party appealed for aid to the governor of Gujarat, Akbar had an excuse to launch the campaign he had already been planning. The two wars that followed resulted in the Mughal acquisition of Berar, the capture of the ruler of Ahmadnagar, and the defeat and annexation of Khandesh. A group of nobles, however, led by the Abyssinian Malik 'Ambār, raised a member of the royal family to the throne at Daulatabad and continued to fight the Mughals.

Golconda, whose area by the mid-17th century approximated that of the Telugu linguistic and cultural region, was built up as a strong state by the Quṭb Shāhīs from 1512. It developed a distinct regional culture with the founding of Hyderabad in 1590–91 by Muḥammad Qulī Quṭb Shah and evolved a political system to suit the indigenous sociopolitical structure. Golconda enjoyed a high level of economic prosperity owing to the productive agricultural plains of Andhra and the busy trade of such ports as Masulipatam, as well as to the diamond mines near Vijayawada.

The Quṭb Shāhīs steadily expanded the area under their control during the 16th century at the expense of the politically fragmented Telugu kings and Nayakas and held their own against the Vijayanagar rulers and the Gajapatis of Orissa. Vijayanagar interests in Andhra and its intervention in Golconda politics through encouragement to the rebel Nayakas under Krishna Deva Raya and his successors ceased after the Talikota debacle in 1565. Consolidation was achieved by Ibrāhīm Quṭb Shah (reigned 1550–80) and enhanced under Muḥammad Qulī early in the 17th century. A conciliatory policy toward the Nayakas, as well as the regime's desire to preserve the Telugu warrior ethos, brought Telugu warrior groups into Golconda's service. Special attention to large-scale irrigation and agriculture, promotion of interregional trade, and administrative centralization were the basic factors in Golconda's stability.

In the struggle for control of the Deccan after the decline of the Bahmani sultanate, the two southernmost states, Bijapur and Golconda, ultimately found themselves in the most advantageous position, because they were farthest away from the growing power of the Mughal Empire in north India. The Mughal's southward

movement, which began under Akbar (reigned 1556–1605) with a successful onslaught against Ahmadnagar, was to end with the annexation of Bijapur (1686) and Golconda (1687) during the reign of Aurangzeb (reigned 1658–1707). During the intervening period, the Mughal presence became increasingly important to the remaining Deccan kings, who struggled to maintain or expand their position within the Deccan while trying to fend off the advancing Mughal arms.

THE VIJAYANAGAR EMPIRE, 1336–1646

Founded in 1336 in the wake of the rebellions against Tughluq rule in the Deccan, the Hindu Vijayanagar empire lasted for more than two centuries as the dominant power in south India. Its history and fortunes were shaped by the increasing militarization of peninsular politics after the Muslim invasions and the commercialization that made south India a major participant in the trade network linking Europe and East Asia. Urbanization and monetization of the economy were the two other significant developments of the period that brought all the peninsular kingdoms into highly competitive political and military activities in the race for supremacy.

DEVELOPMENT OF THE STATE

The kingdom of Vijayanagar was founded by Harihara and Bukka, two of five brothers (surnamed Sangama) who had served

VIJAYANAGAR

Vijayanagar (Sanskrit: "City of Victory") is a great ruined city in southern India and also the name of the empire ruled first from that city and later from Penukonda (in Anantapur district, Andhra Pradesh) between 1336 and about 1614. The site of the city, on the Tungabhadra River, is now partly occupied by the village of Hampi in eastern Karnataka state.

The city and its first dynasty were founded in 1336 by five sons of Sangama, of whom Harihara and Bukka became the city's first kings. In time Vijayanagar became the greatest empire of southern India. By serving as a barrier against invasion by the Muslim sultanates of the north, it fostered the reconstruction of Hindu life and administration after the disorders and disunities of the 12th and 13th centuries. Contact with the Muslims (who were not personally disliked) stimulated new thought and creative productivity. Sanskrit was encouraged as a unifying force, and regional literatures thrived. Behind its frontiers the country flourished in unexampled peace and prosperity.

The first dynasty, the Sangama, lasted until about 1485, when—at a time of pressure from the Bahmani sultan and the raja of Orissa—Narasimha of the Saluva family usurped power. By 1503 the Saluva dynasty had been supplanted by the Tuluva dynasty. The outstanding Tuluva king was Krishna Deva Raya. During his reign (1509–29) the land between the Tungabhadra and Krishna rivers (the Raichur doab) was acquired (1512), the Orissa Hindus were subdued by the capture of Udayagiri (1514) and other towns, and severe defeats were inflicted on the Bijapur sultan (1520). Krishna Deva's successors, however, allowed their enemies to unite against them. In 1565 Rama Raya, the chief minister of Vijayanagar, led the empire into the fatal battle at Talikota, in which its army was routed by the combined forces of the Muslim states of Bijapur, Ahmadnagar, and Golconda and the city of Vijayanagar was destroyed. Tirumala, brother of Rama Raya, then seized control of the empire and founded the Aravidu dynasty, which established a new capital at Penukonda and kept the empire intact for a time. Internal dissensions and the intrigues of the sultans of Bijapur and Golconda, however, led to the final collapse of the empire about 1614.

Lotus Mahal in Hampi, Karnataka, India. Photographer: John Henry Rice; Courtesy: Encyclopædia Britannica, Inc.

in the administrations of both Kakatiya and Kampili before those kingdoms were conquered by the armies of the Delhi sultanate in the 1320s. When Kampili fell in 1327, the two brothers are believed to have been captured and taken to Delhi, where they converted to Islam. They were returned to the Deccan as governors of Kampili for the sultanate with the hope that they would be able to deal with the many local revolts and invasions by neighbouring Hindu kings. They followed a conciliatory policy toward the landholders of the area, many of whom had not accepted Muslim rule, and began a process of consolidation and expansion. Their first campaign was against the neighbouring Hoysala king, Ballala III of Dorasamudra, but it stagnated; after the brothers reconverted to Hinduism under the influence of the sage Madhavacarya (Vidyaranya) and proclaimed their independence from the Delhi sultanate, however, they were able to defeat Ballala and thereby secure their home base. Harihara I (reigned 1336–56) then established his new capital, Vijayanagar, in an easily defensible position south of the Tungabhadra River, where it came to symbolize the emerging medieval political culture of south India. The kingdom's expansion in the first century of its existence made it the first south Indian state to exercise enduring control over different linguistic and cultural regions, albeit with subregional and local chiefly powers exercising authority as its agents and subordinates.

Consolidation

Harihara was succeeded by Bukka (I; reigned 1356–77), who during his first decade as king engaged in a number of costly wars against the Bahmani sultans over control of strategic forts in the Tungabhadra-Krishna Doab, as well as over the trading emporia of the east and west coasts. The Bahmanis generally prevailed in these encounters and even forced Vijayanagar to pay a tribute in 1359. The major accomplishments of Bukka's reign were the conquest of the short-lived sultanate of Maḥbar (Madurai; 1370) and the maintenance of his kingdom against the threat of decentralization. During Harihara's reign the government of the outlying provinces of the growing state had been entrusted to his brothers—usually to the brother who had conquered that particular territory. By 1357 some of Bukka's nephews had succeeded their fathers as governors of those provinces, and there was a possibility that the state would become less and less centralized as the various branches of the family became more firmly ensconced in their particular domains. Bukka, therefore, removed his nephews and replaced them with his sons and favourite generals so that centralized authority (and his own line of succession) could be maintained. However, the succession of Bukka's son Harihara II (reigned 1377–1404) precipitated a repetition of the same action. A rebellion in the Tamil country at the beginning of his reign probably was aided by the disaffected sons and officers of Bukka's deceased eldest son, Kumara Kampana, who were not ready to acknowledge Harihara's authority. Harihara was able to put down the rebellion and subsequently to replace his cousins with his own sons as governors of the provinces. Thus, the circle of power was narrowed once again. The question of succession to the throne had not been settled, however. On many occasions, the conflict resumed between the king and his lineal descendant, who tried to centralize the state, and the collateral relatives (cousins and brothers), who tried to establish ruling rights over some portion of the kingdom.

The temporary confusion that followed the assassination of the Bahmani sultan ʿAlāʾ al-Dīn Mujāhid in 1378 gave Harihara the opportunity to recapture Goa and some other western ports and impose his authority southward along the Malabar Coast. During the next decade, pressure increased for expansion against the Reddi kingdom of Kondavidu in the northeast. Prince Devaraya captured Panagal fort and made it a base of operations in the region. The slight gains made in 1390–91 against an alliance of the Velama chieftain of Rajakonda and the Bahmanis were more than offset when the Bahmani sultan besieged Vijayanagar in 1398–99, slaughtered a large number of people, and exacted a promise to pay tribute. The tribute was withheld two years later, however, when Vijayanagar made alliances with the sultans of Malwa and Gujarat.

Nevertheless, Harihara's reign was relatively successful, because he expanded the state, maintained internal order, and managed to fend off the Bahmani sultans. The control of ports on both coasts provided opportunities for the acquisition of increased wealth through trade.

WARS AND RIVALRIES

Harihara II's death in 1404 was followed by a violent succession dispute among his three surviving sons. Only after two of them had been crowned and dethroned was the third, Devaraya I (reigned 1406–22), able to emerge victorious. Continuing instability, however, coupled with the involvement of Vijayanagar and the Bahmani sultanate as backers of different claimants to the throne of Kondavidu, led to further confrontation between the two powers (each joined by various of the rivalrous Telugu chiefs). Sultan Fīrūz Shah Bahmani supported a Reddi attack on Udayagiri. In a related move, the sultan himself mounted another siege of Vijayanagar city, imposing tributary conditions that included his marriage to Devaraya's daughter. Despite Bahmani successes, Vijayanagar managed to hold Panagal, Nalgonda, and other forts and to regain Udayagiri. The defeat of Fīrūz Shah in 1419 and the death of his Vema ally led to the eventual partition of Kondavidu between Vijayanagar and the Velamas of Rajakonda, who had switched sides with the Vemas during the protracted struggle. This extensive involvement in Andhra and Telingana—inspired by the ambition to expand farther up the eastern seaboard (an area that the Bahmanis to the west also sought to control)—brought Vijayanagar into conflict for the first time with the kingdom of Orissa to the north. Although a war was temporarily averted, there began a rivalry that was to last more than a century.

Perhaps Devaraya's most significant achievement was his reorganization of the army. Realizing the value of cavalry and well-trained archers, he imported many horses from Persia and Arabia and hired Turkish bowmen, as well as troopers who were skilled in mounted warfare. Thus, although it appears that he was seldom able to best the Bahmanis in the field, he had begun to narrow the strategic and technological gap between north and south and to build an army that would be better suited to warfare on open plains.

The short reigns of Devaraya's two sons, Ramcandra and Vijaya, were disastrous. In a war against the Bahmanis, many temples were destroyed, and Vijaya was forced to pay a huge indemnity. A combined invasion by the king of Orissa and the Velamas of Andhra resulted in the loss of the territories newly gained in the partition of the Reddi kingdom of Kondavidu. Vijaya's son and successor, Devaraya II (reigned 1432–46), reconquered the lost Reddi territories and incorporated them into his kingdom, thus establishing the Krishna River as the northeastern boundary. Wars with the Bahmanis in 1435–36 and 1443–44 over

control of Raichur and Mudgal forts in the Tungabhadra-Krishna Doab ended inconclusively. Those campaigns, however, led to further improvements in Vijayanagar's military forces when Devaraya II proclaimed that Muslims would be welcome in his service and assigned Muslim archers already in Vijayanagar service to instruct his Hindu troops. Devaraya also levied tribute from Sri Lanka and campaigned successfully in the Kerala country of the far south, where his victories over local chieftains suggest a process of consolidation. His reign saw both the greatest territorial extension and the greatest centralization of the first period of the history of Vijayanagar.

DECENTRALIZATION AND LOSS OF TERRITORY

During the first 40 years after Devaraya's death in 1446, the centralized power of the state declined, and a considerable amount of territory along both coasts was lost to the Bahmani sultans and to the suddenly powerful Gajapati ruler of Orissa. In the 1450s and 1460s Kapilendra (Kapileshvara), the great king of Orissa, together with his son Hamvira, conquered the Reddi kingdom of Rajahmundry and the Vijayanagar province of Kondavidu, captured Warangal and Bidar from the Bahmanis, eventually occupied Udayagiri, and sent a victorious army down the east coast as far south as the Kaveri (Cauvery) River, where he was repulsed by the able Vijayanagar general and governor of Chandragiri, Saluva Narasimha.

The Orissan raid had a considerable effect upon Vijayanagar. It not only weakened the empire in the east but also indicated that provincial governors might have to fend for themselves if they expected to retain their territories. The fact that Devaraya's son Mallikarjuna (reigned 1446–65) was succeeded by a cousin rather than by his own son was another indication of lessened central control and of the failure of the king and his immediate family to secure their own future, as had been done by many of his ancestors when they removed their cousins from positions of power. The new ruler, Virupaksha (reigned 1465–85), had been a provincial governor. His usurpation was not accepted by many of the provincial governors on the east and west coasts or by the direct descendants of Mallikarjuna, who retired to the banks of the Kaveri and ruled much of the southern part of the kingdom in a semi-independent fashion.

Beginning in 1470, the Bahmanis, under the vizier Maḥmūd Gāwān, began a campaign that succeeded in taking much of the west coast and the northern Karnataka from Vijayanagar. The loss of Goa and other ports was especially disconcerting, because it cut off not only an important source of trade and state income but the principal source of supply of Middle Eastern horses for the military as well. The death in 1470 of Kapilendra of Orissa temporarily relieved military pressure in the east; but it was Saluva

Narasimha (since transferred to Penukonda), rather than Virupaksha, who took advantage of the resultant civil war in Orissa to regain lost territory. He reconquered the Tamil region and became master of the east coast up to the Godavari River. Bahmani aid to Hamvira, in return for the surrender of all the captured forts in Telingana, drew Narasimha into a war with the sultanate. A two-pronged attack by Muḥammad Shah and Maḥmūd Gāwān on Narasimha's territories—Penukonda and the coastal region—and the plunder of Kanchipuram in 1481 were only temporarily successful, for Ishvara Nayaka, a Vijayanagar general, recovered the loot from the returning Bahmani forces at Kandukur, and Narasimha recaptured Penukonda after turning back the Bahmani forces.

LATER DYNASTIES

Beginning as a small chieftain about 1456, Narasimha had put together a large dominion by 1485 as a result of conquests in the south, as well as campaigns against Orissa; and, although nominally subordinate to Virupaksha, he was performing more extensive military and administrative functions than was his superior. It is not surprising that when Virupaksha was murdered by one of his sons—who was in turn murdered by his brother—Saluva Narasimha (reigned 1485–90) stepped in to remove the new ruler and to begin his own dynasty. Usurpation was easier than consolidation, however, and Narasimha spent his reign in relatively successful campaigns to reduce his vassals throughout the kingdom to submission and in unsuccessful attempts to stop the encroachment of the king of Orissa. Narasimha also opened new ports on the west coast so that he could revive the horse trade, which had fallen into Bahmani hands, and he generally revitalized the army. By 1490 the process of centralization had begun again, and both internal and external political circumstances soon would combine to create better opportunities than ever before.

RECONSOLIDATION

At his death in 1491, following the siege of Udayagiri (and his own imprisonment there) by Orissa, Narasimha left his kingdom in the hands of his chief minister, Narasa Nayaka, whom he had appointed regent for his two young sons the previous year. The minister in effect ruled Vijayanagar from 1490 until his own death in 1503. Court intrigues led to the murder of the elder prince by one of Narasa's rivals and to the capture and virtual imprisonment of the younger prince (officially enthroned as Immadi Narasimha) by Narasa in 1492. The usurpation resulted in opposition from provincial governors and chiefs that lasted for the rest of Narasa's life. Early in his regency, however, he had the opportunity to take advantage of the beginning of the disintegration of the Bahmani sultanate. He invaded the disputed Tungabhadra-Krishna Doab in 1492–93 at the invitation of the Bahmani minister,

Qāsim Barīd, who was trying to subdue the newly independent Yūsuf ʿĀdil Khan of Bijapur. Narasa took the strategic forts of Raichur and Mudgal; and, although they were lost again in 1502, the growing disunity of the emerging Muslim polities would provide many similar opportunities in the future.

Narasa also campaigned in the south to restore effective control, which had not existed in many areas since the raid from Orissa in 1463–64. He compelled most of the chiefs and provincial governors to recognize his suzerainty in both Tamil country and Karnataka and nearly restored the old boundaries of the kingdom (some eastern districts were still held by Orissa). By 1503 Narasa had practically completed the process of reconsolidation with which Saluva Narasimha had charged him, although trade restrictions and other impositions by the Portuguese had significantly compromised Vijayanagar's prestige. He also had made virtually certain that his own line rather than that of his old master would continue to rule. It was during the reigns of his sons that Vijayanagar rose to new heights of political power and cultural eminence.

Narasa's eldest son and successor, best known as Vira Narasimha (reigned 1503–09), ended the sham of regency. After ordering the by-then grown Immadi Narasimha's murder in 1505, he ascended the throne and inaugurated the Tuluva dynasty, the third dynasty of Vijayanagar. The usurpation again provoked opposition, which the new king spent most of his reign attempting to quell. He was successful except in subduing the rebellious chiefs of Ummattur and Seringapatam in the south and in recovering Goa from the Portuguese, with whom, however, he was able to establish relations to obtain a supply of better horses. By this time the Bahmani wars, in which the successor states had joined, had become a series of annual jihads, or holy wars, maintaining the Bahmani's virtual control over the doab forts.

GROWTH OF POWER

Vira Narasimha was succeeded by his brother Krishna Deva Raya (reigned 1509–29), generally regarded as the greatest of the Vijayanagar kings. During his reign the kingdom became more powerful than ever before, and internal consolidation reached a new peak. Krishna Deva spent the first 10 years of his reign solidly establishing his authority over his subordinate chieftains and governors while fending off invasions from the northeast.

In an effort to achieve centralization and effective political control, Krishna Deva Raya appointed Brahmans and capable nonkinsmen as commanders, garrisoned the forts with Portuguese and Muslim mercenary gunners, and recruited foot soldiers from local forest tribes; he also created the rank of lesser chiefs known as poligars (*palaiyakkarars*) in the Vijayanagar service.

After decisively defeating an invading coalition of Bahmani forces (who by

this time were virtually separated into five states) and capturing Raichur fort, Krishna Deva took advantage of a quarrel between Bijapur and the Bahmani ruler to subdue both Gulbarga and Bidar and to restore the imprisoned Bahmani sultan to his throne in 1512. During the same period he conducted a successful campaign to subdue Ummattur in the south, and a new province was established from it. From 1513 to 1520, Krishna Deva campaigned against the Gajapati ruler of Orissa, conquering all that king's territory up to the Godavari and raiding as far as the Orissan capital at Kataka. Orissa then sued for peace, and its king gave his daughter in marriage to Krishna Deva, who consequently returned to Orissa all the conquered territory north of the Krishna River.

While Krishna Deva was fighting in the east, Ismā'īl 'Ādil Shah of Bijapur had retaken Raichur fort. In 1520 Krishna Deva decisively defeated Ismā'īl with some aid from Portuguese gunners and recaptured Raichur. In 1523 he carried the attack further, invading Bijapur and capturing several forts. Krishna Deva razed Gulbarga and once again claimed to have restored the Bahmani sultanate by setting one of the three sons of Maḥmūd Shah II on the throne. One result of these successful campaigns and of Krishna Deva's subsequent haughty behaviour was to point out vividly to the Muslim rulers the dangers posed by Vijayanagar, so that in years to come they thought increasingly of taking concerted action against that kingdom. Krishna Deva's

Tiruvengalanatha Temple complex, Vijayanagar, Karnataka, India. Frederick M. Asher

highly successful reign thus led to increased danger to his realm.

During most of his reign Krishna Deva maintained a mutually advantageous relationship with the increasingly powerful Portuguese, whereby he retained access to trade goods, especially to horses from the Middle East, while the Portuguese were allowed to trade in his dominions. The accounts from this period by the Portuguese travelers Domingos Pais and Duarte Barbosa depict a thriving city and kingdom under a highly venerated and capable ruler. Krishna Deva Raya's scholarship and patronage of Telugu and Sanskrit literature have become symbols of Telugu pride and cultural traditions.

About 1524–25 Krishna Deva abdicated and had his young son crowned king. His son died shortly thereafter, however, reportedly poisoned by the jealous former chief minister. Krishna Deva imprisoned the minister and his family and dealt successfully with a serious rebellion three years later—when one of the minister's sons escaped—as well as with Ismāʿīl ʿĀdil Shah's attempt to take advantage of Krishna Deva's troubles to recoup his position. Krishna Deva's death in 1529 ended the period of the kingdom's greatest military and administrative success.

RENEWED DECENTRALIZATION

Krishna Deva had passed over his infant son and his young nephew and picked his half brother Achyuta Deva Raya (reigned 1529–42) to succeed him. Following a brief succession dispute, Achyuta Deva Raya was able to reach the capital from Chandragiri, where Krishna Deva had kept him and other princes confined, and to ascend the throne. Although he probably was not as dissolute a ruler as the Portuguese traveler and writer Fernão Nuniz described him to be, the severe challenges he faced made a successful reign difficult. Krishna Deva's death had precipitated renewed attacks by Bijapur, Golconda, and Orissa and a revolt by the king's minister, Saluva Viranarasimha, and the southern chieftains of Ummattur and Tiruvadi. Achyuta dealt successfully with all his enemies until the late 1530s, when he was imprisoned by Rama Raya, the chief minister, with whom he had agreed to share power. Opposition by some of the nobles to Achyuta's imprisonment, combined with a revolt in the south, led to his release and the beginnings of civil war; but the new

ruler of Bijapur, Ibrāhīm ʿĀdil Shah, after early attempts to create divisiveness in Vijayanagar, arbitrated a settlement between Achyuta and Rama Raya. Under the settlement, Achyuta virtually handed over his sovereignty to the regent, retaining nominal kingship.

Achyuta's reign ended with about the same external boundaries of the kingdom as in 1529, but the struggle with Rama Raya plus the activities of other nobles and chieftains weakened the hold of the centre over some of the provinces. The process of decentralization had set in again, but now the strongman who would pull the kingdom together was already on the scene. Rama Raya brought himself to the undisputed pinnacle of power in 1542–43, when he defeated his rival in the succession struggle following Achyuta's death and crowned his own candidate, Achyuta's nephew Sadashiva (reigned 1542–76). After seven or eight years, Rama Raya also assumed royal titles, but from the first Sadashiva was kept under guard, and Rama Raya, together with his brothers Tirumala and Venkatadri, ruled the kingdom.

Rama Raya was able to control, although not to subdue entirely, rebellious nobles in the east and the extreme south. He also concluded a treaty with the Portuguese (1546), whose settlements had been expanding and who had caused no small amount of damage to indigenous settlements over the past few years. The treaty was broken in

1558, however, and Rama Raya then exacted tribute in compensation for damage to temples caused by the Portuguese.

Relations with the Muslim States

Most crucial during the period of Rama Raya's rule, however, were Vijayanagar's relations with the Muslim successor states to the Bahmani sultanate. At least since Krishna Deva Raya's time, Vijayanagar had usually competed on a more than equal basis and in the same system of state rivalries with the five Muslim states. Thus, an invasion from Bijapur was repulsed in 1543; in 1548 Rama Raya aided Burhān Niẓām Shah of Ahmadnagar in taking a fort from Bidar, but in 1557 Rama Raya allied himself with Bijapur against the Niẓām Shah and Golconda. The result of the last war was a collective treaty, by which any of the four parties, attacked unjustly by another, could call upon the other allies to stop the aggressor. When Ḥusayn Niẓām Shah broke the treaty by invading Bijapur in 1560, Vijayanagar and Golconda responded with an attack that resulted not only in Ahmadnagar's loss of the fort of Kalyani to Bijapur but also in an invasion of Bidar and the defeat of its ruler by Rama Raya. Soon, however, the ruler of Golconda, Ibrāhīm Quṭb Shah, allied himself with Ahmadnagar against Bijapur, and Rama Raya allied Vijayanagar with Bijapur to severely defeat the aggressors.

Decline of Vijayanagar

It is likely that the sultans of Golconda and Ahmadnagar, who had lost much at the hands of Rama Raya, were primarily responsible for the formation of an alliance that destroyed Vijayanagar's power forever. By 1564 at least four of the five sultans (Berar is questionable) had begun their march on Vijayanagar, which resulted early in 1565 in the disastrous defeat of the Vijayanagar forces in the Battle of Talikota and in the subsequent sack and destruction of much of the city of Vijayanagar. Rama Raya was captured and killed, but his brother Tirumala escaped to the south with the king and much of the royal treasure.

Military Policies

Although Rama Raya's efforts toward centralization were not entirely successful, it was his military policies that ultimately led to disaster. There were rebellions when he replaced many members of the old nobility with relatives and close associates, but they appear to have been no more serious than many other rebellions of previous periods under similar circumstances. Indeed, judging on the basis of the number and size of the military campaigns that Rama Raya was able to launch outside Vijayanagar in later years, it would seem that his internal control was relatively secure. Rama Raya has been criticized for allowing

Muslims to hold important positions within his administration, and, although his final defeat at Talikota was at least partly attributable to the defection of two of his Muslim generals, the policy appears to have worked well up to that time. Rama Raya's early experiences as an official at the court of Golconda appear to have given him ideas for improving the Vijayanagar administration and army. As early as 1535 he had hired 3,000 Muslim soldiers from Bijapur, and he later tried to make the Vijayanagar state apparatus more like that of the neighbouring Muslim states. In short, he was building a state that would be as competitive as possible in that time and place. It is likely that at first Vijayanagar's Muslim neighbours took a similar view of state relations and that Vijayanagar was seen as just another competing state. Rama Raya's military successes and his skill in diplomacy, together with his arrogance in the knowledge that Vijayanagar was stronger than any one of the sultanates, led to the Muslim alliance against him. Despite a Muslim historian's claim that the alliance was formed because of Rama Raya's bad treatment of Muslims, there is little evidence to indicate that the principal motives were other than political. Furthermore, the subsequent behaviour of the sultans suggests that, once Vijayanagar had been humbled, they were willing to return to a system of shifting alliances among all the Deccan powers.

LOSS OF CENTRAL CONTROL

The Battle of Talikota did not result in the destruction of the kingdom of Vijayanagar, although the capital city never fully recovered from the ravages it suffered. Rama Raya's brother Tirumala established a new headquarters at Penukonda and attempted to rebuild the army. Much of the south and southeast was lost, however, as the Nayakas of Madura, Thanjavur (Tanjore), and Jinji effectively asserted their independence. Rebellions and banditry arose in many areas. Tirumala appealed to Niẓām Shah of Ahmadnagar for aid against a Bijapuri invasion that reached Penukonda. He then joined with Ahmadnagar and Golconda in a campaign against Bijapur. Tirumala accepted the new states of the Nayakas of the south, retained the allegiance of Mysore and Keladi, and appointed his three sons as governors of the three linguistic regions of his kingdom—Telugu, Kannada, and Tamil. In 1570 he had himself crowned and thus officially inaugurated the Aravidu dynasty, the fourth and last dynasty of Vijayanagar.

When Tirumala retired, his son Shriranga I (reigned 1572–85) tried to continue the process of rebuilding while struggling to maintain his place among the Muslim sultanates without any support from the major Telugu houses. An invasion by Bijapur was repulsed with the aid of Golconda, but subsequent invasions by Golconda resulted in the loss of a substantial amount of territory in the east. The Vijayanagar government relocated from Penukonda, which had sustained two sieges, to Chandragiri. Shriranga's difficulties stemmed partly from the lack of aid from his brothers, who ruled their separate regions, and partly from the dissensions of his nobles and the semi-independent status of some of them. Many nobles had apparently decided that it was no longer in their best interests to give full support to the larger state and that, in the absence of overwhelming power, the development of smaller subregional states was both possible and potentially more profitable.

Shriranga died childless and was succeeded by his younger brother Venkata II (reigned 1585–1614), whose ability and constant activity, combined with a relative dearth of interference by the Muslim sultanates, prevented the further disintegration of centralized authority over the next 28 years. A series of wars between 1580 and 1589 resulted in the reacquisition of some of the territory that had been lost to Golconda in the east and the eventual restoration of the Krishna River as Vijayanagar's northern boundary, but Venkata spent most of his time attempting to retain his hold over his rebellious chieftains and nobles. Most of the east and the Tamil south was in rebellion at one time or another; the most serious threat occurred in 1601, when the Nayakas of Madura, Tanjore, and Jinji came to the aid of the rebellious Lingama Nayaka of Vellore. Venkata defeated the Nayakas and later made Vellore his capital, but his authority was not restored

in the far south. The process of decentralization, although halted for a time, could not be reversed. In the northern areas that had been laid to waste by invading armies, Venkata undertook a program of restoration by offering lower revenue payments. His tact and firmness led to cordial relations with the Portuguese, who established a Jesuit mission in 1607. The Dutch were permitted to build a factory at Devapattana and a fort at Pulicat, notwithstanding Portuguese opposition to the latter. It would appear that by the time of his death in 1614 Venkata had accomplished enough so that a revival of imperial power and prosperity was possible, but instead rivalries among the nobility rapidly led to further decentralization and to the diminution of the state.

BREAKUP OF THE EMPIRE

Venkata's nephew and successor, Shriranga II, ruled for only four months. He was murdered, along with all but one of the members of his family, by one of the two contending parties of nobles. A long civil war resulted and finally degenerated into a series of smaller wars among a number of contending parties. The surviving member of the dynasty, Rama Deva Raya, finally ascended the throne in 1617. His reign was marked by factional warfare and the constant struggle to maintain a much-truncated kingdom along the eastern coast. Although some chieftains continued to recognize his nominal suzerainty and that of his successor, Venkata III (1630–42), real political power resided at the level of chieftains and provincial governors, who were carving out their own principalities. The fourth Vijayanagar dynasty had become little more than another competing provincial power.

Bijapur and Golconda took advantage of the decline in Vijayanagar's strength to make further inroads into the south, while Venkata III's own nephew Shriranga allied himself with Bijapur. Interestingly, it was Venkata who granted the Madraspatna fort to the English as the site for a factory (trading post). In 1642 an expedition from Golconda drove the king from his capital at Vellore. Hearing that his uncle was dying, Shriranga deserted Bijapur and had himself crowned. Although he was able to play Bijapur and Golconda against each other for a time, he could not gain control over the provincial Nayakas, who were by then virtually independent; and, when Bijapur and Golconda finally struck at the same time, Shriranga and the handful of chieftains who came to his aid were powerless to stop them. A last appeal to his Nayakas to come to the defense of Hinduism resulted instead in his defeat by their combined forces in 1645. Meanwhile, Bijapur and Golconda advanced, with the blessings of the Mughal emperor at Delhi, who had suggested that they should partition Karnataka between themselves. The Nayakas realized the danger too late, and by 1652 the Muslim sultans had completed their conquest of Karnataka. Shriranga retired to Mysore, where he kept an exile court until his death in 1672.

ADMINISTRATION OF THE EMPIRE

Vijayanagar was the first southern Indian state to have encompassed three major linguistic and cultural regions and to have established a high degree of political unity among them. The administration of the kingdom sporadically achieved a relatively high degree of centralization, although centrifugal tendencies regularly appeared. To the original five *rajyas* (provinces) held by the Sangama brothers, new ones were added as territories were acquired. Within and among these regions, a complex mosaic of great chiefly houses exercised power to varying degrees, though not with the virtual autonomy that some historians have suggested. The central administration had both a revenue and a military side, but the actual business of raising taxes and troops was mostly the responsibility of the provincial governors and their subordinates. The central government maintained a relatively small body of troops, but it assigned a value to the lands held by the provincial governors and determined the number of troops that were to be supplied from the revenues of each province. This administrative plan led to the development of the nayankara system, in which prominent commanders received land grants and privileged status, becoming Nayakas (local lords or governors). The system, which has been characterized as a kind of military feudalism, worked well enough when the central authority was strong but provided territorial bases for the

Elephant stables, Vijayanagar, Karnataka, India. Frederick M. Asher

Nayakas to build semi-independent hereditary holdings in times of imperial weakness. The imperial rulers were aware of the power of the provinces and tried to counter it by appointing members of the royal family as governors of the militarily more important (but not necessarily more lucrative) provinces. On the whole, however, the device was not successful, because succession rivalries, as in the Muslim kingdoms to the north, tended to produce filial disloyalty to the throne and even rebellion.

Although exact figures are unavailable, the evidence suggests that the level of taxation was close to half of the produce in many areas. Much of the revenue collected did not go to the state, however, because various layers of local landholders took their share first. Although most revenue came from agrarian taxes, commercial and artisan taxes and tributary duties from foreign traders were levied as well.

Under Vijayanagar rule, temples, which exhibited such singularly imperial features as huge enclosures and entrance gateways (*gopuras*), emerged as major political arenas. Monastic organizations (*mathas*) representing various religious traditions also became focal points of local authority, often closely linked with the Nayaka chieftaincies. A fairly elaborate and specialized administrative infrastructure underlay these diverse local and regional religio-political forms.

Vijayanagar the city was a symbol of vast power and wealth. It was a royal ceremonial and administrative centre and the nexus of trade routes. Foreign travelers and visitors were impressed by the variety and quality of commodities that reached the city, by the architectural grandeur of the palace complex and temples, and by the ceremonial significance of the annual Mahanavami celebrations, at which the Nayakas and other chiefs assembled to pay tribute.

Vijayanagar was, to some extent, consciously represented by its sovereigns as the last bastion of Hinduism against the forces of Islam. As with similar Muslim religio-political claims, however, this one often appeared to be more rhetorical than real. The shifting patterns of alliances among Vijayanagar and the sultanates, the occasions on which a rival party of nobles or a claimant to the throne of Vijayanagar would enlist the aid of a Muslim sultan, and the employment of both Hindus and Muslims in the sultanates and in Vijayanagar suggest that rivalries were more political than religious. The various progressive reforms of the Vijayanagar army suggest also that efforts were made to transform at least one aspect of the state in order to make it more competitive with its Muslim and other rivals.

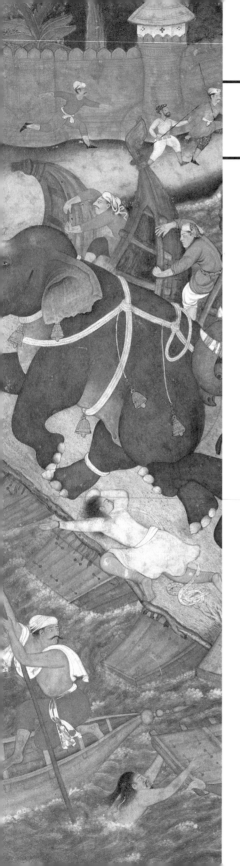

CHAPTER 6

THE MUGHAL EMPIRE, 1526–1761

The Mughal Empire at its zenith commanded resources unprecedented in Indian history and covered almost the entire subcontinent. From 1556 to 1707, during the heyday of its fabulous wealth and glory, the Mughal Empire was a fairly efficient and centralized organization, with a vast complex of personnel, money, and information dedicated to the service of the emperor and his nobility.

THE SIGNIFICANCE OF MUGHAL RULE

Much of the empire's expansion during that period was attributable to India's growing commercial and cultural contact with the outside world. The 16th and 17th centuries brought the establishment and expansion of European and non-European trading organizations in the subcontinent, principally for the procurement of Indian goods in demand abroad. Indian regions drew close to each other by means of an enhanced overland and coastal trading network, significantly augmenting the internal surplus of precious metals. With expanded connections to the wider world came also new ideologies and technologies to challenge and enrich the imperial edifice.

The empire itself, however, was a purely Indian historical experience. Mughal culture blended Perso-Islamic and regional Indian elements into a distinctive but variegated whole. Although by the early 18th century the regions had begun to reassert their independent positions, Mughal manners and ideals outlasted imperial central authority. The imperial centre, in fact, came to be controlled by the regions. The trajectory of the Mughal Empire over roughly its first two centuries (1526–1748) thus provides a fascinating illustration of premodern state building in the Indian subcontinent.

The individual abilities and achievements of the early Mughals—Bābur, Humāyūn, and later Akbar—largely charted this course. Bābur and Humāyūn struggled against heavy odds to create the Mughal domain, whereas Akbar, besides consolidating and expanding its frontiers, provided the theoretical framework for a truly Indian state. Picking up the thread of experimentation from the intervening Sūr dynasty (1540–56), Akbar attacked narrow-mindedness and bigotry, absorbed Hindus in the high ranks of the nobility, and encouraged the tradition of ruling through the local Hindu landed elites. This tradition continued until the very end of the Mughal Empire, despite the fact that some of Akbar's successors, notably Aurangzeb (1658–1707), had to concede to contrary forces.

THE ESTABLISHMENT OF THE MUGHAL EMPIRE

BĀBUR

The foundation of the empire was laid in 1526 by Ẓahīr al-Dīn Muḥammad Bābur, a Chagatai Turk (so called because his ancestral homeland, the country north of the Amu Darya [Oxus River] in Central Asia, was the heritage of Chagatai, the second son of Genghis Khan). Bābur was a fifth-generation descendant of Timur on the side of his father and a 14th-generation descendant of Genghis Khan. His idea of conquering India was inspired, to begin with, by the story of the exploits of Timur, who had invaded the subcontinent in 1398.

Bābur inherited his father's principality in Fergana at a young age, in 1494. Soon he was literally a fugitive, in the midst of both an internecine fight among the Timurids and a struggle between them and the rising Uzbeks over the erstwhile Timurid empire in the region. In 1504 he conquered Kabul and Ghaznī. In 1511 he recaptured Samarkand, only to realize that, with the formidable Ṣafavid dynasty in Iran and the Uzbeks in Central Asia, he should rather turn to the southeast toward India to have an empire of his own. As a Timurid, Bābur had an eye on the Punjab, part of which had been Timur's possession. He made several excursions in the tribal habitats there. Between 1519 and 1524—when he invaded Bhera, Sialkot, and Lahore—he showed his definite intention to conquer Hindustan, where the political scene favoured his adventure.

CONQUEST OF HINDUSTAN

Having secured the Punjab, Bābur advanced toward Delhi, garnering support from many Delhi nobles. He routed two advance parties of Ibrāhīm Lodī's troops and met the sultan's main army at Panipat. The Afghans fought bravely, but they had never faced new artillery, and their frontal attack was no answer to Bābur's superior arrangement of the battle line. Bābur's knowledge of western and Central Asian war tactics and his brilliant leadership proved decisive in his victory. By April 1526 he was in control of Delhi and Agra and held the keys to conquer Hindustan.

Bābur, however, had yet to encounter any of the several Afghans who held important towns in what is now eastern Uttar Pradesh and Bihar and who were backed by the sultan of Bengal in the east and the Rajputs on the southern borders. The Rajputs under Rana Sanga of Mewar threatened to revive their power in northern India. Bābur assigned the unconquered territories to his nobles and led an expedition himself against the rana in person. He crushed the rana's forces at Khanua, near Fatehpur Sikri (March 1527), once again by means of the skillful positioning of troops. Bābur then continued his campaigns to subjugate the Rajputs of Chanderi. When Afghan risings turned him to the east, he had to fight, among others, the joint forces of the Afghans and the sultan of Bengal in 1529 at Ghagra, near Varanasi. Bābur won the battles, but the expedition there too, like the one on the southern borders, was left unfinished. Developments in Central Asia and Bābur's failing health forced him to withdraw. He died near Lahore in December 1530.

BĀBUR'S ACHIEVEMENTS

Bābur's brief tenure in Hindustan, spent in wars and in his preoccupation with northwest and Central Asia, did not give him enough time to consolidate fully his conquests in India. Still, discernible in his efforts are the beginnings of the Mughal imperial organization and political culture. He introduced some Central Asian administrative institutions and, significantly, tried to woo the prominent local chiefs. He also established new mints in Lahore and Jaunpur and tried to ensure a safe and secure route from Agra to Kabul. He advised his son and successor, Humāyūn, to adopt a tolerant religious policy.

HUMĀYŪN

Humāyūn's rule began badly with his invasion of the Hindu principality of Kalinjar in Bundelkhand, which he failed to subdue. Next he became entangled in a quarrel with Sher (or Shīr) Khan (later Sher Shah of Sūr, founder of the Sūr dynasty), the new leader of the Afghans in the east, by unsuccessfully besieging the fortress of Chunar (1532). Thereafter he conquered Malwa and Gujarat, but he could not hold them. Leaving the fortress of Chunar unconquered on the way, Humāyūn proceeded to Bengal to assist Sultan Maḥmūd of that province against Sher Khan. He lost touch with Delhi and Agra, and, because his brother Hindal began to openly behave like an independent ruler at Agra, he was obliged to leave Gaur, the capital of Bengal. Negotiations with Sher Khan fell through, and the latter forced Humāyūn to fight a battle at Chausa, 10 miles (16 km) southwest of Buxar (Baksar; June 26, 1539), in which Humāyūn was defeated. He did not feel strong enough to defend Agra, and he retreated to Bilgram near Kannauj, where he fought his last battle with Sher Khan, who had now assumed the title of shah. Humāyūn was again defeated and was compelled to retreat to Lahore; he then fled from Lahore to the Sindh (or Sind) region, from Sindh to Rajputana, and from Rajputana back to Sindh. Not feeling secure even in Sindh, he fled (July 1543) to Iran to seek military assistance from its ruler, the Ṣafavid Shah Ṭahmāsp I. The shah agreed to assist him with an army on the condition that Humāyūn become a Shī'ite Muslim and return Kandahār, an important frontier town and commercial centre, to Iran in the event of his successful acquisition of that fortress.

Humāyūn had no answer to the political and military skill of Sher Shah and had to fight simultaneously on the southern borders to check the sultan of Gujarat, a refuge of the rebel Mughals. Humāyūn's failure, however, was attributable to inherent flaws in the early Mughal political organization. The armed clans of his nobility owed their first allegiance to their respective chiefs. These chiefs, together with almost all the male members of the royal family, had a claim to sovereignty. There was thus always a lurking fear of the emergence of another

centre of power, at least under one or the other of his brothers. Humāyūn also fought against the heavy odds of his opponents' rapport with the locality.

SHER SHAH AND HIS SUCCESSORS

During Humāyūn's exile Sher Shah established a vast and powerful empire and strengthened it with a wise system of administration. He carried out a new and equitable revenue settlement, greatly improved the administration of the districts and the parganas (groups of

Tomb of Sher Shah of Sūr, Sasaram, Bihar, India. Frederick M. Asher

villages), reformed the currency, encouraged trade and commerce, improved communication, and administered impartial justice.

Sher Shah died during the siege of Kalinjar (May 1545) and was succeeded by his son Islam Shah (ruled 1545–53). Islam Shah, preeminently a soldier, was less successful as a ruler than his father. Palace intrigues and insurrections marred his reign. On his death his young son, Fīrūz, came to the Sūr throne but was murdered by his own maternal uncle, and subsequently the empire fractured into several parts.

RESTORATION OF HUMĀYŪN

After his return to Kabul from Iran, Humāyūn watched the situation in India. He had been preparing since the death of Islam Shah to recover his throne. Following the capture of Kandahār and Kabul from his brothers, he had reasserted his unique royal position and assembled his own nobles. In December 1554 he crossed the Indus River and marched to Lahore, which he captured without opposition the following February. Humāyūn occupied Sirhind and captured Delhi and Agra in July 1555. He thus regained the throne of Delhi after an interval of 12 years, but he did not live long enough to recover the whole of the lost empire; he died as the result of an accident in Shermandal in Delhi (January 1556). His death was concealed for about a fortnight to enable the peaceful accession of his son Akbar, who was away at the time in the Punjab.

THE REIGN OF AKBAR THE GREAT

Akbar (ruled 1556–1605) was proclaimed emperor amid gloomy circumstances. Delhi and Agra were threatened by Hemu—the Hindu general of the Sūr ruler, 'Ādil Shah—and Mughal governors were being driven from all parts of northern India. Akbar's hold over a fraction of the Punjab—the only territory in his possession—was disputed by Sikandar Sūr and was precarious. There was also disloyalty among Akbar's own followers.

EXTENSION AND CONSOLIDATION OF THE EMPIRE

The task before Akbar was to reconquer the empire and consolidate it by ensuring control over its frontiers and, moreover, by providing it with a firm administrative machinery. He received unstinting support from the regent, Bayram Khan, until 1560. The Mughal victory at Panipat (November 1556) and the subsequent recovery of Mankot, Gwalior, and Jaunpur demolished the Afghan threat in upper India.

THE EARLY YEARS

Until 1560 the administration of Akbar's truncated empire was in the hands of Bayram Khan. Bayram's regency was

Agra fort, built by Akbar the Great, in Uttar Pradesh state, India. Frederick M. Asher

momentous in the history of India. At its end the Mughal dominion embraced the whole of the Punjab, the territory of Delhi, what are now the states of Uttar Pradesh and Uttarakhand in the north (as far as Jaunpur in the east), and large tracts of what is now Rajasthan in the west.

Akbar, however, soon became restless under Bayram Khan's tutelage. Influenced by his former wet nurse, Maham Anaga, and his mother, Ḥamīdah Bānū Begam, he was persuaded to dismiss him (March 1560). Four ministers of mediocre ability then followed in quick succession. Although not yet his own master, Akbar took a few momentous steps during that period. He conquered Malwa (1561) and marched rapidly to Sarangpur to punish Adham Khan, the captain in charge of the expedition, for improper conduct. Second, he appointed Shams al-Dīn Muḥammad Atgah Khan as prime minister (November 1561). Third, at about the same time, he took possession of Chunar, which had always defied Humāyūn.

The most momentous events of 1562 were Akbar's marriage to a Rajput princess, daughter of Raja Bharmal of Amber, and the conquest of Merta in Rajasthan. The marriage led to a firm alliance between the Mughals and the Rajputs.

By the end of June 1562, Akbar had freed himself completely from the influence of the harem party, headed by Maham Anaga, her son Adham Khan, and some other ambitious courtiers. The harem leaders murdered the prime minister, Atgah Khan, who was then succeeded by Mun'im Khan.

From about the middle of 1562, Akbar took upon himself the great task of shaping his policies, leaving them to be implemented by his agents. He embarked on a policy of conquest, establishing control over Jodhpur, Bhatha (present-day Rewa), and the Gakkhar country between the Indus and Beas rivers in the Punjab. Next he made inroads into Gondwana. During this period he ended discrimination against the Hindus by abolishing pilgrimage taxes in 1563 and the hated *jizyah* (poll tax on non-Muslims) in 1564.

STRUGGLE FOR FIRM PERSONAL CONTROL

Akbar thus commanded the entire area of Humāyūn's Indian possessions. By the mid-1560s he had also developed a new pattern of king-noble relationship that suited the current need of a centralized state to be defended by a nobility of diverse ethnic and religious groups. He insisted on assessing the arrears of the territories under the command of the old Tūrānī (Central Asian) clans and, in order to strike a balance in the ruling class, promoted the Persians (Irānī), the Indian Muslims, and the Rajputs in the imperial service. Akbar placed eminent clan leaders in charge of frontier areas and staffed the civil and finance departments with relatively new non-Tūrānī recruits. The revolts in 1564–74 by the members of the old guard—the Uzbeks, the Mirzās, the Qāqshāls, and the Atgah Khails—showed the intensity of their indignation over the change. Utilizing the Muslim orthodoxy's resentment over Akbar's liberal views, they organized their last resistance in 1580. The rebels proclaimed Akbar's half-brother, Mirzā Ḥakīm, the ruler of Kabul, and he moved into the Punjab as their king. Akbar crushed the opposition ruthlessly.

SUBJUGATION OF RAJASTHAN

Rajasthan occupied a prominent place in Akbar's scheme of conquest; without establishing his suzerainty over that region, he would have no title to the sovereignty of northern India. Rajasthan also bordered on Gujarat, a centre of commerce with the countries of western Asia and Europe. In 1567 Akbar invaded Chitor, the capital of Mewar; in February 1568 the fort fell into his hands. Chitor was constituted a district, and Āṣaf Khan was appointed its governor. But the western half of Mewar remained in the possession of Rana Udai Singh. Later, his son Rana Pratap Singh, following his defeat by the Mughals at Haldighat (1576), continued to raid until his death in 1597, when his son Amar Singh assumed the mantle. The fall of Chitor and then of Ranthambor (1569) brought almost all of Rajasthan under Akbar's suzerainty.

CONQUEST OF GUJARAT AND BENGAL

Akbar's next objective was the conquest of Gujarat and Bengal, which had connected Hindustan with the trading world of Asia, Africa, and Europe. Gujarat had lately been a haven of the refractory Mughal nobles, and in Bengal and Bihar the Afghans under Dā'ūd Karrānī still posed a serious threat. Akbar conquered Gujarat at his second attempt in 1573 and celebrated by building a victory gate, the lofty Buland Darwāza ("High Gate"), at his new capital, Fatehpur Sikri. The conquest of Gujarat pushed the Mughal Empire's frontiers to the sea. Akbar's encounters with the Portuguese aroused his curiosity about their religion and culture. He did not show much interest in what was taking place overseas, but he appreciated the political and commercial

Buland Darwāza ("High Gate"), built during the reign of Akbar the Great, in Fatehpur Sikri, Uttar Pradesh state, India. Frederick M. Asher

significance of bringing the other gateway to his empire's international trade—namely, Bengal—under his firm control. He was in Patna in 1574, and by July 1576 Bengal was a part of the empire, even if some local chiefs continued to agitate for some years more. Later, Man Singh, governor of Bihar, also annexed Orissa and thus consolidated the Mughal gains in the east.

THE FRONTIERS

On the northwest frontier Kabul, Kandahār, and Ghaznī were not simply strategically significant; these towns linked India through overland trade with central and western Asia and were crucial for securing horses for the Mughal cavalry. Akbar strengthened his grip over these outposts in the 1580s and 1590s.

Following Hakīm's death and a threatened Uzbek invasion, Akbar brought Kabul under his direct control. To demonstrate his strength, the Mughal army paraded through Kashmir, Baluchistan, Sindh, and the various tribal districts of the region. In 1595, before his return, Akbar wrested Kandahār from the Ṣafavids, thus fixing the northwestern frontiers. In the east, Man Singh stabilized the Mughal gains by annexing Orissa, Cooch Behar, and a large part of Bengal. Conquest of Kathiawar and later of Asirgarh and the northern territory of the Niẓām Shāhī kingdom of Ahmadnagar ensured a firm command over Gujarat and central India. At Akbar's death in

October 1605, the Mughal Empire extended to the entire area north of the Godavari River, with the exceptions of Gondwana in central India and Assam in the northeast.

THE STATE AND SOCIETY UNDER AKBAR

More than for its military victories, the empire under Akbar is noted for a sound administrative framework and a coherent policy that gave the Mughal regime a firm footing and sustained it for about 150 years.

CENTRAL, PROVINCIAL, AND LOCAL GOVERNMENT

Akbar's central government consisted of four departments, each presided over by a minister: the prime minister (*wakīl*), the finance minister (*dīwān*, or vizier [*wazīr*]), the paymaster general (*mīr bakhshī*), and the chief justice and religious official combined (*ṣadr al-ṣudūr*). They were appointed, promoted, and dismissed by the emperor, and their duties were well defined.

The empire was divided into 15 provinces (subahs)—Allahabad, Agra, Ayodhya (Avadh), Ajmer, Ahmedabad (Ahmadabad), Bihar, Bengal, Delhi, Kabul, Lahore, Multan, Malka, Qhandesh, Berar, and Ahmadnagar. Kashmir and Kandahār were districts of the province of Kabul. Sindh, then known as Thatta, was a district in the province of Multan.

Orissa formed a part of Bengal. The provinces were not of uniform area or income. There were in each province a governor, a *dīwān*, a *bakhshī* (military commander), a *ṣadr* (religious administrator), and a *qāḍī* (judge) and agents who supplied information to the central government. Separation of powers among the various officials (in particular, between the governor and the *dīwān*) was a significant operating principle in imperial administration.

The provinces were divided into districts (*sarkārs*). Each district had a *fowjdār* (a military officer whose duties roughly corresponded to those of a collector); a *qāḍī*; a *kotwāl*, who looked after sanitation, the police, and the administration; a *bitikchī* (head clerk); and a *khazānedār* (treasurer).

Every town of consequence had a kotwāl. The village communities conducted their affairs through *pancayats* (councils) and were more or less autonomous units.

THE COMPOSITION OF THE |MUGHAL NOBILITY

Within the first three decades of Akbar's reign, the imperial elite had grown enormously. As the Central Asian nobles had generally been nurtured on the Turko-Mongol tradition of sharing power with the royalty—an arrangement incompatible with Akbar's ambition of structuring the Mughal centralism around himself—the emperor's principal

goal was to reduce their strength and influence. The emperor encouraged new elements to join his service, and Iranians came to form an important block of the Mughal nobility. Akbar also looked for new men of Indian background. Indian Afghans, being the principal opponents of the Mughals, were obviously to be kept at a distance, but the Sayyids of Baraha, the Bukhārī Sayyids, and the Kambūs among the Indian Muslims were specially favoured for high military and civil positions. More significant was the recruitment of Hindu Rajput leaders into the Mughal nobility. This was a major step, even if not completely new in Indo-Islamic history, leading to a standard pattern of relationship between the

The Dīwān-e Khass at Fatehpur Sikri, Uttar Pradesh state, India, built c. 1585. P. Chandra

Mughal autocracy and the local despotism. Each Rajput chief, along with his sons and close relatives, received high rank, pay, perquisites, and an assurance that they could retain their age-old customs, rituals, and beliefs as Hindu warriors. In return the Rajputs not only publicly expressed their allegiance but also offered active military service to the Mughals and, if called upon to do so, willingly gave daughters in marriage to the emperor or his sons. The Rajput chiefs retained control over their ancestral holdings and additionally, in return for their services, received *watans* (land assignments outside their homelands) in the empire. The Mughal emperor, however, asserted his right as a "paramount." He treated the Rajput chiefs as *zamindars* (landholders), not as rulers. Like all local *zamindars*, they paid tribute, submitted to the Mughals, and received a patent of office. Akbar thus obtained a wide base for Mughal power among thousands of Rajput warriors who controlled large and small parcels of the countryside throughout much of his empire.

The Mughal nobility came to comprise mainly the Central Asians (Tūrānīs), Iranians (Irānīs), Afghans, Indian Muslims of diverse subgroups, and Rajputs. Both historical circumstances and a planned imperial policy contributed to the integration of this complex and heterogeneous ruling class into a single imperial service. The emperor saw to it that no single ethnic or religious group was large enough to challenge his supreme authority.

ORGANIZATION OF THE NOBILITY AND THE ARMY

In order to organize his civil and military personnel, Akbar devised a system of ranks, or manṣabs, based on the "decimal" system of army organization used by the early Delhi sultans and the Mongols. The *manṣabdārs* (rank holders) were numerically graded from commanders of 10 to commanders of 5,000. Although they fell under the jurisdiction of the *mīr bakhshī*, each owed direct subordination to the emperor.

The *manṣabdārs* were generally paid in nonhereditary and transferable *jāgīrs* (assignments of land from which they could collect revenues). Over their *jāgīrs*, as distinct from those areas reserved for the emperor (*khāliṣah*) and his personal army (*aḥadīs*), the assignees (*jāgīrdārs*) normally had no magisterial or military authority. Akbar's insistence on a regular check of the manṣabdārs' soldiers and their horses signified his desire for a reasonable correlation between his income and obligations. Most *jāgīrdārs* except the lowest-ranking ones collected the taxes through their personal agents, who were assisted by the local moneylenders and currency dealers in remitting collections by means of private bills of exchange rather than cash shipments.

REVENUE SYSTEM

A remarkable feature of the Mughal system under Akbar was his revenue administration, developed largely under the supervision of his famed Hindu minister Todar Mal. Akbar's efforts to develop a revenue schedule both convenient to the peasants and sufficiently profitable to the state took some two decades to implement. In 1580 he obtained the previous 10 years' local revenue statistics, detailing productivity and price fluctuations, and averaged the produce of different crops and their prices. He also evolved a permanent schedule circle by grouping together the districts having homogeneous agricultural conditions. For measuring land area, he abandoned the use of hemp rope in favour of a more definitive method using lengths of bamboo joined with iron rings. The revenue, fixed according to the continuity of cultivation and quality of soil, ranged from one-third to one-half of production value and was payable in copper coin (*dāms*). The peasants thus had to enter the market and sell their produce in order to meet the assessment. This system, called *ẓabṭ*, was applied in northern India and in Malwa and parts of Gujarat. The earlier practices (e.g., crop sharing), however, also were in vogue in the empire. The new system encouraged rapid economic expansion. Moneylenders and grain dealers became increasingly active in the countryside.

FISCAL ADMINISTRATION

All economic matters fell under the jurisdiction of the vizier, assisted principally by three ministers to look separately after the crown lands, the salary drafts and *jāgīrs*, and the records of fiscal transactions. At almost all levels, the revenue and financial administration was run by a cadre of technically proficient officials and clerks drawn mainly from Hindu service castes—Kayasthas and Khatris.

More significantly, in local and land revenue administration, Akbar secured support from the dominant rural groups. With the exception of the villages held directly by the peasants, where the community paid the revenue, his officials dealt with the leaders of the communities and the superior landrights holders (zamindars). The zamindar, as one of the most important intermediaries, collected the revenue from the peasants and paid it to the treasury, keeping a portion to himself against his services and zamindari claim over the land.

COINAGE

Akbar reformed Mughal currency to make it one of the best known of its time. The new regime possessed a fully functioning trimetallic (silver, copper, and gold) currency, with an open minting system in which anyone willing to pay the minting charges could bring metal or old or foreign coin to the mint and have it struck. All monetary exchanges, however, were expressed in copper coins in Akbar's time. In the 17th century, following the silver influx from the New World, silver rupee with new fractional denominations replaced the copper coin as a common medium of circulation. Akbar's aim was to establish a uniform coinage throughout his empire; some coins of the old regime and regional kingdoms also continued.

EVOLUTION OF A
NONSECTARIAN STATE

Mughal society was predominantly non-Muslim. Akbar therefore had not simply to maintain his status as a Muslim ruler but also to be liberal enough to elicit active support from non-Muslims. For that purpose, he had to deal first with the Muslim theologians and lawyers (*'ulamā'*) who, in the face of Brahmanic resilience, were rightly concerned with the community's identity and resisted any effort that could encourage a broader notion of political participation. Akbar began his drive by abolishing both the *jizyah* and the practice of forcibly converting prisoners of war to Islam and by encouraging Hindus as his principal confidants and policy makers. To legitimize his nonsectarian policies, he issued in 1579 a public edict (*mahzar*) declaring his right to be the supreme arbiter in Muslim religious matters—above the body of Muslim religious scholars and jurists. He had by then also undertaken a number of stern measures to reform the administration of religious grants, which were now available to learned and pious men of all religions, not just Islam.

The *mahzar* was proclaimed in the wake of lengthy discussions that Akbar had held with Muslim divines in his famous religious assembly 'Ibādat-Khāneh, at Fatehpur Sikri. He soon became dissatisfied with what he considered the shallowness of Muslim learned men and threw open the meetings to non-Muslim religious experts, including Hindu pandits, Jain and Christian missionaries, and Parsi priests. A comparative study of religions convinced Akbar that there was truth in all of them but that no one of them possessed absolute truth. He therefore disestablished Islam as the religion of the state and adopted a theory of rulership as a divine illumination incorporating the acceptance of all, irrespective of creed or sect. He repealed discriminatory laws against non-Muslims and amended the personal laws of both Muslims and Hindus so as to provide as many common laws as possible. While Muslim judicial courts were allowed as before, the decision of the Hindu village pancayats also was recognized. The emperor created a new order commonly called the Dīn-e Ilāhī ("Divine Faith"), which was modeled on the Muslim mystical Sufi brotherhood. The new order had its own initiation ceremony and rules of conduct to ensure complete devotion to the emperor; otherwise, members were permitted to retain their diverse religious beliefs and practices. It was devised with the object of forging the diverse groups in the service of the state into one cohesive political community.

AKBAR IN HISTORICAL PERSPECTIVE

By 1600 the Mughals in India had achieved a fairly austere and efficient state system, for which Akbar's genius deserves much credit. However, the Mughal system must be studied in the context of broad historical developments of the 16th and 17th centuries. Long before Akbar's schemes, Sher Shah of Sūr's short-lived reforms had included demand for cash payment from the peasants, surveys of agricultural lands and of crops grown, and a reliable, standardized, and high-quality coinage. The Sūr ruler insisted on a uniform rate for the entire empire, which was certainly a major flaw in contrast to Akbar's consideration for regional variations. It is striking, however, that the chief *zabt* territories under Akbar were largely made up of the provinces already controlled by Sher Shah.

Another major development of Sher Shah's brief period—namely, the building of a network of roads to improve the connections already started by Bābur between Hindustan and the great trading routes extending into central and western Asia via Kabul and Kandahār—foreshadowed in a measure the later imperial edifice and economy. By laying a road between Sonargaon (in Bengal) and Attock (near present-day Rawalpindi, Pak.), the Sūr ruler had made a first attempt at bringing the economy of Bengal into closer contact with that of northern India. The expansion under Akbar followed in logical sequence

what had already occurred. The network based on Sher Shah's routes had extended considerably by 1600. Agra came to be linked not only to Burhanpur but also to Cambay, Surat, and Ahmedabad. Lahore and Multan were now the gateway to Kabul as well as to the ports of the mouth of the Indus. The link with Sonargaon became a far more secure control over the ports of Bengal. Many other changes initiated in the late 16th century were to be consolidated only later, in conjunction with further political unification.

THE EMPIRE IN THE 17TH CENTURY

The Mughal Empire in the 17th century continued its conquest and territorial expansion, with a dramatic increase in the numbers, resources, and responsibilities of the Mughal nobles and *manṣabdārs*. There were also attempts at tightening imperial control over the local society and economy. The critical relationship between the imperial authority and the zamindars was regularized and generally institutionalized through thousands of *sanads* (patents) issued by the emperor and his agents. These centralizing measures imposed increasing demands upon both the Mughal officials and the local magnates and therefore generated tensions expressed in various forms of resistance. The century witnessed the rule of the three greatest Mughal emperors: Jahāngīr (ruled 1605–27), Shah Jahān (1628–58), and Aurangzeb (1658–1707).

The reigns of Jahāngīr and Shah Jahān are noted for political stability, brisk economic activity, excellence in painting, and magnificent architecture. The empire under Aurangzeb attained its greatest geographic reach; however, the period also saw the unmistakable symptoms of Mughal decline.

Political unification and the establishment of law and order over extensive areas, together with extensive foreign trade and the ostentatious lifestyles of the Mughal elites, encouraged the emergence of large centres of commerce and crafts. Lahore, Delhi, Agra, and Ahmedabad, linked by roads and waterways to other important towns and the key seaports, were among the leading cities of the world at the time. The Mughal system of taxation had expanded both the degree of monetization and commodity production, which in turn promoted a network of grain markets (*mandīs*), bazaars, and small fortified towns (*qaṣbahs*), supplied by a highly differentiated peasantry in the countryside.

Increasing use of money was illustrated, in the first place, by the growing use of bills of exchange (*hundīs*) to transfer revenue to the centre from the provinces and the consequent meshing of the fiscal system with the financial network of the money changers (ṣarrāfs; commonly rendered "shroff" in English) and, second, by the increasing interest of and even direct participation by the Mughal nobles and the emperor in trade. Thatta, Lahore, Hugli, and Surat were great centres for such activity in the

1640s and 1650s. The emperor owned the shipping fleets, and the governors advanced funds to merchants from state treasuries and the mints.

The shift in the attitude toward trade in the course of the 17th century owed a good deal to the growing Iranian influence in the Mughal court. The Iranians had a long tradition of combining

The feast of Nōrūz at Jahāngīr's court, painting in the Mughal miniature style, early 17th century. P. Chandra

political power and trade. Shah ʿAbbās I had espoused greater state control of commerce. Because the contemporary Muslim empires—including the Mughals, the Ṣafavids, and the Ottomans—were conscious of one another as competitors, mutual borrowings and emulations were more frequent than the chroniclers would indicate.

JAHĀNGĪR

Within a few months of his accession, Jahāngīr had to deal with a rebellion led by his eldest son, Khusraw, who was reportedly supported by, among others, the Sikh Guru Arjun. Khusraw was defeated at Lahore and was brought in chains before the emperor. The subsequent execution of the Sikh Guru permanently estranged the Sikhs from the Mughals.

Khusraw's rebellion led to a few more risings, which were suppressed without much difficulty. Shah ʿAbbās I of Iran, taking advantage of the unrest, besieged the fort of Kandahār (1606) but abandoned the attack when Jahāngīr promptly sent an army against him.

LOSS OF KANDAHĀR

In 1622 Shah ʿAbbās again attacked Kandahār, and Prince Khurram (later Shah Jahān) was directed to relieve that fortress. However, the prince was planning a rebellion against his father and failed to take effective action. The fortress fell after a 45-day siege. Shah ʿAbbās justified its capture on the plea that it belonged to Iran. Jahāngīr accused the shah of treachery and sent forces to recover the fortress. This effort failed, owing to Shah Jahān's rebellion and the illness and death of Jahāngīr himself. The loss of Kandahār was a grievous blow to the prestige of the empire. Jahāngīr, however, commanded full control over Kabul, having reinforced it now by inducting the Afghans under Khan Jahān Lodī into the Mughal nobility. Khan Jahān had close connections with the tribesmen in the northwestern frontiers.

SUBMISSION OF MEWAR

Jahāngīr's most significant political achievement was the cessation of the Mughal-Mewar conflict, following three consecutive campaigns and his own arrival in Ajmer in 1613. Prince Khurram was given the supreme command of the army (1613), and Jahāngīr marched to be near the scene of action. The Rana Amar Singh then initiated negotiations (1615). He recognized Jahāngīr as his suzerain, and all his territory in Mughal possession was restored, including Chitor—although it could not be fortified. Amar Singh was not obliged to attend the imperial court, but his son was to represent him; nor was he required to enter into a matrimonial alliance with the Mughal royal family. Further, the Rajput rulers of Kangra, Kishtwar (in Kashmir), Navanagar, and Kutch (Kachchh; in western India) accepted the Mughal supremacy. Bir Singh Bundela was given a high rank, and a Bundela princess entered the Mughal harem. Also significant was the subjugation of the last Afghan domains in eastern Bengal (1612) and Orissa (1617).

DEVELOPMENTS IN THE DECCAN

Toward the last years of Akbar's reign, the Niz̤ām Shāhīs of Ahmadnagar in the Deccan had engaged the attention of the emperor considerably. The main objective of his intervention in Ahmadnagar was to gain Berar, which had been recently acquired by Ahmadnagar from Khandesh, and Balaghat, which had been a bone of contention between Ahmadnagar and Gujarat. By 1596 Berar was conquered and Ahmadnagar had accepted Mughal suzerainty. However, the issue of a clearly defined frontier could not be resolved, and Mughal attacks continued. Under Jahāngīr the rise of Malik 'Ambār, a Habshi (Abyssinian) general of unusual ability, at the Ahmadnagar court and his alliance with the 'Ādil Shāhīs of Bijapur cemented a united front of the Deccan sultanates and initially forced the Mughals to retreat.

At this time the Marathas also had emerged as a force in the Deccan. Jahāngīr appreciated their importance and encouraged many Marathas to defect to his side (1615). Later, two successive Mughal victories against the combined Deccani armies (1618 and 1620) restrained the Habshi general. However, the Deccan expedition remained unfinished as a result of the rise to power of the emperor's favourite queen, Nūr Jahān, and her relatives and associates. The queen's alleged efforts to secure the prince of her choice as successor to the ailing emperor resulted in the rebellion of Prince Khurram in 1622 and later of Mahābat Khan, the queen's principal ally, who had been deputed to subdue the prince.

REBELLION OF KHURRAM (SHAH JAHĀN)

After failing to take Fatehpur Sikri in April 1623, Khurram retreated to the Deccan, then to Bengal, and from Bengal back again to the Deccan, pursued all the while by an imperial force under Mahābat Khan. His plan to seize Bihar, Ayodhya, Allahabad, and even Agra failed. At last Khurram submitted to his father unconditionally (1626). He was forgiven and appointed governor of Balaghat, but the three-year-old rebellion had caused a considerable loss of men and money.

Mahābat Khan Mosque, Peshawar, Pak. Frederic Ohringer—Nancy Palmer Agency/EB Inc.

MAHĀBAT KHAN'S COUP

Immediately upon the conclusion of peace with Khurram, the imperious queen decided to punish Mahābat Khan for his refusal to take orders from anyone but Jahāngīr. She ordered Mahābat Khan to Bengal and framed charges of disloyalty and disobedience against him. Instead of complying, he proceeded to the Punjab, where the emperor was encamped. Jahāngīr refused to see him. Mahābat Khan placed both the emperor

Detail from The Emperor Shah Jahan, *oil painting by Bichitr, 1631.* Courtesy of the Victoria and Albert Museum, London; photographs, EB Inc.

and the queen under surveillance, but he was finally overcome. The ordeal greatly impaired the emperor's health, and he died in November 1627.

SHAH JAHĀN

On his accession, Khurram assumed the title Shah Jahān (ruled 1628–58). Shahryār, his younger and only surviving brother, had contested the throne but was soon blinded and imprisoned. Under Shah Jahān's instructions, his father-in-law, Āsaf Khan, slew all other royal princes, the potential rivals for the throne. Āsaf Khan was appointed prime minister, and Nūr Jahān was given an adequate pension.

THE DECCAN PROBLEM

Shah Jahān's reign was marred by a few rebellions, the first of which was that of Khan Jahān Lodī, governor of the Deccan. Khan Jahān was recalled to court after failing to recover Balaghat from Ahmadnagar. However, he rose in rebellion and fled back to the Deccan. Shah Jahān followed, and in December 1629 he defeated Khan Jahān and drove him to the north, ultimately overtaking and killing him in a skirmish at Shihonda (January 1631).

The next rebellion was led by Jujhar Singh, a Hindu chief of Orchha, in Bundelkhand, who commanded the crucial passage to the Deccan. Jujhar was compelled to submit after his kinsman Bharat Singh defected and joined the

Mughals. His refusal to comply with subsequent conditions led, after a protracted conflict, to his defeat and murder (1634). Unrest in the region persisted.

The chronic volatility of the Deccan prompted Shah Jahān to seek a comprehensive solution. His first step was to offer a military alliance to Bijapur, with the objective of partitioning troublesome Ahmadnagar. The result was both the total annihilation of the province and the accord of 1636, by which Bijapur was granted one-third of its southern territories. The accord reconciled the Deccan states to a pervasive Mughal presence in the Deccan. Bijapur agreed not to interfere with Golconda, which became a tacit ally of the Mughals. The treaty limited further Mughal advance in the Deccan and gave Bijapur and Golconda respite to conquer the warring Hindu principalities in the south. Within a span of a dozen years, Bijapuri and Golcondan armies overran and annexed a vast and prosperous tract beyond the Krishna River up to Thanjavur and including Karnataka. The Mughals, on the other hand, maneuvered to regain Kandahār (1638) and consolidated and extended their eastern position on the Assamese border (1639) and also in Bengal, where Shah Jahān had become involved in a dispute over Portuguese piracy and abduction of Mughal slaves. In 1648 he moved his capital from Agra to Delhi in an effort to consolidate his control over the northwestern provinces of the empire.

The Mughal attitude of benevolent neutrality toward the Deccan states began to change gradually after 1648, culminating in the invasion of Golconda and Bijapur in 1656 and 1657. A factor in this change was the inability of the Mughals to manage the financial affairs of the Deccan. Subsequently, Bijapur was compelled to surrender the Ahmadnagar areas it had received in 1636, and Golconda was to cede to the Mughals the rich and fertile tract on the Coromandel Coast as part of the *jāgīr* of Mīr Jumla, the famous Golconda vizier who had now joined the Mughal service. To a great extent Shah Jahān's new policy in the Deccan also was propelled by commercial considerations. The entire area had acquired an added value because of the growing importance of the Coromandel Coast as the centre for the export of textiles and indigo.

CENTRAL ASIAN POLICY

Following in the footsteps of his predecessors, Shah Jahān hoped to conquer Samarkand, the original homeland of his ancestors. The brother of Emām Qulī, ruler of Samarkand, invaded Kabul and in 1639 captured Bamiyan, which gave offense to Shah Jahān. The emperor was on the lookout for an opportunity to move his army to the northwest borders. In 1646 he responded to the Uzbek ruler's appeal for aid in settling an internal dispute by sending a huge army. The campaign cost the Mughals heavily. They suffered serious initial setbacks in Balkh, and, before they could recover fully, an alliance between the Uzbeks and the shah

TAJ MAHAL

The Taj Mahal is a mausoleum complex on the southern bank of the Yamuna River, outside Agra, India. It was built by the Mughal emperor Shah Jahān in memory of his wife, Mumtāz Maḥal, who died in 1631. The Taj complex, begun c. 1632, took 22 years to complete.

At its centre lies a square garden area bounded by two smaller, oblong sections, one comprising the mausoleum and the other an entrance gateway. The mausoleum, of pure-white marble inlaid with semiprecious stones, is flanked by two red sandstone buildings, a mosque on

one side and an identical building for aesthetic balance on the other. It stands on a high marble plinth with a minaret at each corner. It has four identical facades, each with a massive central arch 108 feet (33 metres) high, and is surmounted by a bulbous double dome and four domed kiosks.

Its interior, with fine, restrained stone decoration, centres on an octagonal chamber containing the marble tombs, enclosed by a perforated marble screen, with sarcophagi below. Regarded as one of the world's most beautiful buildings, it was designated a UNESCO World Heritage site in 1983. Steps have been taken since the late 1990s to reduce air pollution that has damaged the facade of the building.

The Taj Mahal in Agra, India, one of the world's great architectural masterpieces. Brand X Pictures/Jupiterimages

of Iran complicated the situation. Kandahār was again taken by Iran, even though the Mughals reinforced their hold over the other frontier towns.

WAR OF SUCCESSION

The events at the end of Shah Jahān's reign did not augur well for the future of the empire. The emperor fell ill in September 1657, and rumours of his death spread. He executed a will bequeathing the empire to his eldest son, Dārā. His other sons, Shujā', Aurangzeb, and Murād, who were grown men and governors of provinces, decided to contest the throne. From the war of succession in 1657–59 Aurangzeb emerged the sole victor. He then imprisoned his father in the Agra fort and declared himself emperor.

Shah Jahān died a prisoner on Feb. 1, 1666, at the age of 74. He was, on the whole, a tolerant and enlightened ruler, patronizing scholars and poets of Sanskrit and Hindi as well as Persian. He systematized the administration, but he raised the government's share of the gross produce of the soil. Fond of pomp and magnificence, he commissioned the casting of the famous Peacock Throne and erected many elegant buildings, including the dazzling Taj Mahal outside Agra, a tomb for his queen, Mumtāz Maḥal; his remains also are interred there.

AURANGZEB

The empire under Aurangzeb (ruled 1658–1707) experienced further growth but also manifested signs of weakness. For more than a decade, Aurangzeb appeared to be in full control. The Mughals suffered a bit in Assam and Cooch Behar, but they gainfully invaded Arakanese lands in coastal Myanmar (Burma), captured Chittagong, and added territories in Bikaner, Bundelkhand, Palamau, Assam, and elsewhere. There was the usual display of wealth and grandeur at court.

LOCAL AND PEASANT UPRISINGS

Soon, however, regional disturbances again rocked the empire. The Jat peasantry of Mathura rebelled in 1669; the tribal Pathans plundered the northwestern border districts and caravan routes, declaring war on Aurangzeb in 1667 and again in 1672; a rising occurred among the Satnami sect in Narnaul in 1672; and the Sikhs in the Punjab revolted under their Guru Tegh Bahadur, who was brutally put to death in 1675. The most prolonged uprising, however, was the Rajput rebellion, sparked by Aurangzeb's annexation of the Jodhpur state and his seizure of its ruler's posthumous son Ajit Singh with the alleged intention of converting him to Islam. This rebellion spread to Mewar, and Aurangzeb himself had to proceed to Ajmer to fight the Rajputs, who had been joined by the emperor's third son, Akbar (January 1681). By a stratagem, Aurangzeb managed to isolate Akbar, who fled to the Deccan and thence to Persia. The war with Mewar came to an end (June 1681) because Aurangzeb had to pursue Akbar to the Deccan, where the prince had joined the Maratha king Sambhaji. Jodhpur remained in a state of rebellion for 27 years more, and Ajit Singh occupied his ancestral dominion immediately after Aurangzeb's death.

Aurangzeb spent the last 25 years of his reign in the Deccan. Upon his arrival in the region in 1681, he attempted to cut off the Hindu Marathas from Muslim Bijapur and Golconda, which were, as a result of earlier Mughal offensives, similarly predisposed against Aurangzeb. Failing in this effort, the emperor invaded and annexed Bijapur (1686) and Golconda (1687) with the objective of conquering the Marathas outright, which he achieved, in his own estimation, by capturing and executing Sambhaji. Maratha resistance proved so stubborn, however, that even after nearly two decades of struggle Aurangzeb failed to completely subdue them (see below). The aged emperor died on March 3, 1707.

ASSESSMENT OF AURANGZEB

Aurangzeb possessed natural gifts of a high order. He had assiduously cultivated learning, self-knowledge, self-esteem, and self-control. He was extremely industrious, methodical, and disciplined in habits and thoughts, and his private life was virtuous. However, his religious bigotry made him ill-suited to rule the mixed population of his empire.

Aurangzeb deliberately reversed the policy of his predecessors toward non-Muslim subjects by trying to enforce the principles and practices of the Islamic state. He reimposed the *jizyah* on non-Muslims and saddled them with religious, social, and legal disabilities. To begin with, he forbade their building new temples and repairing old ones. Next, he issued orders to demolish all the schools and temples of the Hindus and to put down their teaching and religious practices. He doubled the customs duties on the Hindus and abolished them altogether in the case of Muslims. He granted stipends and gifts to converts from Hinduism and offered them posts in public service, liberation from prison in the case of convicted criminals, and succession of disputed estates. He also persecuted some Shī'ites and Sufis, who veered from his strict interpretation of Muslim orthodoxy.

All these efforts failed miserably at shoring up the sprawling Mughal political structure. Many of Aurangzeb's orders were not implemented, largely because his nobles did not support them. His bigotry strengthened the hand of those sectors that opposed him for political or other reasons. Of further detriment was his prolonged absence from the heartland of the empire. While he captured the forts of the Marathas, facing his own nobles' connivance at their escape, many of his *jāgīrdārs* in the north were unable to collect their dues from the villages. In the regions that experienced economic growth in the 17th century, the local power-mongers and their followers in the community felt increasingly confident to stand on their own. The abundant commissioning of manṣabdārs with which the leadership addressed this situation far outstripped the empire's growth in area or revenues. The Mughal centre thus began to collapse under its own weight. In 1707, when Aurangzeb died, serious threats from the peripheries had begun to accentuate the problems at the core of the empire.

MUGHAL DECLINE IN THE 18TH CENTURY

The new emperor, Bahādur Shah I (or Shah 'Ālam; ruled 1707–12), followed a policy of compromise, pardoning all nobles who had supported his dead rivals and granting them appropriate postings. He never abolished *jizyah*, but the effort to collect the tax became ineffectual. There was no destruction of temples in Bahādur Shah's reign. In the beginning he tried to gain greater control over the Rajput states of the rajas of Amber (later Jaipur) and Jodhpur, but, when his attempt met with firm resistance, he realized the necessity of a settlement. Because Rajput demands for high *manṣabs* and important governorships were never conceded, however, the settlement did not restore them to fully committed warriors for the Mughal cause. The emperor's policy toward the Marathas was also that of halfhearted conciliation. They continued to fight among themselves as well as against the Mughals in the Deccan. Bahādur Shah was, however, successful in conciliating

Chatrasal, the Bundela chief, and Curaman, the Hindu Jat chief; the latter also joined him in the campaign against the Sikhs.

THE SIKH UPRISINGS

Bahādur Shah attempted to make peace with the Sikh Guru, Gobind Singh. But when, after the death of the Guru, the Sikhs once again raised the banner of revolt in the Punjab under the leadership of Banda Singh Bahādur, the emperor decided to take strong measures and himself led a campaign against the rebels. Practically the entire territory between the Sutlej and the Jamuna rivers, reaching the immediate vicinity of Delhi, was soon under Sikh control. Newly prosperous Jat zamindars and peasants, anxious for recognition, responded to Banda's egalitarian appeal. They, along with numerous other low-caste poor cultivators, traveled to Banda's camp, converted to Sikhism, and took the name Singh as members of the faith. Banda also had support among the Khatris, the caste of the Sikh Gurus. The Sikh movement was an open challenge to Mughal royalty. Banda adopted the title of Sacha Badshah ("True King"), started a new calendar, and issued coins bearing the names of Guru Nanak, the founder of the Sikh religion, and Guru Gobind. The Himalayan Rajput chiefs, secretly in sympathy with any resistance against the Mughals, also supplied Banda with information, material, and refuge when needed. However, the plains Rajputs, the

Muslim elite, and the wealthy townsfolk, including some Khatri traders, opposed Banda. The imperial forces under Bahādur Shah captured some important Sikh strongholds but could not crush the movement; they only swept the Sikhs from the plains back into the Himalayan foothills. In 1715, during Farrukh-Siyar's reign, however, Banda, together with hundreds of his followers, was captured by the governor of the Punjab. They were all executed in Delhi. Thus ended the threat of the emergence of an autonomous non-Mughal state in the Punjab in the early 18th century.

When Bahādur Shah died (February 1712), the position of state finances had deteriorated further as a result of his reckless grants of *jāgīrs* and promotions. During his reign the remnants of the royal treasure were exhausted. Failure to assign productive *jāgīrs* strained the loyalties of the members of the nobility and of the manṣabdārs and reduced the efficiency of the state machinery.

CRACKS IN THE CORE

A new element entered Mughal politics in the ensuing wars of succession. While previously such contests had occurred among royal princes—the nobles merely aiding one rival or another—ambitious nobles now became direct aspirants to the throne. The leading contender to succeed Bahādur Shah was his second son, ʿAẓīm al-Shān, who had accumulated a vast treasure as governor of Bengal and Bihar and had been his father's chief

adviser. His principal opponent was Ẕulfiqār Khan (Dhū al-Fiqār Khan), a powerful Iranian noble, who was the chief bakhshī of the empire and the viceroy of the Deccan. Ẕulfiqār negotiated an unusual agreement allying the three other princes against ʿAẓīm al-Shān and setting forth a partitioned, jointly ruled empire with Ẕulfiqār as imperial vizier. He later shifted his support to Jahāndār Shah, the most pliable of the three brothers, but his proposal, in a measure, demonstrated the increasing potency of regional aspirations.

Jahāndār Shah (ruled 1712–13) was a weak and degenerate prince, and Ẕulfiqār Khan assumed the executive direction of the empire with power unprecedented for a vizier. Ẕulfiqār believed that it was necessary to establish friendly relations with the Rajputs and the Marathas and to conciliate the Hindu chieftains in general in order to save the empire. He reversed the policies of Aurangzeb. The hated *jizyah* was abolished. Only toward the Sikhs did he continue the old policy of suppression. His goal was to reconcile all those who were willing to share power within the Mughal institutional framework.

Ẕulfiqār Khan made several attempts at reforming the economic system, but, in the brief course of his ascendancy, he could do little to redress imperial fiscal decay. When Farrukh-Siyar, son of the slain prince ʿAẓīm al-Shān, challenged Jahāndār Shah and Ẕulfiqār Khan with a large army and funds from Bihar and Bengal, the rulers found their coffers depleted. In desperation they looted their own palaces, even ripping gold and silver from the walls and ceilings, in order to finance an adequate army.

STRUGGLE FOR A NEW POWER CENTRE

Farrukh-Siyar (ruled 1713–19) owed his victory and accession to the Sayyid brothers, 'Abd Allāh Khan and Ḥusayn 'Alī Khan Bāraha. The Sayyids thus earned the offices of vizier and chief *bakhshī* and acquired control over the affairs of state. They promoted the policies initiated earlier by Ẕulfiqār Khan. In addition to the *jizyah*, other similar taxes were abolished. The brothers finally suppressed the Sikh revolt and tried to conciliate the Rajputs, the Marathas, and the Jats. However, this policy was hampered by divisiveness between the vizier and the emperor, as the groups tended to ally themselves with one or the other. The Jats had once again started plundering the royal highway between Agra and Delhi; however, while Farrukh-Siyar deputed Raja Jai Singh to lead a punitive campaign against them, the vizier negotiated a settlement over the raja's head. As a result, throughout northern India zamindars either revolted violently or simply refused to pay assessed revenues. On the other hand, Farrukh-Siyar compounded difficulties in the Deccan by sending letters to some Maratha chiefs urging them to oppose the forces of the Deccan governor, who happened to be the deputy and an associate of Sayyid Ḥusayn 'Alī Khan. Finally, in 1719, the Sayyid brothers brought Ajit

Singh of Jodhpur and a Maratha force to Delhi to depose the emperor.

The murder of Farrukh-Siyar created a wave of revulsion against the Sayyids among the various factions of nobility, who also were jealous of their growing power. Many of these, in particular the old nobles of Aurangzeb's time, resented the vizier's encouragement of revenue farming (selling the right to collect taxes), which in their view was mere shopkeeping and violated the age-old Mughal notion of statecraft. In Farrukh-Siyar's place the brothers raised to the throne three young princes in quick succession within eight months in 1719. Two of these, Rafī' al-Darajāt and Rafī' al-Dawlah (Shah Jahān II), died of consumption. The third, who assumed the title Muḥammad Shah, exhibited sufficient vigour to set about freeing himself from the brothers' control.

A powerful group under the leadership of Chīn Qilich Khan, who held the title Niẓām al-Mulk, and his father's cousin Muḥammad Amīn Khan, the two eminent "Tūrānīs," emerged finally to dislodge the Sayyid brothers (1720). However, this did not signal the restoration of imperial authority.

THE EMPEROR, THE NOBILITY, AND THE PROVINCES

By the time Muḥammad Shah (ruled 1719–48) came to power, the nature of the relationship between the emperor and the nobility had almost completely changed. Individual interests of the nobles had come to guide the course of

Tomb of the Mughal emperor Muḥammad Shah, in Delhi. Frederick M. Asher

politics and state activities. In 1720 Muḥammad Amīn Khan replaced Sayyid ʿAbd Allāh Khan as vizier; after Amīn Khan's death (January 1720), the office was occupied by the Niẓām al-Mulk for a brief period until Amīn Khan's son Qamar al-Dīn Khan assumed the title in July 1724 by a claim of hereditary right. The nobles themselves virtually dictated these appointments. However, because no faction of the nobility, nor for that matter the nobility as a whole, was capable of ruling on its own, the symbols of imperial power—most pointedly the person of the dynastic emperor—had to be preserved with a rather exaggerated emphasis. The nobles in control of the central offices maintained an all-empire outlook, even if they were more concerned with the stability of the regions where they had their *jāgīrs*. *Farmāns* (mandates granting certain rights or special privileges) to governors, fowjdārs, and other local officials were sent, in conformity with tradition, in the name of the emperor.

Individual failings of Aurangzeb's successors also precipitated the decline of royal authority. Jahāndār Shah lacked dignity and decency; Farrukh-Siyar was fickle-minded; Muḥammad Shah was frivolous and overly fond of ease and luxury. The rise to power of the latter's favourite consort, Kokī Jio, and her relations and associates showed that a position at the Mughal court no longer depended on administrative ability, office, or military achievements. Opinions of the emperor's favourites weighed in the appointments, promotions, and dismissals even in the provinces.

The steadily increasing vulnerability of the centre in the face of agrarian unrest, combined with the aforementioned irregularities, set in motion a new type of provincial government. Nobles with ability and strength sought to build a regional base for themselves. The vizier himself, Chīn Qilich Khan, showed the path. Having failed to reform the administration, he relinquished his office in 1723 and in October 1724 marched south to found the state of Hyderabad in the Deccan. In the east, Murshid Qulī Khan had long held Bengal and Orissa, which his family retained after his death in 1726. In the heartland of the empire, the governors of Ayodhya and the Punjab became practically independent. The court needed money from the governors in order to maintain both its functional structure and the necessary pomp and majesty. As the court was not in a position to militarily enforce its regulations in the empire, different provinces—in proportion to their internal conditions and geographic distance from Delhi, as well as the ambition and capability of their governors—reformulated their links with the court. The Mughal court's chief concern at this stage was to ensure the flow of the necessary revenue from the provinces and the maintenance of at least the semblance of imperial unity. Seizing upon the disintegration of the empire, the Marathas now began their northward expansion and overran Malwa, Gujarat, and Bundelkhand. Then, in 1738–39, Nādir Shah, who had established himself as the ruler of Iran, invaded India.

NĀDIR SHAH'S INVASION

The obvious weakness of the Mughal Empire invited Nādir Shah's descent upon the plains of northern India for plunder and spoil. For years the defenses of the northwest had been neglected. Nādir captured Ghaznī and Kabul, crossed the Indus at Attock (December 1738), and occupied Lahore virtually unopposed. Hurried preparations were then made to defend Delhi, but the faction-ridden nobles could not agree on a strategy. Nādir defeated the Mughals at the Battle of Karnal (February 1739), took Emperor Muḥammad Shah prisoner, and marched to Delhi. As a reprisal against the killing of some of his soldiers, Nādir ordered the massacre of some 30,000 Delhi citizens. The invader left Delhi in May laden with booty. His plunder included the famous Koh-i-noor diamond and the jewel-studded Peacock Throne of

Shah Jahān. He compelled Muḥammad Shah to cede to him the province of Kabul.

The Iranian invasion paralyzed Muḥammad Shah and his court. Maratha raids on Malwa, Gujarat, Bundelkhand, and the territory north of these provinces continued as before. The emperor was compelled to appoint the Maratha chief minister (*peshwa*), Balaji Baji Rao, as governor of Malwa. The province of Katehar (Rohilkhand) was seized by an adventurer, ʿAlī Muḥammad Khan Ruhela, who could not be suppressed by the feeble government of Delhi. The loss of Kabul opened the empire to the threat of invasions from the northwest; a vital line of defense had disappeared. The Punjab was again invaded, this time by Aḥmad Shah Durrānī (Abdālī), an Afghan lieutenant of Nādir Shah's forces, who became king of Kabul after Nādir's death (June 1747); Aḥmad Shah sacked Lahore, and, even though a Delhi army compelled him to retreat, his repeated invasions eventually devastated the empire.

THE AFGHAN-MARATHA STRUGGLE FOR NORTHERN INDIA

Muḥammad Shah died in April 1748, and within the next 11 years four princes ascended the Mughal throne. Muḥammad Shah's son, Aḥmad Shah (ruled 1748–54), was deposed by his vizier, ʿImād al-Mulk. ʿĀlamgīr II (ruled 1754–59), the next emperor, was assassinated, also by the vizier, who now proclaimed Prince Muḥī al-Millat, a grandson of Kām Bakhsh, as emperor under the title of Shah Jahān III

(November 1759); he was soon replaced by ʿĀlamgīr II's son Shah ʿĀlam II. In one way or another, the Marathas played a role in all these accessions. Maratha power had by then reached its zenith in northern India. Maratha efforts to dominate the Mughal court were, however, stubbornly contested by the Afghans, newly risen in power under the leadership of Najīb al-Dawlah. The Afghans also had the advantage of support from Aḥmad Shah Durrānī. The period thus saw a fierce struggle between the Marathas and the Afghans for control over Delhi and northern India. The Afghans enjoyed the blessings of the Sunni Muslim theologians, who saw in the rise of the Marathas the eclipse of the power of Islam. The Marathas, however, were never able to mobilize the Hindu chiefs of northern India to side with them collectively. The Jats and the Rajputs, who had emerged as effective rulers of a sizable part of northern India, preferred to stay neutral. To the people of northern India, including the Hindus, the Marathas were alien plunderers from the south, comparable to the Pathans (Pashtuns) from the northwest.

Meanwhile, Aḥmad Shah Durrānī had invaded and plundered repeatedly the northern plains down to Delhi and Mathura. The peshwa then dispatched a strong army under his cousin Sadashiva Rao to drive away the invader and establish the Maratha supremacy in northern India on a firm footing. The final battle, in which the forces of Aḥmad Shah Durrānī routed the Marathas, was fought near

Panipat on Jan. 14, 1761. This defeat shattered the Maratha dream of controlling the Mughal court and thereby dominating the whole of the empire. Durrānī did not, however, found a new kingdom in India. The Afghans could not even retain the Punjab, where a regional confederation was emerging again under the Sikhs. With Shah 'Ālam II away in Bihar, the throne in Delhi remained vacant from 1759 to 1771. During most of this period, Najīb al-Dawlah was in charge of the dwindling empire, which was now effectively a regional kingdom of Delhi.

POLITICAL AND ECONOMIC DECENTRALIZATION DURING THE MUGHAL DECLINE

With the decline of Mughal central authority, the period between 1707 and 1761 witnessed a resurgence of regional identity that promoted both political and economic decentralization. At the same time, intraregional as well as interregional trade in local raw materials, artifacts, and grains created strong ties of economic interdependence, irrespective of political and military relations. Bengal, Bihar, and Avadh (Ayodhya) in northern India were among the regions where these developments were most pronounced. These provinces saw a rise in revenue figures and also the emergence and increasing affluence of a number of towns served by long-distance trade routes.

In due course, the enrichment of the regions emboldened local land- and power-holders to take up arms against external authority. However, parochial goals prevented these rebels from consolidating their interests into an effective challenge to the empire. They relied on support from kinsfolk, peasants, and smaller zamindars of their own castes. Each local group strove to maximize its share of the prosperity at the expense of the others. In conditions of conflict and the absence of coordination among the local elements, the Mughal nobles assumed the role of mediating between Delhi and the localities; as the imperial group weakened further, the nobles found themselves virtually independent, if collectively so, controlling the centre from without.

The necessity of emphasizing imperial symbols was inherent in the kind of power politics that emerged. As each of the contenders in the regions, in proportion to his strength, looked for and seized opportunities to establish his dominance over the others in the neighbourhood, each also apprehended and resisted any such attempt by the others. They all needed for their spoliations a kind of legitimacy, which was so conveniently available in the long-accepted authority of the Mughal emperor. They had no fear in collectively accepting the symbolic hegemony of the Mughal centre, which had come to coexist with their ambitions.

CHAPTER 7

REGIONAL STATES, C. 1700–1850

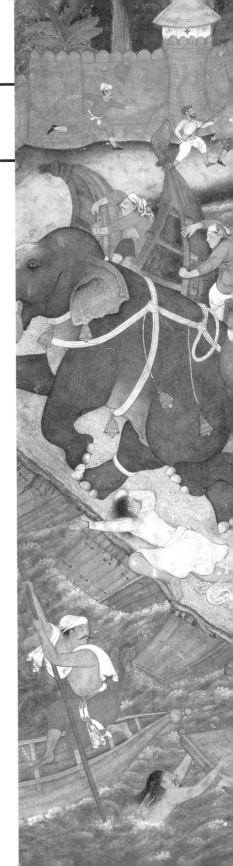

The states that arose in India during the phase of Mughal decline and the following century (roughly 1700 to 1850) varied greatly in terms of resources, longevity, and essential character. Some of them—such as Avadh (Ayodhya) in the north and Hyderabad in the south—were located in areas that had harboured regional states in the immediate pre-Mughal period and thus could hark back to an older local or regional tradition of state formation. Others were states that had a more original character and derived from very specific processes that had taken place in the course of the late 16th and 17th centuries. In particular, many of the post-Mughal states were based on ethnic or sectarian groupings—the Marathas, the Jats, and the Sikhs, for instance—which had no real precedent in medieval Indian history.

THE MARATHAS

There is no doubt that the single most important power to emerge in the long twilight of the Mughal dynasty was the Maratha confederacy. Initially deriving from the western Deccan, the Marathas were a peasant warrior group that rose to prominence during the rule in that region of the sultans of Bijapur and Ahmadnagar.

EARLY HISTORY

The most important Maratha warrior clan, the Bhonsles, had held extensive *jāgīrs* (land-tax entitlements) under the 'Ādil Shāhī rulers, and these were consolidated in the course of the 1630s and 1640s, as Bijapur expanded to the south and southwest. Shahji Bhonsle, the first prominent member of the clan, drew substantial revenues from the Karnataka region, in territories that had once been controlled by the rulers of Mysore and other chiefs who derived from the collapsing Vijayanagar kingdom. One of his children, Shivaji Bhonsle, emerged as the most powerful figure in the clan to the west, while Vyamkoji, half-brother of Shivaji, was able to gain control over the Kaveri (Cauvery) River delta and the kingdom of Thanjavur in the 1670s.

Shivaji's early successes were built on a complex relationship of mixed negotiation and conflict with the 'Ādil Shāhīs on the one hand and the Mughals on the other. His raids brought him considerable returns and were directed not merely at agrarian resources but also at trade. In 1664 he mounted a celebrated raid on the Gujarat port city of Surat, at that time the most important of the ports under Mughal control. The next year he signed a treaty with the Mughals, but this soon broke down after a disastrous visit by the Maratha leader to Aurangzeb's court in Agra. Between 1670 and the end of his life (1680), Shivaji devoted his time to a wide-ranging set of expeditions, extending from Thanjavur in the southeast to Khandesh and Berar in the north. This was a portent of things to come, for the mobility of the Marathas was to become legendary in the 18th century.

RISE OF THE *PESHWAS*

The good fortune of Shivaji did not fall to his son and successor, Sambhaji, who was captured and executed by the Mughals in the late 1680s. His younger brother, Rajaram, who succeeded him, faced with a Mughal army that was now on the ascendant, moved his base into the Tamil country, where Shivaji too had earlier kept an interest. He remained in the great fortress of Jinji (earlier the seat of a Nayaka dynasty subordinate to Vijayanagar) for eight years in the 1690s, under siege by a Mughal force, and for a time it may have appeared that Maratha power was on the decline. But a recovery was effected in the early 18th century, in somewhat changed circumstances. A particularly important phase in this respect is the reign of Shahu, who succeeded Rajaram in 1708 with some acrimony from his widow, Tara Bai.

Lasting some four decades, to 1749, Shahu's reign was marked by the ascendancy of a lineage of Citpavan Brahman ministers, who virtually came to control central authority in the Maratha state, with the Bhonsles reduced to figureheads. Holding the title of *peshwa* (chief minister), the first truly prominent figure of this line is Balaji Vishvanath, who had aided Shahu in his rise to power. Vishvanath and his successor, Baji Rao I (*peshwa* between 1720 and 1740), managed to bureaucratize the Maratha state to a far greater extent than had been the case under the early Bhonsles. On the one hand, they systematized the practice of tribute gathering from Mughal territories, under the heads of *sardeshmukhi* and *cauth* (the two terms corresponding to the proportion of revenue collected). But, equally, they seem to have consolidated methods of assessment and collection of land revenue and other taxes, which were derived from the Mughals. Much of the revenue terminology used in the documents of the *peshwa* and his subordinates derives from Persian (the language of Mughal administration), which suggests a far greater continuity between Mughal and Maratha revenue practice than might have been imagined.

By the close of Shahu's reign, a complex role had been established for the Marathas. On the one hand, in the territories that they controlled closely, particularly in the Deccan, these years saw the development of sophisticated networks of trade, banking, and finance; the rise of substantial banking houses based at Pune, with branches extending into Gujarat, the Ganges River valley, and the south; and an expansion of the agricultural frontier. At the same time, maritime affairs were not totally neglected either, and Balaji Vishvanth took some care to cultivate the Angria clan, which controlled a fleet of vessels based in Kolaba and other centres of the west coast. These ships posed a threat not only to the new English settlement of Bombay (Mumbai) but to the Portuguese at Goa, Bassein, and Daman.

On the other hand, there also emerged a far larger domain of activity away from the original heartland of the Marathas, which was either subjected to raiding or given over to subordinate chiefs. Of these chiefs, the most important were the Gaekwads (Gaikwars), the Sindhias, and the Holkars. Also, there were branches of the Bhonsle family itself that relocated to Kolhapur and Nagpur, while the main line remained in the Deccan heartland, at Satara. The Kolhapur line derived from Rajaram and his wife, Tara Bai, who had refused in 1708 to accept Shahu's rule and who negotiated with some Mughal court factions in a bid to undermine Shahu. The Kolhapur Bhonsles remained in control of a limited territory into the early 19th century, when the raja allied himself with the British against the *peshwas* in the Maratha Wars.

Unlike the Kolhapur Bhonsles and the descendants of Vyamkoji at Thanjavur, both of whom claimed a status equal to that of the Satara raja, the line at Nagpur was clearly subordinate to the Satara rulers. A crucial figure from this line is Raghuji Bhonsle (ruled 1727–55), who was responsible for the Maratha incursions on Bengal and Bihar in the 1740s and early 1750s. The relations of his successors, Janoji, Sabaji, and Mudoji, with the *peshwas* and the Satara line were variable, and it is in this sense that these domains can be regarded as only loosely confederated, rather than tightly bound together.

Subordinate Maratha Rulers

Other subordinate rulers who emerged under the overarching umbrella provided by the Satara ruler and his *peshwa* were equally somewhat opportunistic in their use of politics. The Gaekwads, who came to prominence in the 1720s with the incursions of Damaji and Pilaji Gaekwad into Gujarat, were initially subordinate not only to the Bhonsles but also to the powerful Dabhade family. Their role in this period was largely confined to the collection of the *cauth* levy, and they consolidated their position by taking advantage of differences between the *peshwa* and the Dabhades. The fact that various interests at the Mughal court were at loggerheads with each other also worked to the Gaekwads' advantage. However, it was only after the death of Shahu, when the power of the *peshwas* was further enhanced, that the position of the Gaekwads truly improved. By the early 1750s, the rights of the family to an extensive portion of the revenues of Gujarat were recognized by the *peshwa*, and an amicable division was arranged. The expulsion of the Mughal governor of the Gujarat *subah* (province) from his capital of Ahmedabad in 1752 set the seal on the process. The Gaekwads preferred, however, to establish their capital in Baroda, causing a realignment in the network of trade and consumption in the area.

The rule of Damaji (died 1768) at Baroda was followed by a period of some turmoil. The Gaekwads still remained partly dependent on Pune and the *peshwa*, especially to intervene in moments of succession crisis. The eventual successor of Damaji, Fateh Singh (ruled 1771–89), did not remain allied to the *peshwa* for long, though. Rather, in the late 1770s and early 1780s, he chose to negotiate a settlement with the English East India Company, which will be discussed at greater length later in this book. This settlement eventually led to increased British interference in his affairs. By 1800 the British rather than the *peshwa* were the final arbiters in determining succession among the Gaekwad, who became subordinate rulers under them in the 19th century.

In the mid-18th century a great part of the holdings of the Gaekwads was described in the *peshwa's* correspondence and papers as *saranjam* (nonhereditary grants to maintain troops), and the ruler himself was termed *saranjamdar*, or at times *jāgīrdār*. The same was broadly true of the Holkars and Sindhias and also of another relatively minor dynasty of chiefs, the Pawars of Dhar. In the case of the Holkars, the rise in status and wealth was particularly rapid and marked. From petty local power brokers, they emerged by the 1730s into a position in which Malhar Rao Holkar could be granted a large share of the cauth collection in Malwa, eastern Gujarat, and Khandesh. Within a few years, Malhar Rao consolidated his own principality at Indore, from which his successors controlled important trade routes as well as the crucial trading centre of Burhanpur. After him, control of the dynastic fortunes fell largely to his son's widow, Ahalya Bai, who ruled from 1765 to 1794 and brought Holkar power to its apogee. Nevertheless, their success could not equal that of the last great chieftain family, the Sindhias, who carved a prominent place for themselves in north Indian politics in the decades following the third battle of Panipat (1761). Again, like the Holkars, the Sindhias were based largely in central India, first at Ujjain, and later (from the last quarter of the 18th century) in Gwalior. It was during the long reign of Mahadaji Sindhia, which began after Panipat and continued to 1794, that the family's fortunes were truly consolidated.

Mahadaji, employing in the 1780s a large number of European mercenaries in his forces, proved an effective and innovative military commander who went beyond the usual Maratha dependence on light cavalry. His power, however, had already grown in the 1770s, when he managed to make substantial inroads into a north India that had been weakened by Afghan attacks. He intervened with some effect in the Mughal court during the reign of Shah 'Ālam II, who made him the "deputy regent" of his affairs in the mid-1780s. His shadow fell not only across the provinces of Delhi and Agra but also on Rajasthan and Gujarat, making him the most formidable Maratha leader of the era. He caused trepidation among the personnel of the East India Company and also at Pune, where his relations with the acting *peshwa*, Nana Fadnavis, were fraught with tension. Eventually, the momentum generated by Mahadaji could not be maintained by his successor, Daulat Rao Sindhia (ruled 1794–1827), who was defeated by the British and forced under the Treaty of Surji-Arjungaon (1803) to surrender his territories both to the north and to the west.

MUGHAL MYSTIQUE IN THE 18TH CENTURY

The careers of some of these potentates, especially Mahadaji Sindhia, illustrate the potency of Mughal symbols even in the phase of Mughal decline. For instance, after recapturing Gwalior from the British, Mahadaji took care to have his control of the town sanctioned by the Mughal emperor. Equally, he zealously guarded the privileges and titles granted to him by Shah 'Ālam, such as *amīr al-umarā* ("prince of princes," or commander-in-chief) and nā'ib wakīl-e mutlaq (deputy regent). In this he was not alone. Instances in the 18th century of states that wholly threw off all pretense of allegiance to the Mughals are rare. Rather, the Mughal system of honours and titles, as well as Mughal-derived administrative terminology and fiscal practices, spread apace despite the deterioration of imperial power.

THE CASE OF MYSORE

Theoretically, in the 1720s, the Mughals claimed rights over a far larger area than had ever been the case under Akbar, Jahāngīr, or Shah Jahān. This area included large parts of southern India, over which central rule was never actually consolidated. Taking advantage of their somewhat ambiguous relations with the Mughals and claiming to be the agents of Delhi, the Marathas often made partial claims on the revenues of these areas, as *cauth* and *sardeshmukhi*. This was the case, for example, in Mysore in the 1720s and 1730s. Mysore had come under the sovereign umbrella of the Mughals in the late 1690s, as the result of an embassy sent to Aurangzeb by Cikka Deva Raja Vadiyar, the ruler of Mysore at the time. In effect, this meant that Mysore was to pay a periodic tribute (*peshkash*) to Mughal representatives in the south, but there was a problem in doing so. As Mughal authority in the Deccan and the south was itself fragmented, several possible channels of tribute existed. Mysore thus sought to make use of this ambiguity, playing off Chīn Qilich Khan (still known as Niẓām al-Mulk, a title his descendants would inherit), a powerful Mughal noble who in these years founded a dynasty at Hyderabad, against the Mughal representative at Arcot, thereby putting off the tribute payment. A further variable in the fiscal politics of Mysore was the presence of the Marathas; and some clans, such as the Ghorpades, made it a regular practice to raid the Mysore capital of Seringapatam. In this way, overlapping and at times conflicting claims were justified with reference to a Mughal centre that was distant and for the most part lacked interest in these affairs.

As such, then, few if any of the states discussed above made a direct attack on Mughal legitimacy or sought to challenge Mughal claims head-on. To the extent that such a frontal challenge (as distinct from a rebellion conducted within a shared understanding of the framework of authority) can be located in the period, it comes from the far northwest of the Mughal domain. Eventually, however, this challenge was to have repercussions that were felt by the Marathas and other groups.

CHALLENGE FROM THE NORTHWEST

The northwestern frontier between the Mughals and Ṣafavids had always harboured elements that possessed the potential to destabilize the balance between these states. The area, which falls largely in present-day Afghanistan, also had a tradition of religio-political movements, often intended to provide a direct challenge to the Mughals or Ṣafavids. An important instance is the Roshani movement of Bāyazīd Anṣārī and his successors, which was crushed by the Mughals in the late 16th and early 17th centuries. Again, in the reign of Aurangzeb, a frontal attack on the legitimacy of his rule was made by the Pashtun leader, Khushḥāl Khan Khatak, though in this case from the standpoint of orthodox Islam. Significantly, in Khushḥāl Khan's poetic and other literary works, there was also an explicit and nostalgic yearning for the time of Sher Shah of Sūr, the Afghan who had expelled the Mughal ruler Humāyūn from Hindustan. The spirit of these writings was translated into action in the early 18th century, when Mīr Vays Khan Hotak, a leader of the Hotaki clan of Ghilzays, succeeded in carving out a Pashtun state based at Kandahār, under the nose of the Ṣafavid governor of the area. Between 1709 and 1715, Mīr Vays ruled Kandahār unofficially, but his successors were not so modest. His son, Mīr Maḥmūd, first attacked Kermān in Iran and then, in 1722, took the Ṣafavid capital Eṣfahān itself and proclaimed himself its ruler. However, the success of the Ghilzays was not to last long, as they were challenged both by their fellow Pashtuns—the Abdālīs (Durrānīs)—and by the plans of Nādr Qolī Beg (later Nādir Shah), a Ṣafavid subordinate who harboured substantial ambitions of his own.

Between Mīr Maḥmūd's death (1725) and 1731, Nādr Qolī Beg rapidly consolidated his hold over eastern Iran and placed a severe check on the rise of Pashtun power. Subsequently he marched into Afghanistan and later the Mughal territories, sacking Delhi in 1739. Nādir Shah's success in welding together a disparate set of territories while operating outside the system of Mughal sovereignty provided a model for the Pashtuns after his assassination in 1747. Many from the Abdālīs and Ghilzays had been employed by him, and they had had an opportunity to learn at close quarters. Among those who had been subordinate in this way to Nādir Shah was Aḥmad Khan, a member of the relatively small Sadozai lineage of Abdālī (Durrānī). In the wake of the Persian conqueror's death, a congregation of Pashtun khans at a shrine near Kandahār elected Aḥmad Khan to be their leader. His trajectory took him into conflict with the Mughals and then the Marathas, and finally he acted as a crucial catalyst in the formation of the Sikh state in north India.

THE AFGHAN FACTOR IN NORTHERN INDIA, 1747–1772

Unlike Nādir Shah, Aḥmad Shah Durrānī (or Aḥmad Shah Abdālī—as Aḥmad Khan came to be known after 1747—had little interest in the area west of Afghanistan. Rather, his principal endeavour was to create a state that would lie astride the major overland trade routes that passed from northern India to central and western Asia. Kandahār naturally had an important place in this scheme, but a great deal of attention also had to be paid to centres in north India, such as Multan and Lahore. It is no coincidence that Aḥmad Shah mounted 9 and possibly 10 expeditions to the Punjab, beginning with the first year of his reign, after he had taken Kabul. His campaigns bear an obvious similarity to the seasonal migration of the *powindah* (pastoral nomads) from Afghanistan to India, which normally took place in the agricultural off-season. It was always in autumn and winter that the Durrānī-led armies set out to the east; when summer's heat approached, they beat a tactical retreat to the hills from which they had come.

The ability of the Pashtuns to form a lasting state in this process was severely curtailed by the opposition that Aḥmad Shah faced within his own home territories. In the 1750s, when the first concerted challenge to his authority in the Punjab was posed by an alliance of Mughals, Sikhs, and Marathas, Aḥmad Shāh was too preoccupied with the rebellion of Nāsir Khan Balūch, to the west, to devote attention to the threat in the east. Thus, in 1757 Aḥmad Shah's son Tīmūr, appointed governor of the Punjab, was forced to retreat from Lahore to Peshawar under the force of attacks from Sikhs and Marathas. It was only in 1760 that Aḥmad Shah returned to fight a campaign in northern India, which culminated in his defeat of the Marathas at Panipat in January 1761. However, even this did not turn the tide in his favour. The large-scale attacks that were unleashed on the villages of Sikh peasantry led only to intensified resistance, and Aḥmad Shah found his area of control in the 1760s constantly under threat. His campaigns of 1768 and 1769 were accompanied by widespread desertions on the part of his allies and levies, who thought the Punjab project to be an unviable one. His death in 1772 thus left his son and successor, Tīmūr Shah, with many problems to resolve.

The Afghan presence in northern India during this period was of course not simply restricted to Aḥmad Shah's campaigns. In the course of the middle decades of the 18th century, several Afghan lineages had carved a place for themselves in northern India in the area known as Rohilkhand, to the east and northeast of Delhi and Agra. They diverted trade from these older imperial cities to their own centres and also helped create a new set of routes to Lahore and the northwest. In so doing, they helped weaken further the economic power of the Mughal centre and accelerated the consolidation of regional states on the Gangetic plain itself.

THE SIKHS IN THE PUNJAB

However, a vacuum still existed in the Punjab, which neither the Mughals nor the Durrānī were able to fill. It was in this context that a Sikh kingdom came to be consolidated in the late 18th century.

EARLY HISTORY

The origins of the Sikhs, a religious group initially formed as a sect within the larger Hindu community, lie in the Punjab in the 15th century. The Sikh founder, Guru Nānak (1469–1539), was roughly a contemporary of the founder of Mughal fortunes in India, Bābur, and belonged to the Khatri community of scribes and traders. From an early career as a scribe for an important noble of the Lodī dynasty, Nānak became a wandering preacher before settling down at Kartarpur in the Punjab at about the time of Bābur's invasion. By the time of his death, he had numerous followers, albeit within a limited region, and, like many other religious leaders of the time, founded a fictive lineage (i.e., one not related by blood) of Gurus who succeeded him. His immediate successor was Guru Angad, chosen by Nānak before his death. He too was a Khatri, as indeed were all the remaining Gurus, though of various subcastes.

In practice, the essential teachings of Nānak, collected in the *Adi Granth* (Punjabi: "First Book"), represented a syncretic melding of elements of Vaishnava devotional Hinduism and Sufi Islam, with a goodly amount of social criticism thrown in. No political program is evident in the work, but—as has already been remarked with regard to the Roshanis—religious movements in the period had a tendency to assume political overtones, by virtue of the fact that they created bonds of solidarity among their adherents, who could then challenge the authority of the state in some fashion. The Sikh challenge to the Mughal state could be seen as prefigured in Nānak's own critical remarks directed at Bābur, but in reality it took almost three-quarters of a century to come to fruition. It was in the early 17th century—when under somewhat obscure circumstances Guru Arjun (or Arjun Mal) was tortured and killed by Mughal authorities—that the first signs of a major conflict appeared. Guru Arjun was accused of abetting a rebel Mughal prince, Khusraw, and, more significantly, found mention in Jahāngīr's memoirs as someone who ran a "shop" where religious falsehoods were sold (apparently a reference to the Khatri origins of the Guru). His successor, Hargobind (1595–1644), then began the move toward armed assertion by constructing a fortified centre and holding court from the so-called Akal Takht ("Throne of the Timeless One"). After a brief imprisonment by the Mughals for these activities, Hargobind was released, and he once more entered into armed conflict with Mughal officials. He was forced to spend the last years of his life in the Rajput principality of Hindur, outside direct Mughal jurisdiction, where he maintained a small military force.

A brief period of relative quiet followed Hargobind's death. However, under his son Tegh Bahadur, who became ninth Guru in 1664, conflicts with the Mughals once again increased, partly as a result of Tegh Bahadur's success as a preacher and proselytizer and partly because of the rather orthodox line of Sunni Islam espoused by Aurangzeb. In 1675 Tegh Bahadur was captured and executed upon his refusal to accept Islam, thus laying the path for the increased militancy under the last of the Gurus, Gobind Singh (1675–1708). It should be stressed that it was the very success of the Sikh Gurus in attracting followers and acquiring temporal power that prompted such a response from the Mughals. However, rather than suppressing Sikhism, the policy of Aurangzeb backfired. Guru Gobind Singh assumed all the trappings of a chieftain, gave battle to Mughal forces on more than one occasion, and founded a new centre at Anandpur in 1689. His letters also suggest the partial assumption of temporal authority, being termed *hukmnamas* (loosely, "royal orders"). However, he still chose to negotiate with the Mughals, first with Aurangzeb and then, after the latter's death, with Bahadur Shah I.

Ironically, with Gobind Singh's death, the Sikh threat to Mughal dominance increased. In a further twist, this resulted from the assumption of leadership in the Punjab by Banda Singh Bahadur, a Maratha who had come under the Guru's influence during the latter's last days at Nanded in Maharashtra. Between 1709 and late 1710 the Sikhs under Banda enjoyed dramatic successes in the *sarkars* (districts) of Sirhind, Hisar, and Saharanpur, all of them ominously close to Delhi. Banda set up a capital at Mukhlispur, issued coins in the names of the Gurus (a particularly bold lèse-majesté), and began to use a seal on his orders even as the Mughals did. In late 1710 and 1711 the Mughal forces counterattacked, and Banda and his forces retreated. Expelled from Sirhind, he then moved his operations west into the vicinity of Lahore. Here too he was unsuccessful, and eventually he and his forces were forced to retreat to the fort of Gurdas Nangal. There they surrendered to Mughal forces after a prolonged siege, and Banda was executed in Delhi in 1716.

This phase of activity is especially important for two reasons. First, as distinct from the sporadic militancy exhibited under Hargobind and then Gobind Singh, it was in this period that a full-scale Sikh rebellion against Mughal authority broke out for the first time. Second, Banda's role in the matter itself, which was somewhat enigmatic, lends the affair a curious flavour. Some of Banda's letters speak of orthodox Islam as an enemy to be rallied against, thus suggesting that the Sikhs at this time were moving somewhat away from their initial orientation as mediators between popular Hinduism and Islam. Further, this early Maratha-Sikh alliance prefigures later coalitions that were to emerge in the context of the Durrānī attacks on Punjab.

FROM BANDA SINGH BAHADUR TO RANJIT SINGH

The quelling by Mughal forces of the Sikhs under Banda did not mean an end to Sikh resistance to Mughal claims. In the 1720s and 1730s Amritsar emerged as a centre of Sikh activity, partly because of its preeminence as a pilgrimage centre. Kapur Singh, the most important of the Sikh leaders of the time, operated from its vicinity and gradually set about consolidating a revenue-cum-military system, based in part on compromises with the Mughal governors of the province. Other Sikhs were, however, less willing than Kapur Singh to deal with the Mughal authorities and took the paths of social banditry and raiding. These activities served as a damper on the attempts by the Mughal governors of Lahore *subah* to set up an independent power base for themselves in the region. First 'Abd al-Ṣamad Khan and then his son Ẓakariyyā Khan attempted the twin tracks of conciliation and coercion, but all to little avail. After the latter's demise in 1745, the balance shifted still further in favour of the Sikh warrior-leaders, such as Jassa Singh

Ahluwalia, later the founder of the kingdom of Kapurthala. The mushrooming of pockets under the authority of Sikh leaders was thus a feature of the two decades preceding Durrānī's invasion of the Punjab and took place not merely in the eastern Punjab but in the Bari Doab, not far from Lahore itself. A unique centre was yet to emerge, and the end of the line of Gurus with Gobind Singh ensured that spiritual and temporal authority could not be combined in a single person as before.

Nevertheless, the principal opposition faced by Durrānī in his campaigns of the 1750s and 1760s in the Punjab came from the Sikhs, even if the Mughal forces and Marathas played a role of significance on occasion. These were sanguinary engagements, which cost the Sikhs many thousands of lives, as the Afghan chroniclers themselves testify. Eventually, by the mid-1760s, Sikh authority over Lahore had been established, and the Afghans had been unable to consolidate their early gains. Under Aḥmad Shah's successor, Tīmūr Shah (ruled 1772–93), some of the territories and towns that had been taken by the Sikhs (such as Multan) were recovered, and the descendants of Aḥmad Shah continued to harbour ambitions in this direction until the end of the century. But by the 1770s they were dealing with a confederation of about 60 Sikh chieftains, some of whom founded what were to remain princely states under the British—such as Nabha and Patiala. However, rather as in the case of the Marathas, the confederate structure did not mean that there were never differences or conflicts between these chiefdoms. Nevertheless, at least in the face of their major adversary, the Durrānī clan and its allies, these chiefdoms came together to present a united front.

The Sikh chiefdoms continued many of the administrative practices initiated by the Mughals. The main subordinates of the chiefs were given *jāgīr* assignments, and the Persianized culture of the Mughal bureaucracy continued to hold sway. Unlike the Gurus themselves, who, as has been noted, were exclusively drawn from Khatri stock, the bulk of the Sikh chieftains tended to be of Jat origin, a fact that drew disparaging remarks from at least some contemporary writers, who spoke of them as Sudras (the lowest of the four varnas, or social classes). Thus, besides the states set up in other regions, such as Bharatpur, the Jats can be said to have dominated state building in the Punjab in this period as well.

It was one such chief, Ranjit Singh, grandson of Charhat Singh Shukerchakia, who eventually welded these principalities for a brief time into a larger entity. Ranjit Singh's effective rule lasted four decades, from 1799 to 1839, and was realized in a context already dominated by the growing power of the English East India Company. Within 10 years of his death, the British had annexed Punjab, and so this period can be seen as the last gasp of the old-regime polities in India. His rise to power was based on superior military force, partly serviced by European mercenaries and by the strategic location of the territories that he had inherited from his father.

Ranjit Singh's kingdom combined disparate elements. On the one hand, it represented the culmination of nearly a century of Sikh rebellions against Mughal rule. On the other hand, it was based on intelligent application of the principles of statecraft learned from the Afghans. This emerges from the fact that he used as his capital the great trading city of Lahore, which he captured in 1799, in the aftermath of invasions by Shah Zamān, the successor of Tīmūr Shah. Having gained control of the trade routes, he imposed monopolies on the trade in salt, grain, and textiles from Kashmir to enhance his revenues. Using the cash he was able to collect by these means, he built up an army of 40,000 cavalry and infantry, and by 1809 he was undisputed master of most of Punjab.

Over the remaining three decades of his rule, Ranjit Singh continued to consolidate his territories, largely at the expense of Afghan and Rajput, as well as lesser Sikh, chieftains. In 1818 he took Multan, and the next year he made major gains in Kashmir. At the time of his death, the territory that he controlled sat solidly astride the main trade routes extending from north India to Central Asia, Iran, and western Asia. However, in a number of areas, he established tributary relations with chieftains, thus not wholly subverting their authority. Once again, therefore, the model around which the Sikh state was built bears a striking resemblance to that of the Mughals. *Jāgīrs* remained a

crucial form of remuneration for military service, and, in the directly taxed lands, officials bearing the title of kārdār (agent) were appointed at the level of a unit called—as elsewhere in Mughal domains—the ta'alluqa (district).

However strong the state of Ranjit Singh might have appeared, it was in fact based on a fragile system of alliances, as became apparent soon after his death. At the level of the palace, a dispute broke out in the early 1840s between two factions, one supporting Chand Kaur, daughter-in-law of Ranjit Singh, who wished to be regent, and the other supporting Shīr Singh. But such disputes could scarcely have been the real reason for the collapse of Sikh power within a decade. Rather, it would appear that the state created by Ranjit Singh never really made the transition from being a conquering power to being a stable system of alliances between conflicting social groups and regional interests. In any event, the process of disintegration was accelerated and given a helping hand by the British between 1845 and 1849.

RAJASTHAN IN THE 18TH CENTURY

Such relatively ephemeral successes at state building as that of Ranjit Singh are rare. However, one can find other instances in the context of the 18th century in which consolidation was rapidly followed by reversals. Such instances can be divided into two categories: those in which the consolidation of a particular

SIKHISM

Sikhism is an Indian religion founded in the late 15th century by Nānak, the first of the Sikh leaders titled Guru. Most of the religion's some 25 million members, called Sikhs, live in the Punjab region—the site of their holiest shrine, the Golden Temple, and the principal seat of Sikh religious authority, the Akal Takht. The Adi Granth is the canonical scripture of Sikhism. Its theology is based on a supreme God who governs with justice and grace. Every human being, irrespective of caste or gender, has the opportunity to become one with God. The basic human flaw of self-centredness can be overcome through proper reverence for God, commitment to hard work, service to humanity, and sharing the fruits of one's labour. Sikhs consider themselves disciples of the 10 human Gurus; the Adi Granth assumed the position of Guru after the death of the last human Guru, Gobind Singh (1666–1708). Sikhs accept the Hindu ideas of samsara and karma. The dominant order of Sikhism, into which most Sikh boys and girls are initiated at puberty, is the Khalsa. The emblems of the Khalsa, called the Five Ks, are kes or kesh (uncut hair), kangha (a comb), kachha (long shorts), kirpan (a ceremonial sword), and kara (a steel bracelet).

state proved a threat to British power and hence was undermined (e.g., the case of Mysore, which will be explained in the next section) and others in which the logic of consolidation and decline appears not to have concerned the British. In the latter category can be placed the case of Jaipur (earlier Amber) in eastern Rajasthan, a Rajput principality controlled by the Kachwaha clan. From the 16th century the Kachwahas had been subordinate to the Mughals and had, as a consequence, gradually managed to consolidate their hold over the region around Amber in the course of the 17th century. The crucial role played in high Mughal politics by such members of the clan as Raja Man Singh thus paid dividends, and the chiefs were permitted to maintain a large cavalry and infantry force. In the early 18th century the ruler Jai Singh Sawai took steps to increase his power manyfold. This was done by arranging to have his *jāgīr* assignment in the vicinity of his home territories and by taking on parcels of land in which the tax rights were initially rented from the state and then gradually made permanent. By the time of his death in 1743, Jai Singh (for whom Jaipur came to be named) had emerged as the single most important Rajput ruler.

This example was followed some years later in the 1750s by Suraj Mal, the Jat ruler of Bharatpur, who—like Jai Singh—adopted a modified form of Mughal revenue administration in his territories. However, by this time, the fortunes of the Jaipur kingdom were seriously in question. Under threat from the Marathas, recourse had to be taken more and more

Hawa Mahal (Hall of Winds), Jaipur, Rajasthan, India. Frederick M. Asher

to short-term fiscal exactions, while at the same time a series of crop failures in the 1750s and 1760s spread a pall over the region's fragile agriculture. The second half of the 18th century was thus marked by an economic depression, accompanied by a decline in the political power of Jaipur, which became a vulnerable target for the ambitions of the Marathas, and of Mahadaji Sindhia in particular.

THE SOUTH: TRAVANCORE AND MYSORE

The states discussed so far, with the exception of some of those of the Maratha confederacy, were all landlocked. This does not mean that trade was not an important element in their makeup, for the kingdom of Ranjit Singh was crucially linked to trade. However, lack of access to the sea greatly increased the vulnerability of a state, particularly in an era when the major power was the English East India Company, itself initially a maritime enterprise. In the south, unlike the areas discussed so far, several states did make a determined bid in this period to consolidate their power by the use of maritime outlets. Principal among these were Travancore in Kerala under Martanda Varma and Rama Varma, and Mysore under Hyder Ali and Tippu Sultan.

These states rose to prominence, however, only in the latter half of the 18th century, or at least after 1740. Before that, the southern Indian scene had been dominated by a group of Muslim notables who had accompanied the Mughal

expansion into the region in the 1680s and 1790s or else had come in a second wave that followed immediately after 1700. Among these notables, many of whom set themselves up as tribute-paying chiefs under Mughal authority, can be counted the relatively petty *nawabs* (deputies) of the Balaghat, or northern Karnataka (such as 'Abd al-Rasūl Khan of Sira), but there were also far more substantial men, such as the Niz̤ām al-Mulk and Sazd Allah Khan at Arcot. The Niz̤ām al-Mulk had consolidated his position in Hyderabad by the 1740s, whereas the Arcot principality had emerged some three decades earlier. Neither of these rulers, while establishing dynastic succession, claimed full sovereignty, and thus they continued to cast themselves as representatives of Mughal authority. Southern Indian politics in the 1720s emerged, therefore, as a game with many petty players and three formidable ones: the Marathas (both at Thanjavur and elsewhere), the Niz̤ām, and the Arcot (or Karnatak) nawab.

In the second half of the 18th century, the power of all three of these centres declined. The succession struggle at Arcot in the 1740s and early 1750s left its rulers open to financial manipulation by private British merchants, to whom they were increasingly in debt for war expenses. In the 1750s the power of Hyderabad also declined (after the death of its founder, the Niz̤ām al-Mulk), and control of the coastal districts was soon lost, leaving the kingdom landlocked and relatively sparsely populated. The reign of Pratapasimha

Wall painting in the summer palace of Tippu Sultan, Seringapatam, Karanataka, India.
Frederick M. Asher

(1739–63) marks the beginning of Thanjavur's slide into fiscal ruin. Here again it was the mounting costs of war and the intrusive presence of the Europeans on the coast that triggered the crisis.

In this context the only route remaining was for states to build an elaborate and well-organized war machine while keeping external supply lines open. The control of trade was also seen as crucial in the statecraft of the period. These principles were put into practice in the southern Kerala state of Venad (Travancore) by Martanda Varma (ruled 1729–58). He built a substantial standing army of about 50,000, reduced the power of the Nayar aristocracy on which rulers of the area had earlier been dependent militarily, and fortified the northern limits of his kingdom at the so-called "Travancore line." It was also the policy of this ruler to extend patronage to the Syrian Christians, a large trading community within his domains, as a means of limiting European involvement in trade. The key commodity was pepper, but other goods also came to be defined as royal monopoly items, requiring a license for trade. These policies were continued in large measure by Martanda's successor, Rama Varma (ruled 1758–98), who was able, moreover, to defend his kingdom successfully against a dangerous new rival power—Mysore.

The rise of Mysore to importance dates to the mid-17th century, when rulers of the Vadiyar dynasty, such as Kanthirava Narasaraja and Cikka Deva Raja, fought campaigns to extend Vadiyar control over parts of what is now interior Tamil Nadu (especially Dharmapuri, Salem, and Coimbatore). Until the second half of the 18th century, however, Mysore was a land-locked kingdom and dependent therefore on trade and military supplies brought through the ports of the Indian east coast. As these ports came increasingly under European control, Mysore's vulnerability increased. From the 1760s, steps were taken to change this situation. A cavalry commander of migrant origin, Hyder Ali, assumed effective power in the kingdom in 1761, reducing the Vadiyars to figure-heads and displacing the powerful Kalale family of ministers. First Hyder and then, after 1782, his son, Tippu Sultan, made attempts to consolidate Mysore and make it a kingdom with access to not one but both coasts of peninsular India. Against the Kodavas, the inhabitants of the upland kingdom of Kodagu (Coorg), they were relatively successful. Coastal Karnataka and northern Kerala came under their sway, enabling Tippu to open diplomatic and commercial relations on his own account with the Middle East.

Tippu's ambitions apparently greatly exceeded those of his father, and he strove actively to escape the all-pervasive shadow of Mughal suzerainty, as discussed earlier. However, as in the Sikh kingdom of Ranjit Singh, the problem with the Mysore of Hyder and Tippu was their inability to build an internal consensus. Their dependence on migrants and mercenaries for both military and fiscal expertise was considerable, and they were always resisted by local chiefs, the so-called *poligars*. More crucial was the fact that by the 1770s Mysore faced a formidable military adversary in the form of the English East India Company, which did not allow it any breathing room. It was the English who denied Mysore access to the relatively rich agricultural lands and ports of the Coromandel coastal plain in eastern India, and, equally as significant, it was at the hands of an English attacking force that Tippu finally was killed in 1799 during the fourth of the Mysore Wars.

POLITICS AND THE ECONOMY

The 18th century was a period of considerable political turmoil in India, one in which states rose and fell with some rapidity, and that there was a great deal of fluidity in the system. Did this political turmoil have a clear counterpart in terms of economic dislocation? This does not seem to have been unambiguously the case. It is of course true that raids by military forces would have caused dislocation, and the practice of destroying standing crops was followed by armies throughout most of the century. On the other hand, economic warfare and the attempt to destroy the productive base of a rival state were relatively uncommon in the first half of the 18th century. But, after 1750, such means were exploited to the harshest degree. The destruction of irrigation tanks, the forcible expropriation of cattle wealth, and even the forced march of masses of people were not unknown in the wars of the 1770s and thereafter. All these must have had a deleterious effect on economic stability and curtailed the impulse toward growth.

Such negative effects also can be exaggerated, however. When viewed from Delhi, the 18th century is certainly a gloomy period. The attacks of Nādir Shah and then of Aḥmad Shah Durrānī, and finally the attempts by the Rohillas (who controlled Delhi in 1761–71) to hold the Mughals to ransom left the inhabitants of the city with a sense of being under permanent siege. This perspective can hardly have been shared by the inhabitants of other centres in India, whether Trivandrum, Pune, Patna, or Jaipur. There was a process of economic reorientation that accompanied the political decentralization of the era, and it is on account of this that the experience of Delhi and Agra cannot be generalized. However, even the trajectory of the regions was mixed. In some, the first half of the 18th century witnessed continued expansion—Bengal, Jaipur, and Hyderabad,

for example—while others were late bloomers, as in the case of Travancore, Mysore, or the Punjab. No single chronology of economic prosperity and decline is likely therefore to fit all the regions of India in the epoch.

It would also appear for a variety of reasons, some obvious and others less so, that the mid-18th century marks a significant point of inflection in key processes. For example, the engrossing by the English East India Company of the revenues of Bengal *subah* had the effect of reversing the direction of flow of precious metals into the area; whereas Bengal had earlier absorbed gold and silver in exchange for its exports, this pattern no longer held. Similarly, on the external trade front, the latter half of the 18th century saw the growth, under the company's aegis, of semicoerced forms of crop production, the case of indigo being a prominent one. But another reason why the latter half of the 18th century differs from the period before about 1750 is the changing character of war. In the post-1750 period, warfare became more disruptive of civil life and economic production than before, and at the same time the new technologies in use made it a far more expensive proposition. The use of firearms on a large scale, the employment of mercenaries, and the maintenance of standing armies all are likely to have had profound ramifications. But it does appear hyperbolic to describe the processes of the post-1750 period as a total inversion of what went before.

CULTURAL ASPECTS OF THE
LATE PRECOLONIAL ORDER

Even as it has sometimes been maintained that the 18th century witnessed a general decline in material life, the cultural life of the period also has often been denigrated. In fact, there appears to be scant justification for such a portrayal of trends. Even Delhi, whose economic condition unequivocally declined, housed a number of major poets, philosophers, and thinkers in this epoch, from Shah Walī Allah to Mīr Tāqī Mīr. Further, as regional courts grew in importance, they tended to take on the function of the principal patrons of high culture, whether in music, the visual arts, or literature. It is thus also in relatively dispersed centres, ranging from Avadh to Bikaner and Lahore to Thanjavur, that one finds the courtly traditions of culture persisting. Thanjavur under the Marathas is a particularly fine example of cultural efflorescence, in which literary production of a high quality in Tamil, Telugu, Sanskrit, and Marathi continued, with some of the Maratha rulers themselves playing a significant direct role. Similarly, it is in 18th-century Thanjavur that the main compositions of what is today known as the Karnatak tradition of Indian classical music came to be written, by such men as Tyagaraja, Muttuswami Diksitar, and Syama Sastri. Finally, the period brought the development of a distinct style of painting in Thanjavur, fusing elements imported from the north with older local traditions of textile painting.

This vitality was not restricted purely to elite culture. To begin with, many of the theatre and musical traditions, as well as formal literary genres of the period, picked up and incorporated folk influences. At the same time, the melding of popular Hinduism and Islam gave a particular flavour to cultural productions associated with pilgrimages and festivals. More than in earlier centuries, the tradition of long-distance pilgrimages to major centres from Varanasi to Rameswaram increased and can be seen to fit in with a general trend of increasing mobility. It was common for post-Mughal states to employ mercenary soldiers and imported scribes and clerks. In 18th-century Hyderabad, for example, Kayasthas from the north were employed in large numbers in the bureaucracy, while in Mysore the Maharashtrian Brahmans were given fiscal offices as early as the 1720s. It is apparent that the mobility of musicians, men of letters, and artists was no less than that of these scribal classes. When a major new political centre emerged, it rapidly attracted talent, as evidenced in Ranjit Singh's Lahore. Here, Persian literature of high quality was produced, but not at the cost of literary output in Punjabi. At the same time, new developments were visible in the fields of architecture and painting. Farther to the north, the principality of Kangra fostered an important new school of painting, devoted largely to Vaishnava themes. Indeed, a surprisingly large proportion of the surviving corpus of what is understood today to be part of India's traditional culture is attributable to the 17th and 18th centuries.

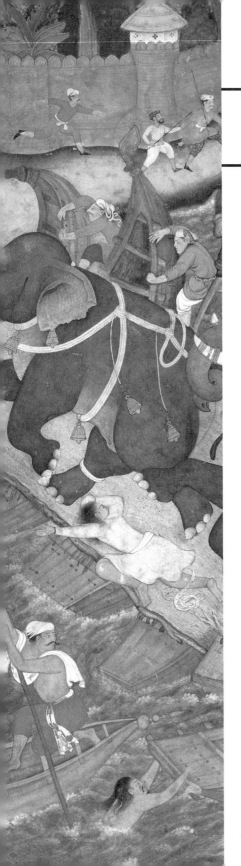

CHAPTER 8

EUROPEAN ACTIVITY IN INDIA, 1498–c. 1765

When the Portuguese navigator Vasco da Gama landed at Calicut (now Kozhikode) in 1498, he was restoring a link between Europe and the East that had existed many centuries previously. The first known connection between the two regions was Alexander the Great's invasion of the Punjab, 327–325 BCE. In the 2nd century BCE, Greek adventurers from Bactria founded kingdoms in the Punjab and the bordering Afghan hills; these survived into the late 1st century. This territorial contact in the north was succeeded by a lengthy commercial intercourse in the south, which continued until the decline of the Roman Empire in the 4th century CE. Trade with the East then passed into Arab hands, and it was mainly concerned with the Middle Eastern Islamic and Greek worlds until the end of the European Middle Ages. The only physical contact with Europe came from occasional travelers, such as the Italians Marco Polo and Niccolò dei Conti and the Russian Afanasy Nikitin in the 15th century, and these were few because of commotions within the tolerant Arab-Islamic world created by successive incursions of Turks and Mongols. For Europe in 1498, therefore, India was a land of spices and of marvels attested to by imaginative Greek authors. For Muslims, Europe was the land of Rūm (Rome) or the Greek empire of Constantinople (Turkish after 1453), and, for Hindus, it was the abode of the foreigners called Yavanas, a corruption of the Greek word *Ionian*.

THE PORTUGUESE

The Portuguese were the first agents of this renewed contact, because they were among the few Europeans at that time to possess both the navigational know-how and the necessary motivation for the long sea voyage. During the 15th century the direct routes for the Indian trade—via the Red Sea and Egypt or across Persia, Iraq, Syria, and Anatolia—had become increasingly blocked, mainly by activities of the Ottoman Empire. The surviving Egyptian route was subject to increasing exploitation by a line of middlemen, ending with the Venetian near-monopoly of the European trade in the eastern Mediterranean, and in 1517 it likewise passed under Ottoman suzerainty. The motive for finding a new route was therefore strong, especially among the Portuguese and the Spanish, who had inherited crusading zeal from wars against the Muslims (Moors) in Iberia and North Africa. Both countries sought an indirect route to the East, but Spain became focused on exploiting the wealth of the New World (discovered while seeking a new route to Asia) while the Portuguese—bolstered by navigational techniques learned from the Genoese (rivals of the Venetians)—sought a route to the East around southern Africa.

Vasco da Gama, upon his arrival in Calicut, hoped to find Christians cut off by Muslim expansion, to deal a blow at Muslim power from their maritime rear, as it were, and hoped to corner the European spice trade. He found his Christians in the Syrian communities of Cochin and Travancore, he found the spices, and he found Muslim Arab merchants entrenched at Calicut. It was his successors, Francisco de Almeida and Afonso de Albuquerque, who established the Portuguese empire in the East. Almeida set up a number of fortified posts; but it was Albuquerque (governor 1509–15) who gave the empire its characteristic form. He took Goa in western India in 1510, Malacca in the East Indies in 1511, and Hormuz (Ormuz) in the Persian Gulf in 1515, and he set up posts in the East Indian Spice Islands (Indonesia). The object of these moves was to establish for Portugal a strategic command of the Indian Ocean, so as to control the maritime spice trade and thereby cripple the economy of the Ottoman-controlled Middle East. While Malacca was the nerve centre for the spice-producing islands of Indonesia and the exchange mart for the trade with the Far East (East Asia), Goa, not Malacca, was the capital because of Portuguese concern with the Ottoman threat.

The Portuguese method was to rely on sea power based on fortified posts and backed by settlements. Portuguese ships, sturdy enough to survive Atlantic gales and mounted with cannon, could easily dispose of Arab and Malay shipping. The bases enabled the Portuguese to dominate the main sea-lanes; but Portugal, with fewer than one million people and involved in Africa and South America as well, was desperately short of manpower. Albuquerque turned his fortresses into settlements to provide a resident population for defense. Intermarriage was encouraged. At the same time, Christianity was encouraged through the church. Goa became an archbishopric. St. Francis Xavier started from Goa on his mission to the south Indian fishermen. The Inquisition was established in 1560. The new mixed population thus became firmly Roman Catholic and provided a stubborn resistance to attacks.

A lack of resources precluded any attempt to establish a land empire. Portugal's control of the Indian Ocean—its period of empire—lasted through the 16th century. During this time it attained great prosperity. Goa acquired the title of Golden, and it became one of the world's wonder cities. Trade with Europe was a royal monopoly, and, in addition, a system of licenses for all inter-Asian trade enriched the royal exchequer. Inter-Asian trade was free to individual Portuguese; and it was the profits of this, combined with trimmings from the royal monopoly, that gave them their affluence.

The three marks of the Portuguese empire continued to be trade, anti-Islamism, and religion. The Portuguese early considered that no faith need be kept with a non-Christian, and to this policy of perfidy they added a tendency of cruelty beyond the normal limits of what was a cruel age; the result was to deprive them of Indian sympathy. In religion the Portuguese were distinguished by missionary fervour and intolerance. Examples of the former are the Madura mission of Roberto de Nobili (1577–1656), nicknamed the White Brahman, and the Jesuit missions to the court of the Mughal emperor

Akbar. Of the latter, there was the Inquisition at Goa and the forcible subjection of the Syrian church to Rome at the Synod of Diamper in 1599.

The Portuguese thus had few friends in the East to help them in a crisis, and in 1580 the Portuguese kingdom was annexed to Spain; thenceforth until 1640, Portuguese interests were sacrificed to those of Spain. Because of the Spanish failure to quell a Dutch rising in the Netherlands, and after the English defeated the Spanish Armada in 1588, the route to the East was opened to both English and Dutch.

This first real impact that Europeans had on India left distinct though not extensive traces. The first is the mixed population of Goans and other Luso-Indians along the western coast of India and in Sri Lanka and with them a lingua franca in the ports and markets. Then came Roman Catholicism, which today has millions of followers and an array of churches, convents, and colleges all over India. More tangible traces include imported commodities such as tobacco, potatoes, pineapples, tomatoes, papayas, cashew nuts, and chilies.

THE DUTCH

In the race to the East after the Spanish obstacle had been removed, the Dutch, having ample resources, were the first to arrive after the Portuguese. Their first voyage was in 1595, helped by the local knowledge of Jan Huyghen van Linschoten, who had worked for six years in Goa. Jacob van Neck's voyage to the

East Indies (Indonesia) in 1598–1600 was so profitable (400 percent for all of his ships) that the die was cast for a great Eastern adventure. The Dutch objective was neither religion nor empire but trade, and the trade in mind was the spice trade. The Dutch were monopolists rather than imperialists. Empire came later, in the 18th century, as a safeguard for monopoly.

The Dutch therefore went directly to the East Indies, the main source of spices, and only secondarily to southern India for pepper and cardamom and to Ceylon (Sri Lanka) for these and cinnamon. From 1619 their headquarters were fixed at Batavia (Jakarta) in Java, from which they developed a series of outlying stations in the East Indian islands (e.g., Celebes [Sulawesi] and the Moluccas) and intermediate ones such as Cape Town in South Africa, along with Ceylon for supply. This was the work of the governor-general Jan Pieterzoon Coen (served 1618–23; 1627–29), and the whole system may be said to have been completed under the governor-general Joan Maetsuyker (served 1653–78).

The Dutch system demanded the control of the eastern seas, and this meant the elimination of European rivals, beginning with the Portuguese. The Dutch succeeded with superior resources and better seamanship, but the Portuguese, though defeated, were not destroyed. Ousted from most strongholds, the Portuguese retained their capital, Goa, in spite of blockades and sieges; they did not cede the area to India until 1961. The second European obstacle was the English, who followed the Dutch to the East Indies; no match for

the Dutch in resources, the English were virtually excluded from the East Indies when, in 1623, the Dutch seized their "factory" (trading post) at Amboina (present-day Ambon) and executed its agents and allies—an action the English later dubbed the Amboina Massacre.

It remained for the Dutch to organize their trade, which was operated through the Dutch East India Company, a complicated organization dominated by the maritime state of Zeeland. Much larger than the English company, it had the character of a national concern. Dutch sea power, more efficient than that of the Portuguese, secured monopoly conditions in the islands and sea-lanes. It was only in land areas such as Travancore that resort had to be made to competition. But there remained the problem of trade, for the Dutch, like the English, were short of exchange goods. Textiles were needed to buy spices in Indonesia, and silver was needed to buy textiles (cotton or silk) in India and China. To work the spice monopoly, the Dutch developed an elaborate system of Eastern trade from the Persian Gulf to Japan, the ultimate object of which was to secure the goods with which to secure the spices without recourse to scarce European resources. It was this trade that brought the Dutch to India at Surat, on the Coromandel Coast (Negapatam), in Bengal, and up-country at Agra.

THE BRITISH, 1600–1740

The English venture to India was entrusted to the (English) East India

Company, which received its monopoly rights of trade in 1600. The company included a group of London merchants attracted by Eastern prospects, not comparable to the national character of the Dutch company. Its initial capital was less than one-tenth of the Dutch company's. Its object, like that of the Dutch, was to trade in spices; and it was at first modestly organized on a single-voyage basis. These separate voyages, financed by groups of merchants within the company, were replaced in 1612 by terminable joint stocks, which covered operations over a term of years. Not until 1657 was a permanent joint stock established.

The company's objective was the spices of the East Indies, and it went to India only for the secondary purpose of securing cottons for sale to the spice growers. The British East Indian venture met with determined Dutch opposition, culminating in the massacre at Amboina in 1623.

In India the English found the Portuguese enjoying Mughal recognition at the western Indian port of Surat. Portuguese command of the sea nullified the English embassy to the Mughal court in spite of its countenance by the emperor Jahāngīr. However, the English victory at Swally Hole in 1612 over the Portuguese, whose control of the pilgrim sea route to Mecca was resented by the Mughals, brought a dramatic change. The embassy of Sir Thomas Roe (1615–18) to the Mughal court secured an accord (in the form of a *farmān*, or grant of privileges) by which the English secured the right to trade and to establish factories in return for

becoming the virtual naval auxiliaries of the empire. This success, with England's exclusion from Indonesia by the Dutch in the same period, determined that India, not the Far East, should be the chief theatre of English activity in Asia.

There followed through the 17th century a period of peaceful trading through factories operating under Mughal grants. This held good for Surat and later for Hugli (1651) in Bengal. In the south the factory at Masulipatam (1611) was moved to the site of Madras (now Chennai), granted by a Hindu raja (1640); it shortly (1647) came under the control of the sultans of Golconda and thence passed to the Mughals in 1687. The only exception to this arrangement was the island port of Bombay (now Mumbai); although independently held, its trade was small because the Marathas, soon locked in combat with the Mughals, held the hinterland.

The trade the company developed differed radically from that of the Dutch. It was a trade in bulk instead of in highly priced luxury goods; the profits were a factor of volume rather than scarcity; it worked in competitive instead of monopolistic conditions; it depended upon political goodwill instead of intimidation. The English trade became more profitable than that of the Dutch, because the smaller area covered and the lack of armed forces necessary to enforce monopoly reduced overhead charges. But it encountered its own difficulties. The Indians would take little other than silver in exchange for their goods, and the export of bullion was anathema to

This painting shows the 1599 meeting of the Mughal emperor Akbar meeting with Sir John Mildenhall. Mildenhall was sent by Queen Elizabeth I to obtain privileges for the setting up of the East India Company. Hulton Archive/Getty Images

the concept of mercantilism, then England's reigning political economy. Lack of military power meant management of Asian governments instead of their coercion. Lack of home dominance meant compromise and hazard of fortune.

To solve the silver problem, the English developed a system of country trade not unlike that of the Dutch, the profits of which helped to pay for the annual investment of goods for England. Madras and Gujarat supplied cotton goods, and Gujarat supplied indigo as well; silk, sugar, and saltpetre (for gunpowder) came from Bengal, while there was a spice trade along the Malabar Coast from 1615 on a competitive basis with the Dutch and Portuguese. Opium was shipped to East Asia, where it later became the basis of the Anglo-Chinese tea trade. The merchants lived in factories (trading houses) or in a collegiate type of settlement where life was confined, colourful, and often short.

The company had many difficulties in England. There was mercantilist disapproval and mercantile jealousy of the company's monopoly; moreover, government instability threatened the company's privilege. King Charles I encouraged the rival Courteen Association (1635), and Oliver Cromwell allowed virtual free trade until 1657. Under the later Stuarts the company prospered, only to have its hopes dashed by a war in India and by the Whigs' Glorious Revolution of 1688–89. The Whigs promoted a new company in 1698, which, however, failed to oust the old one after some years of struggle. In 1702 the government insisted on a merger, which was completed in 1708–09 under the name of the United Company of Merchants of England Trading to the East Indies. This was the body that 40 years later launched on the sea of Indian politics.

A way for rivals to harass the company, besides attacks on the export of bullion, was to limit the sale of cotton goods in England. In 1700 the sale of Asian silks and printed or dyed cottons was forbidden, but trade continued for reexport to continental Europe. After 1700 the company found a new profitable line in the Chinese tea trade, whose imports increased more than 40-fold by 1750.

In India the company suffered a serious setback when it resolved, under the inspiration of Sir Josiah Child, to resort to armed trade and to attack the Mughals. The emperor Aurangzeb was too strong, however, and the venture (1686–90) ended in disaster. Out of this fiasco came both the foundation of Calcutta (now Kolkata) by Job Charnock in 1690—a mudflat that had the advantage of a deep anchorage—and the age of fortified factories surrounded by satellite towns. These were the answers, with Mughal consent, to increasing Indian insecurity. The Madras factory was already fortified, and Fort William in Calcutta followed in 1696. The company thus had, with independent Bombay, three centres of Indian power.

For the next half century the company confined its relations with the Mughals, who had now spread to the deep south beyond Madras, to disputes over rights and terms of trade at local levels. Fresh

KOLKATA

The city of Kolkata (formerly Calcutta), the capital of West Bengal state, is in northeastern India. Formerly the capital (1772–1911) of British India, it has long been one of India's largest metropolitan areas. It is located on the Hugli (Hooghly) River, about 96 miles (154 km) north of the river's mouth in the Bay of Bengal. The English East India Company established a trading centre at the site in 1690, which grew and became the seat of the British province called the Bengal Presidency. It was captured by the nawab (local ruler) of Bengal, who in 1756 imprisoned a number of British there (in a prison known as the Black Hole of Calcutta); the city was retaken by the British under Robert Clive. Calcutta was an extremely busy 19th-century commercial centre, but it began to decline with the removal of the colonial capital to Delhi in 1911. The decline continued when Bengal was partitioned between India and Pakistan in 1947 and when Bangladesh was created in 1971. The flood of refugees from those political upheavals boosted the city's population but also significantly added to its widespread poverty. Despite its problems, Kolkata remains the dominant urban area of eastern India and a major educational and cultural centre.

privileges were obtained in Delhi, and these they were content to argue about rather than fight for. The factors were learning the art of Indian diplomacy as they had formerly to learn the arts of Indian commercial management.

THE FRENCH

The French had shown an interest in the East from the early years of the 16th century, but individual efforts had been checked by the Portuguese. The first viable French company, the French East India Company, was launched by the minister of finance Jean-Baptiste Colbert, with the support of Louis XIV, in 1664. After some false starts, the French company acquired Pondicherry (now Puducherry), 85 miles (137 km) south of Madras, from a local ruler in 1674. It obtained Chandernagore (now Chandannagar), 16 miles (26 km) north of Calcutta, from the Mughal governor in 1690–92. At first the French initiatives suffered from the mixing of grandiose political and colonial schemes with those of trade, but, under the care of François Martin from 1674, the company turned increasingly to trade and began to prosper.

The progress of the settlements was interrupted by events in Europe. The Dutch captured Pondicherry in 1693; when the French regained it under the Peace of Ryswick (1697), they gained the best fortifications in India but lost their trade. By 1706 the French enterprise seemed moribund. The company's privileges were let to a group of Saint-Malo merchants from 1708–20. After 1720, however, came a dramatic change. The company was reconstituted, and over the next 20 years its trade was expanded, and new stations were opened. The Indian Ocean island of Mauritius was finally settled in 1721; Mahe in Malabar and Karaikal on the eastern coast were acquired in 1725 and 1739, respectively. Chandarnagar was revived. The French company remained under the close supervision of the government, which nominated the directors and, from 1733, guaranteed fixed dividends. In spite of the company's growth and its fostering by government, its sales in Europe in 1740 were only about half those of England's East India Company. Its trade was large enough to be worth seizing but not great enough to rival that of the English.

Other enterprises in India included a Danish East India Company, which operated intermittently from 1616 from Tranquebar in southern India, acquiring Serampore (now Shrirampur) in Bengal in 1755, and the Ostend Company of Austrian Netherlands merchants from 1723, a serious rival until eliminated by diplomatic means in 1731. Efforts by Swedes and Prussians proved abortive.

THE ANGLO-FRENCH STRUGGLE, 1740–63

In 1740 India appeared to be relatively tranquil. In the north the Persian Nādir Shah's invasion (1739) had proved to be only a large-scale raid. In the Deccan the Niẓām al-Mulk provided some measure of stability. In western India the Marathas were dominant. However, there was competition between Marathas, Mughals, and local rulers for political supremacy in the Deccan. There was a sense of impending change in the air; the Mughal emperor was sickly, the nizam was aged, and the Marathas were active and ambitious.

It was on this scene that events in Europe precipitated an Anglo-French struggle in India. The War of the Austrian Succession began with Frederick II of Prussia's seizure of Silesia in 1740; France supported Prussia, and from 1742 England supported Austria. The stage thus set, the English decided that the French Indian trade was too powerful to be left alone; the neutrality of previous years was therefore abandoned. Both sides depended on sea power for success, but it was the French who moved first—with an improvised fleet from Mauritius, Bertrand-François Mahé, comte de La Bourdonnais, drove the British in alarm to Bengal and captured Madras after a week's siege in September 1746. Quarrels between La Bourdonnais and the governor of Pondicherry, Joseph-François Dupleix, marred this unexpected success, but an English attack on Pondicherry was repelled. Then the Treaty of Aix-la-Chapelle (1748), which ended the war, returned Madras to the British in exchange for Cape Breton Island in North America.

It would thus appear that the status quo had been restored. In fact the situation had radically changed. Madras was now recognized as British by European treaty, and this was accepted by one of the rival Indian chiefs. The French had grown in prestige as skillful soldiers and in power by detachments of the French fleet left behind on La Bourdonnais's departure. Above all, the astute Dupleix had seen the opportunity offered for exploiting the new French reputation in the confused politics of the region. For some years there had been a disputed succession to the governorship of Karnataka (the Carnatic), itself a dependency of the Niẓām al-Mulk of Hyderabad. The nizam had installed a new Carnatic nawab (deputy; from the Arabic *nawwāb)* in 1743, but the dispute smouldered on between the partisans of the two rival families, who looked impartially to Marathas, Mughals, and Europeans for help.

In 1748, on the morrow of Aix-la-Chapelle, an occasion for French interference occurred with the death of the aged Niẓām al-Mulk. There was a disputed succession between his second son and a grandson, Muẓaffar Jang. Dupleix, encouraged by his easy repulse of the Carnatic nawab from the walls of Madras, decided to support both Muẓaffar and the claimant to the Carnatic nawabship, Chanda Sahib. Dupleix's reward for success would be the means of ruining the British trade in southern India and gaining an indefinite influence over the affairs of the whole Deccan. At first fortune favoured him. The Carnatic nawab was killed in the Battle of Ambur (1749), which demonstrated convincingly the superiority of European arms and methods of warfare. The threatening invasion of the new nizam (now a hereditary title), Nās.ir Jang, ended with the

nizam's murder in December 1750. French troops conducted Muẓaffar Jang toward Hyderabad; when Muẓaffar in turn was murdered three months later, the French succeeded in placing the late nizam's third son, Ṣalābat Jang, on the Hyderabad throne. Thenceforward, in the person of the skillful Charles, marquis de Bussy-Castelnau, Dupleix had a kingmaker at the centre of Muslim power in the Deccan.

The British response to these dramatic successes was to support for the Carnatic nawabship the late nawab's son, Muḥammad ʿAlī, who had taken refuge in the rock fortress of Trichinopoly (now Tiruchchirappalli). They had already interfered in the affairs of Tanjore (Thanjavur) and were no strangers to Indian politics. The French supported Chanda Sahib for the nawabship. There thus developed what was really a private war between the two companies.

Bussy-Castelnau was established at Hyderabad, with the revenues of the Northern Sarkars (six coastal districts) to support his army. In the south the French had only Muḥammad ʿAlī to remove. But from 1751 Dupleix's star began to wane. Robert Clive (later 1st Baron Clive of Plassey), a discontented young British factor who had left the countinghouse for the field, seized the fort of Arcot, political capital of the Carnatic, with 210 men in August 1751. This daring stroke had the hoped-for effect of diverting half of Chanda Sahib's army to its recovery. Clive's successful 50-day defense permitted Muḥammad ʿAlī to procure allies from Tanjore and the Marathas. The French were worsted, and they were eventually forced to surrender in June 1752. Dupleix never recovered from this blow; he was superseded in August 1754 by the director Charles-Robert Godeheu, who made a not unfavourable settlement with the British.

The French gained but a brief respite; the Seven Years' War in Europe, in which Britain and France were once more on opposite sides, broke out in 1756. Both sides sent armaments to the East. The first British force was diverted to Bengal, so that the French general Thomas-Arthur Lally had an advantage on his arrival in 1758. Lally was brave but head-strong and tactless; after taking Fort St. David, he lost time and credit marching to Tanjore, where he forfeited Indian sympathy by executing temple Brahmans. Then his attack on Madras (1758–59) miscarried, while Clive's troops from Bengal defeated the French garrison of the Northern Sarkars. When Sir Eyre Coote arrived with reinforcements, the British defeated Lally decisively at the Battle of Wandiwash in January 1760. Bussy-Castelnau, who had been recalled from Hyderabad, was captured; and Lally retreated to Pondicherry, where, after an eight-month siege made tense by bitter recrimination, he surrendered in January 1761. The French threat to British power in India had come to a temporary close.

This defeat could be partly blamed on Lally, but there were also other, more vital causes. An overriding factor was the British command of the sea. Lally could get no allies for lack of money and no money for lack of supply from France.

The British could supply Madras from both Britain and Bengal. The French company was under the control of the French government, and the company suffered from the vicissitudes of its politics.

EUROPEAN MILITARY SUPERIORITY

The supremacy in Indian politics, which seemed to come so suddenly to the Europeans in India, also requires explanation. There was the matter of arms. The Mughals imported their cavalry tactics from Turkestan and their artillery from Turkey. Their firearms remained slow-firing and cumbersome, so that they were outclassed both in rate of fire and in range by the 18th-century European musket and the cannon landed from European fleets. In the face of charging Mughal cavalry, infantry armed with such faster and more accurate weapons could fire three times instead of once, thus destroying the traditional dominance held by heavy cavalry in Indian warfare. Moreover, beyond this technical advantage, the Europeans also had the advantage of discipline. Troops with loyalty guaranteed by regular pay were more than a match for the personal retinues or mercenary soldiers of the Indian chiefs, however brave the latter might be individually. A chronic problem with Indian armies at that time was the lack of means to pay them; campaigns would be diverted for collecting revenue for this purpose (when Europeans later trained Indians in the European manner, their advantage increased; discipline removed the uncertain factor of personal leadership, and regular pay removed the Indian general's bugbear of mutiny). A further advantage was civil discipline; the European forces were directed by men themselves under discipline, who were without hereditary connections or ties to the local population (though to modern eyes European company men often seemed refractory or disloyal, by standards of India at that time they were regularity itself). Indian loyalty was to an individual leader who might be killed, to relatives who might back the wrong side in a conflict, and to governments that might (and often did, for various reasons) fail to pay their troops. On the Indian side, whatever the situation, someone was nearly always looking over his shoulder thinking of the chances of a change of leadership or a successful coup and what this might mean to him personally. Thus, the European possessed not only an expertise denied to the Indians but also a spirit of confidence, a tenacity, and a will to win that was rare in the Indian forces of the time.

REVOLUTION IN BENGAL

The revolution in Bengal was the product of a number of unrelated causes. The imminence of the Seven Years' War prompted the British to send out Clive with a force to Madras in 1755. Succession troubles in Bengal combined with British mercantile incompetence to produce a crisis at a moment when the French in

south India were still awaiting reinforcements from France.

'Alī Vardī Khan—the nawab and virtual ruler of Bengal—died in April 1756, leaving his power to his young grandson Sirāj al-Dawlah. The latter's position was insecure because of discontent among his officers, both Hindu and Muslim, and because he himself was at the same time both headstrong and vacillating. On an exaggerated report that the British were fortifying Calcutta, he attacked and took

This dramatic engraving shows British prisoners being kept in the Black Hole of Calcutta after Bengal forces captured Fort William in 1756. Rischgitz/Hulton Archive/Getty Images

the city after a four-day siege, on June 20, 1756. The flight of the British governor and several councillors added ignominy to defeat. The survivors were held for a night in the local lockup, known as the Black Hole of Calcutta; many were dead the next morning.

News of this disaster caused consternation in Madras. A force preparing to oust Bussy-Castelnau from the Deccan was diverted to Bengal, giving Clive an army of 900 Europeans and 1,500 Indians. He relieved the Calcutta survivors and recovered the city on Jan. 2, 1757. An indecisive engagement led to a treaty with Sirāj al-Dawlah on February 9, which restored the company's privileges, gave permission to fortify Calcutta, and declared an alliance.

This was a decisive point in British Indian history. According to plan, Clive should have returned to Madras to pursue the campaign against the French; but he did not. He sensed both the hostility and insecurity of Sirāj al-Dawlah's position and began to receive overtures to support a military coup. The chance of installing a friendly and dependent nawab seemed too good to be missed. Having taken this decision, Clive chose the right candidate in Mīr Ja'far, an elderly general with much influence in the army. In so acting, Clive was probably influenced by the example of Bussy-Castelnau at Hyderabad; for six years Bussy-Castelnau had maintained himself with an Indo-French force, sustaining the nizam, S. alābat Jang, and maintaining French influence in the largest south

Indian state with outstanding success. This system of a "sponsored" Indian state, controlled but not administered, was the one Clive had in mind for Bengal.

The prospects for success seemed good. The event, however, proved otherwise, and there were reasons for this not realized at the time. The chiefs were so lacking in vigour that they made little resistance to British encroachments. External danger could come from only one direction and source—the Mughal authority—and that was at the moment in dissolution. While Bussy-Castelnau had no French merchants to satisfy, the British merchants in Calcutta were ready and eager to exploit the situation. And, because the British company's government was made up entirely of merchants, it is easy to understand why the sponsored state of 1757 became the virtually annexed state of 1765.

Before breaking with Sirāj al-Dawlah, Clive took the French settlement of Chandernagore, which the nawab left to its fate lest he need British help to repulse an Afghan attack from the north. The actual conflict with Sirāj al-Dawlah, at Plassey (June 23, 1757), was decided by Clive's resolute refusal to be overawed by superior numbers, by dissensions within the nawab's camp, by Mīr Ja'far's failure to support his superior, and by Sirāj al-Dawlah's own loss of nerve. Plassey was, in fact, more of a cannonade than a battle. It was followed by the flight and execution of Sirāj al-Dawlah, by the occupation of Murshidabad, the capital, and by the installation of Mīr Ja'far as the new nawab.

Robert Clive, India's British governor, receives a decree from India's Mughal ruler Shah 'Ālam II allowing the East India Company the administration of the revenues of Bengal, Bihar, and Orissa. Hulton Archive/Getty Images

Clive now controlled a sponsored state, and he played the part with great skill. His position was prejudiced at the outset by the nawab's failure to find the expected hoarded treasure with which to fulfill his financial promises to the British. The nawab therefore looked for financial support toward his Hindu deputies, with whom saving was second nature. Clive had therefore to intervene repeatedly. In 1759 he defended Patna from attack by the heir to the Mughal throne, 'Alī

Gauhar (later Shah 'Ālam II), who hoped to strengthen his position in the confused world of Delhi politics by acquiring Bihar. Clive also had to deal with the Dutch, who, hearing of Mīr Ja'far's restiveness and alarmed by the growth of British power in Bengal, sent an armament of six ships to their station at Chinsura on the Hooghly River. Though Britain was at peace with the Netherlands at the time, Clive maneuvered the Dutch into acts of aggression, captured their fleet, defeated them on land,

and exacted compensation. They retained Chinsura but could never again challenge the British position in Bengal.

Clive left Calcutta on Feb. 25, 1760, at the height of his fame and aged only 34, looking forward to an English political career. The nawab was completely dependent on the British, to whose trade it seemed that the rich resources of Bengal were now open. But the prospect was less brilliant than it looked; and for this, and for the troubles that ensued in the next few years, Clive had a direct responsibility. Two measures undermined the plan of a sponsored state, leading to the company's bankruptcy on the one hand and to the virtual annexation of Bengal on the other. The first of these was an understanding with Mīr Ja'far, not mentioned in the actual treaty, that personal domestic trade (i.e., trade within India) of company employees would be exempted from the usual tolls and customs duties. The company's trade with Europe had since 1717 been exempt from such taxes, but the application of such concessions to individual employees—or to anyone, for that matter, who held an exemption pass (dastak)—was a fiscal disaster, since the pass system was widely abused. Local Indian traders were soon unable to compete against rivals with such an advantage, and the company itself was soon out-positioned by its own employees (who received little compensation from the company and relied on their own entrepreneurial skills to make ends meet.) From free trade many company employees passed to intimidation, employing agents who used the British name to terrorize the countryside and infringe on the company's monopoly.

The second measure was the acceptance of gifts. This was not forbidden by the company and was, in fact, a recognized custom; but it opened the floodgates of corruption. On the strength of rumours regarding the vast sum of the Murshidabad treasury, large amounts were paid to the armed forces and to the company leaders following the city's capitulation. In addition, Clive obtained a further Mughal title and then claimed a revenue assignment, or jāgīr, for its upkeep, which was worth a large annual sum. In the context of contemporary values these grants equaled nearly one-fourth of the average annual Bengal revenue and represented some 6 percent of the then annual revenue of Great Britain. With such a vigorous opening of the floodgates, it is not surprising that the other servants of the company asked for more almost as a matter of right and that the company's directors in London, with relatives and connections on the spot, preferred verbal denunciations to any resolute or sustained action. The effects became speedily apparent when in fact the Murshidabad treasure turned out to be only a fraction of its rumoured value, so that (as Clive later admitted to a parliamentary enquiry), the nawab had to sell jewels, goods, and furniture to meet his obligations. The results of these measures unfolded in the next decade and continued to be felt for a generation.

THE PERIOD OF DISORDER, 1760–72

The departure of Clive signaled the release of acquisitive urges by the company's Bengal servants. These urges were so strong that the governor, Henry Vansittart (served 1760–64), found himself unable to control them. Under the company's constitution, he had only one vote in a council of up to a dozen and could be overruled by any knot of determined men. During these years, a body of British merchants, long separated from British standards and social restraints, suddenly found themselves with real but undefined authority over the whole of a large and rich province. It is not surprising that they thought mainly of getting rich quickly.

The first step was the deposition of the nawab Mīr Ja'far on the grounds of old age and incompetence. He was supplanted by his son-in-law, Mīr Qāsim, after the latter had paid a large gratuity to the company and to Vansittart personally. In addition, he ceded to the British the districts of Burdwan, Midnapore, and Chittagong. Both sides wanted power, and both sides were short of money. The nawab had lost substantial land revenue and the lucrative tolls on the British merchants' private trade; the company was receiving no remittances from Britain, because the directors considered that Bengal should pay for itself. A clash was inevitable.

Mīr Qāsim removed his capital to distant Munger where he could not be so easily overseen, asserted his authority in the districts, and raised a disciplined force under an Armenian officer. He then turned to the company and negotiated a settlement with Vansittart, by which the company's merchants were to pay an ad valorem duty of 9 percent, against an Indian merchant's duty of 40 percent. At this the Calcutta council revolted, reducing the company's duty to 2.5 percent and on salt only. The breach came in 1763, when Mīr Qāsim, after defeat in four pitched battles, murdered his Indian bankers and British prisoners and fled to Avadh. The next year Mīr Qāsim returned with the emperor Shah 'Ālam II and his minister Shujā' al-Dawlah to be finally defeated at the Battle of Buxar (Baksar). That conflict, rather than Plassey, was the decisive battle that gave Bengal to the British.

These events had been viewed with growing alarm in London. The news of the Mīr Qāsim campaign coincided with the victory of Clive's faction in the company over that of Lawrence Sulivan. Clive used it to appoint himself governor with power to act over the head of the council; he intended an administrative reformation and a political settlement. He arrived in May 1765 to find that the British victory at Buxar had placed Shah 'Ālam in his hands but had created a situation of deep confusion in other respects. Mīr Ja'far had been restored to power but soon died; his second son succeeded him after bestowing lavish gratuities to the company. The British merchants and their agents were the unresisted predators of the Bengal economy, and no one knew the next step to take.

Clive acted with extraordinary vigour. Within four days of arrival he had set up a Select Committee; and, when he left less than two years later, he had effected another revolution. Turning to India's political situation, Clive had to decide where to stop. No one barred his way to Delhi, and he could at that moment have turned the whole Mughal Empire into a company-sponsored state. But he realized that Delhi was easier to have than to hold. He fixed his frontier at the borders of Bihar and Avadh. Shah 'Ālam was given the districts of Kora and Allahabad, and he settled in the latter city, with a tribute (or subsidy) from Bengal that was nearly 10 percent of its estimated revenue. Shujā' al-Dawlah received back Avadh, with a guarantee of its security, in return for paying the troops involved and a cash indemnity. These two were to be buffers between the company and the Marathas and possible marauders from the north.

Clive's next step was to settle Bengal's own status. The Mughal emperor still had much influence, though little power; his complete disfavour might therefore have done the company more harm than good. Clive's solution was to obtain from Shah 'Ālam the "dewanee," or revenue-collecting power, in Bengal and Bihar (the company was thus the imperial divan [*dīwān*] for those two provinces). The nawab was left in charge of the judiciary and magistracy, but he was helpless because he had no army and could get money to raise one only from the company.

This was Clive's system of "dual government." The actual administration remained in Indian hands, and for superintendence Clive appointed a deputy divan, Muḥammad Riḍā Khan, who was at the same time appointed the nawab's deputy. The chain was thus complete. The company, acting in the name of the emperor and using Indian personnel and the traditional apparatus of government, now ruled Bengal. The company's agent was Riḍā Khan; the success of the experiment turned on his efficiency and the extent of the governor's support.

Within the company, Clive enforced his authority by accepting some resignations and enforcing others. Gifts amounting to a value of more than 4,000 rupees were forbidden, and those between that figure and 1,000 rupees were only to be received with official consent. The regulation of private trade was more difficult, for the company paid virtually no salaries. Clive formed a Society of Trade, which operated the salt monopoly, to provide salaries on a graduated scale; but the company directors disallowed this on the ground of expense, and two years later they replaced it by commissions on the revenue, which cost the company more. Finally, Clive dealt with overgrown military allowances with equal vigour, overcoming a mutiny headed by a brigade commander. He used a legacy from Mīr Ja'far to start the first pension fund for the Indian army.

Clive left Calcutta in February 1767. His work—diplomatic, political, and administrative—was a beginning rather than a complete settlement. But in each direction, instead of looking back to the past, it reached out to the future. This creative

View across the Hughli (Hooghly) River to Fort William, Calcutta (now Kolkata), c. 1760.
Hulton Archive/Getty Images

period exacted a heavy price. Clive was pursued to England by his enemies, who launched a parliamentary attack, which, though triumphantly repulsed in 1773, led to his suicide the following year.

It is worth noting how the company's servants so enriched themselves at that time that they undermined the economy of Bengal, and those who returned to Britain became a byword for ostentation. Apart from the great political prizes already mentioned, it must be remembered that all the company's servants were engaged in private trade on their own account. Their new authority and the company's power enabled them to exploit their trade with little hindrance. They had the means of using intimidation (through their agents) against Indian rivals such as the indigo growers and Indian police, customs, revenue, and judicial officials.

Presents and bribes were the price Indians had to pay for freedom from harassment. They were able, through their connection with the administration, to arrange virtual monopolies for particular articles in particular districts, fixing a low purchase price as well as a high selling price. They could arrange commissions on revenue collection, mercantile transactions, and any form of commercial activity. What was not done through agents could be arranged through intermediaries, who also, of course, had their own compensation. Thus, a man could make a fortune, lose it in Britain, return for another, lose it again, and return for a third. It is significant that from the time of Clive's second governorship lamentations increased that the opportunities for quick fortunes were slipping away.

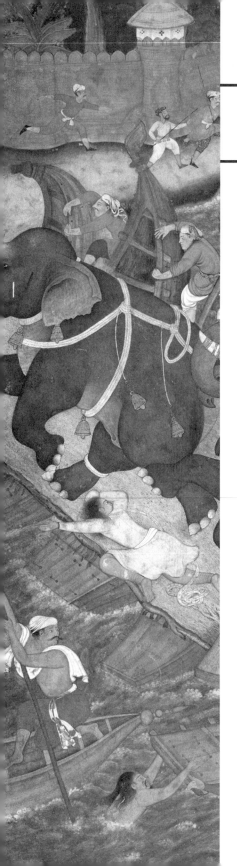

CHAPTER 9

THE EXTENSION OF BRITISH POWER, C. 1765–1856

The year 1765, when Clive arrived in India, can be said to mark the real beginning of the British Empire in India as a territorial dominion. However, the regime he established was really a private dominion of the East India Company. It was not a British colony, and it fitted into the highly flexible structure of the dying Mughal Empire. The structure of the administration was Mughal, not British, and its operators were Indian, personified by the deputy nawab Muḥammad Riḍā Khan.

THE COMPANY BAHADUR

The company was a continuation of the traditional state under British control, and it can be aptly described by its popular title, the Company Bahadur—the Valiant, or Honourable, Company. This Company Bahadur state continued through the governorship of Warren Hastings and in essence until the early 19th century, although Lord Cornwallis (governor-general, 1786–93 and 1805) substituted largely British for Indian personnel. The revenue was collected by the officers of the deputy nawab; the law administered was the current Mughal (Islamic) criminal code, with the traditional personal codes of the Hindu and Muslim communities; the language of administration was Persian. Only the army broke with the past, with its British officers, its discipline, and its Western organization and tactics.

It was this state that Warren Hastings inherited when he became governor of Bengal in 1772. Noteworthy in his 13-year

Warren Hastings, oil painting by Tilly Kettle. Courtesy of The National Portrait Gallery, London

experience some security and a settled order, if not yet an equitable society. Next, the company took over the responsibility for the revenue collection from Riḍā Khan, who was arraigned for corruption; the charges could not be proved, however, even with the approving support of the British authorities. Hastings substituted British for Indian collectors working under a Board of Revenue. In a way this was a retrograde step, for the new collectors were often as corrupt as their predecessors and more powerful; but the change gave legal power to those who already wielded it in fact, and in the future their irregularities could more easily be dealt with than could the surreptitious dealings through the old Indian collectors. Finally, Hastings instituted a network of civil and criminal courts in place of the deputy nawab's. The same law was administered by British judges, who were often incompetent, but a model was provided into which Western ideas and practices could later be fed.

These changes held good through the period of Hastings' rule and may be said to have provided a viable, though not yet very competent or equitable, state. Criminal and personal law cases were virtually in the hands of Indian assessors to British judges who did not know Persian; revenue administration was distorted by the collectors' desire for both personal gain and increased returns for the company. Hastings was least successful in his revenue administration, in which he never advanced beyond a condition of trial and error; a five-year settlement made in ignorance proved unsuccessful, and he was

rule were his internal administration, his dealings with his council, and his foreign policy. Hastings inherited a state that in the five years since Clive's departure had stepped back toward the corruption from which Clive had rescued it. But Hastings was armed with authority by the directors, so that the first two years of his government were a period of real reform. He first dealt with the *dastaks*, or free passes, the use of which had crept in again since Clive's departure; they were abolished, and a uniform tariff of 2.5 percent was enforced on all internal trade. Private trade by the company's servants continued but within enforceable limits. The Bengalis began to

finally reduced to annual settlements, which meant hit-and-miss arrangements with the traditional zamindars.

Hastings was personally incorrupt, but he had to tolerate a good deal in others and to resort to extensive jobbing to placate his supporters both in Bengal and in London. He left a personal legend behind him, but his administration was disorderly as well as strong. A reason for this can be found in his relations with his council. Under the Regulating Act of 1773, Hastings became governor-general of Fort William in Bengal, with powers of superintendence over Madras and Bombay. He was also given a supreme court, administering English law to the British and those connected with them, and a council of four, appointed in the Regulating Act. The leading council member, Sir Philip Francis, hoped to succeed him, and, because Hastings had no power of veto, Francis was able with two supporters to overrule him. For two years Hastings was outvoted, until the death of one member enabled him to use his casting vote. But the struggle continued until Francis—wounded by Hastings in a duel—returned to London in 1780, to continue his vendetta there. The conflict culminated with charges against Hastings of corruption by an Indian official, Nand Kumar (Nandakumar), and with the latter's conviction before the supreme court of perjury and his execution under English law. The episode exposed the moral weakness of the council majority, which failed to reprieve Nand Kumar, and convinced the Indians of Hastings' overriding power.

This struggle, lasting for years, left Hastings triumphant but also embittered; he had to deal not only with the opposition in Calcutta, which never ceased, but also with the constant threat of supersession in the involved politics of London at that time. This strain probably accounts for the acts that formed important items in Hastings's subsequent impeachment—these were the dunning (demands for money) of Raja Chait Singh of Varanasi and his deposition in 1781 and the pressuring of the Begums of Avadh (the mother and grandmother of the nawab Āṣaf al-Dawlah) for the same reason. Hastings's financial difficulties at the time were great, but such actions were harsh and high-handed.

The impeachment of Hastings at the behest of Edmund Burke and the Whigs, which followed his return from India and ended in his acquittal but retirement in 1795, was a kind of very rough justice. Hastings had saved for the company its Indian dominions, and he was relatively incorrupt. But the charges served notice that the company's servants were responsible for their actions toward those they governed, and for these actions they were answerable to Parliament. Hastings was so identified with the company's rule that he was the inevitable target for any such assertion of principle.

THE COMPANY AND THE STATE

During the first half of the 18th century, the East India Company was a trading corporation with a steady annual dividend of 8–10 percent, offering its employees prospects of a modest fortune through private trade, along with great hazards to health and life. It was directed in London by 24 directors—elected annually by the shareholding body, the Court of Proprietors—who worked through a series of committees.

The Bengal adventure from 1757 turned the two courts—of directors and proprietors—into political bodies, because they now controlled a great eastern state. Shares became political counters, the purchase of which might secure votes needed to change the company's policy. A second result was the return to Britain of the company's servants with fortunes; their ostentation and lack of restraint earned them the title nabob (the English version of nawab). These events soon produced reactions. The shareholders wanted to share in this new wealth, in the guise of increased dividends, and the directors wanted the company as well as its servants to benefit from this wealth. Two processes were thus set in motion—one a rising pressure for increased dividends and the other an attempt by the company to discipline its servants and to secure some profit for itself. Broadly speaking, it was the success of the first and the failure of the second that provoked state intervention in the company's affairs.

The close personal connection between the "direction" and the company's servants themselves weighed heavily and eventually stultified the directors' efforts. It produced an infirmity of purpose, which led to the return to Bengal by one faction of servants dismissed for irregularities by another—a factionalism epitomized by the struggle between Clive and Lawrence Sulivan for control of the company. These developments occupied the 1760s, drastically reducing the prestige of the company. On the side of discipline, alarm at the overruling of Henry Vansittart and the wars against Mīr Qāsim and Shah 'Ālam led to the dispatch of Clive as governor in 1765. As the effect of Clive's measures diminished after his return to England in 1767, three "supervisors" were dispatched to Bengal in 1769 with plenary powers, but they were lost at sea. Then Hastings was appointed in 1772 with a reform mandate. But it was too late, for bankruptcy was now knocking at the door.

The company had hoped for large profits from Clive's first control of Bengal. The hopes then shortly dashed were revived by his second governorship. Clive believed that he had secured an ample revenue surplus for the company. On the strength of these expectations, the company's dividend was raised to 12.5 percent in 1767; in the same year the first signs of parliamentary opposition were bought off by the offer of a large annual cash incentive to the state in return for undisturbed possession of Bengal. As the expectations withered, this became a financial millstone that compelled the company in 1772 to ask for a loan to avert bankruptcy. This opened the floodgates of parliamentary criticism, leading to committees of inquiry and revelations of malpractices, to Clive's suicide (1774), and to the beginning of state intervention.

In 1773 the British government gave a substantial loan to the company, but its price was the Regulating Act, passed the same year. The act sought to "regulate" the affairs of the company, in both London and India. In London the qualifications fee for a vote was doubled, and the directors' terms were extended from one to four years, with a year's gap before reelection. This ended the soliciting of votes for the control of policy by private interests and gave continuity of policy to the direction. In India a governor-generalship of Fort William in Bengal was established, with supervisory control over the other Indian settlements and Warren Hastings as its first incumbent. Hastings was given four named councillors, but future appointments were to be made by the company. Finally, a supreme court with a chief justice and three judges was set up. The Regulating Act was a first step toward taking the political direction of British India out of the hands of the company and of securing a unified overall control. But it had serious defects, which bedeviled administration in Bengal and made India (despite British preoccupation with the American Revolution) a leading subject of controversy over the next 20 years.

The governor-general possessed no veto in his council. With three political councillors from Britain, each ready to take Warren Hastings's place, this led to his virtual supersession by the majority for two years and to a paralysis of the executive. Hastings used the energy in fighting his council that should have gone to reforming Bengal. The superintending power added responsibility with little power to enforce it. The supreme court decided to administer English law (the only law it knew) and to apply it not only to all the British in Bengal but also to all Indians connected with them; in practice this meant those Indians in Calcutta, and it led to such grave abuses as the hanging of Nand Kumar for an offense not recognized as being capital in any Indian code.

In 1780 the company's privileges ran out, but this was during the crisis of the American Revolution, so a decision was delayed until 1784. Charles James Fox's radical measure to transfer the control of British India to seven commissioners was defeated by the influence of King George III in the House of Lords, but the next year the matter was settled for more than 70 years by Prime Minister William Pitt the Younger's India Act of 1784. Its essence was the institution of a dual control. The directors were left in charge of commerce and as political executants, but they were politically superintended by a new Board of Control, the president of which, in the person of Henry Dundas, soon became the virtual minister for India. The directors dealt with the board through a secret committee of three, but their dispatches to India could be altered, vetoed, and dictated by the board. The governor-general could be recalled by the crown. In India the governor's council was reduced to three, including the commander in chief, and by an amending act he acquired the veto, which Warren Hastings had missed so much. Finally, there was to be a parliamentary inquiry before each 20-year renewal of the company's charter.

Pitt's India Act proved to be a landmark because it gave the British government control of policy without patronage. The cumbrous dual system developed into a seesaw arrangement of give and take, becoming ever stronger on the government side as greater ability, influence, and power had their effect. The inquiry provision produced a national inquest on Indian affairs every 20 years, marking successive stages in the diminution of the company's political power. On the first such inquiry, in 1793, the company repelled an attempt to compel it to support Christian missionary work; this incident led to the foundation of the Church Missionary Society in 1799. In 1813 the company was obliged by Parliament to admit missionaries and was deprived of its monopoly on trade. By the Act of 1833 it lost its trade altogether and was thenceforth a governing corporation under increasing state surveillance. In 1853, with the introduction of competitive examinations, the company lost most of its patronage and also had to admit nominated directors. Policies were increasingly dictated to a sulky or apathetic board. The last case of the recall of a governor-general by the company was that of Lord Ellenborough in 1844; this was the real swan song of the company, because it was recognized that such a thing could never happen again. The company had become a managing agency of the British government.

RELATIONS WITH THE MARATHAS AND MYSORE

After Clive's settlement in 1765, the East India Company had no desire for any further acquisitions. Its object was still trade; it regarded the acquisition of Bengal as a political framework for the safe conduct of trade, justified by the danger of near anarchy in its most profitable scene of operations. But such a resolution was easier to make than to keep. Indian states were ever ready to seek European help in achieving their own projects; many of the company's servants looked longingly at territorial revenues that might assist their own enrichment, and the exigencies of Indian politics at times made nonalignment difficult to observe.

In 1765 the three centres of the company's power were independent of each other, but the post-Mughal Indian pattern was becoming clear. In the north there were the Mughal fragments of Allahabad, Avadh, and Delhi, with the Sikhs resurgent in the Punjab. In the Deccan the nizam of Hyderabad maintained his Mughal regime uneasily, sometimes overwhelmed by two vigorous and expansive powers—the Marathas and Mysore.

The Marathas had made their bid for the Mughal succession in the previous decade, and they were now recovering from a disastrous defeat at Panipat (1761). The unified leadership of the *peshwa* had given way to a confederacy of the *peshwa* and four military dictatorships developing into monarchies. The

This painting shows the English settlement of Fort St. George on the Coromandel Coast in 1785. The city of Madras (now Chennai), founded by the East India Company, grew up around this seaport. Edward Gooch/Hulton Archive/Getty Images

Marathas were restless, energetic, and acquisitive; their greatest enemy was their own divisions.

In the south the old Hindu state of Mysore had passed into the hands of Hyder Ali in 1762. When Warren Hastings took overall control of the company's possessions in 1774, Madras had already stumbled into war with Hyder Ali and had submitted to a virtually dictated peace under the walls of Madras in 1769. The nawab of the Carnatic had become by degrees dependent on the company because he needed its support against the threat of Hyder and the nizam. Ingenious and feckless, the nawab involved Madras in south Indian politics and the company in his affairs by borrowing from company employees.

Hastings had a natural gift for realpolitik, but he was tied to a policy of nonaggression. Much of his diplomatic skill was spent repairing the blunders of others. His major work for British India was preserving the company's dominion against a coalition of country (Indian) powers, virtually unaided from home, at a time when Britain was itself hard pressed both in America and by a European coalition. His first work was to safeguard Bengal from the reviving power of the Marathas, who had conducted Shah 'Ālam II to Delhi in 1771. Hastings intervened and handed Allahabad and Kora to Shujā' al-Dawlah of Avadh in return for a subsidy and a treaty. The following year he found himself assisting the nawab of Avadh to crush the Afghan Rohillas in the Ganges–Yamuna Doab (this stroke was the first item in the indictment at his impeachment, but its effect was to stabilize the north Indian situation for the next 10 years).

In western India, Hastings was the victim of Bombay brashness and of directorial blunders. A succession struggle in Pune for the *peshwa*-ship led Bombay to support Raghunatha Rao in the hope of securing the island of Salsette and town of Bassein. When this was countermanded by Calcutta, London intervened to renew the venture. In 1779 a British army was surrounded on its way to Pune, one month before a force sent by Hastings completed a brilliant march across India at Surat. This precipitated the Convention of Wadgaon, the terms of which were likewise repudiated by British officials. In 1782 the British made peace with the *peshwa*, abandoning Raghunatha and having only Salsette to show for seven years of war. This first round of what came to be called the Maratha Wars was a draw.

While this war was in progress, Hastings was confronted with a far greater menace. In 1780 the ineptitude of Madras provoked a coalition of the nizam, Hyder Ali, and the Marathas, which defeated the company's armies and swept over the Carnatic. Though without hope of succour from Britain, itself hard-pressed, Hastings set about sustaining the Madras forces and dividing his foes. In 1781 the military balance was restored, and the next year the Marathas made peace (the Treaty of Salbai). Hyder Ali died (1782), French help arrived too late to affect the issue, and in 1784 the Treaty of Mangalore with Hyder Ali's son Tippu Sultan restored the status quo. Hastings thus had little to show in the way of empire building. His feat of defense without external aid was nevertheless remarkable. He preserved the British dominion in India, and by so doing he made it possible for others to extend it. The company had become one of the recognized great powers of India.

Pitt's Act of 1784 reiterated the company's own intentions by forbidding aggressive wars and annexations. Lord Cornwallis and his successor Sir John Shore (governor-general 1793–98) were eager to comply, but Cornwallis nevertheless found himself involved in the third Mysore war (1790–92) with Tippu Sultan, who possessed his father's ability without his judgment. The cause was a combination of Tippu Sultan's intransigence with conflicting obligations undertaken by the Madras government. It took three campaigns before Cornwallis could bring

Tippu Sultan to bay. Half his dominions were annexed, more as a precaution than as an exercise in imperialism. But Tippu Sultan remained formidable and, not unnaturally, more hostile than ever.

THE ASCENT TO PARAMOUNTCY

At that point a radical change occurred in British policy. Two causes were principally responsible. There was a growing body of opinion within the company that only British control of India could end the constant wars and provide really satisfactory conditions for trade; full dominion would be economical as well as salutary. The more-compelling immediate cause was the transformation of European politics by the French Revolution. A new French threat to India emerged, this time overland, with Napoleon I's Egyptian expedition of 1798–99. It was certain that a French army under such a leader would find many friends in India to welcome it, not least Tippu Sultan.

THE GOVERNMENT OF LORD WELLESLEY

The next governor-general, Lord Mornington (later Richard Colley Wellesley, Marquess Wellesley), combined the convictions of the imperialist group with a mandate to deal with the French. Wellesley was thus able to use this fear of the French as a cover for his imperialism until he was near to complete success. His term of office (1798–1805)

was therefore a decisive period in the rise of the British dominion.

Wellesley decided first to strike at Mysore, still a formidable military power and avowedly hostile. He had little difficulty getting the nizam for an ally and securing the neutrality of the *peshwa*. The nizam, hard pressed by the Marathas, was persuaded to disband his contingent of French-trained troops in return for a promise of protection. This was the first of Wellesley's subsidiary treaties. Tippu Sultan had entertained French republican envoys and had planted a tree of liberty at Seringapatam, but when the British stormed Seringapatam in May 1799 he was isolated and at bay, and he found too late that concessions, in the Indian tradition, would not save him. Tippu Sultan died fighting in the breach. Wellesley tempered his imperialism with diplomacy by restoring the child head of the old Hindu reigning family as the ruler of half of Tippu Sultan's dominions; the other half was divided between the nizam and the company. This substantially enlarged the area of the Madras presidency.

For the next three years Wellesley was occupied with certain exercises in realpolitik and with developing his device of the subsidiary treaty. The realpolitik was evidenced in four directions. On the death (1801) of the reigning Carnatic nawab, Wellesley took over his territories, pensioning the new nawab with one-fifth of the revenue. The same fate befell the small but highly cultivated state of Tanjore (1799) and the port city of Surat on a disputed succession.

The biggest of these exercises concerned the Mughal successor state of Avadh in northern India, which had been in treaty relationship with the company since 1765. This rich state had fallen into disorder under the listless though cultured rule of Āṣaf al-Dawlah; on his death in 1797 a succession dispute and an Afghan invasion of the Punjab gave Wellesley a welcome opportunity for interference. He pressed the nawab to disband his troops and increase his payment to the company for his subsidiary force. When the nawab made an offer to abdicate, it was accepted immediately; but, on finding that abdication would mean annexation and not his son's succession, he withdrew it, and Wellesley treated him as rebellious. In 1801 Wellesley annexed half the state, including the Ganges–Yamuna Doab and almost all of Rohilkhand. Whatever the verdict on the means employed, this move had important consequences. Avadh was isolated, and a jumping-off place was secured for an attack on the northern Marathas. The company was no longer looking for buffer states as shields against attack but for territory that would serve as springboards for offensive action.

This change of attitude applies to Wellesley's development of the subsidiary system. In the hands of Clive and Hastings, it was a defensive instrument to safeguard the company's possessions; in the hands of Wellesley, it became an offensive device with which to subject independent states to British control. The essence of the system was that the company undertook to protect a state from external attack in return for control of its foreign relations. For this purpose it provided a subsidiary force of company troops, who were commonly stationed in a cantonment near the state capital. The state paid for this force by means of a subsidy, which was often commuted into ceding territory. In order to protect itself from an external enemy, the state in question bound itself irrevocably to the British power, providing at the heart, as it were, the means of its own coercion should it ever wish to resume independence.

Wellesley first applied this system in 1798 to Hyderabad, when the aging Niẓām 'Alī Khan was in dire fear of the Marathas. In 1800 the subsidy was compounded for the nizam's share of the Mysore annexations. The same system was applied to Avadh, when the great annexation of 1801 was said to be on account of the subsidiary force. It was then the turn of the Marathas—one of the few remaining bastions of Indian independence. Had the Maratha chiefs remained united, Wellesley could have accomplished little; the death of the young *peshwa* released fresh dissensions, however, heightened by the death of the minister Nana Fadnavis in 1800. The chiefs Holkar and Dawlat Rao Sindhia contended for power over the *peshwa*, Baji Rao II. On Holkar's success in 1802, Baji Rao fled to Bassein and applied for British aid. Such an opportunity at the centre of Maratha power was not to be missed; there was also the justification that Dawlat Rao Sindhia, in the north, had 40,000 French-trained troops under a

French commander. The Treaty of Bassein (Dec. 31, 1802) placed, as it were, a time bomb at the heart of the Maratha confederacy; British troops were stationed at Pune, at the price of a cession of territory, and the *peshwa* was reduced to dependency on the British.

This action provoked the Second Maratha War—at first against Dawlat Rao Sindhia and Raghuji Bhonsle and then against Holkar. At first the British won resounding victories. Wellesley's brother Arthur (later Arthur Wellesley, 1st duke of Wellington) defeated the Sindhia-Bhonsle coalition in west-central India, while Lord Lake (Gerard Lake, 1st Viscount Lake)

Duke of Wellington, portrait by Francisco de Goya, 1812. In the National Gallery, London. Courtesy of the Trustees, The National Gallery, London

broke up Sindhia's French army, occupied Delhi, and took the aged emperor Shah ʿĀlam II under protection. Then came a check, however, with the intervention of Holkar using the old Maratha cavalry tactics, forcing the British to retreat, and besieging Delhi. Though Holkar was later defeated, this was the signal for which exasperated directors and a doubting ministry had been waiting. Wellesley was recalled. His race for hegemony had been lost in the last lap. But Wellesley's work, avowedly imperialistic, made ultimate supremacy inevitable. The Marathas were too broken to reunite, and there was no one to take their place.

THE GOVERNMENT OF LORD MINTO

The next 10 years were an interlude, not a new era. During that period both Sindhia and Holkar plundered the chiefs of Rajasthan, thus preparing them mentally for future British overlordship. Meanwhile, bands of freebooters known as Pindaris raided the Nagpur (home of the Bhonsle dynasty) and Hyderabad states in widening circles and thence entered British territory. These were dispossessed villagers and discarded soldiers—the human flotsam and jetsam of the frequent wars. They had the elusiveness of guerrillas, and they received the tacit countenance of the Maratha princes but not the goodwill of the population, who were their principal victims.

Lord Minto (governor-general 1807–13) was occupied with the revived French danger, which was once again serious with the Treaty of Tilsit (1807) and Napoleon I's resulting alliance with Russia. To guard against a French-sponsored Russian attack, British missions were sent to Afghanistan, to Persia, and to Ranjit Singh, the Sikh ruler of the Punjab. The first two proved fruitless, but the Treaty of Amritsar (1809) with Ranjit Singh defined British and Sikh spheres of influence and settled relations for a generation. Minto's other achievement was the capture of the Île de France (Mauritius) and Java from the French-controlled Dutch; the former island became a colony, and the latter was restored to the Dutch under the peace treaty. One result of this episode was the acquisition of the key point of Singapore by Sir Stamford Raffles in 1819.

THE GOVERNMENT OF LORD HASTINGS

The end of the Napoleonic Wars in 1815 opened a new era in India by strengthening the commercial and economic arguments for completing supremacy and by removing all fear of the French. The Pindari raids, which grew year by year until they affected both the Bengal and Madras presidencies, added further reasons for action. The final act was directed by Francis Rawdon-Hastings, 1st marquess of Hastings (governor-general 1813–23), who came to India as a consolation for his failure to attain the premiership under his friend the prince regent (later King George IV). Lord Hastings, however, first had to deal in 1814–16 with the Gurkhas of the northern kingdom of Nepal, who inflicted a series of defeats on a Bengal army unprepared for mountain warfare. Each side earned the respect of the other. The resulting Treaty of Segauli (1816) gave the British the tract of hill country where Shimla (Simla), the site of the future summer capital of British India, was situated, and it settled relations between Nepal and British India for the rest of the British period. Nepal remained independent and isolated, supported by the export of soldiers to strengthen the British military presence in India.

Lord Hastings then turned to the Pindaris. By a large-scale and well-planned enveloping movement, he hoped to enclose them in an iron net. But this involved entering Maratha territories and seeking the cooperation of their princes. Sindhia agreed after agonizing indecision, and this really settled the issue. Holkar's state was in disorder and was easily defeated. Both the raja of Nagpur and the *peshwa* resisted and attacked the British forces stationed under their respective subsidiary treaties. Nagpur quickly collapsed, but the *peshwa* kept up a running fight before surrendering in June 1818. The Pindari bands themselves, chased hither and thither, broke up or surrendered.

The East India Company was thus the undisputed master of India, as far as the Sutlej River in the Punjab. This episode was completed by the acceptance of British suzerainty by the Rajput chiefs of Rajasthan, central India, and Kathiawar, as they had formerly accepted the Mughals. Thus the year 1818 marks a watershed, when the British Empire in India became the British Empire of India.

THE SETTLEMENT OF 1818

The diplomatic settlement of 1818, except for a few annexations before 1857, remained in force until 1947 and is therefore worth some attention. The company, under the influence of its guiding star of economy, wished to be saved as much of the expense of administering India as possible, especially the less fertile portions. Having controlled the larger states by its subsidiary forces (for which they paid), it was content with tribute from the remainder, with control posts at strategic points. Thus, Kathiawar was controlled from Baroda and Rajasthan from Ajmer. There was no thought of integration as in Mughal days. The states were isolated and excluded from any connection with the British. About half of India remained under Indian rulers, robbed of any power of aggression and deprived of any opportunity of cooperation: in the south were the large units of Mysore, Hyderabad, and Travancore; in the west, the states of Shivaji's family; across the centre to the east, Nagpur and a number of poor "jungle" states; in the west and west-central areas, numerous Rajput and other Hindu chiefs with the surviving Maratha states of Sindhia, Holkar, and the Gaekwar; west of the Yamuna River, some Sikh princedoms; and in the Ganges valley, the still prosperous and disorderly state of Avadh. In all there were more than 360 units; politically, they were like the surviving fragments of a broken jigsaw puzzle, with all its complexity but without its unity.

The subjection of a whole subcontinent containing a unique civilization has long been a source of historical wonderment. The one-time explanations of innate superiority and of mere fate are no longer seriously entertained. But analysis goes far to dissipate the mystery. In the first place, the feat was not unique; the Turkish Muslims had twice done much the same—for shorter periods, it is true, but also with fewer resources. All these achievements were made possible by the innate divisiveness of Hindu society, rent by class and caste divisions, which rendered it unusually willing to call in unwelcome outsiders to defeat the still more unwelcome neighbour. The foreigners, asked in the first resort to assist in defeating a rival, were in the last resort accepted as masters in preference to dominance by a rival. Thus, Marathas preferred the British to the Mughals, and the nizam preferred the British to the Marathas. Long historical memories can be inhibiting as well as inspiring. Against this setting can be set the company's urge toward unity in the interests of trade. Even when its Indian trade was no longer profitable, India gave profits to others, and its opium bought the Chinese tea, which gave the East India Company its overall profits. Given the fact of expansion, Britain enjoyed the advantage of overseas reinforcement through its sea power and of reserves of power, far greater than that of any Indian prince, through its rapidly expanding industrial economy. A lost battle for the British was an incident in a campaign, for the Indian prince usually the end of the chapter. Then there were the technical advantages of arms and military discipline and the immense general advantage of a disciplined civilian morale. In the later stages this was boosted by the rising self-confidence of Europeans in general, with their belief that the western European civilization was the only truly progressive one that had ever existed. For the Hindu, on the other hand, his world was at its lowest ebb—in the Kali Yuga, or Dark Age—while the Muslim believed in inscrutable fate. The Hindu's heart was in his religio-cultural complex, and political dominion meant little to the ordinary Hindu so long as this remained untouched.

ORGANIZATION AND POLICY IN BRITISH INDIA

The realization of supremacy in 1818 made urgent the problem of the organization of and determination of policy for British India. So far only Bengal had been deliberately organized; the extensive areas annexed after 1799 in the north and the south were still under provisional arrangements. Now the *peshwa's* dominions in the west awaited settlement. The administrators of the first 30 years of the 19th century gave British India the form it retained until 1947. Outstanding among them were Sir Thomas Munro in

Madras, Mountstuart Elphinstone in western India, and Sir Charles T. Metcalfe in Delhi; to this trio must be added a fourth—Holt MacKenzie, whose planning determined the lines of settlement from Banaras (Varanasi) to the Yamuna River.

ORGANIZATION

The only areas so far definitely settled were those of Bengal, Bihar, and Orissa. Lord Cornwallis had been charged by Pitt with the reorganization of Bengal under the new act. Besides being a soldier of distinction, Cornwallis was a man of outstanding integrity, a landlord with rural tastes, and an instinctive

Lord Cornwallis, undated engraving. Encyclopædia Britannica, Inc.

Whig. Cornwallis first undertook a cleansing of the existing system. Discipline among the company's servants was enforced at the price of dismissal. Private trade was forbidden to all government officers, and the service was divided into administrative and commercial branches. These measures (which, with others, became known as the Cornwallis Code) were coupled with a generous salary system, which removed the temptation to corruption. From this time the company's service began to gain its later reputation for efficiency and integrity. All this could be done because the governor-general, with his council of three and his veto power, was now unassailable to the attacks that had ruined Vansittart and frustrated Warren Hastings.

From this base Cornwallis built up the Bengal system. Its first principle was Anglicization. In the belief that Indian officials were corrupt (and that British corruption had been cured), all posts worth more than £500 a year were reserved for the company's covenanted servants. Next came the government. The 23 districts each had a British collector with magisterial powers and two assistants, who were responsible for revenue collection. The judicial system was organized with district judges for both civil and criminal cases. In civil cases there were four courts of appeal; and in criminal, four circuit courts. Criminal justice was taken over from the nawab's deputy, thus removing the last shred of Mughal authority. The criminal code was

the Islamic one, humanely modified. A new police force replaced the former local constables of the zamindars. This new system, which, with its division of authority, showed its Whig influence, was rounded off by the proclamation of the rule of law, making all governmental acts answerable in the ordinary courts of law. Though hardly noticed at the time by Indians, it was a radical innovation with far-reaching effects. It was a charter of civil—as distinct from political—liberty.

Cornwallis's permanent settlement of the land revenue is the measure that most deeply affected the life and structure of Indian society, three-quarters of the revenue coming from the land. He found a system of hereditary zamindars, who had acquired police and magisterial powers as well and who were much shaken by the frequent changes of revenue policy under the British. The "settlement" was the decision in 1793 to stabilize the revenue demand at a fixed annual figure, with a commission to the zamindar for collection, and to regard him as the owner of his zamindari; he had the disposal of wastelands within his jurisdiction, but these lands were liable to be sold for arrears of payment. Thus, the land revenue collector became a landlord, with the Achilles' heel that the lands he administered could be sold for arrears, while the tiers of lesser landholders became his tenants. The zamindar reaped the profit of rising prices and of cultivation of wasteland, while the classes below him lost their occupancy rights. The intended protection of these tenants proved illusory because their rights were customary, unsupported by documents. The legal cases that ensued clogged the courts to the point of breakdown. Initially, the zamindar often lost his holding because the fixed demand was pitched too high. The net result of this measure was the creation of a landlord class, loyal to the British connection but divorced from touch with the cultivators. The government, receiving the revenue from the zamindars, knew little of the people and could do little for them.

At first the Bengal system was thought to provide the key to Indian administration, but doubts multiplied with the years. In Madras, Sir Thomas Munro retained the paternal framework of government but introduced a radically differing method of revenue management known as the ryotwari system, in which the settlement was made directly with the cultivator, each field being separately measured and annually assessed. The system eliminated the middleman but sometimes placed the cultivators at the mercy of lower officials, who often formed cliques of caste groups. Munro considered that innovation and ignorance were the ruling British vices. His system tended to be static and to allow the subordinate tail to wag the directing British dog.

In western India, Mountstuart Elphinstone had the problem of reconciling to British control the resentful Marathas of the *peshwa's* dominions. With a masterly mixture of tact and firmness, he largely succeeded. He retained Indian agency as far as possible, and he allowed the Maratha nobles, or *jāgīrdārs,*

to retain most of their land and many of their privileges. He even continued some donations to Hindu temples. He used the *ryotwari* method of assessing land revenue, collecting through local officials from the village headmen. In Bombay he encouraged Western learning and science, tempting suspicious Brahmans to open their minds to the West. He foresaw the ultimate end of British rule through voluntary Westernization, and he took the first steps toward introducing the new world without antagonizing the old.

In the north, Sir Charles Metcalfe discovered the largely autonomous village with its joint ownership and cultivation by caste oligarchies. He believed this to be the original pattern of rural organization throughout India, and it became his passion to preserve it as far as possible in current conditions. Like Munro and Elphinstone, he was suspicious of change and wished to leave the villagers alone as far as possible. In this he was powerfully supported by the work of Holt MacKenzie, the Bengal secretary whose memorandum of 1819 set a course of recognition and record of village rights for the whole of the northwestern provinces (as later revised and codified, this marked the end of the Bengal system of permanent revenue settlement).

The resulting system of administration of British India was still largely Indian in pattern, though it was now British in direction and superintendence. It was paternalistic and hierarchical, and it suffered, like its immediate predecessors, from a chronic tendency to overassess.

The Mughal emperor was replaced by the mystical entity the Company Bahadur, and its representative, the governor-general, moved about with almost equal pomp. The higher direction was exclusively European, but the officers acted in a Mughal spirit, and the administration at subdistrict and village level went on much as before. But there were also large changes. The British established on a national scale the idea of property in land, and the resulting buying and selling caused large class changes. Their new security benefited the commercial classes generally, but the deliberate sacrifice of Indian industry to the claims of the new machine industries of Britain ruined such ancient crafts as cotton and silk weaving. The new legal system, with its network of courts, proved efficient on the criminal justice side but was heavily overloaded on the civil.

The strain and the scandal of this situation created a demand for increased Indian agency and caused the first breaches in the British monopoly of higher office. Indianization began with the confessed inefficiency of the British legal system. The picture is completed by the company's army, separately organized in the three presidencies and officered, like the civil service, exclusively by the British. It was backed by contingents of the British army. The Bengal army preponderated in numbers and fighting spirit. By European standards it was cumbrous and inefficient; some of its defects were exposed in the early days of the war with Nepal. But it was more than a match for anything that could be brought against it. Of other powers in the region, only the Russians, could they have moved so far in force, might have made short work of it.

THE DETERMINATION OF POLICY

The administration of British India thus established was impressive though ponderous. But it was essentially static; it was a repair of the machinery of government without any decision about its direction. Such a situation in a subcontinent could not be viable for long.

In the early 19th century a great debate went on in Britain about the nature of the

This 1858 illustration shows plainclothes sepoys, Indian soldiers from the Bengal army of the British East India Company. Hulton Archive/Getty Images

government in India. The company wanted India to be regarded as a field for British commercial exploitation, with the company holding the administrative whip with one hand and exploiting with the other. This pleased no one but the company itself. As an extension of this, the new regime could be regarded as a law-and-order or police state, holding the ring while British merchants in general traded profitably. But this was assailed from several quarters. There was the Whig demand, first voiced by Edmund Burke in his campaign against Warren Hastings, that the Indian government must be responsible for the welfare of the governed. This was reinforced by Evangelicals in England, both Anglican and Baptist, who added the rider that, as the ruler, Britain was responsible for India's spiritual and moral welfare as well. The Evangelicals were a rising force, influential in the British "establishment." Their remedy for India, as a preparation for conversion, was English education. They were reinforced in this by the rising group of freethinking utilitarians—followers of Jeremy Bentham and John Stuart Mill—who were influential in the company's service, who wished to use India as a laboratory for their theories, and who thought Indian society could be transformed by legislation. Finally, there were radical rationalists who had borrowed the doctrine of human rights from France and wished to introduce them into India, and on the practical side there was a body of British merchants and manufacturers who saw in India both a market and a profitable theatre of activity and who chafed at

the restraints of the East India Company's monopoly.

Some of these influences seeped into the Tory ascendancy, which lasted until 1830. In 1813 the East India Company lost its monopoly of trade with India and was compelled to allow free entry of missionaries. British India was declared to be British territory, and money was to be set aside annually for the promotion of both Eastern and Western learning. But the real breakthrough came with the governor-generalship of Lord William Bentinck (served 1828–35) and with the Whig government that from 1830 carried the great Reform Bill.

Bentinck was a radical aristocrat. His administrative reforms were in line with utilitarian theory but with deference to local conditions and in harmony with his own military sense of command. In Bengal the collector was made the real head of his district by the addition of civil judgeship to his magistracy; he was also disciplined by the institution of commissioners to superintend him. The judiciary was overhauled with the same eye to a chain of authority.

But it was as a social reformer that Bentinck made an indelible mark on the future of India. He was commissioned by the directors to effect economies in order to show a balanced budget in the approaching charter-renewal discussions. In doing this he incurred much odium, but he was able to take the first steps in Indianizing the higher judicial services. On his arrival Bentinck was confronted with an agitation against suttee, the burning of Hindu widows on the funeral pyres of their husbands. In suppressing the practice, he had to face the reproaches of both Hindus and Europeans on the grounds of religious interference. But he was also fortified by the support of the Hindu reformer Ram Mohun Roy. In thus acting and in prohibiting child sacrifice on Sagar Island and discouraging infanticide—a widespread practice among the Rajputs—Bentinck established the principle that the general good did not permit violations of the universal moral law, even if done in the name of religion. The same principle applied to the suppression of ritual murder and robbery by gangs of *thagi* (thugs) in central India in the name of the goddess Kali.

Bentinck also substituted English for Persian as the language of record for government and the higher courts, and he declared that government support would be given primarily to the cultivation of Western learning and science through the medium of English. In this he was supported by Thomas Babington (later Lord) Macaulay.

This period saw the British in India committed to promoting the positive welfare of India instead of merely holding a ring for trade and exploitation; to introducing Western knowledge, science, and ideas alongside the Indian with a view to eventual absorption and adoption; and to the promotion of Indian participation in the government with a view to eventual Indian self-government. It was the changeover from the concept of a Mughal successor state—the Company Bahadur—to that of a Westernized self-governing dominion. In the former case, the British were wardens of a stationary society; in the latter, trustees of an evolving one.

A word should be added about the Indian states. Their place in British India was also a subject of the great debate on the future of India. On the whole, the argument for subordinate isolation held, and no great change occurred in their status until after the revolt of 1857. Out of the discussions, however, came the de facto principle of British paramountcy, which was increasingly assumed though not openly proclaimed. The only important change before 1840 was the takeover of Mysore in 1831 on the ground of misgovernment; it was not annexed, but it was administered on behalf of the raja for the next 50 years.

THE COMPLETION OF DOMINION AND EXPANSION

After the settlement of 1818, the only parts of India beyond British control were a fringe of Himalayan states to the north, the valley and hill tracts of Assam to the east, and a block of territory in the northwest covering the Indus valley, the Punjab, and Kashmir. To the south Ceylon was already occupied by the British, but to the east the Buddhist kingdom of Myanmar (Burma) straddled the Irrawaddy River.

The Himalayan states were Nepal of the Gurkhas, Bhutan, and Sikkim. Nepal and Bhutan remained nominally independent throughout the British period, though both eventually became British protectorates—Nepal in 1815 and Bhutan in 1866. Sikkim came under British protection in 1890; earlier it had ceded the hill station of Darjiling (Darjeeling) to the British. The valley and hill tracts of Assam were taken under protection to save them from attack by Burmans from Myanmar. Beginning in 1836, the Indian tea plant was cultivated, after the failure of Chinese imported ones, and thus commenced the great Indian tea industry.

In the early 19th century the Burmans were in an aggressive mood, having defeated the Thais (1768) and subjected Arakan and hill states on either side of the river valleys. Attacks on British protected territory in 1824 started the First Anglo-Burmese War (1824–26), which, though mismanaged, led to the British annexation of the coastal strips of Arakan and Tenasserim in 1826. The Second Anglo-Burmese War (1852) was caused by disputes between merchants (trading in rice and teak timber) and the Rangoon governor. The governor-general, Lord Dalhousie (served 1848–56), intervened, annexing the maritime province of Pegu with the port of Rangoon (now Yangon) in a campaign—this time well-managed and economical. Commercial imperialism was the motive for this campaign.

To the northwest, British India was bounded by the Sikh kingdom of Ranjit Singh, who added the Vale of Kashmir and Peshawar to his state in 1819. Beyond was confusion, with the Afghan monarchy in dissolution and its lands parcelled between several chiefs and Sind (Sindh),

controlled by a group of emirs, or chiefs. British indifference changed to action in the 1830s, owing to the advance of Russia in Central Asia and to that nation's diplomatic duel with Lord Palmerston about its influence in Turkey. Afghanistan was seen as a point from which Russia could threaten British India or Britain could embarrass Russia. Lord Auckland (served 1836–42) was sent as governor-general, charged with forestalling the Russians, and from this stemmed his Afghan adventure and the First Anglo-Afghan War (1838–42). The method adopted was to restore Shah Shojā', the exiled Afghan king, then living in the Punjab, by ousting the ruler of Kabul, Dūst Muḥammad. Ranjit Singh cooperated in the enterprise but cleverly avoided any military commitment, leaving the British to bear the whole burden. The route of invasion lay through Sind, because of Sikh occupation of the Punjab.

The emirs' treaty of 1832 with the British was brushed aside, and Sind was forced to pay arrears of tribute to Shah Shojā'. At first things went well, with victories and the occupation of Kabul in 1839. But then it was discovered that Shah Shojā' was too unpopular to rule the country unaided; the British restoring force thus became a foreign occupying army—anathema to the liberty-loving Afghans—and was regularly engaged in putting down sporadic tribal revolts. After two years a general revolt in the autumn of 1841 overwhelmed and virtually annihilated the retreating British garrison. Meanwhile, the Russian menace

RANJIT SINGH

Raujit Singh (1780–1839; also spelled Runjit Singh, byname Lion of the Punjab) was the founder and maharaja (1801–39) of the Sikh kingdom of the Punjab.

He was the only child of Maha Singh, on whose death in 1792 he became chief of the Shukerchakias, a Sikh group. His inheritance included Gujranwala town and the surrounding villages, now in Pakistan. At 15 he married the daughter of a chieftain of the Kanhayas, and for many years his affairs were directed by his ambitious mother-in-law, the widow Sada Kaur. A second marriage, to a girl of the Nakkais, made Ranjit Singh preeminent among the clans of the Sikh confederacy.

In July 1799 he seized Lahore, the capital of the Punjab (now the capital of Punjab province, Pak.). The Afghan king, Shah Zaman, confirmed Ranjit Singh as governor of the city; in 1801, however, Ranjit Singh proclaimed himself maharaja of the Punjab. He had coins struck in the name of the Sikh Gurus, the revered line of Sikh leaders, and proceeded to administer the state in the name of the Sikh commonwealth. A year later he captured Amritsar, the most important commercial entrepôt in northern India and sacred city of the Sikhs. Thereafter he proceeded to subdue the smaller Sikh and Pashtun (Afghan) principalities that were scattered over the Punjab. But his later forays east were checked by the English, with whom he signed the Treaty of Amritsar (1809), fixing the Sutlej River as the eastern boundary of his territories.

Ranjit Singh then turned his ambitions toward the north and west, against the Pashtuns. In the summer of 1818 his troops captured the city of Multan and six months later entered the Pashtun citadel, Peshawar. In July 1819 he finally expelled the Pashtuns from the Vale of Kashmir. By 1820 he had consolidated his rule over the whole Punjab between the Sutlej and Indus rivers.

All of Ranjit Singh's conquests were achieved by Punjabi armies composed of Sikhs, Muslims, and Hindus. His commanders were also drawn from different religious communities, as were his cabinet ministers. In 1820 Ranjit Singh began to modernize his army, using European officers to train the infantry and the artillery. The modernized Punjabi army fought well in campaigns in the North-West Frontier (on the Afghanistan border). Ranjit Singh added Ladakh (a region of eastern Kashmir) to his kingdom in 1834, and his forces repulsed an Afghan counterattack on Peshawar in 1837.

In 1838 he agreed to a treaty with the British viceroy Lord Auckland to restore Shah Shojā' to the Afghan throne at Kabul. In pursuance of this agreement, the British Army of the Indus entered Afghanistan from the south, while Ranjit Singh's troops went through the Khyber Pass and took part in the victory parade in Kabul.

Shortly afterward, Ranjit Singh was taken ill, and he died at Lahore in June 1839, almost exactly 40 years after he had entered the city as a conqueror. In little more than six years after his death, the Sikh state he had created collapsed because of the internecine strife of rival chiefs.

in eastern Europe had receded. Auckland's successor, Lord Ellenborough (served 1842–44), arranged for a brief reoccupation and sack of Kabul by means of a converging march from Kandahār in the south and Jalālābād in the east and a return through the Khyber Pass. Thus, honour was satisfied, and the fact of defeat was glossed over. Shah Shojāʿ was shortly thereafter murdered. The episode demonstrated, at a heavy price in terms of money and human suffering, both the ease with which Afghanistan could be overrun by a regular army and the difficulty of holding it. The enterprise, though conceived as an insurance against Russian imperialism, developed into a species of imperialism itself. Economics joined with Afghan spirit to put a limit on British expansion in this direction.

After the Afghans came Sind. There was little to be said for the emirs themselves—a group of related chiefs who had come to power in the late 18th century and had kept the country in poverty and stagnation. A treaty in 1832 threw the Indus River open to commerce except for the passage of armed vessels or military stores; at the same time, the integrity of Sind was recognized. Thus, Auckland's march through Sind was a clear violation of a treaty signed only seven years before. Sore feelings at the turn of events in Afghanistan produced a final breach. On a charge of unfriendly feelings by the emirs during the First Anglo-Afghan War, Karachi, occupied in 1839, was retained. Further demands were then made; the moderate resident James

Outram was superseded by the militant general Sir Charles James Napier; and resistance was provoked, to be crushed at the Battle of Miani (1843). Sind was then annexed to the Bombay Presidency; after four years of rough-and-ready rule by Napier, its economy was put in order by Sir Bartle Frere.

There remained the great Sikh state of the Punjab, the single-handed creation of Ranjit Singh. Succeeding to a local chiefship in 1792 at the age of 12, he occupied Lahore in 1799 under a grant from Zamān Shah, the Afghan king. He could thus pose as a legitimate ruler, not only to his own people (the Sikhs) but to the majority of Muslims of the Punjab. From this start he extended his dominions northwestward as far as the Afghan hills and including the Kashmir region and southwestward well beyond Multan, toward the Sindh region. The Treaty of Amritsar with the British in 1809 barred his expansion southeastward; besides directing Ranjit's expansionism northwestward, it produced an admiration for the disciplined company's troops, who coolly repelled the Sikh Akali suicide squads when they attacked the British at Amritsar. From that time dates the formation of the formidable Sikh army with its 40,000 disciplined infantry, 12,000 cavalry, and powerful artillery—as well as large numbers of foreign mercenary officers. It was generally agreed that the Sikh army compared favourably for efficiency with the company's forces.

Ranjit Singh employed Hindus and Muslims besides Sikhs, but his regime was in fact a Sikh dominion based on tacit Hindu support and Muslim acquiescence. It used most of the revenue to support the army, which made it apparently powerful but retarded development. It was a highly personal system, centred on Ranjit himself. It was thus one that the company would not lightly attack but that had inner weaknesses behind its formidable facade. These weaknesses began to be exposed on the morrow of Ranjit's death in 1839; within six years the state was on the verge of dissolution. Army disbandment or foreign adventure seemed the only way for the Sikhs to deal with this crisis. The former being impossible, at length the Rani Jindan, regent for the boy prince Dalip Singh, the chief minister, and the commander in chief agreed on a move against the British. The frontier was crossed in December 1845, and a sharp and bloody war ended in a British victory at the Battle of Sobraon in February 1846. The British feared to annex outright a region full of former soldiers and wished to retain a buffer state against possible attack from the northwest. By the Treaty of Lahore they took Kashmir and its dependencies, with the fertile Jullundur (now Jalandhar) area, reduced the regular army to 20,000 infantry and 12,000 cavalry, and exacted a sizable cash indemnity. The British then sold Kashmir to the Hindu chief Gulab Singh of Jammu, who had changed sides at precisely the right moment. Thus were sown the seeds of a chronic political problem for the subcontinent.

Sikh nobles chafed under the conditions of the peace, and two years later a rising at Multan became a national Sikh revolt; the Sikh court was helpless. Another brief and still bloodier war, with the Sikhs this time fighting resolutely, ended with their surrender in March 1849 and the British annexation of the state.

Annexation this time proved viable, perhaps because of the underlying tension between Sikhs and Muslims. The Sikhs may have preferred the British to a Muslim raj. The British repressed the *sirdars*, or Sikh leaders, but left the rest of the community and its religion untouched.

Whatever the reason, the Sikhs sided with the British during the 1857 mutiny; the Muslims, however, could not forget their loss of power to the Sikhs. There was little commercial exploitation of the state, and the Sikhs found employment in the army. Lord Dalhousie closely supervised the administration through a like-minded agent, Sir John Lawrence. The pair produced a new model administration, establishing what was known as the Punjab school. It was noted for strong personal leadership, on-the-spot decisions, strong-arm methods, impartiality between the communities, and material development, including irrigation. A canal, a road, or a bridge was the Punjabi official's delight. The cultivator was preferred to the *sirdar*; the countryman was preferred to the townsman. The Punjab system was strong and efficient, creating prosperity, but it never reconciled the two main confessional communities or welded them into unity.

Lord Dalhousie's reign is often regarded as an exercise in imperialism; in fact it was more an exercise in Westernism.

Dalhousie was a man of great drive and strong conviction. In general, he considered Western civilization to be far superior to that of the Indian, and the more of it that could be introduced, the better. Along these lines he pushed Western education—introducing a grant-in-aid system, which later proliferated Indian private colleges—and planned three universities. Socially, he allowed Christian converts to inherit the property of their Hindu families. Materially, he extended irrigation and the telegraph and introduced the railway.

Politically, British administration was preferable to Indian, and it was to be imposed where possible. Externally, this led to annexation, as in the Punjab and in Myanmar, rather than to the control of foreign relations or to a British-superintended native regime. Internally, it led to the annexation of Indian states on the ground of misgovernment or the doctrine of lapse. The leading case of misgovernment was the disorderly but prosperous Muslim state of Avadh—one of the oldest allies of the British. The doctrine of lapse concerned Hindu states where rulers had no direct natural heirs. Hindu law allowed adoption to meet these cases, but Dalhousie declared that such must be approved by the supreme government; otherwise there was "lapse" to the paramount power, which meant the imposition of the usual British administration. The three principal cases were Satara in 1848 (the descendants of the Maratha king Shivaji), Jhansi (1853), and the large Maratha state of Nagpur (1854). Finally, Dalhousie abolished the titular

sovereignties of the Carnatic and Tanjore and declined to continue the former *peshwa's* pension to his adopted son.

THE FIRST CENTURY OF BRITISH INFLUENCE

The onset of British influence in India differed both in manner and in kind from that of other historical invasions. The British came neither as migrating hordes seeking new homes nor, originally, as armies seeking plunder or empire. They had no missionary zeal. Yet eventually they did more to transform India than did any previous ruling power. This apparent paradox requires some explanation.

POLITICAL EFFECTS

At first the British were only one group of foreign traders among several, fortunate to find in the Mughals a firm government ready to foster trade. Their entry into politics was gradual, first as allies of country powers, then as their virtual directors, and only finally as masters. At each step they were assisted by local powers who preferred British influence to that of their neighbours. It was mainly in the 20 years from 1798 to 1818 that they were consciously imperialistic and only thereafter that they treated India as a conquered rather than an acquired country. The effect of this was to replace the defunct Mughal regime and the abortive Maratha successor empire with a veiled but very real hegemony.

Indians were accustomed to the idea of political unity and overlordship. They admired the British for being more successful than themselves, while reprobating many of the British habits and doctrines. But the old ruling classes showed little sign of adopting British institutions; after 1818 they withdrew within themselves, nursing their memories rather than feeding their hopes. The Indian regimes of 1857 all assumed a traditional form. The one department in which Western influence was effective was the military. From the time of Mir Qasim in Bengal (1760–63), Indian princes began to train troops in the European manner and to form parks of artillery. Some of these bodies, culminating in Ranjit Singh's Sikh army, attained a high degree of efficiency. Their problem was maintenance, for most princes lacked the necessary resources to pay their men and officers regularly and maintain their arms. Indian opinion, in general, saw the British as the latest holders of the traditional paramount power. There was no novelty in the fact that there were foreign personnel within the government, for this had been a Mughal practice too. What was new was the artificial division between British India and Indian-governed India, with little contact between the two. The Mughals had practiced partnership for a century; the Turks and Afghans, subordinate cooperation; but the British, it seemed, wished to forget the Indian leaders altogether.

ECONOMIC EFFECTS

Things were quite different in the economic field. Up to 1750 the effect of the East India Company's operations was marginal. Production of cotton and silk goods, indigo, saltpetre, and, later, opium was stimulated in particular areas such as Bengal, Gujarat, and Malwa, with some gain to the middlemen but no sign of any general rise in living standards. India was then, as now, mainly agricultural, and its industries, though significant, were marginal to its whole economy. The latter changed, however, with the acquisition of Bengal. The bias in favour of British merchants diverted trade from their Indian counterparts, though some of the profit went back to the British merchants' Indian agents. The extravagant present giving, a large abuse of a traditional system, diverted much money to Britain. Still more, the pressure on the zamindars for more revenue, and theirs in turn on the cultivators, further diminished the Bengali income. To this must be added the operation of monopolies, public and private. When the Bengal famine of 1770 occurred, a famine reckoned to have swept away one-third of the population, little attempt at relief was made, though it would have been practicable given Bengal's network of waterways. The cruel severity with which the revenue was still collected at this time delayed recovery for many years. Economic recovery was further delayed by Warren Hastings's makeshift revenue arrangements; and much dislocation was caused in the social structure, with its own effect on economic life.

Cornwallis's permanent settlement (1793), after an initial period of dislocation, gave relief and security to the zamindars, who benefited by the rise in prices and the cultivation of wastelands; the cultivators themselves, now the zamindars' tenants-at-will, remained as poor as before. Apart from the zamindars, the principal class to benefit from the British was that of the entrepreneurs of Calcutta, who acted as agents and bankers to the British. Thus, both Clive's and Hastings's business managers became wealthy landowners. In Madras little could be done until the burden of the Carnatic nawab's debts was removed and the country was settled after the Cornwallis-Wellesley annexations (1792–99). There, economic settlement turned on the working of the *ryotwari* revenue system; regularity of collection was offset by severity of assessment, and the same may be said of both western and northern India.

After about 1800 there was a new factor: machine-made cotton goods from Britain. These steadily undermined the Indian handicraft industries until all but the highest and coarsest grades of cloth were squeezed out. The district of Dacca (now Dhaka, Bangl.) was especially illustrative of this process. Beginning in 1836, tea was grown in Assam and coffee was cultivated in the south. Coal mining was begun, but its growth, with that of the jute and cotton machine industries, had to wait for the second half of the century. The average Indian was far more secure than before (except for famine) but generally was not much more prosperous. India drifted toward the status of a colonial economy, a supplier of raw materials, a market for manufactured articles, to the profit of the foreigner.

SOCIAL EFFECTS

The social effects of this period were considerable. They took mainly the form of the displacement of classes. As already noted, there was a general disturbance in Bengal caused by the permanent settlement, whereby the lesser landholders were reduced to the condition of tenants-at-will. But there was also disturbance among the zamindars. The first upset followed the famine of 1770, when the cultivators were often too few for the revenue demand to be met, and "farming" the revenue—that is, selling the right of taxation to a second party—for some time took the place of a revenue settlement. The second upset came with the permanent settlement of 1793, when the revenue figure fixed was in many cases too high for the existing cultivation. By 1820 it was calculated that more than one-third of the estates had changed hands through sale for arrears of land tax. The purchasers were in the main the Calcutta entrepreneurs newly enriched by their contacts with the British. Many were absentees. The social link between landholder and cultivator had been broken, cash nexus replacing traditional rights.

In Calcutta itself, these same rentiers formed a fashionable and intellectual society from which came the first significant cultural contacts with the West. It was composed of the prosperous section of the three upper Bengali castes, with such others as gained acceptance by their wealth or education. Collectively, this literate class of gentry was known as the *bhadralok* ("respectable people").

In the north there was less dislocation, though the landholders, many of whom had no title but the sword, tended to be repressed. There was a general recognition of rights and broadly of their protection. The chief sufferers were ruling families, who lost power, and the official aristocracy, who lost office. In the south, chiefs whom Sir Thomas Munro dispossessed were largely in the class of robber barons.

In western India a balance between aristocratic and cultivating rights was perhaps better-maintained than elsewhere, and relations were more harmonious. Of significance was the rapid development of Bombay from the time it came to possess a large hinterland in 1818. With it came the rise of the enterprising Parsi community (Zoroastrians of Persian heritage).

In general, apart from Bengal, there was some repression of the old aristocracy, a regulation and preservation of lesser landholders' rights, and an encouragement of the commercial classes. Communities did not break up, but their fortunes rose and fell with their ability to adjust to changing conditions.

CULTURAL EFFECTS

The cultural effects of British influence during the century from 1757 to 1857, though less spectacular, were in the long run farther-reaching. At first there was little enough. But as the Europeans grew in political importance, Indians became interested in the causes of the growth, so that the first examples of cultural influence were in the military field. Some Europeans, in their turn, early interested themselves in Indian culture, as evident from the foundation of the Asiatic Society of Bengal in 1784 by Sir William Jones and from the translation of Sanskrit works such as the *Bhagavadgita* and Kalidasa's *Abhijnanashakuntala* and of Persian works such as the *Āʾīn-e Akbarī* by Abū al-Faḍl ʿAllāmī.

As the British completed their supremacy, four Indian attitudes could be discerned. There were Indians who rejected all things Western, retiring to their houses and estates to dream of the past. There were those who were clients and employees of the British, as they had been of the Mughals and the Turks before them, without any intention of giving up their traditional culture. But there were also those who, while remaining good Hindus or Muslims, began to study Western ways and thought for careerist purposes. And there was, finally, a small group who sought to study the ideas and spirit of the West with a view to incorporating in their own society anything that seemed desirable.

The agents of Western influence were government officials, who carried Western ideas such as utilitarianism and equality before the law and Western concepts of property into their administration of revenue and the law, and missionaries, who combined hostility to Hinduism and Islam with the presentation of a new ethic—the practice of good works and the promotion of English education as preliminaries for conversion. It was at this point that the Indian careerist and inquirer met the new Western stream of thought. The English language was popular because it opened paths to employment and influence; orthodox Hindus patronized the English schools and promoted the Hindu College (now Presidency College) in Calcutta (1816). This college, along with Alexander Duff's Scottish Church College, also in Calcutta, became a centre of Western influence and saw the rise of the Young Bengal movement, the Westernizing zeal of which denied the Hindu religion itself.

But between the complete Westernizers and the careerists was a third group, which found a leader of genius in Ram Mohun Roy. Making a moderate fortune in Calcutta finance, which he invested in zamindaris, from 1815 Roy advocated reforms in Hindu society and the acceptance of some features of Western thought. He denounced suttee (the burning of widows) and championed the cause of the Indian widow and wife. He advocated English education as a means of bringing Western knowledge to India. He denounced idolatry and preached monotheism. With his Precepts of Jesus, he both introduced the Christian ethic into Hindu society and drew the sting of missionary attacks. He finally founded a reforming Hindu body, the Brahmo Samaj ("Society of Brahma"), in 1828. Both careerists and Roy's followers cooperated in the spread of English education, but it was the latter who began the movement of borrowing from the West without any feeling of disloyalty to their past.

Princely India remained, for the most part, in a stagnant traditionalism. In British India land settlements had produced much social dislocation while purporting to respect traditional rights and to learn from the past; in particular, the Western concept of property in land had led to much social displacement. The Westernized legal system was efficient in suppressing crime but dilatory in upholding rights and incomprehensible for most natives in its working. Social evils like suttee and infanticide and practices such as those of the thugs had been suppressed or discouraged, but Hinduism and Islam were still by and large respected. The revolutionary aspect of the British presence was the decision, taken about the time of the tenure of Lord William Bentinck as governor-general, to introduce Western knowledge and science through the medium of the English language. Western inventions like the telegraph, modern irrigation, railways, and steamships followed, throwing India open to the industrial mechanistic and democratic world of the developing West. Along with education came the Christian missionary intrusion, with its moral and ideological challenge. This, in its turn, provoked a creative response from Ram Mohun Roy's circle, who were laying the foundations of a modernized Hinduism, which was later to find political expression in the Indian National Congress.

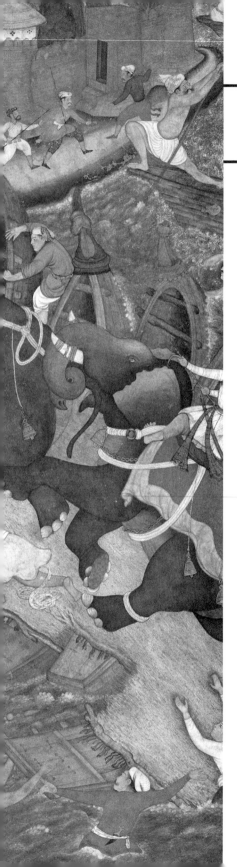

CHAPTER 10

BRITISH INDIA FROM THE MUTINY TO WORLD WAR I

By the year 1857 the British had established complete political control of the Indian subcontinent, which they ruled directly or through subordinate princes. They had established an authoritarian system of government, making use of Mughal practice and tradition and supported by an efficient civil service and a relatively efficient army.

THE MUTINY AND GREAT REVOLT OF 1857–59

When soldiers of the Bengal army mutinied in Meerut on May 10, 1857, tension had been growing for some time. The immediate cause of military disaffection was the deployment of the new breech-loading Enfield rifle, the cartridge of which was purportedly greased with pork and beef fat. When Muslim and Hindu troops learned that the tip of the Enfield cartridge had to be bitten off to prepare it for firing, a number of troops refused, for religious reasons, to accept the ammunition. These recalcitrant troops were placed in irons, but their comrades soon came to their rescue. They shot the British officers and made for Delhi, 40 miles (65 km) distant, where there were no British troops. The Indian garrison at Delhi joined them, and by the next nightfall they had secured the city and Mughal fort, proclaiming the aged titular Mughal emperor, Bahādur Shah II, as their leader. There at a stroke was an army, a cause, and a national leader—the only Muslim who appealed to both Hindus and Muslims.

NATURE AND CAUSES OF THE REBELLION

This movement became much more than a military mutiny. There has been much controversy over its nature and causes. The British military commander Sir James Outram thought it was a Muslim conspiracy, exploiting Hindu grievances. Or it might have been an aristocratic plot, set off too soon by the Meerut outbreak. But the only evidence for either of these was the circulation from village to village of chapatis, or cakes of unleavened bread, a practice that, though it also occurred on other occasions, was known to have taken place at any time of unrest. The lack of planning after the outbreak rules out these two explanations, while the degree of popular support argues more than a purely military outbreak.

Nationalist historians have seen in it the first Indian war of independence. In fact, it was rather the last effort of traditional India. It began on a point of caste pollution; its leaders were traditionalists who looked to reviving the past, while the small new Westernized class actively supported the British. And the leaders were not united, because they sought to revive former Hindu and Muslim regimes, which in their heyday had bitterly clashed. But something important was required to provoke so many to seize the opportunity of a military uprising to stage a war of independence.

The military cause was both particular and general. The particular reason, the greased cartridges for the Enfield rifles, was a mistake rectified as soon as it was discovered; but the fact that explanations and reissues could not quell the soldiers' suspicions suggests that the troops were already disturbed by other causes. The Bengal army of some 130,000 Indian troops may have contained as many as 40,000 Brahmans as well as many Rajputs. The British had accentuated caste consciousness by careful regulations, had allowed discipline to grow lax, and had failed to maintain understanding between British officers and their men. In addition, the General Service Enlistment Act of 1856 required recruits to serve overseas if ordered, a challenge to the castes who composed so much of the Bengal army. To these points may be added the fact that the British garrison in Bengal had been reduced at this time to 23,000 men because of troop withdrawals for the Crimean and Persian wars.

The general factors that turned a military mutiny into a popular revolt can be comprehensively described under the heading of political, economic, social, and cultural Westernization. Politically, many princes of India had retired into seclusion after their final defeat in 1818. But the wars against the Afghans and the Sikhs and then the annexations of Dalhousie alarmed and outraged them. The Muslims had lost the large state of Avadh; the Marathas had lost Nagpur, Satara, and Jhansi. Further, the British were becoming increasingly hostile toward traditional survivals and contemptuous of most things Indian. There was therefore both resentment and unease among the old governing class, fanned in Delhi by the British decision to end the Mughal imperial title on Bahādur Shah's death.

Economically and socially, there had been much dislocation in the landholding class all over northern and western India as a result of British land-revenue settlements, setting group against group. There was thus a suppressed tension in the countryside, ready to break out whenever governmental pressure might be reduced.

Then came the Western innovations of the now overconfident British. Their educational policy was a Westernizing one, with English instead of Persian as the official language; the old elites, schooled in the traditional pattern, felt themselves slighted. Western inventions such as the telegraph and railways aroused the prejudice of a conservative society (though Indians crowded the trains when they had

This illustration from the Illustrated London News *shows armed forces in the street and ruined buildings during the* sepoy *uprising, part of the Indian mutiny (1857–1859).* Hulton Archive/Getty Images

them). More disturbing to traditional sensibilities were the interventions, in the name of humanity, in the realm of Hindu custom—e.g., the prohibition of suttee, the campaign against infanticide, the law legalizing remarriage of Hindu widows. Finally, there was the activity of Christian missionaries, by that time widespread. Government was ostentatiously neutral, but Hindu society was inclined to regard the missionaries as eroding Hindu society without openly interfering. In sum, this combination of factors produced, besides the normal tensions endemic in India, an uneasy, fearful, suspicious, and resentful frame of mind and a wind of unrest ready to fan the flame of any actual physical outbreak.

THE REVOLT AND ITS AFTERMATH

The dramatic capture of Delhi turned mutiny into full-scale revolt. The whole episode falls into three periods: first came the summer of 1857, when the British, without reinforcements from home, fought with their backs to the wall; the second concerned the operations for the relief of Lucknow in the autumn; and the third was the successful campaign of Sir Colin Campbell (later Baron Clyde) and Sir Hugh Henry Rose (later Baron Strathnairn of Strathnairn and Jhansi) in the first half of 1858. Mopping-up operations followed, lasting until the British capture of rebel leader Tantia Topi in April 1859.

From Delhi the revolt spread in June to Kanpur (Cawnpore) and Lucknow. The surrender of Kanpur, after a relatively brief siege, was followed by a massacre of virtually all British citizens and loyal Indian soldiers at Kanpur. The Lucknow garrison held out in the residency from July 1, in spite of the death of Sir Henry Lawrence on July 4. The campaign then settled down to British attempts to take Delhi and relieve Lucknow. In spite of their apparently desperate situation, the British possessed long-term advantages: they could and did receive reinforcements from Britain; they had, thanks to the resolution of Sir John Lawrence, a firm base in the Punjab, and they had another base in Bengal, where the people were quiet; they had virtually no anxiety in the south and only a little in the west; and they had an immense belief in themselves and their civilization, which gave resolution to their initial desperation. The mutineers, on the other hand, lacked good leadership until nearly the end, and they had no confidence in themselves and suffered the guilt feelings of rebels without a cause, making them frantic and fearful by turns.

In the Punjab were some 10,000 British troops, which made it possible to disarm the Indian regiments; and the recently defeated Sikhs were so hostile to the Muslims that they supported the British against the Mughal restoration in Delhi. A small British army was improvised, which held the ridge before Delhi against greatly superior forces until Sir John Lawrence was able to send a siege train under John Nicholson. With this, and the aid of rebel dissensions, Delhi was stormed and captured by the British on September 20, while the emperor Bahādur Shah surrendered on promise of his life.

Down-country operations centred on the relief of Lucknow. Setting out from Allahabad, Sir Henry Havelock fought through Kanpur to the Lucknow residency on September 25, where he was besieged in turn. But the back of the rebellion had been broken and time gained for reinforcements to restore British superiority. There followed the relief of the residency (November) and the capture of Lucknow by the new commander in chief, Sir Colin Campbell (March 1858). By a campaign in Avadh and Rohilkhand, Campbell cleared the countryside.

The next phase was the central Indian campaign of Sir Hugh Rose. He first defeated the Gwalior contingent and then, when the rebels Tantia Topi and Rani Lakshmi Bai of Jhansi had seized Gwalior, broke up their forces in two more battles. The rani found a soldier's death, and Tantia Topi became a fugitive. With the British recovery of Gwalior (June 20, 1858), the revolt was virtually over.

The restoration of peace was hindered by British cries for vengeance, often leading to indiscriminate reprisals. The treatment of the aged Bahādur Shah, who was sent into exile, was a disgrace to a civilized country; also, the whole population of Delhi was driven out into the open, and thousands were killed after perfunctory trials or no trials at all. Order was restored by the firmness of Charles John Canning (later Earl Canning), first viceroy of India (governed 1858–62), whose title of

"Clemency" was given in derision by angry British merchants in Calcutta, and of Sir John Lawrence in the Punjab. Ferocity led to grave excesses on both sides, distinguishing this war in horror from other wars of the 19th century.

Measures of prevention of future crises naturally began with the army, which was completely reorganized. The ratio of British to Indian troops was fixed at roughly 1:2 instead of 1:5—one British and two Indian battalions were formed into brigades so that no sizable station should be without British troops. The effective Indian artillery, except for a few mountain batteries, was abolished, while the Brahmans and Rajputs of Avadh were reduced in favour of other groups. The officers continued to be British, but they were more closely linked with their men. The army became an efficient professional body, drawn largely from the northwest and aloof from the national life.

CLIMAX OF THE RAJ, 1858–85

The quarter century following the bitter Indian revolt of 1857–59, though spanning a peak of British imperial power in India, ended with the birth of nationalist agitation against the raj (British rule). For both Indians and British, the period was haunted with dark memories of the mutiny, and numerous measures were taken by the British raj to avoid another conflict. In 1885, however, the founding of the Indian National Congress marked the beginnings of effective, organized protest for "national" self-determination.

GOVERNMENT OF INDIA ACT OF 1858

On Aug. 2, 1858, less than a month after Canning proclaimed the victory of British arms, Parliament passed the Government of India Act, transferring British power over India from the East India Company, whose ineptitude was primarily blamed for the mutiny, to the crown. The merchant company's residual powers were vested in the secretary of state for India, a minister of Great Britain's cabinet, who would preside over the India Office in London and be assisted and advised, especially in financial matters, by a Council of India, which consisted initially of 15 Britons, 7 of whom were elected from among the old company's court of directors and 8 of whom were appointed by the crown. Though some of Britain's most powerful political leaders became secretaries of state for India in the latter half of the 19th century, actual control over the government of India remained in the hands of British viceroys—who divided their time between Calcutta (Kolkata) and Simla (Shimla)—and their "steel frame" of approximately 1,500 Indian Civil Service (ICS) officials posted "on the spot" throughout British India.

SOCIAL POLICY

On Nov. 1, 1858, Lord Canning announced Queen Victoria's proclamation to "the Princes, Chiefs and Peoples of India," which unveiled a new British policy of perpetual support for "native princes" and nonintervention in matters of religious belief or worship within British India. The announcement reversed Lord Dalhousie's prewar policy of political unification through princely state annexation, and princes were left free to adopt any heirs they desired so long as they all swore undying allegiance to the British crown. In 1876, at Prime Minister Benjamin Disraeli's prompting, Queen Victoria added the title Empress of India to her regality. British fears of another mutiny and consequent determination to bolster Indian states as "natural breakwaters" against any future tidal wave of revolt thus left more than 560 enclaves of autocratic princely rule to survive, interspersed throughout British India, for the entire nine decades of crown rule. The new policy of religious nonintervention was born equally out of fear of recurring mutiny, which many Britons believed had been triggered by orthodox Hindu and Muslim reaction against the secularizing inroads of utilitarian positivism and the proselytizing of Christian missionaries. British liberal socioreligious reform therefore came to a halt for more than three decades—essentially from the East India Company's Hindu Widow's Remarriage Act of 1856 to the crown's timid Age of Consent Act of 1891, which merely raised the age of statutory rape for "consenting" Indian brides from 10 years to 12.

The typical attitude of British officials who went to India during this period was, as the English writer Rudyard Kipling put it, to "take up the white man's burden." By and large, throughout the interlude of their Indian service to the crown, Britons lived as super-bureaucrats, "Pukka Sahibs," remaining as aloof as possible from "native contamination" in their private clubs and well-guarded military cantonments (called camps), which were constructed beyond the walls of the old, crowded "native" cities in this era. These new British military towns were initially erected as secure bases for the reorganized British regiments and were designed with straight roads wide enough for cavalry to gallop through whenever needed. The old company's three armies (located in Bengal, Bombay [Mumbai], and Madras [Chennai]), which in 1857 had only 43,000 British to 228,000 native troops, were reorganized by 1867 to a much "safer mix" of 65,000 British to 140,000 Indian soldiers. Selective new British recruitment policies screened out all "nonmartial" (meaning previously disloyal) Indian castes and races from armed service and mixed the soldiers in every regiment, thus permitting no single caste or linguistic or religious group to again dominate a British Indian garrison. Indian soldiers were also restricted from handling certain sophisticated weaponry.

After 1869, with the completion of the Suez Canal and the steady expansion of steam transport reducing the sea passage between Britain and India from about three months to only three weeks, British women came to the East with ever greater alacrity, and the British officials they married found it more appealing to return home with their British wives during furloughs than to tour India as their predecessors had done. While the intellectual calibre of British recruits to the ICS in this era was, on the average, probably higher than that of servants recruited under the company's earlier patronage system, British contacts with Indian society diminished in every respect (fewer British men, for example, openly consorted with Indian women), and British sympathy for and understanding of Indian life and culture were, for the most part, replaced by suspicion, indifference, and fear.

Queen Victoria in 1887. Alexander Bassano/Hulton Archive/Getty Images

Queen Victoria's 1858 promise of racial equality of opportunity in the selection of civil servants for the government of India had theoretically thrown the ICS open to qualified Indians, but examinations for the services were given only in Britain and only to male applicants between the ages of 17 and 22 (in 1878 the maximum age was further reduced to 19) who could stay in the saddle over a rigorous series of hurdles. It is hardly surprising, therefore, that by 1869 only one Indian candidate had managed to clear these obstacles to win a coveted admission to the ICS. British royal promises of equality were thus subverted in actual implementation by jealous, fearful bureaucrats posted "on the spot."

GOVERNMENT ORGANIZATION

From 1858 to 1909 the government of India was an increasingly centralized paternal despotism and the world's largest imperial bureaucracy. The Indian Councils Act of 1861 transformed the viceroy's Executive Council into a miniature cabinet run on the portfolio system, and each of the five ordinary members was placed in charge of a distinct department of Calcutta's government—home, revenue, military, finance, and law. The military commander in chief sat with this council as an extraordinary member. A sixth ordinary member was assigned to the viceroy's Executive Council after 1874, initially to preside over the Department of Public Works, which after 1904 came to be called Commerce and Industry.

Though the government of India was by statutory definition the "Governor-General-in-Council" (governor-general remained the viceroy's alternate title), the viceroy was empowered to overrule his councillors if ever he deemed that necessary. He personally took charge of the Foreign Department, which was mostly concerned with relations with princely states and bordering foreign powers. Few viceroys found it necessary to assert their full despotic authority, since the majority of their councillors usually were in agreement, but in 1879 Viceroy Lytton (governed 1876–80) felt obliged to overrule his entire council in order to accommodate demands for the elimination of his government's import duties on British cotton manufactures, despite India's desperate need for revenue in a year of widespread famine and agricultural disorders.

From 1854 additional members met with the viceroy's Executive Council for legislative purposes, and by the act of 1861 their permissible number was raised to between 6 and 12, no fewer than half of whom were to be nonofficial. While the viceroy appointed all such legislative councillors and was empowered to veto any bill passed on to him by this body, its debates were to be open to a limited public audience, and several of its nonofficial members were Indian nobility and loyal landowners. For the government of India the legislative council sessions thus served as a crude public-opinion barometer and the beginnings of an advisory "safety valve" that provided the viceroy with early crisis warnings at the minimum possible risk of parliamentary-type opposition. The act of 1892 further expanded the council's permissible additional membership to 16, of whom 10 could be nonofficial, and increased their powers, though only to the extent of allowing them to ask questions of government and to criticize formally the official budget during one day reserved for that purpose at the very end of each year's legislative session in Calcutta. The Supreme Council, however, still remained quite remote from any sort of parliament.

ECONOMIC POLICY AND DEVELOPMENT

Economically, this was an era of increased commercial agricultural production, rapidly expanding trade, early industrial development, and severe famine. The total cost of the mutiny of 1857–59, which was equivalent to a normal year's revenue, was charged to India and paid off from increased revenue resources in four years. The major source of government income throughout this period remained the land revenue, which, as a percentage of the agricultural yield of India's soil, continued to be "an annual gamble in monsoon rains." Usually, however, it provided about half of British India's gross annual revenue, or roughly the money needed to support the army. The second most lucrative source of revenue at this time was the government's continued monopoly over the flourishing opium trade to China; the third was the tax on salt, also jealously guarded by the crown as its official monopoly preserve. An individual income tax was introduced for five years to pay off the war deficit, but urban personal income was not added as a regular source of Indian revenue until 1886.

Despite continued British adherence to the doctrine of laissez-faire during that period, a 10 percent customs duty was levied in 1860 to help clear the war debt, though it was reduced to 7 percent in 1864 and to 5 percent in 1875. The above-mentioned cotton import duty, abolished in 1879 by Viceroy Lytton, was not reimposed on British imports of piece goods and yarn until 1894, when the value of silver fell so precipitously on the world market that the government of India was forced to take action, even against the economic interests of the home country (i.e., textiles in Lancashire), by adding enough rupees to its revenue to make ends meet. Bombay's textile industry had by then developed more than 80 power mills, and the Indian industrialist Jamsetji (Jamshedji) N. Tata's (1839–1904) huge Empress Mill was in full operation at Nagpur, competing directly with Lancashire mills for the vast Indian market. Britain's mill owners again demonstrated their power in Calcutta by forcing the government of India to impose an "equalizing" 5 percent excise tax on all cloth manufactured in India, thereby convincing many Indian mill owners and capitalists that their best interests would be served by contributing financial support to the Indian National Congress.

Britain's major contribution to India's economic development throughout the era of crown rule was the railroad network that spread so swiftly across the subcontinent after 1858, when there were barely 200 miles (320 km) of track in all of India. By 1869 more than 5,000 miles (8,000 km) of steel track had been completed by British railroad companies, and by 1900 there were some 25,000 miles (40,000 km) of rail laid. By the start of World War I (1914–18) the total reached 35,000 miles (56,000 km), almost the full growth of British India's rail net. Initially, the railroads proved a mixed blessing for most Indians, since by linking India's agricultural, village-based heartland to the British imperial port cities of Bombay, Madras, and Calcutta, they served both to accelerate the pace of raw-material extraction from India and to speed up the transition from subsistence food to commercial agricultural production. Middlemen hired by port-city agency houses rode the trains inland and induced village headmen to convert large tracts of grain-yielding land to commercial crops.

Large sums of silver were offered in payment for raw materials when the British demand was high, as was the case throughout the American Civil War (1861–65); however, but after the Civil War ended, restoring raw cotton from the southern United States to Lancashire mills, the Indian market collapsed. Millions of peasants weaned from grain production now found themselves riding the boom-and-bust tiger of a world-market economy. They were unable to convert their commercial agricultural surplus back into food during depression years, and from 1865 through 1900 India experienced a series of protracted famines, which in 1896 was complicated by the introduction of the bubonic plague (spread from Bombay, where infected rats were brought from China). As a result, though the population of the subcontinent increased dramatically from about 200 million in 1872 (the year of the first almost universal census) to more than 319 million in 1921, the population may have declined slightly between 1895 and 1905.

The spread of railroads also accelerated the destruction of India's indigenous handicraft industries, for trains filled with cheap competitive manufactured goods shipped from England now rushed to inland towns for distribution to villages, underselling the rougher products of Indian craftsmen. Entire handicraft villages thus lost their traditional markets of neighbouring agricultural villagers, and craftsmen were forced to abandon their looms and spinning wheels and return to the soil for their livelihood. By the end of the 19th century a larger proportion of India's population (perhaps more than three-fourths) depended directly on agriculture for support than at the century's start, and the pressure of population on arable land increased throughout this period. Railroads also provided the military with swift and relatively assured access to all parts of the country in the event of emergency and were eventually used to transport grain for famine relief as well.

The rich coalfields of Bihar began to be mined during this period to help power the imported British locomotives, and coal production jumped from roughly 500,000 tons in 1868 to some 6,000,000 tons in 1900 and more than 20,000,000 tons by 1920. Coal was used for iron smelting in India as early as 1875, but the Tata Iron and Steel Company, which received no government aid, did not start production until 1911, when, in Bihar, it launched India's modern steel industry. Tata grew rapidly after World War I, and by World War II it had become the largest single steel complex in the British Commonwealth. The jute textile industry, Bengal's counterpart to Bombay's cotton industry, developed in the wake of the Crimean War (1853–56), which, by cutting off Russia's supply of raw hemp to the jute mills of Scotland, stimulated the export of raw jute from Calcutta to Dundee. In 1863 there were only two jute mills in Bengal, but by 1882 there were 20, employing more than 20,000 workers.

The most important plantation industries of this era were tea, indigo, and coffee. British tea plantations were started in north India's Assam Hills in the 1850s and in south India's Nilgiri Hills some 20 years later. By 1871 there were more than 300 tea plantations, covering in excess of 30,000 cultivated acres (12,000 hectares) and producing some 3,000 tons of tea. By 1900 India's tea crop was large enough to export 68,500 tons to Britain, displacing the tea of China in London. The flourishing indigo industry of Bengal and Bihar was threatened with extinction during the Blue Mutiny (violent riots by cultivators in 1859–60), but India continued to export indigo to European markets until the end of the 19th century, when synthetic dyes made that natural product obsolete. Coffee plantations flourished in south India from 1860 to 1879, after which disease blighted the crop and sent Indian coffee into a decade of decline.

FOREIGN POLICY

THE NORTHWEST FRONTIER

British India expanded beyond its company borders to both the northwest and the northeast during this initial phase of crown rule. The turbulent tribal frontier to the northwest remained a continuing source of harassment to settled British rule, and Pathan (Pashtun) raiders served as a constant lure and justification to champions of the "forward school" of imperialism in the colonial offices of Calcutta and Simla and in the imperial government offices at Whitehall, London. Russian expansion into Central Asia in the 1860s provided even greater anxiety and incentive to British proconsuls in India, as well as at the Foreign Office in London, to advance the frontier of the Indian empire beyond the Hindu Kush and, indeed, up to Afghanistan's northern border along the Amu Darya. Lord Canning (governed 1856–62), however, was far too preoccupied with trying to restore tranquillity within India to consider embarking upon anything more ambitious than the northwest frontier punitive expedition policy (commonly called "butcher and bolt"), which was generally regarded as the simplest, cheapest method of "pacifying" the Pathans. As viceroy, Lord Lawrence (governed 1864–69) continued the same border-pacification policy and resolutely refused to be pushed or lured into the ever-simmering cauldron of Afghan politics. In 1863, when the popular old emir, Dūst Muḥammad Khan, died, Lawrence wisely refrained from attempting to name his successor, leaving the Dūst's 16 sons to fight their own fratricidal battles until 1868, when Shīr 'Alī Khan finally emerged victorious. Lawrence then recognized and subsidized the new emir. The viceroy, Lord Mayo (governed 1869–72), met to confer with Shīr 'Alī at Ambala in 1869 and, though reaffirming Anglo-Afghan friendship, resisted all requests by the emir for more permanent and practical support for his still precarious regime. Lord Mayo, the only British viceroy killed in office, was assassinated by an Afghan prisoner on the Andaman Islands in 1872.

THE SECOND AFGHAN WAR

Russia's glacial advance into Turkistan sufficiently alarmed Prime Minister Disraeli and his secretary of state for India, Robert Salisbury, that by 1874, when they came to power in London, they pressed the government of India to pursue a more vigorous interventionist line with the Afghan government. The viceroy, Lord Northbrook (governed 1872–76), resisting all such cabinet promptings to

reverse Lawrence's noninterventionist policy and to return to the militant posture of the First Afghan War era, resigned his office rather than accept orders from ministers whose diplomatic judgment he believed to be disastrously distorted by Russophobia. Lord Lytton, however, who succeeded him as viceroy, was more than eager to act as his prime minister desired, and, soon after he reached Calcutta, he notified Shīr 'Alī that he was sending a "mission" to Kabul. When the emir refused Lytton permission to enter Afghanistan, the viceroy bellicosely declaimed that Afghanistan was but "an earthen pipkin between two metal pots." He did not, however, take action against the kingdom until 1878, when Russia's General Stolyetov was admitted to Kabul while Lytton's envoy, Sir Neville Chamberlain, was turned back at the border by Afghan troops. The viceroy decided to crush his neighbouring "pipkin" and launched the Second Afghan War on Nov. 21, 1878, with a British invasion. Shīr 'Alī fled his capital and country, dying in exile early in 1879. The British army occupied Kabul, as it had in the first war, and a treaty signed at Gandamak on May 26, 1879, was concluded with the former emir's son, Ya'qūb Khan. Ya'qūb Khan promised, in exchange for British support and protection, to admit to his Kabul court a British resident who would direct Afghan foreign relations, but the resident, Sir Louis Cavagnari, was assassinated on Sept. 3, 1879, just two months after he arrived. British troops trudged back over the passes to Kabul and removed Ya'qūb from the throne, which remained vacant until July 1880, when 'Abd al-Raḥmān Khan, nephew of Shīr 'Alī, became emir. The new emir, one of the shrewdest statesmen in Afghan history, remained secure on the throne until his death in 1901.

The viceroy, Lord Lansdowne (governed 1888–94), who sought to reassert a more forward policy in Afghanistan, did so on the advice of his military commander in chief, Lord Roberts, who had served as field commander in the Second Afghan War. In 1893 Lansdowne sent Sir Mortimer Durand, the government of India's foreign secretary, on a mission to Kabul to open negotiations on the delimitation of the Indo-Afghan border. The delimitation, known as the Durand Line, was completed in 1896 and added the tribal territory of the Afrīdīs, Maḥsūds, Wazīrīs, and Swātīs as well as the chieftainships of Chitral and Gilgit, to the domain of British India. The 9th earl of Elgin (governed 1894–99), Lansdowne's successor, devoted much of his viceregal tenure to sending British Indian armies on punitive expeditions along this new frontier. The viceroy, Lord Curzon (governed 1899–1905), however, recognized the impracticality of trying to administer the turbulent frontier region as part of the large Punjab province. Thus, in 1901 he created a new North-West Frontier Province containing some 40,000 square miles (about 100,000 square km) of trans-Indus and tribal borderland territory under a British chief commissioner responsible directly to the viceroy. By instituting a policy of regular payments to frontier tribes,

the new province reduced border conflicts, though for the next decade British troops continued to fight against Maḥsūds, Wazīrīs, and Zakka Khel Afrīdīs.

THE INCORPORATION OF BURMA

British India's conquest of Burma (Myanmar) was completed during this period. The Second Anglo-Burmese War (1852) had left the kingdom of Ava (Upper Burma) independent of British India, and under the rule of King Mindon (1853–78), who built his capital at Mandalay, steamers bringing British residents and private traders up the Irrawaddy River from Rangoon (Yangon) were welcomed. Mindon, noted for convening the Fifth Buddhist Council at Mandalay in 1871 (the first such council in some 1,900 years), was succeeded by a younger son, Thibaw, who in February 1879 celebrated his ascendancy to the throne by having 80 siblings massacred. Thibaw refused to renew his father's treaty agreements with Britain, turning instead to seek commercial relations with the French, who were then advancing toward his kingdom from their base in Southeast Asia. Thibaw sent envoys to Paris, and in January 1885 the French signed a treaty of trade with the kingdom of Ava and dispatched a French consul to Mandalay. This envoy hoped to establish a French bank in Upper Burma to finance the construction of a railway and the general commercial development of the kingdom, but his plans were thwarted. The viceroy, Lord Dufferin (governed 1884–88)—impatient with Thibaw for delaying a treaty agreement with British India, goaded to action by British traders in Rangoon, and provoked by fears of French intervention in Britain's "sphere"—sent an expedition of some 10,000 troops up the Irrawaddy in November 1885. The Third Anglo-Burmese War ended in less than a month with the loss of hardly 20 lives, and on Jan. 1, 1886, Upper Burma, a kingdom of greater area than Britain and with a population of some 4,000,000, was annexed by proclamation to British India.

INDIAN NATIONALISM AND THE BRITISH RESPONSE, 1885–1920

The Indian National Congress held its first meeting in December 1885 in Bombay city while British Indian troops were still fighting in Upper Burma. Thus, just as the British Indian empire approached its outermost limits of expansion, the institutional seed of the largest of its national successors was sown.

Origins of the Nationalist Movement

Provincial roots of Indian nationalism, however, may be traced to the beginning of the era of crown rule in Bombay, Bengal, and Madras. Nationalism emerged in 19th-century British India both in emulation of and as a reaction against the consolidation of British rule and the spread of Western civilization. There were, moreover, two turbulent

national mainstreams flowing beneath the deceptively placid official surface of British administration: the larger, headed by the Indian National Congress, which led eventually to the birth of India, and the smaller Muslim one, which acquired its organizational skeleton with the founding of the Muslim League in 1906 and led to the creation of Pakistan.

Many English-educated young Indians of the post-mutiny period emulated their British mentors by seeking employment in the ICS, the legal services, journalism, and education. The universities of Bombay, Bengal, and Madras had been founded in 1857 as the capstone of the East India Company's modest policy of selectively fostering the introduction of English education in India. At the beginning of crown rule, the first graduates of these universities, reared on the works and ideas of Jeremy Bentham, John Stuart Mill, and Thomas Macaulay, sought positions that would help them improve themselves and society at the same time. They were convinced that, with the education they had received and the proper apprenticeship of hard work, they would eventually inherit the machinery of British Indian government. Few Indians, however, were admitted to the ICS; and, among the first handful who were, one of the brightest, Surendranath Banerjea (1848–1925), was dismissed dishonourably at the earliest pretext and turned from loyal participation within the government to active nationalist agitation against it. Banerjea became a Calcutta college teacher and then editor

SIR SURENDRANATH BANERJEA

The renowned Indian statesman Surendranath Banerjea (1848–1925) was one of the founders of modern India. As a young man, he attempted unsuccessfully to serve in the Indian Civil Service, at the time virtually closed to ethnic Indians. He then became a teacher and founded a college in Calcutta (now Kolkata), which was later named for him. Banerjea attempted to bring Hindus and Muslims together for political action, and for 40 years he put forward a nationalist viewpoint in his newspaper, The Bengalee. *Twice elected president of the Indian National Congress, he advocated for an Indian constitution on the Canadian model. He was elected in 1913 to two legislative councils and later was knighted (1921); in 1924 he was defeated by an independence candidate, whereupon he retired to write his autobiography,* A Nation in the Making *(1925).*

of *The Bengalee* and founder of the Indian Association in Calcutta. In 1883 he convened the first Indian National Conference in Bengal, anticipating by two years the birth of the Congress on the opposite side of India. After the first partition of Bengal in 1905, Banerjea attained nationwide fame as a leader of the *swadeshi* ("of our own country") movement, promoting Indian-made goods, and the movement to boycott British manufactured goods.

During the 1870s young leaders in Bombay also established a number of provincial political associations, such as the Poona Sarvajanik Sabha (Poona Public Society), founded by Mahadev Govind Ranade (1842–1901), who had graduated at the top of the University of Bombay's first bachelor of arts class in 1862. Ranade found employment in the educational department in Bombay, taught at Elphinstone College, edited the

Indu Prakash, helped start the Hindu reformist Prarthana Samaj (Prayer Society) in Bombay, wrote historical and other essays, and became a barrister, eventually being appointed to the bench of Bombay's high court. Ranade was one of the early leaders of India's emulative school of nationalism, as was his brilliant disciple Gopal Krishna Gokhale (1866–1915), later revered by Mohandas Karamchand Gandhi (1869–1948) as a political guru (preceptor). Gokhale, an editor and social reformer, taught at Fergusson College in Poona (Pune) and in 1905 was elected president of the Congress. Moderation and reform were the keynotes of Gokhale's life, and by his use of reasoned argument, patient labour, and unflagging faith in the ultimate equity of British liberalism, he was able to achieve much for India.

Bal Gangadhar Tilak (1856–1920), Gokhale's colleague at Fergusson

College, was the leader of Indian nationalism's revolutionary reaction against British rule. Tilak was Poona's most popular Marathi journalist, whose vernacular newspaper, *Kesari* ("Lion"), became the leading literary thorn in the side of the British. The Lokamanya ("Revered by the People"), as Tilak came to be called after he was jailed for seditious writings in 1897, looked to orthodox Hinduism and Maratha history as his twin sources of nationalist inspiration. Tilak called upon his compatriots to take keener interest and pride in the religious, cultural, martial, and political glories of pre-British Hindu India; in Poona, former capital of the Maratha Hindu glory, he helped found and publicize the popular Ganesha (Ganapati) and Shivaji festivals in the 1890s. Tilak had no faith in British justice, and his life was devoted primarily to agitation aimed at ousting the British from India by any means and restoring *swaraj* ("self-rule" or independence) to India's people. While Tilak brought many non-English-educated Hindus into the nationalist movement, the orthodox Hindu character of his revolutionary revival (which mellowed considerably in the latter part of his political career) alienated many within India's Muslim minority and exacerbated communal tensions and conflict.

The viceroyalties of Lytton and Lord Ripon (governed 1880–84) prepared the soil of British India for nationalism, the former by internal measures of repression and the futility of an external policy of aggression, the latter indirectly as a result of the European community's rejection of his liberal humanitarian legislation. One of the key men who helped arrange the first meeting of the Congress was a retired British official, Allan Octavian Hume (1829–1912), Ripon's radical confidant. After retiring from the ICS in 1882, Hume, a mystic reformer and ornithologist, lived in Simla, where he studied birds and theosophy. Hume had joined the Theosophical Society in 1881, as had many young Indians, who found in theosophy a movement most flattering to Indian civilization.

Helena Blavatsky (1831–91), the Russian-born cofounder of the Theosophical Society, went to India in 1879 to sit at the feet of Swami Dayananda Sarasvati (1824–83), whose "back to the Vedas" reformist Hindu society, the Arya Samaj, was founded in Bombay in 1875. Dayananda called on Hindus to reject the "corrupting" excrescences of their faith, including idolatry, the caste system, and infant marriage, and to return to the original purity of Vedic life and thought. The Swami insisted that post-Vedic changes in Hindu society had led only to weakness and disunity, which had destroyed India's capacity to resist foreign invasion and subjugation. His reformist society was to take root most firmly in the Punjab at the start of the 20th century, and it became that province's leading nationalist organization. Blavatsky soon left Dayananda and established her own "Samaj," whose Indian headquarters were outside Madras city, at Adyar. Annie

Besant (1847–1933), the Theosophical Society's most famous leader, succeeded Blavatsky and became the first and only British woman to serve as president of the Indian National Congress (1917).

The Early Congress Movement

The first Congress session, convened in Bombay city on Dec. 28, 1885, was attended by 73 representatives, as well as 10 more unofficial delegates; virtually every province of British India was represented. Fifty-four of the delegates were Hindu, only two were Muslim, and the remainder were mostly Parsi and Jain. Practically all the Hindu delegates were Brahmans. All of them spoke English. More than half were lawyers, and the remainder consisted of journalists, businessmen, landowners, and professors. Such was the first gathering of the new India, an emerging elite of middle-class intellectuals devoted to peaceful political action and protest on behalf of their nation in the making. On its last day, the Congress passed resolutions, embodying the political and economic demands of its members, that served thereafter as public petitions to government for the redress of grievances. Among these initial resolutions were calls for the addition of elected nonofficial representatives to the supreme and provincial legislative councils and for real equality of opportunity for Indians to enter the ICS by the immediate introduction of simultaneous examinations in India and Britain.

Economic demands by the Congress started with a call for the reduction of "home charges"—that part of Indian revenue that went toward the entire India Office budget and the pensions of officials living in Britain in retirement. Dadabhai Naoroji (1825–1917), the "grand old man" of the Congress who served three times as its president, was the leading exponent of the popular economic "drain" argument, which offered theoretical support to nationalist politics by insisting that India's poverty was the product of British exploitation and the annual plunder of gold, silver, and raw materials. Other resolutions called for the reduction of military expenditure, condemned the Third Anglo-Burmese War, demanded retrenchment of administrative expenses, and urged reimposition of import duties on British manufactures.

Hume, who is credited with organizing the Indian National Congress, attended the first session of the Congress as the only British delegate. Sir William Wedderburn (1838–1918), Gokhale's closest British adviser and himself later elected twice to serve as president of the Congress, and William Wordsworth, principal of Elphinstone College, both appeared as observers. Most Britons in India, however, either ignored the Congress and its resolutions as the action and demands of a "microscopic minority" of India's diverse millions or considered them the rantings of disloyal extremists. Despite this combination of official disdain and hostility, the Congress quickly won substantial Indian

Helen Keller meets with Indian poet Rabindranath Tagore in New York in 1930. Transcendental Graphics/Hulton Archive/Getty Images

support and within two years had grown to number more than 600 delegates. In 1888, when Viceroy Dufferin on the eve of his departure from India dismissed the Congress as "microscopic," it mustered 1,248 delegates at its annual meeting. Still, British officials continued to dismiss the significance of the Congress, and more than a decade later Viceroy Curzon claimed, perhaps wishfully, that it was "tottering to its fall." Curzon, however, inadvertently helped to infuse the Congress with unprecedented popularity and militant vitality by his own arrogance and by failing to appreciate the importance of human sympathy in his relentless drive toward greater efficiency.

THE FIRST PARTITION OF BENGAL

The first partition of Bengal in 1905 brought that province to the brink of open rebellion. With some 85 million people, Bengal was admittedly much too large for a single province and merited reorganization and intelligent division. The line drawn by Lord Curzon's government, however, cut through the heart of the Bengali-speaking "nation," leaving western Bengal's *bhadralok*, the intellectual Hindu leadership of Calcutta, tied to the much less politically active Bihari- and Oriya-speaking Hindus to their north and south. A new Muslim-majority province of Eastern Bengal and Assam was created with its capital at Dacca (now Dhaka). The leadership of the Congress viewed that partition as an attempt to "divide and rule" and as proof of the government's vindictive antipathy toward the outspoken *bhadralok* intellectuals, especially since Curzon and his subordinates had ignored countless pleas and petitions signed by tens of thousands of Calcutta's leading citizens. Mother-goddess-worshipping Bengali Hindus believed that partition was nothing less than the vivisection of their "mother province," and mass protest rallies before and after Bengal's division on Oct. 16, 1905, attracted millions of people theretofore untouched by politics of any variety.

The new tide of national sentiment born in Bengal rose to inundate India in every direction, and *Bande Mataram* ("Hail to Thee Mother") became the Congress's national anthem, its words taken from *Anandamath*, a popular Bengali novel by Bankim Chandra Chatterjee, and its music composed by Bengal's greatest poet, Rabindranath Tagore (1861–1941). As a reaction against

the partition, Bengali Hindus launched an effective boycott of British-made goods and dramatized their resolve to live without foreign cloth by igniting huge bonfires of Lancashire-made textiles. Such bonfires, re-creating ancient Vedic sacrificial altars, aroused Hindus in Poona, Madras, and Bombay to light similar political pyres of protest. Instead of wearing foreign-made cloth, Indians vowed to use only domestic (*swadeshi*) cottons and other clothing made in India. Simple hand-spun and hand-woven saris became high fashion, first in Calcutta and elsewhere in Bengal and then all across India, and displaced the finest Lancashire garments, which were now viewed as hateful imports. The *swadeshi* movement soon stimulated indigenous enterprise in many fields, from Indian cotton mills to match factories, glass-blowing shops, and iron and steel foundries.

Increased demands for national education also swiftly followed partition. Bengali students and professors extended their boycott of British goods to English schools and college classrooms, and politically active Indians began to emulate the so-called "Indian Jesuits"—Vishnu Krishna Chiplunkar (1850–82), Gopal Ganesh Agarkar (1856–95), Tilak, and Gokhale—who were pioneers in the founding of indigenous educational institutions in the Deccan in the 1880s. The movement for national education spread throughout Bengal, as well as to Varanasi (Banaras), where Pandit Madan Mohan

Malaviya (1861–1946) founded his private Banaras Hindu University in 1910.

One of the last major demands to be added to the platform of the Congress in the wake of Bengal's first partition was *swaraj* (self-rule), soon to become the most popular mantra of Indian nationalism. *Swaraj* was first articulated, in the presidential address of Dadabhai Naoroji, as the Congress's goal at its Calcutta session in 1906.

Sultan Sir Mohammad Shah, Aga Khan III, 1935. Encyclopædia Britannica, Inc.

NATIONALISM IN THE MUSLIM COMMUNITY

While the Congress was calling for *swaraj* in Calcutta, the Muslim League held its first meeting in Dacca. Though the Muslim minority portion of India's population lagged behind the Hindu majority in uniting to articulate nationalist political demands, Islam had, since the founding of the Delhi sultanate in 1206, provided Indian Muslims with sufficient doctrinal mortar to unite them as a separate religious community. The era of effective Mughal rule (c. 1556–1707), moreover, gave India's Muslims a sense of martial and administrative superiority to, as well as a sense of separation from, the Hindu majority.

In 1857 the last of the Mughal emperors had served as a rallying symbol for many mutineers, and in the wake of the mutiny most Britons placed the burden of blame for its inception upon the Muslim community. Sir Sayyid Ahmad Khan (1817–98), India's greatest 19th-century Muslim leader, succeeded, in his *Causes of the Indian Revolt* (1873), in convincing many British officials that Hindus were primarily to blame for the mutiny. Sayyid had entered the company's service in 1838 and was the leader of Muslim India's emulative mainstream of political reform. He visited Oxford in 1874 and returned to found the Anglo-Muhammadan Oriental College (now Aligarh Muslim University) at Aligarh in 1875. It was India's first centre of Islamic and Western higher education, with instruction given in English and modeled on Oxford. Aligarh became the intellectual cradle of the Muslim League and Pakistan.

Sayyid Mahdi Ali (1837–1907), popularly known by his title Mohsin al-Mulk, had succeeded Sayyid Ahmad as leader and convened a deputation of some 36 Muslim leaders, headed by the Aga Khan III, that in 1906 called upon Lord Minto (viceroy from 1905–10) to articulate the special national interests of India's Muslim community. Minto promised that any reforms enacted by his government would safeguard the separate interests of the Muslim community. Separate Muslim electorates, formally inaugurated by the Indian Councils Act of 1909, were thus vouchsafed by viceregal fiat in 1906. Encouraged by the concession, the Aga Khan's deputation issued an expanded call during the first meeting of the Muslim League (convened in December 1906 at Dacca) "to protect and advance the political rights and interests of Mussalmans of India." Other resolutions moved at its first meeting expressed Muslim "loyalty to the British government," support for the Bengal partition, and condemnation of the boycott movement.

REFORMS OF THE BRITISH LIBERALS

In Great Britain the Liberal Party's electoral victory of 1906 marked the dawn of a new era of reforms for British India. Hampered though he was by the viceroy, Lord Minto, the new secretary of state for India, John Morley, was able to introduce several important innovations into the legislative and administrative machinery of the British Indian government. First of all, he acted to implement Queen Victoria's promise of racial equality of opportunity, which since 1858 had served only to assure Indian nationalists of British hypocrisy. He appointed two Indian members to his council at Whitehall: one a Muslim, Sayyid Husain Bilgrami, who had taken an active role in the founding of the Muslim League; the other a Hindu, Krishna G. Gupta, the senior Indian in the ICS. Morley also persuaded a reluctant Lord Minto to appoint to the viceroy's executive council the first Indian member, Satyendra P. Sinha (1864–1928), in 1909. Sinha (later Lord Sinha) had been admitted to the bar at Lincoln's Inn in 1886 and was advocate general of Bengal before his appointment as the viceroy's law member, a position he felt obliged to resign in 1910. He was elected president of the Congress in 1915 and became parliamentary undersecretary of state for India in 1919 and governor of Bihar and Orissa in 1920.

Morley's major reform scheme, the Indian Councils Act of 1909 (popularly called the Morley-Minto Reforms), directly introduced the elective principle to Indian legislative council membership. Though the initial electorate was a minuscule minority of Indians enfranchised by property ownership and education, in 1910 some 135 elected Indian representatives took their seats as members of legislative councils throughout British India. The act of 1909 also increased the maximum additional membership of the supreme council from 16 (to which it had been raised by the Councils Act of 1892) to 60. In the provincial councils of Bombay, Bengal, and Madras, which had been created in 1861, the permissible total membership had been raised to 20 by the act of 1892, and this was increased in 1909 to 50, a majority of whom were to be nonofficial; the number of council members in other provinces was similarly increased.

In abolishing the official majorities of provincial legislatures, Morley was following the advice of Gokhale and other liberal Congress leaders, such as Romesh Chunder Dutt (1848–1909), and overriding the bitter opposition of not only the ICS but also his own viceroy and council. Morley believed, as did many other British Liberal politicians, that the only justification for British rule over India was to bequeath to the government of India Britain's greatest political institution, parliamentary government. Minto and his officials in Calcutta and Simla did succeed in watering down the reforms by writing stringent regulations for their implementation and insisting upon the retention of executive veto power over all legislation. Elected members of the new councils were empowered, nevertheless, to engage in spontaneous supplementary questioning, as well as in formal debate with the executive concerning the annual budget. Members were also permitted to introduce legislative proposals of their own.

Gokhale took immediate advantage of these vital new parliamentary procedures by introducing a measure for free and compulsory elementary education throughout British India. Although defeated, it was brought back again and again by Gokhale, who used the platform of the government's highest council of state as a sounding board for nationalist demands. Before the act of 1909, as Gokhale told fellow members of the Congress in Madras that year, Indian nationalists had been engaged in agitation "from outside," but "from now," he said, they would be "engaged in what might be called responsible association with the administration."

MODERATE AND MILITANT NATIONALISM

In 1907 the Congress held its annual meeting in Surat, but the assembly, plagued by conflict, never came to order long enough to hear the presidential address of its moderate president-elect, Rash Behari Ghose (1845–1921). The division of the Congress reflected broad tactical differences between the liberal evolutionary and militant revolutionary wings of the national organization and those aspiring to the presidency. Young militants of Tilak's New Party wanted to extend the boycott movement to the entire British government, while moderate leaders like Gokhale cautioned against such "extreme" action, fearing it might lead to violence. Those moderates were attacked by the militants as "traitors" to the "motherland," and the Congress split into two parties, which would not reunite for nine years. Tilak demanded *swaraj* as his "birthright," and his newspaper encouraged the young militants, whose introduction of the cult of the bomb and the gun in Maharashtra and Bengal led to Tilak's deportation for "sedition" to Mandalay prison from 1908 to 1914. Political violence in Bengal, in the form of terrorist acts, reached its peak from 1908 through 1910, as did the severity of official repression and the number of "preventive detention" arrests. Although Minto continued to assure Morley that opposition to the partition of Bengal was "dying down," and although Morley tried to convince his Liberal friends that it was a "settled fact," the opposite, in fact, was true. Harsher repression seemed only to breed more violent agitation.

Before the end of 1910, Minto finally returned home, and Morley appointed the liberal Lord Hardinge to succeed him as viceroy (governed 1910–16). Soon after reaching Calcutta, Hardinge recommended the reunification of Bengal, a position accepted by Morley, who also agreed to the new viceroy's proposal that a separate province of Bihar and Orissa should be carved out of Bengal. King George V journeyed to India for his coronation durbar in Delhi, and there, on Dec. 12, 1911, were announced the revocation of the partition of Bengal, the creation of a new province, and the plan to shift the capital of British India from Calcutta to Delhi's distant plain. By shifting their capital to the site of great Mughal glory, the British hoped to placate Bengal's Muslim minority, now aggrieved at the loss of provincial power in eastern Bengal.

Reunification of Bengal indeed served somewhat to mollify Bengali Hindus, but the downgrading of Calcutta from imperial to mere provincial capital status was simultaneously a blow to *bhadralok* egos and to Calcutta real estate values. Political unrest continued, now attracting Muslim as well as Hindu acts of terrorist violence, and Lord Hardinge himself was nearly assassinated by a bomb thrown into his howdah as he entered Delhi atop the viceregal elephant in 1912. The would-be assassin escaped in the crowd.

CHAPTER 11

BRITISH INDIA FROM WORLD WAR I TO 1947

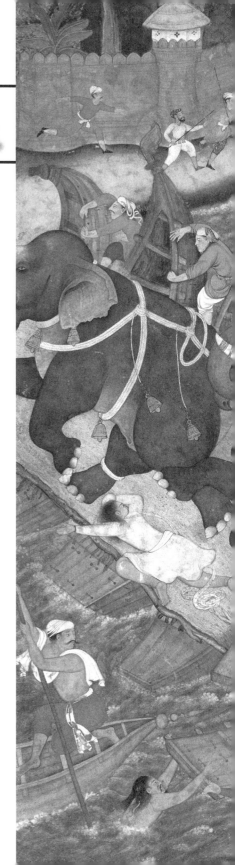

Later in 1912 Edwin Samuel Montagu, Morley's political protégé, who served as parliamentary undersecretary of state for India from 1910 to 1914, announced that the goal of British policy toward India would be to meet the just demands of Indians for a greater share in government. Britain seemed to be awakening to the urgency of India's political demands just as more compelling problems of European war preempted Whitehall's attention. The ultimate goal of the Indian nationalists—the end of the raj and independence—would have to wait for more than three decades while the world experienced two global wars that flanked a crippling economic depression.

WORLD WAR I AND ITS AFTERMATH

In August 1914, Lord Hardinge announced his government's entry into World War I. India's contributions to the war became extensive and significant, and the war's contributions to change within British India proved to be even greater. In many ways—politically, economically, and socially—the impact of the conflict was as pervasive as that of the mutiny of 1857-59.

INDIA'S CONTRIBUTIONS TO THE WAR EFFORT

The initial response throughout India to Lord Hardinge's announcement was, for the most part, enthusiastic support.

Indian princes volunteered their men, money, and personal service, while leaders of the Congress—from Tilak, who had just been released from Mandalay and had wired the king-emperor vowing his patriotic support, to Gandhi, who toured Indian villages urging peasants to join the British army—were allied in backing the war effort. Only India's Muslims, many of whom felt a strong religious allegiance to the Ottoman caliph that had to be weighed against their temporal devotion to British rule, seemed ambivalent from the war's inception.

Support from the Congress was primarily offered on the assumption that Britain would repay such loyal assistance with substantial political concessions—if not immediate independence or at least dominion status following the war, then surely its promise soon after the Allies achieved victory. The government of India's immediate military support was of vital importance in bolstering the Western Front, and an expeditionary force, including two fully manned infantry divisions and one cavalry division, left India in late August and early September 1914. They were shipped directly to France and moved up to the battered Belgian line just in time for the First Battle of Ypres. The Indian Corps sustained extraordinarily heavy losses during the winter campaigns of 1914–15 on the western front. The myth of Indian racial inferiority, especially with respect to courage in battle, was thus dissolved in sepoy blood on Flanders fields. In 1917 Indians were at last admitted to the final bastion of British Indian racial discrimination—the ranks of royal commissioned officers.

In the early months of the war, Indian troops also were rushed to eastern Africa and Egypt, and by the end of 1914 more than 300,000 officers and men of the British Indian Army had been shipped to overseas garrisons and battlefronts. The army's most ambitious, though ill-managed, campaign was fought in Mesopotamia. In October 1914, before Turkey joined forces with the Central Powers, the government of India launched an army to the mouth of the Shatt al-Arab to further Viceroy Curzon's policy of control over the Persian Gulf region. Al-Baṣrah (Basra) was taken easily in December 1914, and by October 1915 the British Indian Army had moved as far north as Al-Kūt (Kūt al-'Amārah), barely 100 miles (160 km) from Baghdad. The prize of Baghdad seemed within reach of British arms, but, less than two weeks after Gen. Sir Charles Townshend's doomed army of 12,000 Indians started north in November 1915, they were stopped at Ctesiphon, then forced to fall back to Al-Kūt, which was surrounded by Turks in December and fell in April 1916. This disaster became a national scandal for Britain and led to the immediate resignation of India's secretary of state, Austin Chamberlain.

Edwin Montagu, Chamberlain's successor at Whitehall's India Office, informed the British House of Commons on Aug. 20, 1917, that the policy of the British government toward India was thereafter to be one of "increasing association of Indians in every branch of the administration . . . with a view to the progressive realization of responsible government in India as an integral part of the Empire." Soon after this stirring promise of political reward for India's wartime support, Montagu embarked upon a personal tour of India. During his tour, Montagu conferred with his new viceroy, Lord Chelmsford (governed 1916–21), and their lengthy deliberations bore fruit in the Montagu-Chelmsford Report of 1918, the theoretical basis for the Government of India Act of 1919.

ANTI-BRITISH ACTIVITY

Anti-British terrorist activity started soon after the war began, sparked by the return to India of hundreds of embittered Sikhs who had sought to emigrate from their Punjab homes to Canada but who were denied permission to disembark in that country because of their colour. As British subjects, the Sikhs had assumed they would gain entry to underpopulated Canada, but, after wretched months aboard an old freighter (the *Komagata Maru*) in cramped and unsanitary conditions with inadequate food supplies, they returned to India as confirmed revolutionaries. Leaders of the Ghadr ("Revolution") party, which had been started by Punjabi Sikhs in 1913, journeyed abroad in search of arms and money to support their revolution, and Lala Har Dayal, the party's foremost leader, went to Berlin to solicit aid from the Central Powers.

Muslim disaffection also grew and acquired revolutionary dimensions as the Mesopotamian campaign dragged on. Many Indian Muslims appealed to Afghanistan for aid and urged the emir to start a holy war against the British and in defense of the caliphate. After the war the Khilāfat movement, an offspring of growing pan-Islamic consciousness in India, was started by two fiery orator-journalists, the brothers Shaukat and Muhammad Ali. It lured thousands of Muslim peasants to abandon their village homes and trudge over frozen high passes in a disastrous *hijrah* ("flight") from India to Afghanistan. In Bengal, terrorist bombings continued to harass officials, despite numerous "preventive detention" arrests made by Indian Criminal Intelligence Division police under the tough martial-law edicts promulgated at the war's inception.

The deaths of Gokhale and of the Bombay political leader Sir Pherozeshah Mehta in 1915 removed the most powerful moderate leadership from the Congress and cleared the way for Tilak's return to power in that organization after its reunification in 1916 at Lucknow. That historic session in December 1916 brought even greater unity to India's nationalist forces, as the Congress and the Muslim League agreed to a pact outlining their joint program of immediate national demands. The Lucknow Pact called first of all for the creation of expanded provincial legislative councils, four-fifths of whose members should be elected directly by the people on as broad a franchise as possible. The league's readiness to unite with the Congress was attributed to the pact's stipulation that Muslims should receive a far higher proportion of separate electorate seats in all legislative councils than they had enjoyed under the act of 1909. Thanks to such generous concessions of political power by the Congress, Muslim leaders, including Mohammad Ali Jinnah (1876–1949), agreed to set aside doctrinal differences and work with the Indian National Congress toward the attainment of national freedom from British rule. This rapprochement between the Congress and the Muslim League was short-lived, however, and by 1917 communal tensions and disagreements once again dominated India's faction-ridden political scene. Tilak and Annie Besant each campaigned for different home-rule leagues, while Muslims worried more about pan-Islamic problems than all-India questions of unity.

THE POSTWAR YEARS

By Armistice Day, Nov. 11, 1918, more than a million Indian troops had been shipped overseas to fight or serve as noncombatants behind the Allied lines on every major front from France to Gallipoli in European Turkey. Nearly 150,000 Indian battle casualties, more than 36,000 of them fatal, were sustained during the war. India's material and financial contributions to the war effort included the shipment of vast amounts of military stores and equipment to various fronts and nearly five million tons of wheat to Great Britain; also supplied by India were raw jute, cotton goods, rough-tanned hides, tungsten (wolfram), manganese, mica, saltpetre, timbers, silk, rubber, and various oils. The government of India paid for all its troops overseas, and, before the war ended, the viceroy presented a gift of £100 million (actually an imperial tax) to the British government. The Tata Iron and Steel Company received Indian government support once the war started and by 1916 was producing 100,000 tons of steel per year. An industrial commission was appointed in 1916 to survey the subcontinent's industrial resources and potential, and in 1917 a munitions board was created to expedite the production of war matériel. Wartime inflation was immediately followed by one of India's worst depressions, which came in the wake of the devastating influenza epidemic of 1918–19, a pandemic that took a far heavier toll of Indian life and resources than all the casualties sustained throughout the war. (Indians accounted for roughly half of the pandemic's total deaths worldwide.)

Politically, the postwar years proved equally depressing to India's great expectations. British officials, who in the first flush of patriotism had abandoned their ICS posts to rush to the front, returned to oust the Indian subordinates acting in their stead and carried on their prewar jobs as though nothing had changed in British India. Indian soldiers also returned from battlefronts to find that back home they were no longer treated as invaluable allies but reverted immediately to the status of "natives." Most of the soldiers recruited during the war had come from the Punjab, which, with less than one-tenth of India's population, had supplied as many as half of the combatant troops shipped abroad. It is thus hardly surprising that the flashpoint of postwar violence that shook India in the spring of 1919 was Punjab province.

The issue that served to rally millions of Indians, arousing them to a new level of disaffection from British rule, was the government of India's hasty passage of the Rowlatt Acts early in 1919. These "black acts," as they came to be called, were peacetime extensions of the wartime emergency measures passed in 1915 and had been rammed through the Supreme Legislative Council over the unanimous opposition of its Indian members, several of whom, including Jinnah, resigned in protest. Jinnah wrote to Viceroy Lord Chelmsford that the enactment of such autocratic legislation, following the victorious conclusion of a war in which India had so loyally supported Britain, was an unwarranted uprooting of the "fundamental principles of justice" and a gross violation of the "constitutional rights of the people."

Mohandas K. Gandhi, the Gujarati barrister who had returned from South Africa shortly after the war started and was recognized throughout India as one of the most promising leaders of the Congress, called upon all Indians to take sacred vows to disobey the Rowlatt Acts and launched a nationwide movement for the repeal of those repressive measures.

Gandhi's appeal received the strongest popular response in the Punjab, where the nationalist leaders Kichloo and Satyapal addressed mass protest rallies both from the provincial capital of Lahore and from Amritsar, sacred capital of the Sikhs. Gandhi himself had taken a train to the Punjab early in April 1919 to address one of those rallies, but he was arrested at the border station and taken back to Bombay by orders of Punjab's lieutenant governor, Sir Michael O'Dwyer. On April 10, Kichloo and

Mohandas K. Gandhi with delegates of the Indian Round Table Conference, London. Encyclopædia Britannica, Inc.

Indian visitors study the bullet-pocked wall in Amritsar. The wall was the site of a massacre on April 13, 1919, in which British officers ordered soldiers to open fire on an unarmed crowd, killing nearly 400 civilians. Narinder Nanu/AFP/Getty Images

Satyapal were arrested in Amritsar and deported from the district by Deputy Commissioner Miles Irving. When their followers tried to march to Irving's bungalow in the camp to demand the release of their leaders, they were fired upon by British troops. With several of their number killed and wounded, the enraged mob rioted through Amritsar's old city, burning British banks, murdering several Britons, and attacking two British women. Gen. Reginald Edward Harry Dyer was sent with Gurkha (Nepalese) and Balochi troops from Jullundur to restore order.

JALLIANWALA BAGH MASSACRE

Soon after Dyer's arrival, on the afternoon of April 13, 1919, some 10,000 or more unarmed men, women, and children gathered in Amritsar's Jallianwala Bagh (*bāgh*, "garden"; but before 1919 it had become a public square) to attend a protest meeting, despite a ban on public assemblies. It was a Sunday, and many neighbouring village peasants also came to Amritsar to celebrate the Hindu Baisakhi festival. Dyer positioned his men at the sole, narrow passageway of the Bagh, which was otherwise entirely enclosed by the backs of abutted brick buildings. Giving no word of warning, he ordered 50 soldiers to fire into the gathering, and for 10 to 15 minutes 1,650 rounds of ammunition were unloaded into the screaming, terrified crowd, some of whom were trampled by those desperately trying to escape. According to official estimates, nearly 400 civilians were killed, and another 1,200 were left wounded with no medical attention. Dyer, who argued his action was necessary to produce a "moral and widespread effect," admitted that the firing would have continued had more ammunition been available.

The governor of the Punjab province supported the massacre at Amritsar and, on April 15, placed the entire province under martial law. Viceroy Chelmsford, however, characterized the action as "an error of judgment," and, when Secretary of State Montagu learned of the slaughter, he appointed a commission of inquiry, headed by Lord Hunter. Although Dyer was subsequently relieved of his command, he returned a hero to many in Britain, especially conservatives, who presented him with a jeweled sword inscribed "Saviour of the Punjab."

The Massacre of Amritsar turned millions of moderate Indians from patient and loyal supporters of the British raj into nationalists who would never again place trust in British "fair play." It thus marks the turning point for a majority of the Congress's supporters from moderate cooperation with the raj and its promised reforms to revolutionary noncooperation. Liberal Anglophile leaders, such as Jinnah, were soon to be displaced by the followers of Gandhi, who would launch, a year after that dreadful massacre, his first nationwide *satyagraha* ("devotion to truth") campaign as India's revolutionary response.

GANDHI'S STRATEGY

For Gandhi, there was no dichotomy between religion and politics, and his unique political power was in great measure attributable to the spiritual leadership he exerted over India's masses, who viewed him as a *sadhu* (holy man) and worshipped him as a *mahatma* (which, in Sanskrit, means "great soul"). He chose *satya* ("truth") and *ahimsa* (nonviolence, or love) as the polar stars of his political movement; the former was the ancient Vedic concept of the real, embodying the very essence of existence itself, while the latter, according to Hindu (as well as Jain) scripture, was the highest religion (*dharma*). With these two weapons, Gandhi assured his followers, unarmed India could bring the mightiest empire known to history to its knees. His mystic faith magnetized millions, and the sacrificial suffering (*tapasya*) that he took upon himself by the purity of his chaste life and prolonged fasting armed

SATYAGRAHA

The concept of satyagraha (Hindi: "insistence on truth" or "zeal for truth") was introduced in the early 20th century by Mahatma Gandhi to designate a determined but nonviolent resistance to evil. Gandhi's satyagraha became a major tool in the Indian struggle against British imperialism and has since been adopted by protest groups in other countries.

According to this philosophy, satyagrahis—practitioners of satyagraha—achieve correct insight into the real nature of an evil situation by observing a nonviolence of the mind, by seeking truth in a spirit of peace and love, and by undergoing a rigorous process of self-scrutiny. In so doing, the satyagrahi encounters truth in the absolute. By his refusal to submit to the wrong or to cooperate with it in any way, the satyagrahi asserts this truth. Throughout his confrontation with the evil, he must adhere to nonviolence, for to employ violence would be to lose correct insight. A satyagrahi always warns his opponents of his intentions; satyagraha forbids any tactic suggesting the use of secrecy to one's advantage. Satyagraha includes more than civil disobedience; its full range of application extends from the details of correct daily living to the construction of alternative political and economic institutions. Satyagraha seeks to conquer through conversion; in the end, there is neither defeat nor victory but rather a new harmony.

Satyagraha draws from the ancient Indian ideal of ahimsa (nonviolence, or love), which is pursued with particular rigour by Jains. In developing ahimsa into a modern concept with broad political consequences, as satyagraha, Gandhi also drew from the writings of Leo Tolstoy and Henry David Thoreau, from the Bible, and from the great Sanskrit epic the Bhagavad Gita. Gandhi first conceived satyagraha in 1906 in response to a law discriminating against Asians that was passed by the British colonial government of the Transvaal in South Africa. In 1917 the first satyagraha campaign in India was mounted in the indigo-growing district of Champaran. During the following years, fasting and economic boycotts were employed as methods of satyagraha, until the British left India in 1947.

Critics of satyagraha, both in Gandhi's time and subsequently, have argued that it is unrealistic and incapable of universal success, since it relies upon a high standard of ethical conduct in the opponent, the representative of "evil," and demands an unrealistically strong level of commitment from those struggling for social amelioration. Nonetheless, satyagraha played a significant role in the civil rights movement led by Martin Luther King, Jr., in the United States and has spawned a continuing legacy in South Asia itself.

him with great powers. Gandhi's strategy for bringing the giant machine of British rule to a halt was to call upon Indians to boycott all British-made goods, British schools and colleges, British courts of law, British titles and honours, British elections and elective offices, and, should the need arise if all other boycotts failed, British tax collectors as well. The total withdrawal of Indian support would thus stop the machine, and nonviolent noncooperation would achieve the national goal of *swaraj*.

The Muslim quarter of India's population could hardly be expected to respond any more enthusiastically to Gandhi's *satyagraha* call than they had to Tilak's revivalism, but Gandhi laboured valiantly to achieve Hindu-Muslim unity by embracing the Ali brothers' Khilāfat movement as the "premier plank" of his national program. Launched in response to news of the Treaty of Sèvres's dismemberment of the Ottoman Empire in 1920, the Khilāfat movement coincided with the inception of *satyagraha*, thus giving the illusion of unity to India's nationalist agitation. Such unity, however, proved as chimerical as the Khilāfat movement's hope of preserving the caliphate itself, and in December 1920 Mohammed Ali Jinnah, alienated by Gandhi's mass following of Hindi-speaking Hindus, left the Nagpur Congress. The days of the Lucknow Pact were over, and by the start of 1921 the antipathetic forces of revivalist Hindu and Muslim agitation, destined to lead to the birth of the independent dominions of India and Pakistan

in 1947, were thus clearly set in motion in their separate directions.

PRELUDE TO INDEPENDENCE, 1920–1947

The last quarter century of British crown rule was racked by increasingly violent Hindu-Muslim conflict and intensified agitation demanding Indian independence. British officials in London, as well as in New Delhi and Simla, tried in vain to stem the rising tide of popular opposition to their raj by offering tidbits of constitutional reform, which proved either too little to satisfy both the Congress and the Muslim League or too late to avert disaster. More than a century of British technological, institutional, and ideological unification of the South Asian subcontinent thus ended after World War II with communal civil war, mass migration, and partition.

CONSTITUTIONAL REFORMS

British politicians and bureaucrats tried to cure India's ailing body politic with periodic infusions of constitutional reform. The separate electorate formula introduced for Muslims in the Government of India Act of 1909 (the Morley-Minto Reforms) was expanded and applied to other minorities in the Government of India Acts (1919 and 1935). Sikhs and Christians, for example, were given special privileges in voting for their own representatives comparable to those vouchsafed to Muslims.

The British raj thus sought to reconcile Indian religious pluralism to representative rule and no doubt hoped, in the process of fashioning such elaborate constitutional formulas, to win undying minority support for themselves and to undermine the arguments of Congress's radical leadership that they alone spoke for India's "united nationalist movement." Earlier official support of, and appeals to, India's princes and great landowners had proved fruitful, especially since the inception of the crown raj in 1858, and more concerted efforts were made in 1919 and 1935 to wean minorities and India's educated elite away from revolution and noncooperation.

The Government of India Act of 1919 (also known as the Montagu-Chelmsford Reforms), under which elections were held in 1920, increased the number of Indian members to the viceroy's Executive Council from at least two to no fewer than three and transformed the Imperial Legislative Council into a bicameral legislature consisting of a Legislative Assembly (lower house) and a Council of State (upper house). The Legislative Assembly, with 145 members, was to have a majority of 104 elected, while 33 of the Council of State's 60 members were also to be elected. Enfranchisement continued to be based on property and education, but under the act of 1919 the total number of Indians eligible to vote for representatives to provincial councils was expanded to five million; just one-fifth of that number, however, were permitted to vote for Legislative Assembly candidates, and only about 17,000 elite were allowed to choose Council of State members. Dyarchy (dual governance) was to be introduced at the provincial level, where executive councils were divided between ministers elected to preside over "transferred" departments (education, public health, public works, and agriculture) and officials appointed by the governor to rule over "reserved" departments (land revenue, justice, police, irrigation, and labour).

The Government of India Act of 1935 gave all provinces full representative and elective governments, chosen by franchise extended now to some 30 million Indians, and only the most crucial portfolios—defense, revenue, and foreign affairs—were "reserved" to appointed officials. The viceroy and his governors retained veto powers over any legislation they considered unacceptable, but prior to the 1937 elections they reached a "gentleman's agreement" with the Congress's high command not to resort to that constitutional option, which was their last vestige of autocracy. The act of 1935 was also to have introduced a federation of British India's provinces and the still autonomous princely states, but that institutional union of representative and despotic rule was never realized, since the princes were unable to agree among themselves on matters of protocol.

The act of 1935 was itself the product of the three elaborate sessions of the Round Table Conference, held in London, and at least five years of bureaucratic labour, most of which bore little fruit. The first session—attended by 58 delegates from British India, 16 from the British Indian states, and 16 from British political parties—was convened by Prime Minister Ramsay MacDonald in the City of Westminster, London, in November 1930. While Jinnah and the Aga Khan III led among the British Indian delegation a deputation of 16 Muslims, no Congress deputation joined the first session, as Gandhi and his leading lieutenants were all in jail at the time. Without the Congress the Round Table could hardly hope to fashion any popularly meaningful reforms, so Gandhi was released from prison before the second session started in September 1931 but, at his own insistence, attended it as the Congress's sole representative. Little was accomplished at the second session, for Hindu-Muslim differences remained unresolved and the princes continued to argue with one another. The third session, which began in November 1932, was more the product of official British inertia than any proof of progress in closing the tragic gaps between so many Indian minds reflected in earlier debate. Two new provinces emerged, however, from those official deliberations. In the east Orissa was established as a province distinct from Bihar, and in the west Sind (Sindh) was separated from the Bombay Presidency and became the first Muslim-majority governor's province of British India since the reunification of Bengal. It was decided that Burma should be a separate colony from British India.

In August 1932 Prime Minister MacDonald announced his Communal Award, Great Britain's unilateral attempt to resolve the various conflicts among India's many communal interests. The award, which was later incorporated into the act of 1935, expanded the separate-electorate formula reserved for Muslims to other minorities, including Sikhs, Indian Christians, Anglo-Indians, Europeans, distinct regional groups (such as the Marathas in the Bombay Presidency), and special interests (women, organized labour, business, landowners, and universities). The Congress was, predictably, unhappy at the extension of communal representation but became particularly outraged at the British offer of separate-electorate seats for "depressed classes," meaning the so-called "untouchables." Gandhi undertook a "fast unto death" against that offer, which he viewed as a nefarious British plot to wean more than 50 million Hindus away from their higher-caste brothers and sisters. Gandhi, who called the untouchables "Children of God" (Harijans), agreed after prolonged personal negotiations with Bhimrao Ramji Ambedkar (1891–1956), a leader of the untouchables, to reserve many more seats for them than the British had promised, as long as they remained within the "Hindu" majority fold. Thus, the offer of separate-electorate seats for the untouchables was withdrawn.

THE CONGRESS'S AMBIVALENT STRATEGY

Gandhi, promising his followers freedom in just one year, launched on Aug. 1, 1920, his first nationwide *satyagraha* campaign, which he believed would bring the British raj to a grinding halt. After more than a year, and even with 60,000 satyagrahis in prison cells across British India, the raj remained firm, and, therefore, Gandhi prepared to unleash his last and most powerful boycott weapon—calling upon the peasants of Bardoli in Gujarat to boycott land taxes. In February 1922, on the eve of that final phase of boycott, word reached Gandhi that in Chauri Chaura, United Provinces, 22 Indian police were massacred in their police station by a mob of *satyagrahis*, who set fire to the station and prevented the trapped police from escaping immolation. Gandhi announced that he had committed a "Himalayan blunder" in launching *satyagraha* without sufficient "soul-cleansing" of India's masses and, as a result, called a halt to the noncooperation movement. He was subsequently arrested, however, and found guilty of "promoting disaffection" toward the raj, for which he was sentenced to six years in prison.

While Gandhi was behind bars, Motilal Nehru (1861–1931), one of northern India's wealthiest lawyers, started within Congress a new politically active "party," the Swaraj Party. Motilal Nehru shared the lead of this new party with C.R. (Chitta Ranjan) Das (1870–1925) of Bengal. Contesting the elections to the new Central Legislative Assembly in 1923, the party sought by antigovernment agitation within the council chambers to disrupt official policy and derail the raj. Though Gandhian noncooperation

remained the Congress's primary strategy, actual partial cooperation in the postwar reforms thus became the alternate tactic of those Congress leaders who were less orthodox Hindu, or more secular-minded, in outlook. The Swarajists won more than 48 out of 105 seats in the Central Legislative Assembly in 1923, but their numbers were never quite enough to prevent the British from passing the legislation they desired or believed was needed to maintain internal "order."

Gandhi was released from jail in February 1924, four years early, after a surgery. Thereafter he focused on what he called his "constructive program" of hand spinning and weaving and overall village "uplift," as well as on Hindu "purification" in seeking to advance the cause of the Harijans, especially through granting them entry to Hindu temples, from which they had always been banished. Gandhi himself lived in village ashrams (religious retreats), which served more as models for his socioeconomic ideals than as centres of political power, though the leaders of the Congress flocked to his remote rural retreats for periodic consultation on strategy.

In many ways Congress policy remained plagued by ambivalence for the remaining years of the raj. Most members of the high command aligned with Gandhi, but others sought what seemed to them more practical or pragmatic solutions to India's problems, which so often transcended political or imperial-colonial questions. It was always easier, of course, for Indian leaders to rally the masses behind emotional religious appeals or anti-British rhetoric than to resolve problems that had festered throughout the Indian subcontinent for millennia. Most Hindu-Muslim differences, therefore, remained unresolved, even as the Hindu caste system was never really attacked or dismantled by the Congress.

Imperial economic exploitation did, however, prove to be an excellent nationalist catalyst—as, for example, when Gandhi mobilized the peasant masses of India's population behind the Congress

Children and women walk during the 240-mile (385-km) Salt March (March–April 1930). The march, organized by Mahatma Gandhi, was the beginning of a satyagraha campaign against British rule in India in 1930–31. Time & Life Pictures/ Getty Images

during his famous march against the salt tax in 1930, which was the prelude to his second nationwide *satyagraha*. The British government's monopoly on the sale of salt, which was heavily taxed, had long been a major source of revenue to the raj, and, by marching from his ashram at Sabarmati (near Ahmedabad, Gujarat) to the sea at Dandi, where he illegally picked up salt from the sands on the shore, Gandhi mobilized millions of Indians to follow him in thus breaking the law. It was an ingeniously simple way to break a British law nonviolently, and before year's end jail cells throughout India were again filled with *satyagrahis*.

Many of the younger members of the Congress were eager to take up arms against the British, and some considered Gandhi an agent of imperial rule for having called a halt to the first *satyagraha* in 1922. Most famous and popular of these militant Congress leaders was Subhas Chandra Bose (1897–1945) of Bengal, a disciple of C.R. Das and an admirer of Hitler and Mussolini. Bose was so popular within Congress that he was elected its president twice (in 1938 and 1939) over Gandhi's opposition and the active opposition of most members of its central working committee. After being forced to resign the office in April 1939, Bose organized with his brother Sarat his own Bengali party, the Forward Bloc, which initially remained within the Congress fold. At the beginning of World War II, Bose was arrested and detained by the British, but in 1941 he escaped their surveillance and fled to Afghanistan, thence to the Soviet Union and Germany, where he remained until 1943.

Jawaharlal Nehru (1889–1964), Motilal's only son, emerged as Gandhi's designated successor to Congress leadership during the 1930s. A Fabian socialist and a barrister, the younger Nehru was educated at Harrow School and at Trinity College, Cambridge, and was drawn into the Congress and the noncooperation movement by his admiration for Gandhi. Though Jawaharlal Nehru personally was more of an Anglophile aristocrat

Jawaharlal Nehru, photograph by Yousef Karsh, 1956. Karsh—Rapho/Photo Researchers

than a Hindu *sadhu* or *mahatma*, he devoted his energies and intellect to the national movement and, at age 41, was the youngest elected president of the Congress in December 1929, when it passed its Purna Swaraj ("Complete Self-Rule") resolution. Jawaharlal's radical brilliance and energy made him a natural leader of the Congress's youth movement, while his Brahman birth and family fortune overcame many of that party's more conservative leadership's misgivings about placing him at the Congress's helm. The Purna Swaraj resolution—proclaimed on Jan. 26, 1930, later to be celebrated as independent India's Republic Day—called for "complete freedom from the British" but was later interpreted by Prime Minister Nehru as permitting India to remain within the British Commonwealth, a practical concession young Jawaharlal had often vowed he would never make.

MUSLIM SEPARATISM

The Muslim quarter of India's population became increasingly wary of the Congress's promises and restive in the wake of the collapse of the Khilāfat movement, which occurred after Kemal Atatürk announced his modernist Turkish reforms in 1923 and disavowed the very title of caliph the following year. Hindu-Muslim riots in Malabar claimed hundreds of lives in 1924, and similar religious rioting spread to every major city in northern India, wherever rumours of Muslim "cow slaughter," the polluting appearance of a dead pig's carcass in a mosque, or other clashing doctrinal fears ignited the tinder of distrust ever lurking in the poorer sections of India's towns and villages. At each stage of reform, as the prospects of real devolution of political power by the British seemed more imminent, separate-electorate formulas and leaders of various parties stirred hopes, which proved almost as dangerous in triggering violence as did fears. The older, more conservative leadership of the pre-World War I Congress found Gandhian *satyagraha* too radical—moreover, far too revolutionary—to support, and liberals like Sir Tej Bahadur Sapru (1875–1949) organized their own party (eventually to become the National Liberal Federation), while others, like Jinnah, dropped out of political life entirely. Jinnah, alienated by Gandhi and his illiterate mass of devoutly Hindu disciples, instead devoted himself to his lucrative Bombay law practice, but his energy and ambition lured him back to the leadership of the Muslim League, which he revitalized in the 1930s. Jinnah, who was also instrumental in urging Viceroy Lord Irwin (later, 1st Earl Halifax; governed 1926–31) and Prime Minister MacDonald to convene the Round Table Conference in London, was urged by many Muslim compatriots, including Liaquat Ali Khan (1895–1951), to become the permanent president of the Muslim League.

By 1930 a number of Indian Muslims had begun to think in terms of separate statehood for their minority community, whose population dominated the northwestern provinces of British India and the eastern half of Bengal, as well as important pockets of the United Provinces and the great princely state of Kashmir. (The princely state of Hyderabad was ruled by a Muslim dynasty but was mostly Hindu.) One of Punjab's greatest Urdu poets, Sir Muḥammad Iqbāl (1877–1938), while presiding over the Muslim League's annual meeting in Allahabad in 1930, proposed that "the final destiny" of India's Muslims should be to consolidate a "North-West Indian Muslim state." Although he did not name it Pakistan, his proposal included what became the major provinces of modern Pakistan—Punjab, Sind, the North-West Frontier Province, and Balochistan. Jinnah, the Aga Khan, and other important Muslim leaders were at the time in London attending the Round Table Conference, which still envisaged a single federation of all Indian provinces and princely states as the best possible constitutional solution for India in the aftermath of a future British withdrawal. Separate electorate seats, as well as special guarantees of Muslim "autonomy" or "veto powers" in dealing with sensitive religious issues, were hoped to be sufficient to avert civil war or any need for actual partition. As long as the British raj remained in control, such formulas and schemes appeared to suffice, for the British army could always be hurled into the communal fray at the brink of extreme danger, and the army had as yet remained apolitical and—since its post-mutiny reorganization—untainted by communal religious passions.

In 1933 a group of Muslim students at Cambridge, led by Choudhary Rahmat Ali, proposed that the only acceptable solution to Muslim India's internal conflicts and problems would be the birth of a Muslim "fatherland," to be called Pakistan (Persian: "Land of the Pure"), out of the Muslim-majority northwestern and northeastern provinces. The Muslim League and its president, Jinnah, did not join in the Pakistan demand until after the league's famous Lahore meeting in March 1940, as Jinnah, a secular constitutionalist by predilection and training, continued to hope for a reconciliation with the Congress. Such hopes virtually disappeared, however, when Nehru refused to permit the league to form coalition ministries with the Congress majority in the United Provinces and elsewhere after the 1937 elections. The Congress had initially entered the elections with the hope of wrecking the act of 1935, but—after it had won so impressive a victory in most provinces and the league had done so poorly, mostly because it had inadequately organized itself for nationwide elections—Nehru agreed to participate in the government and insisted there were but "two parties" in India, the Congress and the British raj.

Jinnah soon proved to Nehru that the Muslims were indeed a formidable "third" party. The years from 1937 to 1939, when the Congress actually ran most of British India's provincial governments, became the seed period for the Muslim League's growth in popularity and power within the entire Muslim community, for many

Muslims soon viewed the new "Hindu raj" as biased and tyrannical and the Hindu-led Congress ministries and their helpers as insensitive to Muslim demands or appeals for jobs, as well as to their redress of grievances. The Congress's partiality toward its own members, prejudice toward its majority community, and jobbery for its leadership's friends and relations all conspired to convince many Muslims that they had become second-class citizens in a land that, while perhaps on the verge of achieving "freedom" for some Indians, would be run by "infidels" and "enemies" to the Muslim minority. The league made the most of the Congress's errors of judgment in governance; by documenting as many reports as it could gather in papers published during 1939, it hoped to prove how wretched a Muslim's life would be under any "Hindu raj." The Congress's high command insisted, of course, that it was a "secular and national" party, not a sectarian Hindu organization, but Jinnah and the Muslim League responded that they alone could speak for and defend the rights of India's Muslims. Thus, the lines of battle were drawn by the eve of World War II, which served only to intensify and accelerate the process of communal conflict and irreversible political division that would split British India.

THE IMPACT OF WORLD WAR II

On Sept. 3, 1939, the viceroy Lord Linlithgow (governed 1936–43) informed India's political leaders and populace that they were at war with Germany. For Nehru and the Congress's high command, such unilateral declarations were viewed as more than insensitive British behaviour, for, in undertaking to run most of British India's provinces, the Congress thought of itself as the viceroy's "partner" in administering the raj. What a "betrayal," therefore, this autocratic declaration of war was judged, and how angry it made Nehru and Gandhi feel. Instead of offering loyal support to the British raj, they demanded a prior forthright statement of Britain's postwar "goals and ideals." Neither Linlithgow nor Lord Zetland, his Tory secretary of state, was prepared, however, to pander to the Congress's wishes at Great Britain's darkest hour of national danger. Nehru's outrage helped convince the Congress's high command to call on all its provincial ministries to resign. Jinnah was overjoyed at this decision and proclaimed Friday, Dec. 22, 1939, a Muslim "Day of Deliverance" from the tyranny of the Congress "raj." Jinnah met regularly with Linlithgow, moreover, and assured the viceroy that he need not fear a lack of support from India's Muslims, many of whom were active members of Britain's armed services. Throughout World War II, as the Congress moved farther from the British, first with passive and later with active noncooperation, the Muslim League in every possible way quietly supported the war effort.

The first meeting of the league after the outbreak of the war was held in Punjab's ancient capital of Lahore in March 1940. The famous Lahore Resolution, later known as the Pakistan Resolution, was passed by the largest gathering of league delegates just one day after Jinnah informed his followers that "the problem of India is not of an inter-communal but manifestly of an international character." The league resolved, therefore, that any future constitutional plan proposed by the British for India would not be "acceptable to the Muslims" unless it was so designed that the Muslim-majority "areas" of India's "North-Western and Eastern Zones" were "grouped to constitute 'independent States' in which the constituent units shall be autonomous and sovereign." Pakistan was not mentioned until the next day's newspapers introduced that word in their headlines, and Jinnah explained that the resolution envisioned the establishment of not two separately administered Muslim countries but rather a single Muslim nation-state—namely, Pakistan.

Gandhi launched his first "individual satyagraha" campaign against the war in October 1940. Vinoba Bhave, Gandhi's foremost disciple, publicly proclaimed his intent to resist the war effort and was subsequently sentenced to three months in jail. Jawaharlal Nehru, who was the next to openly disobey British law, was sentenced to four years behind bars. By June 1941 more than 20,000 Congress *satyagrahis* were in prisons.

It was also in 1941 that Bose fled to Germany, where he started broadcasting appeals to India urging the masses to "rise up" against British "tyranny" and to "throw off" their chains. There were, however, few Indians in Germany, and Hitler's advisers urged Bose to go back to Asia by submarine; he was eventually transported to Japan and then to Singapore, where Japan had captured at least 40,000 Indian troops during its takeover of that strategic island in February 1942. These captured soldiers became Netaji ("Leader") Bose's Indian National Army (INA) in 1943 and, a year later, marched behind him to Rangoon. Bose hoped to "liberate" first Manipur and then Bengal from British rule, but the British forces at India's eastern gateways held until the summer monsoon gave them respite enough to be properly reinforced and drove Bose and his army back down the Malay Peninsula. In August 1945 Bose escaped by air from Saigon but died of severe burns after his overloaded plane crashed onto the island of Formosa.

BRITISH WARTIME STRATEGY

Lord Linlithgow's initial refusal to discuss postwar ideals with the Congress left India's premier national party without an opportunity for constructive debate about any political prospects—that is, other than those it could win by noncooperation or through violence. However, after Japan joined the Axis powers in late 1941 and moved with such rapidity into most of Southeast Asia, Britain feared that the Japanese would soon invade India. In March 1942 the war cabinet of British Prime Minister Winston Churchill sent the socialist Sir Richard Stafford Cripps, a

close personal friend of Nehru, to New Delhi with a postwar proposal. The Cripps Mission offered Indian politicians full "dominion status" for India after the war's end, with the additional stipulation, as a concession primarily to the Muslim League, that any province could vote to "opt out" of such a dominion if it preferred to do so. Gandhi irately called the offer "a post-dated cheque on a bank that was failing," and Nehru was equally negative and angry at Cripps for his readiness to give so much to the Muslims. Cripps's hands had been tied by Churchill before he left London, however, as he was ordered by the war cabinet merely to convey the British offer, not to modify it or negotiate a new formula. He flew home empty-handed in less than a month, and soon afterward Gandhi planned his last *satyagraha* campaign, the Quit India movement. Declaring that the British presence in India was a provocation to the Japanese, Gandhi called upon the British to "quit India" and to leave Indians to deal with the Japanese by nonviolent means, but Gandhi and all members of the Congress high command were arrested before the dawn of that movement in August 1942. In a few months at least 60,000 Indians filled British prison cells, and the raj unleashed massive force against Indian underground efforts to disrupt rail transport and to generally subvert the war effort that followed the crackdown on the Quit India campaign. Parts of the United Provinces, Bihar, the North-West Frontier, and Bengal were bombed and strafed by British pilots as the raj resolved to crush all Indian resistance and violent opposition as swiftly as possible. Many Indians were killed and wounded, but wartime resistance continued as more young Indians, women as well as men, were recruited into the Congress's underground.

Japan's attack on Pearl Harbor in December 1941 brought the United States into the war as Britain's most powerful ally. By late 1942 and throughout the rest of the war, U.S. arms and planes steamed and flew into Calcutta and Bombay, bolstering British India as the major Allied launching pad against Japanese forces in Southeast Asia and China. The British raj thus remained firm despite growing Indian opposition, both violent and nonviolent. Indian industry grew rapidly, moreover, during World War II. Electric power output doubled, and the steel plant at Jamshedpur became the British Empire's foremost by the war's end. Indian shipyards and light-manufacturing plants flourished in Bombay, as well as in Bengal and Orissa, and, despite many warnings, the Japanese never launched major air attacks against Calcutta or Madras. In mid-1943 Field Marshall Lord Wavell, who replaced Linlithgow as viceroy (1943–47), brought India's government fully under martial control for the war's duration. No progress was made in several of the Congress's attempts to resolve Hindu-Muslim differences through talks between Gandhi and Jinnah. Soon after the war's end in Europe, Wavell convened a political conference in Shimla in late June 1945, but there was no meeting of minds, no formula sturdy enough to bridge the gulf between the Congress and the Muslim League.

Two weeks after the Simla talks collapsed in midsummer, Churchill's government was voted out of power by the Labour Party's sweep of London's polls, and Prime Minister Clement Attlee appointed one of Gandhi's old admirers, Lord Pethick-Lawrence, to head the India Office. With the dawn of the atomic age in August and Japan's surrender, London's primary concern in India was how to find the political solution to the Hindu-Muslim conflict that would most expeditiously permit the British raj to withdraw its forces and to extricate as many of its assets as possible from what seemed to the Labour Party to have become more of an imperial burden and liability than any real advantage for Great Britain.

THE TRANSFER OF POWER AND THE BIRTH OF TWO COUNTRIES

Elections held in the winter of 1945–46 proved how effective Jinnah's single-plank strategy for his Muslim League had been, as the league won all 30 seats reserved for Muslims in the Central Legislative Assembly and most of the reserved provincial seats as well. The Congress was successful in gathering most of the general electorate seats, but it could no longer effectively insist that it spoke for the entire population of British India.

In 1946 Secretary of State Pethick-Lawrence personally led a three-man cabinet deputation to New Delhi with the hope of resolving the Congress–Muslim League deadlock and, thus, of transferring British power to a single Indian administration. Cripps was responsible primarily for drafting the ingenious Cabinet Mission Plan, which proposed a three-tier federation for India, integrated by a minimal central-union government in Delhi, which would be limited to handling foreign affairs, communications, defense, and only those finances required to care for such unionwide matters. The subcontinent was to be divided into three major groups of provinces: Group A, to include the Hindu-majority provinces of the Bombay Presidency, Madras, the United Provinces, Bihar, Orissa, and the Central Provinces (virtually all of what became independent India a year later); Group B, to contain the Muslim-majority provinces of the Punjab, Sind, the North-West Frontier, and Balochistan (the areas out of which the western part of Pakistan was created); and Group C, to include the Muslim-majority Bengal (a portion of which became the eastern part of Pakistan and in 1971 the country of Bangladesh) and the Hindu-majority Assam. The group governments were to be virtually autonomous in everything but matters reserved to the union centre, and within each group the princely states were to be integrated into their neighbouring provinces. Local provincial governments were to have the choice of opting out of the group in which they found themselves should a majority of their populace vote to do so.

Punjab's large and powerful Sikh population would have been placed in a particularly difficult and anomalous position, for Punjab as a whole would have belonged to Group B, and much of the Sikh community had become anti-Muslim since the start of the Mughal emperors' persecution of their Gurus in the 17th century. Sikhs played so important a role in the British Indian Army that many of their leaders hoped that the British would reward them at the war's end with special assistance in carving out their own nation from the rich heart of Punjab's fertile canal-colony lands, where, in the kingdom once ruled by Ranjit Singh (1780–1839), most Sikhs lived. Since World War I, Sikhs had been equally fierce in opposing the British raj, and, though never more than 2 percent of India's population, they had as highly disproportionate a number of nationalist "martyrs" as of army officers. A Sikh Akali Dal ("Party of Immortals"), which was started in 1920, led militant marches to liberate gurdwaras ("doorways to the Guru"; the Sikh places of worship) from corrupt Hindu managers. Tara Singh (1885–1967), the most important leader of this vigorous Sikh political movement, first raised the demand for a separate Azad ("Free") Punjab in 1942. By March 1946 many Sikhs demanded a Sikh nation-state, alternately called Sikhistan or Khalistan ("Land of the Sikhs" or "Land of the Pure"). The Cabinet Mission, however, had no time or energy to focus on Sikh separatist demands and found the Muslim League's demand for Pakistan equally impossible to accept.

As a pragmatist, Jinnah—terminally afflicted with tuberculosis and lung cancer—accepted the Cabinet Mission's proposal, as did Congress leaders. The early summer of 1946, therefore, saw a dawn of hope for India's future prospects, but that soon proved false when Nehru announced at his first press conference as the reelected president of the Congress that no constituent assembly could be "bound" by any prearranged constitutional formula. Jinnah read Nehru's remarks as a "complete repudiation" of the plan, which had to be accepted in its entirety in order to work. Jinnah then convened the league's Working Committee, which withdrew its previous agreement to the federation scheme and instead called upon the "Muslim Nation" to launch "direct action" in mid-August 1946. Thus began India's bloodiest year of civil war since the mutiny nearly a century earlier. The Hindu-Muslim rioting and killing that started in Calcutta sent

Muslim women board a train at New Delhi in India to travel to the newly independent Pakistan on August 7, 1947. Keystone Features/Hulton Archive/Getty Images

deadly sparks of fury, frenzy, and fear to every corner of the subcontinent, as all civilized restraint seemed to disappear.

Lord Mountbatten (served March–August 1947) was sent to replace Wavell as viceroy as Britain prepared to transfer its power over India to some "responsible" hands by no later than June 1948. Shortly after reaching Delhi, where he conferred with the leaders of all parties and with his own officials, Mountbatten decided that the situation was too dangerous to wait even that brief period. Fearing a forced evacuation of British troops still stationed in India, Mountbatten resolved to opt for partition, one that would divide Punjab and Bengal, rather than risk further political negotiations while civil war raged and a new mutiny of Indian troops seemed imminent. Among the major Indian leaders, Gandhi alone refused to reconcile himself to partition and urged Mountbatten to offer Jinnah the premiership of a united India rather than a separate Muslim nation. Nehru, however, would not agree to that, nor would his most powerful Congress deputy, Vallabhbhai Jhaverbhai Patel (1875–1950), as both had become tired of arguing with Jinnah and were eager to get on with the job of running an independent government of India.

Britain's Parliament passed in July 1947 the Indian Independence Act, ordering the demarcation of the dominions of India and Pakistan by midnight of Aug. 14–15, 1947, and dividing within a single month the assets of the world's largest empire, which had been integrated in countless ways for more than a century. Racing the deadline, two boundary commissions worked desperately to partition Punjab and Bengal in such a way as to leave the maximum practical number of Muslims to the west of the former's new boundary and to the east of the latter's, but, as soon as the new borders were known, roughly 15 million Hindus, Muslims, and Sikhs fled from their homes on one side of the newly demarcated borders to what they thought would be "shelter" on the other. In the course of that tragic exodus of innocents, as many as a million people were slaughtered in communal massacres that made all previous conflicts of the sort known to recent history pale by comparison. Sikhs, settled astride Punjab's new "line," suffered the highest percentage of casualties. Most Sikh refugees relocated in the relatively small area of what is now the Indian border state of Punjab. Tara Singh later asked, "The Muslims got their Pakistan, and the Hindus got their Hindustan, but what did the Sikhs get?"

CHAPTER 12

THE REPUBLIC OF INDIA

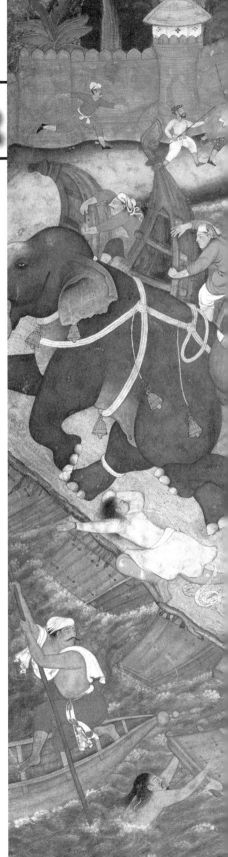

Thus, the new republic was born at the stroke of midnight on August 15. However, India's first years of freedom were plagued by the tragic legacy of partition. Refugee resettlement, economic disruption and inadequate resources for virtually every need, continuing communal conflicts (as more than 10 percent of India's population remained Muslim), and, within a few months of independence, the outbreak of undeclared war with Pakistan over Kashmir were but a few of the major difficulties confronting the newborn dominion.

THE NEHRU ERA, 1947–64

Mountbatten had remained in New Delhi to serve as India's first new governor-general, mostly a ceremonial job. Meanwhile Nehru took charge of free India's responsible government as its first prime minister, heading a Congress cabinet, whose second most powerful figure was Patel.

Gandhi, who accepted no office, chose to walk barefoot through the riot-torn areas of Bengal and Bihar, where he tried through his presence and influence to stop the communal killing. He then returned to Delhi, and there he preached nonviolence daily until he was assassinated by an orthodox Hindu Brahman fanatic on Jan. 30, 1948. "The light has gone out of our lives," Prime Minister Nehru said, "and there is darkness everywhere." Yet Nehru carried on at India's helm, and, owing in part to his secular, enlightened leadership, not

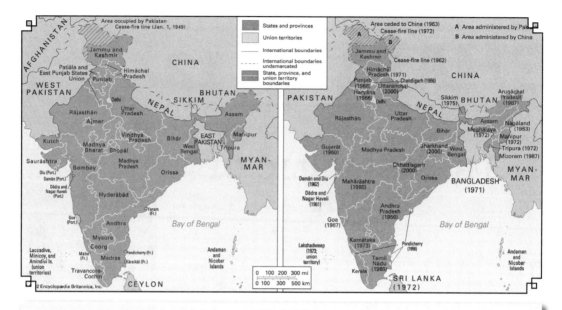

Reorganization of states and union territories since independence. (Left) India in 1955, with the former princely states integrated in the union; (right) India after the States Reorganization Act in 1956 and later administrative changes.

only did India's flood of religious hatred and violence recede but also some progress was made toward communal reconciliation and economic development. Nehru spoke out fearlessly against India's "caste-ridden" and "priest-ridden" society, which, as a Hindu Brahman pandit, he could do without fear of too much upper-caste criticism. His charismatic brilliance, moreover, continued to make him a major vote-winner in each election campaign that he led (1951–52, 1957, 1962) throughout his 17 arduous years in office, as the Congress—opposed only by minor parties and independent candidates—dominated political life. Nehru's modernist mentality and cosmopolitan

popularity helped to hide the traditional continuity of India's internal problems, few of which disappeared under his leadership.

GOVERNMENT AND POLITICS

The Dominion of India was reborn on Jan. 26, 1950, as a sovereign democratic republic and a union of states. With universal adult franchise, India's electorate was the world's largest, but the traditional feudal roots of most of its illiterate populace were deep, just as their religious caste beliefs were to remain far more powerful than more recent exotic ideas, such as secular statehood. Elections were to be held, however, at least every five years, and the major model of government followed by India's constitution was that of British parliamentary rule, with a lower House of the People (Lok Sabha), in which an elected prime minister and his cabinet sat, and an upper Council of States (Rajya Sabha). Nehru led his ruling Congress Party from New Delhi's Lok Sabha until his death in 1964. The nominal head of India's republic, however, was a president, who was indirectly elected. India's first two presidents were Hindu Brahmans, Rajendra Prasad and Sarvepalli Radhakrishnan, the latter a distinguished Sanskrit scholar who had lectured at Oxford. Presidential powers were mostly ceremonial, except for brief periods of "emergency" rule, when the nation's security was believed to be in great danger and normal constitutional procedures and civil rights were feared to be too cumbersome or threatening.

India's federation divided powers between the central government in New Delhi and a number of state governments (crafted from former British provinces and princely states), each of which also had a nominal governor at its head and an elected chief minister with his cabinet to rule its legislative assembly. One of the Congress's long-standing resolutions had called for the reorganization of British provincial borders into linguistic states, where each of India's major regional languages would find its administrative reflection, while English and Hindi would remain joint national languages for purposes of legislation, law,

and service examinations. Pressure for such reorganization increased in 1953, after the former British province of Madras was divided into Tamil Nadu ("Land of the Tamils") and Andhra (from 1956 Andhra Pradesh), where Telugu, another Dravidian tongue, was spoken by the vast majority. Nehru thus appointed the States Reorganization Commission to redesign India's internal map, which led to a major redrawing of administrative boundaries, especially in southern India, by the States Reorganization Act, passed in 1956. Four years later, in 1960, the enlarged state of Bombay was divided into Marathi-speaking Maharashtra and Gujarati-speaking Gujarat. Despite these changes, the difficult process of reorganization continued and demanded attention in many regions of the subcontinent, whose truly "continental" character was perhaps best seen in this ongoing linguistic agitation. Among the most difficult problems was a demand by Sikhs that their language, Punjabi, with its sacred Gurmukhi script, be made the official tongue of Punjab, but in that state many Hindus, fearing they would find themselves disadvantaged, insisted that as Hindi speakers they too deserved a state of their own, if indeed the Sikhs were to be granted the Punjabi *suba* (state) for which so many Sikhs agitated. Nehru, however, refused to agree to a separate Sikh state, as he feared that such a concession to the Sikhs, who were both a religious and a linguistic group, might open the door to further "Pakistan-style" fragmentation.

FOREIGN POLICY

Nehru served as his own foreign minister and throughout his life remained the chief architect of India's foreign policy. The dark cloud of partition, however, hovered for years in the aftermath of India's independence, and India and Pakistan were left suspicious of one another's incitements to border violence.

The princely state of Jammu and Kashmir triggered the first undeclared war with Pakistan, which began a little more than two months after independence. Prior to partition, princes were given the option of joining the new dominion within which their territory lay, and, thanks to the vigorous lobbying of Mountbatten and Patel, most of the princes agreed to do so, accepting handsome pensions (so-called "privy purses") as rewards for relinquishing sovereignty. Of some 570 princes, only 3 had not acceded to the new dominion or gone immediately over to Pakistan—those of Junagadh, Hyderabad, and Kashmir. The nawab of Junagadh and the nizam of Hyderabad were both Muslims, though most of their subjects were Hindus, and both states were surrounded, on land, by India. Junagadh, however, faced Pakistan on the Arabian Sea, and when its nawab followed Jinnah's lead in opting to join that Muslim nation, India's army moved in and took control of the territory. The nizam of Hyderabad was more cautious, hoping for independence for his vast domain in the heart of southern India, but

India refused to give him much more than one year and sent troops into the state in September 1948. Both invasions met little, if any, resistance, and both states were swiftly integrated into India's union.

Kashmir, lying in the Himalayas, presented a different problem. Its maharaja was Hindu, but about three-fourths of its population was Muslim, and the state itself was contiguous to both new dominions, sitting like a crown atop South Asia. Maharaja Hari Singh tried at first to remain independent, but in October 1947 Pashtun (Pathan) tribesmen from the North-West Frontier of Pakistan invaded Kashmir in trucks, heading toward Srinagar. The invasion triggered India's first undeclared war with Pakistan and led at once to the maharaja's decision to opt for accession to India. Mountbatten and Nehru airlifted Indian troops into Srinagar, and the tribesmen were forced to fall back to a line that has, since early 1949, partitioned Kashmir into Pakistan-held Azad Kashmir (the western portion of Kashmir) and the Northern Areas (the northern portion of Kashmir, also administered by Pakistan) and India's state of Jammu and Kashmir, which includes the Vale of Kashmir and Ladakh. Nehru initially agreed to Mountbatten's proposal that a plebiscite be held in the entire state as soon as hostilities ceased, and a UN-sponsored cease-fire was agreed to by both parties on Jan. 1, 1949. No statewide plebiscite was held, however, for in 1954, after Pakistan began to receive arms from the United States, Nehru withdrew his support.

India's foreign policy, defined by Nehru as nonaligned, was based on Five Principles (Panch Shila): mutual respect for other nations' territorial integrity and sovereignty; nonaggression; noninterference in internal affairs; equality and mutual benefit; and peaceful coexistence. These principles were, ironically, articulated in a treaty with China over the Tibet region in 1954, when Nehru still hoped for Sino-Indian "brotherhood" and leadership of a "Third World" of nonviolent nations, recently independent of colonial rule, eager to save the world from Cold War superpower confrontation and nuclear annihilation.

China and India, however, had not resolved a dispute over several areas of their border, most notably the section demarcating a barren plateau in Ladakh—most of which was called Aksai Chin, which was claimed by India as part of Jammu and Kashmir state but never properly surveyed—and the section bordered on the north by the McMahon Line, which stretched from Bhutan to Burma (Myanmar) and extended to the crest of the Great Himalayas. The latter area, designated as the North-East Frontier Agency (NEFA) in 1954, was claimed on the basis of a 1914 agreement between Arthur Henry McMahon, the British foreign secretary for India, and Tibetan officials but was never accepted by China. After China had reasserted its authority over Tibet in 1950, it began appealing to India—but to no avail—for negotiations over the border. This Sino-Indian dispute was exacerbated in the late 1950s after India discovered a road across Aksai Chin built by the Chinese to link its autonomous region of Xinjiang with Tibet. The tension was further heightened when, in 1959, India granted asylum to the Dalai Lama, Tibet's spiritual leader. Full-scale war blazed in October 1962 when a Chinese army moved easily through India's northern outposts and advanced virtually unopposed toward the plains of Assam before Beijing ordered their unilateral withdrawal.

The war was a blow to Nehru's most cherished principles and ideals, though as a result of swift and extensive American and British military support, including the dispatch of U.S. bombers to the world's highest border, India soon secured its northern defenses. India's "police action" of integrating Portuguese Goa into the union by force in 1961 represented another fall from the high ground of nonviolence in foreign affairs, which Nehru so often claimed for India in his speeches to the UN and elsewhere. During his premiership, Nehru tried hard to identify the country's foreign policy with anticolonialism and antiracism. He also tried to promote India's role as the peacemaker, which was seen as an extension of the policies of Gandhi and as deeply rooted in the indigenous religious traditions of Buddhism, Jainism, and Hinduism. Like most foreign policies, India's was, in fact, based first of all on its government's perceptions of national interest and on security considerations.

Economic Planning and Development

As a Fabian Socialist, Nehru had great faith in economic planning and personally chaired his government's Planning Commission. India's First Five-Year Plan was launched in 1951, and most of its funds were spent on rebuilding war-shattered railroads and on irrigation schemes and canals. Food grain production increased from 51 million tons in 1951 to 82 million tons by the end of the Second Five-Year Plan (1956–61). During that same decade, however, India's population grew from about 360 million to 440 million, which eliminated real economic benefits for all but large landowners and the wealthiest and best-educated quarter of India's urban population. The landless and unemployed lower half of India's fast-growing population remained inadequately fed, ill-housed, and illiterate. However, Nehru's wisdom in keeping his nation nonaligned helped accelerate the country's economic development, as India received substantial aid from both sides of the Cold War, with the Soviet Union and eastern Europe contributing almost as much in capital goods and technical assistance as did the United States, Great Britain, and West Germany. The growth of iron and steel industries soon became a truly international example of coexistence, with the United States building one plant, the Soviet Union another, Britain a third, and West Germany a fourth. For the Third Five-Year Plan (1961–66), launched during Nehru's era, an Aid India Consortium of the major Western powers and Japan provided some $5 billion in capital and credits, and, as a result, India's annual iron output rose to nearly 25 million tons by the plan's end, with about three times that amount of coal produced and almost 40 billion kilowatt-hours of electric power generated. India had become the world's 10th most advanced industrial country in terms of absolute value of output, though it remained per capita one of the least productive of the world's major countries.

As modernity brought added comforts and pleasure to India's urban elite, the gap between the larger industrial urban centres and the areas of extensive rural poverty became greater. Various schemes designed to reduce rural poverty were tried, many ostensibly in emulation of Gandhi's *sarvodaya* (rural "uplift") philosophy, which advocated community sharing of all resources for the mutual benefit and enhancement of peasant life. The social reformer Vinoba Bhave started a *bhoodan* ("gift-of-land") movement, in which he walked from village to village and asked large landowners to "adopt" him as their son and to give him a portion of their property, which he would then distribute among the landless. He later expanded that program to include *gramdan* ("gift-of-village"), in which villagers voluntarily surrendered their land to a cooperative system, and *jivandan* ("gift-of-life"), the giving of all one's labour, the latter attracting volunteers as famous as the socialist J.P. (Jaya Prakash) Narayan, founder of the Janata

("People's") opposition to the Congress of the mid-1970s. The Ford Foundation, an American philanthropic organization, began a community development and rural extension program in the early 1950s that encouraged young Indian college students and technical experts to focus their skills and knowledge on village problems. India's half million villages, however, were slow to change, and, though a number of showcase villages emerged in the environs of New Delhi, Bombay, and other large cities, the more-remote villages remained centres of superstition, poverty, caste division, and illiteracy.

It was not until the late 1960s that chemical fertilizers and high-yield food seeds brought the Green Revolution in agriculture to India. The results were mixed, as many poor or small farmers were unable to afford the seeds or the risks involved in the new technology. Moreover, as rice and, especially, wheat production increased, there was a corresponding decrease in other grain production. Farmers who benefited most were from the major wheat-growing areas of Haryana, Punjab, and western Uttar Pradesh.

POST-NEHRU POLITICS AND FOREIGN POLICY

At his death on May 27, 1964, Nehru's only child and closest confidante, Indira Gandhi, was with him. Long separated from her husband—Feroze Gandhi, by then deceased—Indira had moved into Teen Murti Bhavan, the prime minister's mansion, with her two sons, Rajiv and Sanjay. She had accompanied her father the world over and had been the leader of his Congress Party's "ginger group" youth movement, as well as Congress president, but, as a young mother and widow, she had not as yet served in parliament nor on her father's cabinet and, hence, did not put herself forward as a candidate for prime minister. Though it appeared that Nehru was grooming her as his successor, he had denied any such intention, and his party instead chose Lal

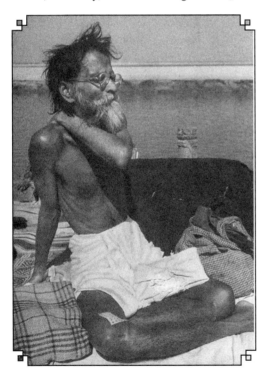

This photo, taken in 1952, shows Gandhi disciple and religious leader Vinobha Bhave, the founder of the Bhoodan Yujna ("land-gift movement"). James Burke/ Time & Life Pictures/Getty Images

Indira Gandhi (left) *rides with her father, India's prime minister Jawaharlal Nehru, in 1961.* Hulton Archive/Getty Images

Bahadur Shastri as India's second prime minister. Shastri had devoted his life to party affairs and had served Nehru well both inside and outside his cabinet. His modesty and simplicity, moreover, appealed to most Indians.

THE 1965 WAR WITH PAKISTAN

Almost immediately after Shastri took office, India was faced with a threat of war from Pakistan. Pakistan's president, Mohammad Ayub Khan, had led a military coup in 1958 that put him in charge

of his country's civil and military affairs, and his regime had received substantial military support from the United States. By 1965 Ayub felt ready to test India's frontier outposts, first in the Sindh (Sind) and then in Kashmir. The first skirmishes were fought in the Rann of Kachchh (Kutch) in April, and Pakistan's U.S.-made tanks rolled to what seemed like an easy victory over India's counterparts. The Commonwealth prime ministers and the UN quickly prevailed on both sides to agree to a cease-fire and withdrawal of forces to the prewar borders. Pakistan, however, believed it had won and that India's army was weak, and Zulfikar Ali Bhutto, Ayub's foreign minister, urged another round in Kashmir that summer, to which Ayub agreed. In mid-August Pakistan launched "Operation Grandslam" with the hope of cutting across the only significant overland route to Kashmir before India could bring up its outmoded tanks. India's forces, however, moved a three-pronged tank attack aimed at Lahore and Sialkot across the international border in Punjab early in September. The great city of Lahore was in range of Indian tank fire by September 23, when a UN cease-fire was agreed on by both sides. Each country's army had suffered considerable losses and had run low on ammunition as a result of the immediate decision by the United Kingdom and the United States to embargo all further military shipments to both armies. Shastri was hailed as a hero in New Delhi.

A Soviet-sponsored South Asian peace conference was held early in January 1966 at Tashkent, in what was then the Uzbek S.S.R., where Ayub and Shastri finally reached an agreement on January 10 to "restore normal and peaceful relations" between India and Pakistan. The next morning, however, Shastri was dead of a heart attack, and the Tashkent Agreement hardly outlived him. Before the month's end, Indira Gandhi, who had served in Shastri's cabinet as minister of information and broadcasting, had been elected by the Congress Party to become India's next prime minister. She easily defeated her only rival, Morarji Desai.

INDIRA GANDHI'S IMPACT

Indira Gandhi's soft-spoken, attractive personality masked her iron will and autocratic ambition, and most of her Congress contemporaries underestimated her drive and tenacity. During her first year in office, she visited Washington, where she won substantial support for India's weakened economy, and her subsequent visit to Moscow reflected the continuation of her father's policy of nonalignment. Trying to defuse Sikh agitation, moreover, and as a reward for Sikh military service in the Kashmir war, she granted the long-standing Sikh demand of a Punjabi *suba* (state), which required partition of the existing state of Punjab but left its newly designed capital of Chandigarh as shared administrative headquarters of the new states of Punjab, with a Sikh majority, and Haryana, with a slight Hindu majority.

Several years of poor monsoons had conspired with wartime spending to undermine India's economy, and Prime Minister Gandhi's subsequent decision to devalue the rupee cost her party considerable losses at the polls in India's fourth general elections, in 1967. Although the Congress, with 283 seats (of 520), was still considerably larger than any of the various left- and right-wing opposition parties, none of which gained more than 44 seats, her overall Lok Sabha majority was reduced from some 200 (which she had inherited) to fewer than 50. The Congress, moreover, lost most of the more than 3,400 elective seats in the state

INDIRA GANDHI

The Indian politician Indira Gandhi (1917–84) served three consecutive terms as prime minister (1966–77) and a fourth (1980–84) before her assassination in 1984. Indira Priyadarshini Nehru, the only child of Jawaharlal Nehru, studied in India and at the University of Oxford. In 1942 she married Feroze Gandhi (d. 1960), a fellow member of the Indian National Congress. In 1959 she was given the largely honorary position of party president, and in 1966 she achieved actual power when she was made leader of the Congress Party and, consequently, prime minister. She instituted major reforms, including a strict population-control program. In 1971 she mobilized Indian forces in East Bengal's secession from Pakistan and rebirth as Bangladesh. She oversaw the incorporation of Sikkim in 1974. Convicted in 1975 of violating election laws, she declared a state of emergency, jailing opponents and passing many laws limiting personal freedoms. She was defeated in the following election but returned to power in 1980. In 1984 she ordered the army to attack the Golden Temple complex of the Sikhs at Amritsar to root out Sikh militants inside the temple; some 450 Sikhs died in the fighting. Later that year she was shot and killed by her own Sikh bodyguards in revenge.

assemblies, and Gandhi felt obliged to invite Desai into her cabinet as deputy prime minister and finance minister. As leader of Gujarat's wealthy banking and business elite, Desai was considered a pillar of economic stability, whose presence in New Delhi would swiftly restore confidence in the Congress government.

India's first Muslim president, Zakir Husain, was also elected in 1967, but his death two years later opened a wider rift in Congress leadership and gave Gandhi the opportunity of taking more power into her own hands, as she began rejecting the advice and support of her father's closest colleagues of the old guard, including Desai, whom she forced out of her cabinet. For president she backed her own candidate, Vice President V.V. (Varahagiri Venkata) Giri, against the majority of her party's leadership, who favoured the Lok Sabha speaker Neelam Sanjiva Reddy; she proved to be a skillful political manager for Giri, who was easily elected. Because of this, the old guard of the Congress Party expelled Gandhi for "indiscipline," but, refusing to be intimidated, she rallied most of the elected members of parliament to her "New Congress" standard and led a left-wing national coalition of communist and provincial Dravidian and Akali parties from Punjab and Tamil Nadu. Desai led the old guard, a minority of Congress members who remained as the prime minister's opposition in the Lok Sabha but who could not thwart any of her major legislation, including a constitutional amendment to abolish former princely pensions in 1970. Gandhi called new elections at the end of 1970,

On June 22, 1971, refugees carry their belongings as they approach the Indian border, after fleeing from fighting in East Pakistan (now Bangladesh). Popperfoto/Getty Images

and—sweeping the polls the following March with the promise "Eliminate poverty!"—her party won 350 seats in a Lok Sabha of 515.

THE BANGLADESH WAR

In December 1970 Pakistan held general elections, its first since independence. The Awami League, headed by East Pakistan's popular Bengali leader Mujibur Rahman (Sheikh Mujib), won a clear majority of seats in the new assembly, but West Pakistan's chief martial law administrator and president, Gen. Agha Mohammad Yahya Khan, refused to honour the democratic choice of his country's majority. At the end of March 1971, after failed negotiations in which Mujib demanded virtual independence for East Pakistan, Yahya Khan ordered a military massacre in Dhaka (Dacca). Though Mujib was arrested and flown to prison in West Pakistan, he called on his followers in the east to rise up and proclaim their independence as Bangladesh ("Land of the Bengalis"). Some 10 million refugees fled across the border from East Pakistan to India in the ensuing eight months of martial rule and sporadic firing by West

Pakistan's army. Soon after the monsoon stopped, India's army moved up to the Bangladesh border and by early December had advanced virtually unopposed to Dhaka, which was surrendered in mid-December. Mujib, released by Pres. Zulfikar Ali Bhutto, who had taken over from the disgraced Yahya Khan, flew home to a hero's welcome, and in January 1972 he became the first prime minister of the People's Republic of Bangladesh.

India's stunning victory over Pakistan in the Bangladesh war was achieved in part because of Soviet military support and diplomatic assurances. The Treaty of Peace, Friendship, and Cooperation, signed in mid-1971 by India with the Soviet Union, gave India the arms it used in the war. With the birth of Bangladesh, India's already dominant position in South Asia was enhanced, and its foreign policy, which remained officially nonaligned, tilted further toward the Soviet Union.

In a last-ditch but futile effort to support Pakistan, a nuclear-armed aircraft carrier of the U.S. Pacific Fleet was sent to the Bay of Bengal, ostensibly to evacuate civilians from Dhaka, but the war ended before any such assistance could be rendered. Many Indians viewed the aircraft carrier's presence so close to their own shores as provocative "nuclear weapons rattling," and by 1972 India launched an atomic program of its own, detonating its first plutonium-armed device under the sands of Rajasthan in May 1974. The atomic explosion was felt in Pakistan's neighbouring Sind province and triggered that country's resolve to produce a bomb

of its own as swiftly as possible. Pakistan subsequently forged stronger ties with China and with Muslim countries to the west but found itself further diminished as a potential challenge to Indian hegemony over South Asia.

EMERGENCY RULE

The Bangladesh war raised Prime Minister Gandhi to virtual "mother goddess" stature at home. She was viewed as a brilliant military strategist and diplomat, and her popularity was never greater than in the years immediately after that brief December war. By late 1974, however, Gandhi's golden image had tarnished, for, despite her campaign rhetoric, poverty was hardly abolished in India. Quite the contrary, with skyrocketing oil prices and consumer-goods inflation, India's unemployed and landless, as well as its large fixed-income labouring population, found itself sinking deeper into starvation's grip and impossible debt. Student strikes and mass protest marches rocked Bihar and Gujarat, as Narayan and Desai joined forces in leading a new Janata Morcha ("People's Front") movement against government corruption and Gandhi's allegedly inept leadership. The mass movement gathered momentum throughout the first half of 1975 and reached its climax that June, when the Congress lost a crucial by-election in Gujarat and Gandhi herself was found guilty by Allahabad's High Court of several counts of election malpractice during the last campaign for her Lok Sabha seat. The mandatory penalty for that crime was exclusion from holding any elective office for six years from date of conviction.

Opposition leaders threatened a civil disobedience campaign to force the prime minister to resign, and many of her oldest cabinet colleagues and Congress Party advisers urged her to step down pending an appeal to India's Supreme Court. Following instead the advice of her ambitious and energetic younger son, Sanjay, on June 26, 1975, Gandhi persuaded Pres. Fakhruddin Ali Ahmed to declare a national emergency, which empowered her to do whatever she considered best for the country for at least six months. The elite Central Reserve Police force, the prime minister's palace guard, was ordered to arrest Desai and the ailing and aged Narayan, as well as hundreds of others who had worked with her father and Mohandas Gandhi in helping India to win its freedom from British rule. She then blacked out the entire region of Delhi in which the press was published and appointed Sanjay as her trusted personal censor of all future news leaders and editorials. Her minister of information and broadcasting, Inder K. Gujral, immediately resigned rather than accept orders from Sanjay, who held no elective office at the time but who clearly was becoming one of the most powerful persons in India. "India is Indira, and Indira is India," was the call of Congress Party sycophants, and soon the country was plastered with her poster image. Practically every leader of India's political opposition was jailed or kept under house arrest for almost two years, and some of India's most prominent journalists, lawyers, educators, and political activists were muzzled or imprisoned.

Gandhi announced her Twenty-Point Program soon after the emergency was proclaimed, and most points were aimed at reducing inflation and energizing the economy by punishing tax evaders, black marketers, smugglers, and other real criminals. Prices did come down, production indexes rose dramatically, and even the monsoon proved cooperative by bringing abundant rains on time two years in a row. At the same time, however, popular discontent was fostered by some of the emergency acts, such as a freeze on wage increases, pressure for increased worker discipline, and a birth-control program initiated by Sanjay that mandated sterilization for families with more than two children. It was perhaps because of the economic gains that the prime minister decided early in 1977 to call general elections, but she may also have believed what she read about herself in her controlled press or feared a military coup had she simply refused to seek a civil mandate for her policies. Most political prisoners were released, and Narayan immediately joined Desai in quickly revitalizing the Janata movement, whose campaign warned Indians that the elections might be their last chance to choose between "democracy and dictatorship." In the elections, held in February, Indira and Sanjay both lost their Lok Sabha seats, as did most of their loyal followers, and the Congress was reduced to just 153 seats, 92 of which were from four of the southern states. The Janata Party's 295 seats (of a total 542) gave it only a modest majority, but opposition candidates together represented more than two-thirds of the Lok Sabha.

THE JANATA INTERLUDE AND THE RETURN OF INDIRA GANDHI

At the age of 80, Desai took the post of prime minister. Although Narayan was too sick to accept any office, there were others in the Janata Party, especially Charan Singh, of the Jat peasant caste, who considered themselves at least as worthy of becoming prime minister as Desai, and the petty squabbling over power and all the perks of high office kept the new leaders in Delhi so preoccupied that little time or vital energy was left with which to address the nation's crying problems and needs. Freedom did return, however, including laissez-faire in all its worst forms, and inflation soon escalated, as did smuggling, black-marketing, and every form of corruption endemic to any poor country with underpaid bureaucrats and undereducated police. Even the rains failed Desai, whose high-spending regime soon used up the substantial surplus in food grains that Gandhi had amassed in new storage facilities.

Politically, perhaps the worst error made by Desai was to insist on punishing Indira Gandhi and Sanjay Gandhi, both of whom were accused of many crimes, none of which would be easy to prove in any Indian court. In November 1978

Indira Gandhi had again been elected to the Lok Sabha, but this time as a member of the Congress (I) Party (the I stood for Indira), which she and her supporters had formed that year. She was expelled from the Lok Sabha the following month and then briefly imprisoned, but this action brought a strong backlash of sympathy for her from millions of Indians, many of whom a year earlier had feared her as a tyrant.

No major legislation was introduced by the new government, which in a year of inaction seemed incapable of solving any of India's problems and lost the confidence of most of the populace. In mid-July 1979, Desai resigned rather than face a no-confidence motion that had been tabled in the Lok Sabha and would easily have passed. Charan Singh was then selected prime minister, but just a few weeks later he too resigned. President Reddy, who had been elected along with Desai in 1977, called for new elections and dissolved parliament in the winter of 1979.

In January 1980 India's seventh general election returned Indira Gandhi to power over New Delhi's central government. The Congress (I) Party, which had run on the slogan "Elect a government that works," won 351 of the 525 contested Lok Sabha seats, as against 31 for Janata. Sanjay Gandhi also won election to the Lok Sabha and resumed his former post as head of the Congress's youth wing (the Youth Congress). Though he remained outside his mother's cabinet, he personally selected half of the Congress's successful Lok Sabha candidates, and it appeared that he was being groomed as her successor. In June 1980, however, Sanjay Gandhi was killed in the crash of a new stunt plane he was flying. Indira Gandhi, who seemed never fully to recover from the loss of Sanjay, immediately recruited her elder son, Rajiv, into political life. Rajiv had been a pilot until his younger brother's death but took up politics at his mother's insistence.

SIKH SEPARATISM

India's problems of poverty, pluralism, inequities in development and gross disparities in wealth and education, and continuing provincial and communal violence did not disappear or diminish. The worst violence erupted in Punjab, where, ironically, the majority of the Sikh population had gained affluence in the wake of India's Green Revolution of the late 1960s. Yet bumper crops and higher per capita incomes brought all the gadgets and toys of modernity, which pulled or lured many younger Sikhs away from ingrained tradition and religious values that others considered sacred. This opened large gaps within Sikh society, almost as wide and deep as those that separated Punjab from the rest of India. Though Indira Gandhi had agreed in 1970 to transfer Chandigarh to the recently divided Punjab as its sole capital, that simple act had never been carried out, for Haryana's mainly Hindu populace vigorously demanded adequate compensation if their state were to be deprived of so valuable an asset. The prime minister tried to appease Sikh frustrations by appointing a Sikh, Zail Singh, as her home minister, in charge of police nationwide, yet most of the leaders in Chandigarh and Amritsar distrusted Singh and soon came to distrust Gandhi even more. Though in 1982 she nominated Zail Singh to be the first Sikh president of India, even that symbolic elevation of a member of the small Sikh minority to the highest office in India's secular republic failed to quell the rising storm over Punjab.

By the early 1980s some Sikhs were calling for more than mere separate provincial statehood, instead demanding nothing less than a nation-state of their own, an autonomous Sikh Khalistan, or "Land of the Pure." More moderate Sikh leaders, such as Harchand Singh Longowal, who was elected president of the Akali Party in 1980, unsuccessfully attempted to avert civil war by seeking to negotiate a settlement of Sikh demands with New Delhi's Congress leaders. Extremists like Jarnail Singh Bhindranwale won the support of many younger devout Sikhs around Amritsar, who were armed with automatic weapons and launched a violent movement for Khalistan that took control of the Sikhs' holiest shrine, the Golden Temple (Harimandir), and its sacred precincts. Gandhi and her government seemed unable to do anything to stop the growing number of politically motivated killings and acts of terror in Punjab, Haryana, and Delhi. She knew that nationwide elections would have to be called by

January 1985, and the overwhelming Hindu majority of India's electorate would likely judge her government too weak to be retained. In 1984, therefore, Gandhi gave her generals permission to launch their "Operation Bluestar," as it was code-named, against the Golden Temple. Early in June, after a night of artillery fire, they moved tanks and troops into the temple precincts, and for four days and nights the battle raged, until Bhindranwale and most of his snipers were dead. Hundreds of innocent people were caught in the cross fire, and at least 100 soldiers died. Khalistan had its first martyrs. In retaliation, on Oct. 31, 1984, Gandhi herself was shot dead by two of her own Sikh guards inside her garden in New Delhi. The next day mobs of blood-thirsty thugs began to roam the Sikh neighbourhoods in and around Delhi, where they set fire to cars, homes, and businesses and launched a massacre of Sikhs that left thousands dead and many more thousands wounded and homeless in the worst religious riot since partition.

INDIA SINCE THE MID-1980S

The night Indira Gandhi died, her son flew back to New Delhi from West Bengal, where he had been on the campaign trail. Pres. Zail Singh also flew home, from a visit to the Persian Gulf, and swore in the 40-year-old Rajiv Gandhi as prime minis-ter, though he had not even been a member of his mother's cabinet. Several days later, on the eve of his mother's funeral, Rajiv decided to call out the army

to stop the orgy of murder and terror in Delhi. Several well-known leaders of the Congress (I) Party in Delhi were accused by human-rights activists of having incited the Hindu mobs to violence, but none was ever accused in any court of law or sentenced to any jail term.

THE PREMIERSHIP OF RAJIV GANDHI

Rajiv Gandhi wisely opted to call for fresh elections nationwide soon after taking office, and, reaping the sympathy vote for his mother's murder, won the December 1984 election by the largest majority ever amassed by any party leader in indepen-dent India. In her own violent death, Indira Gandhi thus assured her son's suc-cession to the post of power for which she had carefully groomed him during the last four years of her life.

With the Congress (I) winning more than 400 seats in the Lok Sabha, Rajiv Gandhi could have passed virtually any legislative program he wanted. He chose to work toward removing onerous licens-ing restrictions and other bureaucratic red tape relating to high-technology imports and the establishment of foreign-funded factories and other businesses in India. The new prime minister hoped to lead India into the computer age, and, departing from his grandfather's Fabian Socialist predisposition toward Great Britain and his mother's leaning toward the Soviet Union—which continued to bolster India's air and sea defenses—Rajiv Gandhi looked more to the United States for help and to American technology as his favoured model for India's development. Though hundreds of millions remained unemployed or underemployed and illiterate, he stopped emphasizing, as his grandfather and mother had done, the need to abolish or even diminish poverty for India's lower half, instead addressing himself more to the captains of Indian industry and commerce and advocating a trickle-down theory of economic growth.

Because of his youth, Gandhi represented the ascension of a new generation to power and brought with him the hope of resolving some of India's long-standing problems. His initial popularity, however, began to diminish after his first two years in office, and charges of mismanagement became common. His greatest political challenge, though, resulted from problems with a member of his own cabinet, Minister of Finance V.P. (Vishwanath Pratap) Singh, who by 1987 had conducted investigations into the machinations of several of India's leading industrial and commercial families and houses whose reputations for tax evasion were notorious. In January of that year, Singh found himself suddenly transferred to the Ministry of Defense, but his crusade against corruption continued in his new ministry, where he found signs of financial kickbacks in the procurement of arms, especially from the Swedish firm of Bofors. A political uproar followed, and Singh, charging that the government was hindering his investigation, resigned from the cabinet in April.

By 1989 Gandhi, as well as the Congress (I), was still tainted by charges of corruption, and recent price increases on essential goods made the Congress (I) even more vulnerable to opposition parties, including the right-wing Bharatiya Janata ("Indian People's") Party (BJP), headed by L.K. (Lal Krishna) Advani, and V.P. Singh's new Janata Dal. In the general elections held in November, Gandhi barely managed to retain his own Lok Sabha seat, as the Congress (I), winning only 193 seats, lost its majority. The Janata Dal (141 seats) emerged with the second largest block, and V.P. Singh, with the support of the BJP (88 seats) and the two main communist parties (44 seats), was able to put together a coalition majority that took office in December.

FOREIGN POLICY

Relations with the United States improved during the last half of the 1980s, with greater trade, scientific cooperation, and cultural exchanges. When civil rule resumed in Pakistan in 1988, India's relations with that country also reached a new level of friendship, though the South Asian thaw proved to be brief.

In December 1985 Rajiv Gandhi had endorsed a bold initiative, helping to launch the seven-nation South Asian Association for Regional Cooperation (SAARC), whose annual meetings thereafter offered the leaders of India and Pakistan, as well as their smaller neighbours, unique opportunities to informally discuss and resolve problems. The problem of Kashmir was among the worst of these, though India had in the late 1980s also accused Pakistan of arming and then sending Pakistani agents across the Punjab border. In late 1989 strikes, terrorism, and unrest escalated in Kashmir, and by early 1990 the area was rocked by a series of violent explosions and fierce exchanges of heavy fire along the line of control that separated the Indian- and Pakistani-administered sectors of Kashmir. A newly vitalized liberation front in Srinagar captured the allegiance of many young Kashmiri Muslims, who may have been inspired by unrest in Israel's West Bank or in eastern Europe or by the Soviet Union's withdrawal from Afghanistan to risk their lives in a struggle for freedom from "Indian occupation." New Delhi responded by proclaiming president's rule, suspending all local elected government, and rushing in additional troops until the entire state of Jammu and Kashmir was under curfew and martial law. New Delhi refused to discuss the matter with any foreign powers, as it insisted that the situation in the state was a purely domestic matter that could be dealt with by Indians alone.

The Indian government was also confronted by unrest in neighbouring Sri Lanka, where in the 1980s conflict between the island's Sinhalese Buddhist majority and its Tamil Hindu minority broke out into civil war. With a large, politically powerful Tamil community of its own, India viewed the unrest with particular concern and had since the 1970s tried diplomacy to no avail. In 1987, after several SAARC meetings between Gandhi and Sri Lanka's president, J.R. (Junius

Richard) Jayewardene, the two leaders signed a peace accord that provided the Tamils with an autonomous province within a united Sri Lanka. India agreed to prevent Tamil separatists from using its territory, notably Tamil Nadu, for training and shelter and agreed to send an Indian Peace-Keeping Force (IPKF) to disarm the Liberation Tigers of Tamil Eelam (Tamil Tigers) and other Tamil forces. The IPKF, however, soon found itself embroiled in fighting the Tamil Tigers. The accord had never been popular among Tamils or Sinhalese, and by 1989 the Indian government was bowing to Sri Lankan pressure to pull out its troops. In March 1990, with its mission unaccomplished, the last of the IPKF had been withdrawn.

V.P. SINGH'S COALITION—ITS BRIEF RISE AND FALL

V.P. Singh, who had initially denied any interest in becoming prime minister, emerged after the 1989 elections as the leader of a loosely knit coalition whose extreme wings were basically antipathetic to each other. Haryana's Jat leader, Devi Lal, who nominated V.P. Singh for prime minister, became deputy prime minister, thus raising fears in Punjab that another period of harsh Delhi rule was about to begin. V.P. Singh's first visit as prime minister, however, was to Amritsar's Golden Temple, where he walked barefoot to announce that he hoped to bring a "healing touch" to Punjab's sorely torn state. Singh promised a political solution for the region's problems, but, reflecting

The Babri Masjid in Ayodhya, India, prior to its destruction in December 1992. Frederick M. Asher

the ambivalence in his new coalition, the move in Amritsar was not followed up by the transfer of Chandigarh, nor indeed by any state elections.

A similar ambivalence within the coalition was seen with respect to events in Ayodhya (in Uttar Pradesh), an ancient capital and—as most orthodox Hindus believe—birthplace of the deity Rama. The Babri Masjid, a mosque erected by the Mughal emperor Bābur in Ayodhya, was said to have been built over the very site of Rama's birthplace, where a more ancient Hindu temple, Ram Janmabhoomi, was supposed to have stood. In the fall of 1990 a mass march of Hindus bearing consecrated bricks to rebuild "Rama's birth temple" won the support of most members of Advani's BJP, as well as of many other Hindus throughout India. V.P. Singh and his government, however, were committed to India as a secular nation and would not permit the destruction of the mosque, which Muslims considered one of their oldest and most sacred places. India's police were thus ordered to stop the more than one million Hindus marching toward Ayodhya, including Advani himself, who rode in a chariot such as King Rama might have used. On October 23, the day that

Advani was stopped and arrested, Singh lost his Lok Sabha majority, as the BJP withdrew its support for the coalition.

Singh had earlier come under severe attack from many upper-caste Hindus of northern India for sponsoring implementation of the 1980 Mandal Commission report, which recommended that more jobs in all services be reserved for members of the lower castes and ex-untouchable outcaste communities. After he announced in August 1990 that the recommendations would be enforced, many young upper-caste Hindus immolated themselves in protests across northern India. V.P. Singh's critics accused him of pandering to the lower castes for their votes, and many members of his own party deserted him on this searing issue, foremost among them Chandra Shekhar, who led a splinter group of Janata Dal dissidents out of Singh's coalition. On Nov. 7, 1990, V.P. Singh resigned after suffering a vote of no confidence by a stunning margin of 356 to 151.

Most of those who voted against the prime minister were members of Rajiv Gandhi's Congress (I) Party, for Gandhi retained the largest single block of party faithful in the Lok Sabha; however, Advani's BJP support also lined up against Singh. The smallest new party bloc in Lok Sabha belonged to Shekhar, whose Janata Dal (S)—the S stood for Socialist—gained the support of Gandhi and thus came to be invited by Pres. Ramaswamy Venkataraman to serve as prime minister before the end of 1990. Devi Lal, who in August had been ousted by Singh, again became deputy prime minister. With fewer than 60 Janata (S) members in the Lok Sabha, however, the new prime minister's hold on power was tenuous and not expected to survive any longer than deemed expedient by Gandhi and the Congress (I) bloc. When the Congress (I) walked out of the Lok Sabha in March 1991, Shekhar had little choice but to resign and call upon President Venkataraman to announce new general elections.

CONGRESS GOVERNMENT OF NARASIMHA RAO

The first round of the elections took place on May 20, but the following day in Tamil Nadu, in a small town just south of Madras (Chennai), Gandhi was assassinated in a suicide bomb attack. A woman apparently of Sri Lankan Tamil origin and bearing a concealed plastic bomb destroyed herself and more than a dozen others crowded around Gandhi, who, though expected to regain the post of prime minister, had abandoned his previous security precautions to campaign more vigorously. The other two rounds of the elections were postponed in respect for the young leader. After Sonia, Rajiv's Italian-born widow, declined an invitation by the central committee of the Congress (I) to replace her husband as party president, the Congress (I) closed ranks behind P.V. (Pamulaparti Venkata) Narasimha Rao, one of its most senior leaders and diplomats, and unanimously elected him Congress (I) president.

"The only way to exist in India is to coexist," Narasimha Rao told his pluralistic nation as election campaigning resumed in early June. Though the younger Gandhi's assassination apparently had ended the Nehru dynasty, the Nehru legacy of secular democratic development for India remained embodied at the head of the Congress (I). Born in the southern presidency of Madras in what is now Andhra Pradesh state, Narasimha Rao had been a disciple of Mohandas Gandhi and of Nehru, had served in the Lok Sabha, and was appointed foreign minister under both Indira Gandhi and Rajiv Gandhi. On June 20, after the Congress (I) won more than 220 of the 524 seats contested for the Lok Sabha, Narasimha Rao was able to form a minority government and became the first Indian prime minister from a southern state. The opposition in the Lok Sabha was led by Advani, whose BJP won some 120 seats, reaching a new peak in popularity, especially in the Hindi-speaking heartland of northern India, where it took control of India's most populous state, Uttar Pradesh. The Janata Dal gained fewer than 60 seats, just slightly more than the approximately 50 seats won by the two communist parties.

The Rao government's nearly five-year rule was marked by many challenges. In 1992 Advani's promise to resume his "sacred pilgrimage" to Ayodhya to erect Rama's temple became an immediate and potentially explosive issue when, despite promises of restraint from Hindu nationalist leaders, an army of Hindu protestors tore down the Babri Masjid in December of that year. The destruction of the 464-year-old mosque ignited the country's worst interreligious rioting since the Indian partition of 1947 and set the stage for severe clashes between Hindu and Muslim extremists during the rest of the decade.

Also in 1992, amid allegations of corruption within the Rao government, a number of bankers, brokers, and political figures were indicted in a wide-scale stock market swindle in which public funds were used to inflate stock prices in order to benefit the conspirators. These financial misdealings took place in a framework of growing economic liberalization, deregulation, and privatization that had begun under the government of Rajiv Gandhi and that continued unabated through the close of the century. India's move toward a more market-oriented economy was fueled largely by an educational system that produced a huge number of graduates in technology and the sciences, and India experienced a dramatic growth in its high-technology and computer sectors.

THE FIRST AND SECOND BJP GOVERNMENTS

Despite a booming national economy, the Congress—the "(I)" was by then dropped—polled poorly in the 1996 general election, falling from 260 seats in the Lok Sabha to only 140 (an all-time low). In part, this drop in Congress support stemmed from accusations of political corruption on the part of Narasimha Rao; to some extent, however, it signaled a rise in Hindu nationalism in the form of the BJP. That party increased its representation in the Lok Sabha from 113 to 161, the overall largest party representation, but no party had sufficient seats to form a government. The BJP, led by Atal Bihari Vajpayee, was unable to form a stable coalition, and Vajpayee held the premiership for scarcely a week.

A hastily contrived coalition, the United Front (UF), under Janata Dal politician H.D. Deve Gowda, soon was able to seat a government. But the UF relied on the support of the Congress from the outside, in exchange for continuing certain Congress policies. The coalition still proved unstable, and Gowda was replaced as prime minister in April 1997 by Inder Kumar Gujral, also of the Janata Dal. However, an interim report on Rajiv Gandhi's assassination released in November stated that the Dravida Munnetra Kazhagam (DMK) party, a member of the UF, shared responsibility in Gandhi's death. The Congress removed its support, and, after the collapse of the UF, new elections were slated for March 1998. (The claims against the DMK were never substantiated.)

Much to the chagrin of the Congress, the BJP polled well in the March elections, increasing its membership in the Lok Sabha from 160 seats to 179. The Congress, now led by Sonia Gandhi, increased their representation slightly, garnering an additional five seats. No single party seemed to be in a position to form a government (Janata Dal had fallen to a mere six seats), and it was only after much politicking that

the BJP was able to form a new governing coalition, again under Vajpayee.

The BJP coalition, called the National Democratic Alliance, crumbled in April 1999 and operated as a caretaker government until elections that fall. The BJP again had a good outing, outpolling all other parties and raising its representation in the Lok Sabha to 182 seats. The Congress representation in the lower house eroded even further, to 112 seats.

India had conducted its first nuclear weapons test in 1974, but its program for developing and fielding such weapons had been covert. Under the BJP, India publicly and proudly declared itself a member of those states possessing nuclear weapons, and in May 1998—within months of the BJP coming to power—India conducted a series of five nuclear weapons tests. This apparently was interpreted as sabre rattling by Pakistan, which responded by detonating its own nuclear devices. The international community harshly condemned both sides and urged the two new nuclear powers to begin a dialogue, particularly on the unresolved question of Kashmir.

Despite several tentative steps toward rapprochement, armed conflict broke out between India and Pakistan in the high mountains of the Kargil region of Jammu and Kashmir state in May 1999. Eventually, intense international pressure induced the Pakistani government to withdraw its troops to its side of the line of control. Nonetheless, Kashmir continued to be a point of contention, and acts of terrorism conducted by extremists hoping to change Indian policy toward the region grew more common and severe.

RETURN OF THE CONGRESS

The BJP espoused a broad Hindu nativism. During the years of BJP government, Hindu products were favoured over imports, names of cities were changed—either to reflect the precolonial name (e.g., Chennai for Madras) or to bring the name more in line with local pronunciation (Kolkata for Calcutta)—and the party openly opposed what it considered non-Hindu values.

Given India's tradition of secular politics, many Indians were uncomfortable with the BJP's pro-Hindu approach, and this discomfort was perhaps one of the reasons why the BJP had such a poor showing at the May 2004 elections. The Congress regained some ground lost in previous general elections, raising its representation in the Lok Sabha to 145 seats; the BJP's membership fell to 137 seats. As had become the pattern in other recent elections, no party was situated to call a government on its own, so the Congress formed a coalition known as the United Progressive Alliance (UPA). Congress leader Sonia Gandhi opted not to take the premiership, however, and instead recommended Manmohan Singh, a Sikh, for the post. The Congress made significant gains in the 2009 parliamentary elections, increasing its seat total in the Lok Sabha to 206; conversely, the BJP's total fell to 116. Singh formed another cabinet and was sworn in for a second term, becoming the first prime minister since Jawaharlal Nehru to do so after having served a full five-year first term.

Singh had been minister of finance under Narasimha Rao until 1996, and he was the man most credited with restructuring the Indian economy during the 1990s. The election was seen by many as a turn away from the pro-urban policies adopted by the BJP. Since the early 1990s, India's economy had boomed, particularly in the high-technology and technical-services sector. The economy in many rural areas, however, had stagnated. Farming remained largely dependent on the monsoon, and many formerly remote areas were opened up merely so that their natural resources might be exploited with little benefit to local inhabitants. The UPA espoused a strongly pro-farmer message and sought to introduce rural programs reminiscent of those of the New Deal era in the United States. The new government aimed to revitalize the agrarian economy, step up investment in agriculture, provide access to credit, and improve the quality of rural infrastructure. The government made employment generation and social equity important features of its agenda. An indication of the government's efforts on the latter point actually began during the BJP era, when Kocheril Raman Narayanan, a Dalit ("untouchable"), served as president (1997–2002). After the Congress came to power, Pratibha Patil became the country's first woman president in 2007, and another Dalit, Meira Kumar, was named the first woman speaker of the Lok Sabha in 2009.

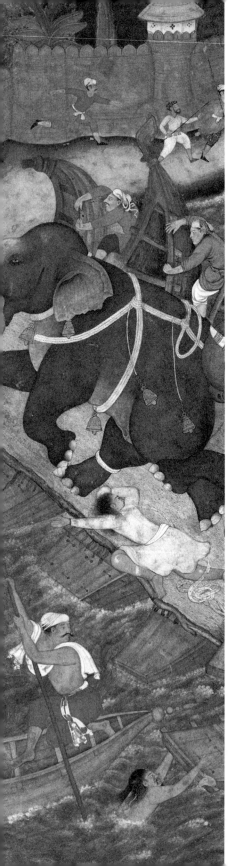

CONCLUSION

As India approaches its 65th year of independence, it faces challenges, but its future also holds great promise. The nation is working to build diplomatic bridges to Pakistan. In October 2008 limited trade resumed between the Indian- and Pakistani-administered segments of Kashmir, the first such commerce through the region in six decades. The resumption of this trade signaled improved relations between the two countries.

India is also making efforts to combat terrorism both at home and abroad. Along with the growth of terror by Muslim extremists, India experienced a rise in violence among communist (mostly Maoist) groups known as Naxalites. First formed in the 1960s, Naxalite groups experienced a revival in the early 21st century, espousing a doctrine of liberation and emancipation. They generally operated on the fringes of society in the most economically backward regions and were highly attractive to marginalized tribal peoples, poor rural residents, and others with grievances. The union government soon acknowledged that Naxalism, along with terrorism, presented significant threats to internal security in India. However, efforts to deter terrorist attacks did not prevent some major deadly incidents, including the bombing of multiple trains in Mumbai in July 2006, bombings in several locations in Delhi in September 2008, and the assault by armed terrorists on several buildings in central Mumbai two months later.

India remains a land of marked contrasts. Economically, it is a world leader in high technology, while at the same time vast numbers of people survive on subsistence agriculture. The country has an enormous and growing population, which has more than tripled since 1947 and has steadily gained ground on that of China, but it also contains some of

Mass celebrations in India commemorate the 150th anniversary of the Indian Mutiny of 1857–58, which in India is often called the first war of independence against British rule. The India Today Group/Getty Images

the most spectacular natural scenery on earth. India has made great strides at reducing the influence of its ancient caste system, but class distinctions and inequities remain, and sectarian tensions—especially between Hindus and Muslims—periodically flair into incidents of remarkable violence. A large, highly educated middle class has emerged, but India remains one of the world's poorest countries per capita, with tens of millions of people living in great poverty. It has developed nuclear weapons, but this action has spurred rival Pakistan to do the same and has been a factor in increasing tensions in the region. Yet, as it struggles with its myriad of challenges, India remains the world's most populous democracy, with a multiparty electoral system that provides a stable government responsible and responsive to the voters. India is a major player on the global diplomatic stage, expanding on its early role as leader of the Nonaligned Movement to one in which it is at the forefront of the world's lower-income countries as they negotiate with the major industrial powers. Throughout it all, India's culture remains vibrant and thriving, a pastiche of ancient traditions, modern popular culture, and numerous combinations of these various elements.

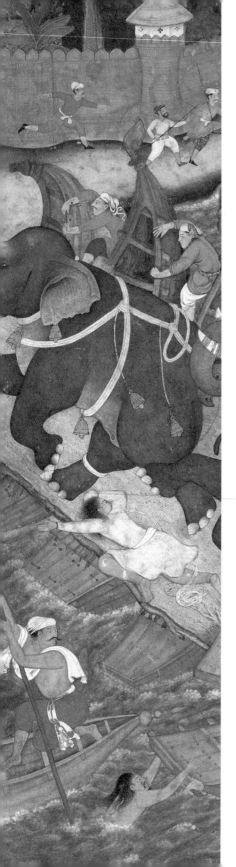

GLOSSARY

alluvial Relating to soil or sediments that are deposited by running water.

amelioration An improvement or the act of making better.

analogous Corresponding in some manner.

arrears An unpaid and overdue debt or unfulfilled obligation.

bastion A projecting part of a fortification that is situated in both corners of a straight wall.

bellicosely Aggressive or hostile in temperament.

bifurcated Divided into two branches or parts.

bitumen A naturally occurring viscous and sticky substance resembling asphalt.

carnelian A reddish-brown semiprecious gemstone used in jewelry making.

centrifugal Moving outward or away from the center.

citadel A stronghold or fortified place in or near a city.

conciliatory Willing to compromise.

concomitant One that occurs or exists concurrently with something else.

cumbrous Difficult to handle.

despotism Government ruled by one individual with absolute power or control.

dramaturgy The techniques of dramatic composition.

endogamous Marriage within one's own group or tribe in accordance with custom or law.

ephemeral Short-lived.

eponymous Describes the giving of one's name to something, such as a city, state, institution, etc.

exchequer A treasury of a state or nation.

feudalistic Relating to a political and economic system in which people provided services to a lord in return for the use of his land.

garrison A military post.

gypsum A mineral used to make plaster or cement.

hegemony Leadership exercised by one nation over another.

ignominy Personal dishonor.

incumbent The current holder of an office.

inorganic Matter that lacks the characteristics of a living organism.

interregnum The time between the end of a sovereign's reign and the reign of his or her successor.

lunate A crescent-shaped, small stone tool.

malleable Impressionable.

mastic Resin from a tree that can serve as an adhesive.

metallurgy The heating of metals to give them desired shapes or properties.

microlith A small stone tool.

monarchical Pertaining to a government led by a sole and absolute ruler, usually for life and by hereditary right.

mutineers People who are openly rebellious and refusing to obey authority.

nexus The core center.

nomenclature A system of names used in a science or art by an individual or community.

numismatic Pertaining to coins or currency.

oligarchic Pertaining to a government led by a few.

ostentation A pretentious show of wealth or importance.

plebiscite A vote by the electorate on some important public question.

plinth A square base of a column or pier, like a pedestal.

postern An entrance other than the main one, such as a back door or gate.

promulgate To formally put a law into operation.

proselytizer One who tries to convert others to a particular religion.

realpolitik Politics based on practical rather than moral considerations.

renascent Being reborn.

satyagraha The form of nonviolent resistance initiated in India by Mahatma Gandhi.

spoliation Robbery or plundering in a time of war.

stupa A dome-shaped monument or structure that houses Buddhist relics.

surreptitious Stealthy and secretive.

suzerainty A relationship between states in which the international affairs of a subservient state are controlled by the more powerful one.

syncretic The fusion of different systems of belief, as in religion or philosophy.

temporal Temporary, earthly.

tripartite Involving three parties.

vizier A high officer in certain Muslim governments.

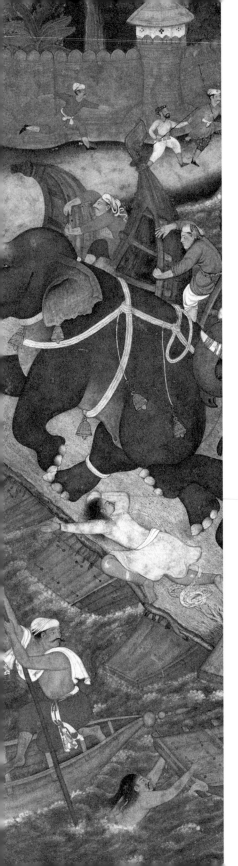

FOR FURTHER READING

Bose, Sumantra. *Kashmir: Roots of Conflict, Paths to Peace*. Cambridge, MA.: Harvard University Press, 2003.

Daniélou, Alain. *A Brief History of India*. Rochester, VT.: Inner Traditions, 2003.

Dettman, Paul R. *India Changes Course: Golden Jubilee to Millenium*. Westport, CT: Prager Publishers, 2001.

Eraly, Abraham. *India*. New York: DK Pub. 2008.

Eraly, Abraham. *The Mughal Throne: The Saga of India's Great Emporers*. London: Phoenix, 2004.

Guha, Ramachandra. *India After Gandhi: The History of the World's Largest Democracy*. New York: Ecco, 2007.

Hardy, Peter. *The Muslims of British India*. London, England: Cambridge University Press, 1972.

Judd, Denis. *The Lion and the Tiger: The Rise and Fall of the British Raj*. Oxford, England: Oxford University Press, 2004.

Kamdar, Mira. *Planet India: How the Fastest-Growing Democracy Is Transforming America and the World*. New York: Scribner, 2007.

Luce, Edward. *In Spite of the Gods: The Rise of Modern India*. New York: Anchor, 2008.

Mansingh, Surjit. *Historical Dictionary of India*. Lanham, MD.: Scarecrow Press, 2006.

Matane, Paulias, and M.L. Ahuja. *India: A Splendour in Cultural Diversity*. New Delhi, India: Anmol Publications Pvt. Ltd., 2004.

Mishra, Pankaj. *Temptation of the West*. New York: Farrar, Straus and Giroux, 2006.

Nilekani, Nandan. *Imagining India: The Idea of a Renewed Nation*. New York: Penguin Press, 2009.

Panagariya, Arvind. *India: The Emerging Giant.* New York: Oxford University Press, 2008.

Robb, Peter. *A History of India.* New York: Palgrave, 2002.

SarDesai, D.R. *India: The Definitive History.* Boulder, CO: Westview Press, 2008.

Thapar, Romila. *Early India: From the Origins to AD 1300.* Berkeley: University of California Press, 2004.

Vohra, Ranbir. *The Making of India: A Historical Survey.* Armonk, NY: ME Sharpe, Inc., 1997.

Watson, Francis. *India: A Concise History.* New York: Thames & Hudson, 2002.

Wolpert, Stanley. *A New History of India.* New York: Oxford University Press, 2004.

Wood, Michael. *India.* New York: Basic Books, 2007.

INDEX

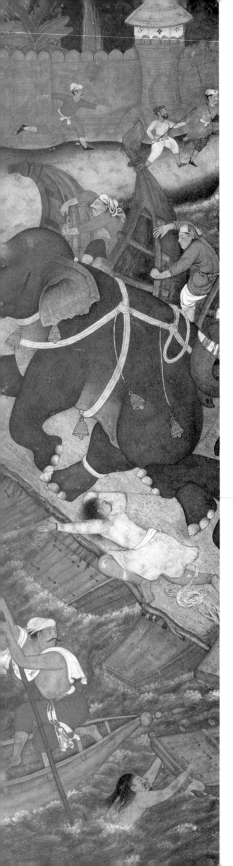